MW01002112

Romans

The other volumes in this series on Romans are:

Romans: Atonement and Justification (3:20-4:25)

Romans: Assurance (5)

Romans: The New Man (6)

Romans: The Sons of God (8:5-17)

Romans: The Final Perseverance of the Saints (8:17-39)

Romans

An Exposition of Chapters 7.1–8.4
The Law: Its Functions and Limits

D. M. Lloyd-Jones

ZONDERVAN
PUBLISHING HOUSE

OF THE ZONDERVAN CORPORATION | GRAND RAPIDS. MICHIGAN 49506

To the faithful and enthusiastic Friday-nighters
at Westminster Chapel 1955-68

Romans
© D. M. Lloyd-Jones   1973

First Zondervan printing   1974

ISBN 0-310-27910-0

Printed in the United States of America

83   84   85   86   87   88 — 20   19   18   17   16   15   14   13   12   11

Contents

Contents

Contents

Preface

This volume deals with what is undoubtedly one of the most controversial chapters in the Bible. Whatever view one may take of it inevitably leads to criticism and disagreement. That, in turn, helps to explain much of the difficulty with respect to it. The danger is to approach it from an entrenched position or tradition with the determination to vindicate that at all costs. Prejudice is one of the greatest enemies of true exposition.

As I see it, and explain at length in my exposition, the greatest cause of trouble is to become obsessed by the so-called 'man of Romans 7', and to approach the entire chapter, as a consequence, from the standpoint of Christian experience. That is to miss the real theme and central object of the chapter and purpose of the Law given by God through Moses to the Children of Israel. This chapter is undoubtedly the 'locus classicus' of the Christian, and especially the Pauline, view of the Law. It was clearly crucial in an evangelistic sense in the time of the Apostle himself, and also from the standpoint of resolving the tension between Jew and Gentile in the early Church. It is also vital to an understanding of how the Christian Bible ever came into being, and as to why a mainly Gentile Church incorporated the Old Testament with their new literature. I have been interested recently to notice that Professor von Campenhausen in his *The Formation of the Christian Bible,* 1967, (English translation published by A & C Black, London, 1972) goes so far as to say that the Christian Bible would never have been possible, were it not for the view of the Law taught here by the Apostle Paul.

I was much encouraged also by a review in the Westminster Theological Journal of a book on Paul by Professor H. N. Ridderbos of Kampen University, Holland, which indicated that Professor Ridderbos takes much the same view as I do. I had hoped that the English translation of that work, by Dr J. R. de Witt, would have been published so that I might have quoted

Preface

from it, but having seen some proof sheets, through the kindness of Dr de Witt, I am confirmed in the impression given by the review of the original Dutch edition.

Once more I do not apologise for much repetition. The text demands it – full weight must be given to each statement, and nothing must be glossed over in the interests of a theory. I make one request of my readers; that is, that if they remain unconvinced by the case I put forward, they suspend final judgment until the next volume appears, and especially until they have read the exposition of chapter 8, verse 15 in that volume.

I decided that this present volume should include verses 1–4 of Chapter 8 because, though verse 1 of that chapter starts a new section, the first four verses seem to me to be, primarily, a summary of the previous argument, and therefore throw great light on it.

It will be clear from the exposition that the theme of this volume is no mere fascinating theological or intellectual problem, but one which is of vital importance to Christian experience, and to the health, well-being and vigour of the Church. To end a reading of Romans 7 in a depressed condition is to fail to understand it; to turn to it as a means of comfort in such a state of depression, or as a justification for such a state, is a travesty of the Apostle's teaching as I understand it.

I plead therefore for a patient and careful reading; and I trust that under the blessing of God, this volume may help to bring many from 'the spirit of bondage again to fear' to an experience of 'the Spirit of adoption whereby we cry Abba Father'.

These sermons were preached on Friday nights in Westminster Chapel, London, during the period April 1959–February 1960, there being an interval during the summer months of 1959.

As with the previous volumes I am deeply indebted to Mrs E. Burney, and Mr S. M. Houghton, and the Publishers for their kind and gracious help. They are in no way responsible for the view presented. My wife, as ever, was my best constructive critic while these sermons were being preached, and has been a constant encouragement during the labour of preparing them for publication.

September 1973   D. M. LLOYD-JONES

One

> *Know ye not, brethren, (for I speak to them that know the law),*
> *how that the law hath dominion over a man as long as he liveth?*
>
> Romans 7: 1

This 7th chapter is one of the famous chapters in the Epistle to the Romans, and indeed in the Bible as a whole. Anyone who knows anything about Christian doctrine and theology will often have talked about and argued over this chapter. No other chapter, perhaps, has been more frequently the cause of discussion and disputation and argument. That is why most people are more familiar with it than with chapter 6, but if I were compelled to compare these chapters with each other I would say that the 6th is a more important chapter than this one. However, that does not matter.

Most people are familiar with this 7th chapter because of the argument that generally takes place with regard to the final section which runs from verse 13 to the end of the chapter. The great point of discussion is as to what exactly Paul is saying there. Is he describing himself as he then was, or as he once was in the past? Is it the description of a man before his conversion, or of a man after his conversion? That is the subject of the great argument.

Let me state now at the very beginning that I shall have but little to say about that, because that is not, as I understand it, the most important question dealt with in this chapter. We shall discover the correct interpretation if we approach the entire chapter in the right way. The wrong approach, as I have just been indicating, is to rush through the earlier verses in order to get to the final section. Most people who fail to understand the final section do so simply because they have never understood the first section. The Apostle Paul had a very logical mind; he

always proceeds step by step. It follows therefore that it is particularly dangerous in his case to isolate or extract any one verse or
paragraph. It is very important, therefore, as we come to consider the teaching of this chapter, that we should remind ourselves of its setting. How did he ever come to write it? What is he
attempting to do as he writes it?

I start then by reminding you of the connection, the setting.
Chapters 6 and 7 of this Epistle, it seems to me – and as we have
seen in connection with chapter 6 – must be regarded as a parenthesis. The Apostle's exposition of the great doctrine of redemption, the main drift of his argument, goes straight on from chapter 5, verse 21, to chapter 8, verse 1, or, perhaps to chapter 8,
verse 5. Chapters 6 and 7 are a parenthesis in which the Apostle
turns aside in order to clear up certain difficulties which he knew
would arise in the minds of the readers of this letter in Rome,
and which had already arisen in the minds of many Christian
people in other churches also. These difficulties arise from the
tremendous statement Paul makes at the end of chapter 5,
verses 20 and 21. 'Moreover', he says, 'the law entered, that the
offence might abound. But where sin abounded, grace did much
more abound: That as sin hath reigned unto death, even so might
grace reign through righteousness unto eternal life by Jesus
Christ our Lord.' That is the fundamental statement which
winds up the argument of chapter 5, and especially verses 12–19.
There, Paul has been dealing with our incorporation into Christ,
and explaining that we now are to Christ what we once were to
Adam, and accordingly our whole future is certain and guaranteed
because 'where sin abounded, grace did much more abound',
and 'as sin hath reigned unto death, even so (will) grace reign
through righteousness unto eternal life through Jesus Christ our
Lord'.

The Apostle is immediately aware of the fact that such a
statement is liable to serious misunderstanding, that indeed it
was being misunderstood. He has already said in chapter 3 that
he is being 'slanderously reported' as saying certain things.
He was frequently wronged in that way. We have also reminded
ourselves that if our preaching does not expose us to these
'slanderous' attacks the probability is that we are not really
preaching the gospel. No man was so slandered as Martin Luther,
who under the guidance of the Spirit rediscovered the great

truth that led to the Protestant Reformation. He was constantly exposed to all sorts of slanderous statements in regard to both his teaching and his personal life. Any man who preaches the doctrine of justification by faith truly will be misunderstood. This is because of the staggering character of the great doctrine.

The Apostle sees at once that there was a likelihood of two main charges being brought against him. The first was the charge of antinomianism, the charge that he is more or less saying 'Live as you like, sin as much as you like. All is well; grace will look after you and cover all your sin.' He takes up that charge in chapter 6: 'What shall we say then? Shall we continue in sin that grace may abound?' In earlier chapters on that text we have seen how he refutes that argument completely. He does so in verses 1–13 of chapter 6 where he shows that the effect of abounding grace is not sin but righteousness. But then in verse 14, he had said that 'sin shall not have dominion over you, for you are not under law, but under grace', and he knows again that that will be misunderstood, and people will say, 'What then? Shall we sin because we are not under the law, but under grace?' He refutes that also in a final and overwhelming manner in the remainder of chapter 6. He demolishes these false suggestions; he proves that the effect of abounding grace, far from encouraging sin, will mean the death of sin, and lead to holiness and righteousness and glory in the presence of God. Indeed he proves that the whole design of grace is to promote holiness, because the purpose of grace is to make us holy, unblameable and perfect in the presence of God.

But there is still another problem to be dealt with, because at the end of chapter 5, in verses 20 and 21, he has not only been making statements about grace, but has also referred to the place and the function of the Law. This also, being misunderstood, led to the second charge that was being brought against the Apostle, namely, that his preaching of justification by faith only, and of our being united to the Lord Jesus Christ, seemed to be doing away altogether with the Law, and the whole notion of law, in God's dealings with the human race. Now it is not surprising that people should say that, because the Apostle has used a somewhat daring phrase about the Law in the 20th verse of that 5th chapter. 'Moreover', he said, 'the law entered'; which we paraphrased, 'the law came in, not on the main line, but as it were, sideways'. Paul knew that people with a legalistic mind and with a Judaistic background were liable to say, 'You should not speak of the Law in that way, you must not speak of the Law as something that comes in as a sort of aside. Is not that to derogate from the greatness and the glory of the Law? Is not that virtually to suggest that the Law is something more or less indifferent?' It was because the Apostle knew that his phrase was liable to misunderstanding that he devotes this 7th chapter to an explanation and explication of what he meant by putting it in that way.

Then the Apostle had repeated this statement, and put it perhaps still more strongly in the 14th verse of chapter 6. In winding up his first argument in chapter 6 he had said, 'For sin shall not have dominion over you', and his reason for saying that is, 'for (because) you are not under the law, but under grace'. He seems to glory in that fact. He seems to be striking another blow at the Law. He has already knocked it down, as it were, in chapter 5, verse 20; he is now trampling on it. At once his opponents take up the cudgels and say, 'Surely these are very wrong and very dangerous statements to make; surely if you are going to abrogate the Law and do away with it altogether, you are doing away with every guarantee of righteous and holy conduct and behaviour. Sanctification is impossible without the Law. If you treat the Law in that way and dismiss it, and rejoice in doing so, are you not encouraging lawlessness, and are you not almost inciting people to live a sinful life?' Law, they believed, was the great guarantee of holy living and sanctification. The Apostle clearly has to safeguard himself, and the truth of the gospel, against that particular misunderstanding and charge.

Now that is exactly the purpose of this 7th chapter. It is to explain what he means when he says that the Law 'came in by the side', and that we should rejoice in the fact that we are not 'under the law but under grace'. This 7th chapter is an expanded exposition or explication of both those statements, or, to put it more positively, its purpose is to show us the function and the purpose of the Law as given by God through Moses to the Children of Israel.

But the Apostle has another particular object in view also, namely, to show that sanctification by the Law is as impossible as was justification by the Law. The theme of the first four chapters of the Epistle is that a sinner can never be justified by the Law. He had already summed that up in a great statement in chapter 3, verse 20: 'Therefore by the deeds of the law shall no man be justified in his sight'. There it is stated categorically. Now, here he is saying in effect in chapter 7, 'Therefore by the deeds of the law shall no man be sanctified in his sight'. As it is impossible to be justified by the Law, it is equally impossible to be sanctified by the Law. As we shall see later, he even puts it as strongly as this, that not only can a man not be sanctified by the Law, but it is actually true to say that the Law is a hindrance to sanctification, and that it aggravates the problem of sanctification. That is the thesis of this 7th chapter; not only can a man not sanctify himself by observance of the Law; the Law is even a hindrance and an obstacle to sanctification. That is his general thesis, the fundamental proposition he sets out to prove; we must keep it very firmly in our minds.

As we proceed to follow the detailed outworking of this proposition, we divide the chapter into three sections. Nowhere is it more important that we should have a bird's-eye view of a chapter before we come to the details than here. It is easy to get muddled and lost in some of the detailed statements if we fail to bear in mind what Paul is basically saying to his readers. The first division consists of verses 1 to 6. Here we have a general statement in which he defines our relationship as believers to the Law. At the same time he shows why a change in our relationship to the Law is as absolutely essential for our sanctification as it was for our justification. The key verse in this first section is verse 4; it is a crucial one. 'Wherefore, my brethren, you also are become dead to the law by the body of Christ.' Why? 'In order that you should be married to another, even to him who is raised from the dead.' But why should you be married to Him? Why should you be married to anyone, and in particular, Why should you be married to Christ? Here is the answer – 'that (in order that) we should bring forth fruit unto God'. That is the real subject matter; that is the vital question. What the Apostle is concerned about is the bringing forth of this fruit unto God; and his case in the whole chapter is that you can never bring forth fruit unto God as long as you are married to the Law. There is only one way to bring forth fruit unto God, and that is, to be married to the Lord Jesus Christ. That is Paul's case! In verses

1 to 6 he puts it in a general way. What is our relationship, as believers, to the Law? It is not what it once was; there has been a change. He tells us how it came about, and he tells us the object and the purpose of it all. We could never produce fruit unto God unless that relationship had been changed and we had entered into a new relationship. That is the first section.

The second section runs from verse 7 to verse 12, and is a vindication of the Law. 'What shall we say then?' If that first statement is correct someone is going to say, 'Very well, that means that the Law is sin'. 'What shall we say then? Is the Law sin?' The answer is, 'God forbid'; and the Apostle proceeds, as far as verse 12, to vindicate the Law in and of itself, and to show that it is not the Law that is responsible for our lack of fruit unto God, but that the trouble is in ourselves. As he had stated the matter in the first section, a careless reader might draw that deduction foolishly and wrongly and say, 'Well then, there was something wrong with the Law if it could not make us bear fruit unto God'. 'Oh no', says Paul, 'the trouble is not in the Law, it is in you.' So he gives us this great vindication of the Law. The Law has been given by God; and therefore the trouble cannot be in the Law, it must be in us. He will later say a similar thing in one great assertion in chapter 8, verse 3, 'For what the law could not do'. Why could it not do it? 'In that it was weak through the flesh'. The weakness was not in the Law but in us; the Law was weak 'through the flesh'. This is what Paul works out in verses 7–12. Chapter 8, verse 3, is but a summary of the theme that he has already argued out here.

The third and final section of the chapter consists of verses 13–25. This is nothing but a working out, in a practical and experimental manner, of the statement that he has already made in the first two sections. The Apostle wants to bring the truth right home to us, so he does not just state it as a general principle; he proceeds to show what our position would be if we were still left under the Law. He shows how utterly impossible our sanctification would be in that condition, and in a final word introduces the only hope in this respect – 'I thank God through Jesus Christ our Lord'.

There, I suggest, is the general lay-out of the contents of this famous chapter. In other words, the business of chapter 7 is to repeat and to re-apply what he has said so grandly in chapter

5, verse 10, which is, 'For if, when we were enemies, we were reconciled to God by the death of his Son, much more, being reconciled, we shall be saved in his life' – saved completely, saved entirely, fully sanctified and perfectly glorified. How? In the life of Jesus Christ! It is the only way, nothing else can do it. The Apostle repeats it here in chapter 7, verses 24 and 25: 'O wretched man that I am! who shall deliver me from the body of this death? I thank God through Jesus Christ our Lord.' As we have indicated earlier, verses 12 to 21 in chapter 5 are but an outworking of that fundamental statement in the 10th verse of chapter 5. And we shall also find, as we work our way through this chapter, that Paul repeats a number of things he has already said in chapter 6, and especially what he was saying towards the end where he introduced this whole notion of fruit-bearing. In verse 21 of chapter 6 he asks, 'What fruit had ye then in those things whereof ye are now ashamed? for the end of those things is death. But now being made free from sin, and become servants to God, you have your fruit unto holiness, and the end everlasting life. For the wages of sin is death; but the gift of God is eternal life through Jesus Christ our Lord.' What he demonstrates in this 7th chapter is that there is only one way of bearing fruit unto God, and that is, to be married to, to be joined to, the Lord Jesus Christ. To be married to the Law means 'fruit unto death'. There is only one way to have 'fruit unto God' and to life, and that is, to be married to, to be joined unto the Lord Jesus Christ. The Apostle is going to prove that. He does so by proving that the Law could not do it, and that Christ can do it. That is the theme of this 7th chapter.

We shall find, at the same time, that this is an amazing chapter in certain respects. It is beyond any doubt the profoundest analysis of sin, and of its ways and its results, which is to be found anywhere in the whole of Scripture. There is no more profound statement about sin, no more profound psychological analysis of sin and what it does, and how it does it, than you find here. It is indeed quite incomparable in that respect. It is also a mighty statement with respect to the function of the Law and the place of the Law in the life of the believer. It is also the greatest statement found anywhere in the whole range of Scripture with regard to the final impotence of the Law in the matter of salvation. So we must keep our eye on that. In doing so we shall also find that it is beyond any question the finest exposure of the utter futility of the position of those who think that morality alone is sufficient. It shows the complete futility of believing in Christian morality or ethics alone while shedding the Christian doctrine of salvation. There is no statement to be found anywhere that so utterly demolishes that position as this 7th chapter of Romans.

It is therefore a chapter that is very much needed at this present time. We are confronted today by numbers of people who take a very superior position as great intellects, great men. They are no longer interested in Christian doctrine. Of course not! They do not believe in the miraculous and supernatural; they do not believe in the absolute necessity of a substitutionary atonement. They have shed all that, but they claim to be holding on to the Christian ethic. Here is the chapter of all chapters which exposes the utter futility of their position. They 'talk loftily', either because they are not familiar with this chapter, or else do not understand it. It is the final refutation of the foolish exaltation of ethics and morality at the expense of the doctrine of salvation. It is a glorious statement in that respect. And finally, in many ways it puts the doctrine of our relationship to the Lord Jesus Christ in its highest form, and certainly in its most mystical form. Here we are taught – of course we are taught it elsewhere also, but it is put very plainly here – that we are married to the Lord Jesus Christ. Such is the particular illustration which the Apostle employs.

There, then, are the leading themes on which we must concentrate. Had you realized that these themes are found here? Or had you thought that there was only one subject dealt with in Romans, chapter 7, namely, the question, Is this a description of a converted man or an unconverted man? Is it Paul in some transitory stage, passing as it were, from being unconverted to the glory of his position in chapter 8? Had you seen anything in it but that? It is tragic that because of a false intellectual interest, and often because of a party spirit, Christians should rob themselves of the riches of this great chapter. How careful we should be in our handling of the Scripture!

I would venture to assert that many, not to say most of our troubles in the Christian life are due to our failure to grasp the teaching of this 7th chapter of the Epistle to the Romans. For instance, what a totally inadequate conception people have of sin these days! How little talk there is about sin; how they dislike preaching that gets to grips with sin! 'Ah', they say, 'we must always be positive. Tell us about salvation. We need not worry our heads about sin and the depths of sin.' This explains why much of our modern Christianity is so superficial! People spend their time in arguing glibly about 'going over from chapter 7 to chapter 8 of Romans' who have never yet been in chapter 7! They have never realized the depths of sin within themselves, they have never really known the power of sin, its awful tyranny and ugliness – this thing that is even able, as it were, to twist the Law of God to suit its own end, and to nullify the Law of God. What a terrible thing sin is! Many have thought that when they believed, or 'took their decision' or 'stepped forward', all was clear, and they were going to 'live happily ever afterwards'. Then, ere long, they find themselves in certain troubles, and they do not understand, the reason being that they have never understood sin. They have been rushed to an untimely and doubtful birth; they have never really known repentance. They may have been told by an evangelist that they need not worry about repentance, that that will come later, that the great thing is to believe positively on the Lord Jesus Christ. But they have neither understood why, nor how, and inevitably they come into trouble later. They have never understood the teaching of this chapter on the depth of sin, the foulness of sin, the power of sin.

But there are also many Christian people who are constantly in trouble about the Law and about their relationship to the Law. We shall come to this in detail later; at the moment I am continuing to give a bird's-eye view. Many Christian people keep on putting themselves back 'under the law'. It generally happens like this. They have believed in the Lord Jesus Christ, they are Christians; but then they fall into sin; and because they fall into sin they begin to think 'Was I ever a Christian at all?' They become uncertain of their salvation, they not only lose their assurance, they even doubt whether they are Christians at all. Other people may feel the same about them, and say, 'The man was never a Christian at all. Had he been a Christian he would never have done a thing like that.' What has happened? It is the result of a complete misunderstanding of the relationship of Christians to the Law. Each time they sin they put themselves back 'under the law', and they find themselves under condemnation again. A Christian should never do that.

I am about to make a statement which is almost certainly going to be misunderstood. I make it in order to expound the passage. I shall be 'slanderously reported' for having said it, even as the Apostle himself was. I put it like this. It does not matter how deeply, how violently you may sin as a believer, you should never come again under condemnation. If you do, it is because you have not understood your relationship to the Law, and you have put yourself back 'under law' again. 'By saying that', says someone, 'you have incited people to go on and sin as much as they like'. Not at all! In reality I have done the exact opposite; because if you but really understand the truth at this point, it will give you great strength to withstand sin. I say again, that however much you may sin, and whatever the character of the sin, you must never put yourself back 'under the law'; you must never have that sense of condemnation again. 'There is therefore now no condemnation to them that are in Christ Jesus' – that is how Paul will sum it all up in the 1st verse of chapter 8. That is the thrust of his entire argument.

But there is another way in which Christian people often put themselves 'under the law'. It is when they fail to attain to the standard which they find set out for the Christian in the New Testament. Now this is positive; the former was negative. They read the various descriptions of the Christian man and they say, 'I am not that; I have not attained to that'. Then, because they have not attained to it, they begin to say, 'I wonder whether I am a Christian at all; for if I were a Christian, surely I would be living in that way'. They begin to test themselves in the light of Scripture. That is good and right; but when they find that they have not attained to the standard of Scripture, instead of saying that they are poor Christians they begin to say that they are not Christians at all; and that is where they go wrong. They put themselves back 'under the law'. They have misused the tests of the Christian to condemn themselves; they are under condemnation again, and that means to be 'under the law'. But as Christians we must never be in that position. What the Apostle is concerned to show in this chapter is that we are dead to the Law, that we have finished with it. We are in a new marriage relationship, and never again can we return to the old.

So whatever you do, or whatever you fail to do, you must never go back 'under the law'; you must never again give place to that sense of condemnation. The moment you have a sense of condemnation you are misinterpreting your relationship to the Law.

How common this is in the experience of every pastor! People come to him constantly along these two lines, and especially in connection with the taking of the Lord's Supper. They say, 'I am not fit to take Communion, I really do not feel that I am good enough'. That is just a proof that they have never understood this doctrine truly. The answer to them is this: 'You will never be good enough.' The Lord's Supper is not for people who are good enough; it is for people who are not 'under the law' but 'under grace'; it is for people who are married to Christ. They come to His banqueting chamber and to His table, unworthy perhaps, but that does not matter; they come as they are because they are married to Him. At His table they are reminded again that, though they are not what they should be, they are no longer 'under condemnation', because of His blood; they are reminded that they are united to Him, and belong to Him; they are in fellowship with Him and can receive strength and power from Him. They are the very people who should come. But how frequently do people misunderstand these things, simply because they do not understand truly their relationship to the Law! That, then, is one illustration of failure to appropriate the lesson of this chapter.

But there is a second cause of failure. Certain people misunderstand the chapter, and what I have just been saying, in such a way as to ignore the Law altogether; and they go headlong into antinomianism, which is a terrible state indeed. 'Ah,' they say, 'you are right when you say that a man must never put himself under condemnation again – absolutely right.' But then they interpret that to mean, It does not matter what I do, I can sin as much as I like; there is no condemnation for me, I am safe, I am secure. That is sheer antinomianism. To say that it does not matter how you live or what you do is to dismiss everything that the Law states. That is an equally fatal misinterpretation of this teaching. We shall have to pay very careful attention to these matters, and we shall have to define very closely what Paul means in verse 4 when he says, 'Wherefore, my brethren, you also are become dead to the law'. The exact interpretation of that statement is a most important matter. Many a man has gone headlong into antinomianism because he has not understood it. There are always these two extremes – the fearful person who puts himself 'under the law' and its condemnation; and the bold, the brazen type, who does the exact opposite, and is guilty of that horrible sin called antinomianism. That is the second group of troubles.

But there is a third group. Many Christian people are in trouble because they have never fully understood the doctrine of their union with the risen Lord. As I have already said, the Apostle first stated this in verse 10 of chapter 5 – 'If, when we were enemies, we were reconciled to God by the death of his Son, much more, being reconciled, we shall be saved in his life.' As we were in Adam, so we are in Christ. Paul has worked that out in the remainder of chapter 5. The whole point of the argument was that it is the power of Christ that produces the fruit. Thank God that it does so! The chief thing in the Christian life, therefore, is to realize our union with the Lord Jesus Christ; that we are joined to Him and married to Him. What is our duty? What has the Christian to do? In a sense the Christian has only one thing to do, namely to be faithful to Christ, to obey Him in terms of the well-known words of the Marriage Service – 'Forsaking all other, to keep thee only unto him'. That is the marriage pledge, the marriage vow. His is the power, His is the only force that can produce the fruit; our business is to realize our relationship to Him, to be faithful to Him, to 'keep ourselves only unto him', and to obey Him implicitly in all the details of our lives.

Those are the great themes of the chapter, and as I have already said, it is because so many Christians fail to realize them, and especially the last, that they are so constantly in trouble. You cannot be a Christian, as we have seen so repeatedly in chapter 6, without being united to Christ. The Apostle has used several illustrations to make this clear, and he is going to use another. He wants to make it so perfectly plain. All who believe in the Lord Jesus Christ have been put 'into Christ', into His death, His burial, His resurrection, His ascended life. 'Reckon ye yourselves also to be dead indeed unto sin, but alive unto God through Jesus Christ our Lord.' We shall find as we work through this 7th chapter that in a sense the Apostle just goes on repeating this. He puts it in a new way in expounding our relationship to the Law, but it is the same fundamental argument. And at the same time he reintroduces us to the cardinal principles of the Faith, and thereby saves us from so many of the diseases of the soul, so many of the failures in practical Christian living, and so much of the unhappiness that results from the lack of assurance of our eternal security in Christ.

Two

*

*Know ye not, brethren (for I speak to them that know the law),
how that the law hath dominion over a man as long as he liveth?
For the woman which hath an husband is bound by the law to her
husband so long as he liveth; but if the husband be dead, she is
loosed from the law of her husband.*

*So then if, while her husband liveth, she be married to another
man, she shall be called an adulteress; but if her husband be dead,
she is free from that law; so that she is no adulteress, though she
be married to another man.*

*Wherefore, my brethren, ye also are become dead to the law by
the body of Christ; that ye should be married to another, even to
him who is raised from the dead, that we should bring forth fruit
unto God.* Romans 7:1–4

We have seen that the great theme of this chapter is the Christian
in his relationship to the Law, and in particular as regards his
sanctification. Having looked at it in general we now come to a
more detailed consideration of the teaching. That brings us
to the first section which runs from the 1st verse to the 6th
verse. Here the particular theme is the relationship of the Christian to the Law – his freedom from the Law, and especially why
this had to take place in order to secure our sanctification. That is,
I repeat, the theme of the whole chapter. The Apostle, as is his
custom, states it in this first section, and then in the other two
sections gives reasons for what he asserts here in this terse and
strong manner. Let us follow him as he works out his argument.

'Know ye not, brethren (for I speak to them that know the
law), how that the law hath dominion over a man as long as he
liveth?' Although, in a sense, the meaning of these words is
obvious, people have argued about them, and have gone astray
in their exposition of the whole chapter because they have not
been clear as to the exact meaning of these words in this 1st
verse. Let us therefore examine them.

We start with the word 'brethren'. 'Know ye not, brethren', says the Apostle. The common error here is to say that he is referring only to the Jews. It is error because if you say that this is a reference only to the Jews you will proceed to say that the whole chapter refers only to the Jews and to their relationship to the Law. But on the whole it is agreed – and to me the matter is beyond dispute – that the Apostle is not here referring to Jews only but to all who are Christians. This is not merely a matter of personal opinion, for elsewhere the Apostle himself helps us to see that that is what he means. In the 9th chapter, verse 3, when he is referring to the Jews in particular, he does so in this way, 'For I could wish that myself were accursed from Christ for my brethren, my kinsmen according to the flesh'. When he is referring to the Jews only as his brethren he makes it clear by adding, 'my kinsmen according to the flesh'. So in the absence of that qualification we are surely fully justified in saying that 'brethren' here is not a reference only to the Jews, but to Jews and Gentiles who had been converted and who had become Christians. We meet with the same thing in verse 4: 'Wherefore, my brethren, ye also are become dead to the law by the body of Christ; that ye should be married to another.' That clearly refers to all who are Christians.

The next word we have to consider is the word 'law'. 'Know ye not, brethren (for I speak to them that know the law), how that the law hath dominion over a man as long as he liveth.' What law is this? Those who have already gone astray about the 'brethren' go wrong about this also. They say that this is a reference only to the Law as given through Moses to the children of Israel, that it refers to the Mosaic Law only. Some even go further and say that it refers to the ceremonial part of that Law alone, and to nothing else. It would be quite unprofitable to spend time in refuting these false expositions. I simply call attention to them. The whole case which is presented by the Apostle surely excludes such an interpretation of the word 'law' altogether. The Apostle here is patently referring to law in general, to universal law. He is stating something which is true of all human society. It is true of the Mosaic Law certainly, but not only of the Mosaic Law. It is a general principle that is true of law in general and of the relationship of men and women everywhere to law.

I must emphasize the word 'dominion' because the Apostle is going to make use of it. 'Know ye not, brethren, that the law hath dominion over a man.' The word 'dominion' means 'to lord it over', 'to have authority upon', 'to be a lord over someone'. Paul says that the law 'lords it' over us as long as we are alive.

That brings us to the last phrase – 'as long as he liveth'. This simply means that the law applies to us as long as we are alive. You cannot contract out of the law as long as you are alive. As long as any man is alive in this country he is subject to the laws of this country. But that leads to the further statement, that the law only applies to him as long as he lives. The moment he dies the law cannot touch him. You cannot sue a dead man in court; the law cannot do anything about a dead man. The moment a man dies the law cannot touch him; he has finished with the law. As long as he is alive he is 'under' it, under its dominion; but the moment he dies the law can say nothing to him at all; its enactments are null and void as far as he is concerned. The Apostle is making a general statement. He says that this is something which is familiar to everyone who knows anything at all about law, a matter of common knowledge to the citizens of any country. That is what he means by the statement in brackets, 'I speak to them that know the law'. The general proposition, then, is that every one of us is subject to the law of the land in which we live as long as we are alive; but the moment we die the law of the land has nothing further to do with us and nothing further to say to us.

That is the way in which the Apostle starts his argument. I must point out that he obviously likes this way of arguing. In going through the epistles of Paul you not only learn about doctrine and theology and spiritual truth, but, if you read carefully, you can learn much about many other things. One thing, in particular, is that you can learn how to argue, how to debate, how to present a case and put it forward. He was a master of that art. Here, he does something that we have seen him doing before. His method is what I call 'the strategy of the indirect approach'. He never comes directly to the point; he always starts from a broad base. He lays down a proposition with which all are going to agree, which all can accept, something which is obvious. Never forget that when you are involved in a discussion. If you can find certain principles which your opponent is likely to accept, which he must accept if he is a reasonable person, start with them. Do not jump immediately to the particular question; approach it in a general manner. Lay a foundation first, then gradually build up your case on it.

Now that is what the Apostle does here. He says in effect, 'Now we shall all agree that with regard to the operation of the law of the land, any land, this is the position . . .' He used the same method exactly in verse 16 of the 6th chapter. There, in taking up the objection, 'What then? shall we sin because we are not under the law, but under grace?' he answers immediately, 'God forbid'. But then he goes on to deal with it in this way, 'Know ye not?' It is the same kind of argument as we have here, an appeal to general knowledge. 'You know perfectly well, of course, everyone agrees with this, that to whom ye yield yourselves servants to obey, his servants ye are to whom ye obey.' That is the general proposition which he proceeds to work out in detail. He adopts exactly the same procedure here. In other words, if you want to convince people, and to help them, you must not be in too much of a hurry. Lay a good foundation for your argument. Carry people with you if you can. Lay down general propositions, truisms, before you come to your particular propositions. What a fascinating man this Apostle is!

Having thus laid down a general proposition about all law in the second and third verses he takes up a particular example of a law and how it works. He moves from the general to the particular. He works out the general principle in the particular case of marriage and the marriage relationship. Here I must point out something that we may very well miss. The Apostle is going to take it for granted, as he has told us in the 1st verse, that we all know this, and are all agreed about this. But if he were alive today, I am afraid it would be doubtful whether he could take it for granted, and alas, even among Christian people. The Apostle, however, takes for granted a general agreement about the whole question of the relationship of husbands and wives, and wives and husbands.

How is he going to use that argument or illustration? Before we answer that question let me ask another question: Why does the Apostle choose this particular illustration of marriage? He always has a very good reason for his procedure; he does not merely take up the first idea that comes into his mind. He has chosen this particular illustration because it is going to serve his purpose in certain respects in a way that no other illustration can. How then does this illustration about marriage, and the marriage relationship, serve in a special way to bring out the Apostle's argument? The first answer is that it emphasizes very clearly, and perhaps more clearly than anything else, the relationship of mankind to the Law of God by nature, and before we are regenerate and come under grace. We must remember that the fundamental point the Apostle is proving is that 'Sin shall not have dominion over you, for (because) you are not under law, but under grace' (chapter 6, verse 14).

This illustration of marriage brings out very clearly the relationship that subsists between man as he is in sin and the Law of God. On this matter the Apostle says things that were universally accepted then but which, alas, are no longer universally accepted. What is the relationship of a wife to her husband? The term he uses is that she is 'married to the husband'. What does marriage mean? The very term the Apostle used, the term that is normally used, is a term which in and of itself suggests a kind of subordination. His phrase in chapter 6, verse 14, was, 'You are not under the law'. The very word which is translated 'married' carries with it the idea of being under authority. Paul is so much concerned about this that he uses a variety of terms. 'The woman which hath an husband is bound by the law to her husband'. 'Bound' carries the same idea again. Indeed, both terms carry forward the idea that is implicit in the word 'dominion' in the first verse. All his terms suggest the same thing – 'dominion', 'married,' 'bound'. They are in contrast, of course, with the word 'loosed' in the second verse, and with 'free from that law' in the third verse.

Such is the idea that the Apostle's illustration is meant to convey. A woman who is married to a man is under the authority of that man; she is under the power and the control of her husband. The very term suggests it, and all these other surrounding terms give emphasis to it. And it is absolutely essential to the Apostle's argument because he is comparing this husband with the law. The relationship of the unbeliever to the law is identical with that of the wife to the husband. He asserts that as long as her husband is alive the woman is under the authority and the power and the control of her husband.

There was no such thing as a feminist movement when the Apostle wrote these words! Whatever we may think or say about the matter, it is abundantly clear that feminism, and the feminist movement, are utterly un-scriptural. That teaching denies one of the cardinal and basic principles of the Bible. Yet you will find that it is quite common among Christians, and it has even invaded evangelical circles. I glance at the matter in passing, because of its bearing upon the Apostle's argument. The protagonists of feminism think that they are exalting women, but actually they are not doing so. Man and woman are different, and are meant to be different, and a truly Christian woman always recognizes this. Now it is quite wrong to say that this is merely the opinion and teaching of the Apostle Paul. The Apostle Paul teaches what the whole Bible teaches; it is because his thinking was governed by the Scriptures that he puts it in this form. Take, for instance, Genesis 3: 16, where God says to Eve, 'Thy desire shall be to thy husband, and he shall rule over thee'. God speaks in this way to Eve because she was first guilty of the transgression, because she first fell into sin. And God's pronouncement runs throughout human history: 'Thy desire shall be to thy husband, and he shall rule over thee.' The Apostle here, as well as in the 5th chapter of the Epistle to the Ephesians, makes that perfectly clear. 'Wives, submit yourselves unto your own husbands, as unto the Lord. For the husband is the head of the wife, even as Christ is the head of the church' (Ephesians 5: 22-33). It is tragic that in a reaction against Victorianism – which I am ready to agree was often quite wrong, for many Victorian husbands misused the Scripture in order to be tyrants – the pendulum should have swung so much to the other extreme as to lead to a denial of Scripture. The husband is the head of the wife, and the head of the family. That is God's ordinance, and Paul compares it with the relationship of Christ to the Church. So the wife is exhorted to submit herself because the husband is her head, even as Christ is the Head of the Church. A Christian man should know how to honour his wife, as the Apostle proceeds to tell us. He does not tyrannize over his wife. He gives her her place, he pays her respect. That is the ideal, and the true, and the Christian relationship; but it is never at the expense of what is laid down so plainly in the Old Testament, and in the New, that the husband is the head of the wife. The

Apostle says here that all know this, and are in agreement with it. This is the position of all mankind by nature. The whole of the human race is under the Law of God.

There are also those who may ask whether the Gentiles who had never received the Law of God through Moses were also under this Law. But the Apostle has dealt with that finally in the 2nd chapter of this Epistle, where he says that 'They have the law written in their hearts'. That chapter has established that the whole of mankind is under the Law of God. God made His will explicit and plain and clear in the case of the Jews by giving the Law through Moses; but God's universal Law for the whole of mankind obtains, and the whole of mankind by nature is under the Law. We have seen also how he explains in chapter 5 that even from Adam to Moses, before the Law was promulgated to the Jews through Moses, the Law of God was there but had not yet been defined in this particular manner. Everyone is under the Law of God; that is why 'death reigned from Adam to Moses'. That is the first reason for using this particular illustration; the marriage relationship helps us to see the universal relationship of man in sin to the Law of God. As the wife is under her husband, under his authority, so the whole human race is under the Law of God.

Secondly, the illustration also bring out the binding character of the relationship. Notice the terms: 'The woman that hath an husband is bound by the law to her husband.' The Apostle uses the perfect tense and therefore we are entitled to translate it thus: 'The woman which hath an husband is permanently bound by the law to her husband'. She goes on being bound, is permanently bound; that is the emphasis of the tense. What Paul means, of course, as he has already told us in verse 1, is that nothing but death can break this relationship. 'What about divorce?' asks someone. The answer is that divorce has come in as a concession, as our Lord Himself teaches. God allowed this, He said, 'because of the hardness of your hearts' (Matthew 19: 8). It is a concession, and therefore does not affect the Apostle's argument at this point. He is stating what God originally ordained and what is the universal principle in law. If the law itself decides to make certain concessions for certain reasons, that is another matter, into which we need not enter. But the principle the Apostle lays down is that marriage as such is something that

is not broken by anything but death. But – and this is what he is
anxious to put clearly – death does end the relationship. We shall
see how he works that out. Marriage is a relationship which is
permanent, but which is ended, and can be ended, only by death.
He chose his illustration to bring out that point also.

Then, in the third place, the Apostle chose it in order to bring
out the idea of the possibility of entering into a new relationship.
His illustration in the previous chapter about the 'slave' also
did that, because one man could buy a slave from another. That
illustration was helpful as far as it went, but it did not go far
enough. The marriage relationship puts it much more clearly;
because here it is not a question of buying and selling; it is a
question of death. The death of either party ends the relationship
and releases the surviving partner for a new relationship. The
Apostle is particularly anxious to show this. That is why he
works out his illustration in a certain amount of detail. Let us
watch him as he does so.

He starts his argument by laying down his universal principle.
Then coming to a particular example he says, 'For instance, a
woman who is married to her husband is bound by the law to
that husband as long as he lives'. Then he begins to work it
out – 'But if the husband be dead, she is loosed from the law
of her husband'. This relationship which seemed so permanent is
suddenly ended by death, and so the wife is 'loosed', is 'set free',
and is in a different position. As Paul wishes to make this clear
to us he devotes the whole of the 3rd verse also to a further explanation. 'So then', he says, 'if, while her husband is still alive,
she be married to another, she shall be called an adulteress'.
There is no question about that. Anyone who knows anything
about the laws concerning marriage is agreed as to that. If
this woman joins herself to another man she is an adulteress.
Why? Because her husband is still alive. 'But if her husband be
dead she is free from that law which bound her to that husband;
so that she is no adulteress, though she be married to another
man.'

The Apostle has worked this out in order that we might understand that all that has happened to us in the Lord Jesus Christ
does not contravene the Law. It is not a setting of law on one
side, it is a 'fulfilling of the law'. We shall see this in greater
detail when we come to the 14th verse. Here is this woman, says

the illustration, who was married to that first husband. She is now married to another husband but she has not broken the law. The death of the first husband had ended that first contract, and she is free, so though she is married to another man you must not say that she is an adulteress. She is entitled to marry again; there is nothing wrong in what she is doing. What she has done is legal and right; the law is honoured because the death of the first husband has set her free. The Apostle's concern is to show the way in which we can pass from one spiritual relationship to God to another relationship – 'Ye are not under the law, but under grace'. The illustration shows us how this happens and it is a very wonderful illustration.

Then, fourthly, I believe that the Apostle chose this particular illustration because it brings out as nothing else can the whole object of this relationship. The object of the relationship, he tells us in verse 4, is 'that we should bring forth fruit unto God'. That is the ultimate purpose of marriage. It is not to gratify lust, it is 'that the earth may be replenished', as God told man at the very beginning. In Genesis, chapter 1, verse 28, we read, 'And God blessed them (the man and the woman), and God said unto them, Be fruitful, and multiply'. Such is the original purpose of marriage.

All these points which are implicit in this illustration are essential to the Apostle's argument about the relationship of men and women to the law. I emphasize especially my fourth point, because what Paul is really concerned to prove is that while we are 'married to the law' we can never truly 'bring forth fruit unto God'. It is only as we are married to the Lord Jesus Christ that that becomes possible. So there has to be a dissolution of the first relationship; and we must enter into the second relationship.

In order to work this out further, let us consider the word 'loosed' in verse 2. 'If the husband be dead she is *loosed* from the law of her husband.' This is a most interesting word. In a different translation we have met it before in the 6th verse of the 6th chapter, 'Knowing this, that our old man is crucified with him, that the body of sin might be *destroyed*'. That is exactly the same Greek word as is translated here by 'loosed'. And we interpreted it as meaning 'to be rendered of no effect', 'to be rendered null and void'. But here we meet the word once more, and it is translated 'loosed'. We must grasp the full significance of this word. It really means 'to do away', 'to become or to make of no effect', 'to bring to nought', 'to put away', 'to make void'. She is 'loosed' from the law of her husband. As far as the law which bound her to her husband is concerned, she has been 'put away', she has been entirely 'set free'. The old relationship has been rendered null and void. The Apostle's meaning is perfectly clear.

In other words, what the Apostle sets himself to prove to us is that we must be delivered from the power and the dominion of the Law if we are to produce fruit unto God, and that that can only be accomplished by a death. It is death alone that can break this relationship. If the relationship is not broken by death it will not be a legal break, it will be an adulterous association. So the Apostle proceeds to show that what has happened to us in and through the Lord Jesus Christ does not violate the Law, but rather fulfils it. But it is not enough that we should be broken from, and separated from, the old relationship; before we can bear fruit to God we must be joined in a new relationship, and the whole procedure must be honouring to the Law and in entire conformity with the Law. That is why Paul took the trouble to work out the details in verse 3: 'If, while her husband liveth, she be married to another man, she shall be called an adulteress: but if her husband be dead, she is free from that law; so that she is no adulteress, though she be married to another man.' He says this in order to show the way in which God has worked out our salvation. It is another way of saying what he said so magnificently in the 3rd chapter, verse 26, with regard to justification – 'That God might be just, and the justifier of him which believeth in Jesus'. God is always just, and what God does is always just. 'Do we then make void the law through faith? God forbid,' he says at the end of that 3rd chapter, 'yea we confirm, we establish the law.' Of course! It is essential that we should see that truth at this point.

Next, having worked out his illustration, the Apostle comes to its application in verse 4. He is now going to apply the illustration about the marriage relationship to all believers, to those who are 'in Christ Jesus'. Here we come to another of Paul's great monumental verses, one of these striking statements of his which we have been encountering from time to time, and which gives us one of those perfect definitions of what it means to be a Christian. Here we have the gospel in a nutshell. In a few words the whole essence of the Christian faith and position is summed up for us.

Before we examine it in detail we have to meet what I call a mechanical difficulty. Certain commentators have said that the Apostle does not quite know how to use the illustration, or that, if he does, he goes back on his own illustration and becomes muddled. They feel and say this because there is, on the surface, an apparent muddle in the application of the illustration. The Apostle seems to switch over his reference from one to another. What he has been telling us so far is that the position of all of us by nature is that we are to the Law what a wife is to her husband, that if her husband dies the wife is free to marry another husband. So when he comes to the application you expect him to say something like this, 'The position now is that the law has died and therefore we are free'. But instead of saying that, he says, 'Wherefore, my brethren, ye also are become dead to the law'. Hence the commentators find themselves in trouble. Before, it was the husband who died; now it is the wife who has died. Why does the Apostle use this illustration, they say, if he is going to twist it round in that manner? Cannot he think of a better illustration? Then they try to explain it, to defend the Apostle, and say, 'Perhaps he is saying that we were married, not to the law, but to the "old man".' But that cannot rightly be said! Thus they try to get the Apostle out of his difficulty. But there is no real difficulty. No illustration is perfect, and no illustration must be pressed in its every detail. The Apostle is concerned to clarify a great principle, and his illustration, it seems to me, does that to perfection. All he is concerned to show is that death alone can terminate the old relationship. And as far as the Law is concerned it does not matter which of the partners dies.

The Apostle switches over the reference for one reason only, namely, that he could not say that the Law had died, because the Law has not died. The Law is still alive. I agree that the idea of our being married to the Law is a strange one in and of itself; but it brings out so well those other aspects which I have been outlining that it seems to me to be a masterly illustration. The Law is still there, so Paul cannot say that the Law has died. But the important thing is that, because of a death which has taken place, we are no longer 'bound to the Law', no longer 'under the dominion of the Law'; we are free from the obligations of this former marriage. In other words, our old relationship to the Law has ended; and, as we shall see, it has ended because of a death. That is what the Apostle is concerned to emphasize.

One further remark must be made in order to clear the ground for a positive exposition of this striking 4th verse. Paul is going to say that we have 'become dead to the law by the body of Christ'. Let me clear up this question as to the way in which the Christian can be said to be 'dead to the law', because this again has been grievously misunderstood. There are those who say that it means that the Christian has nothing to do with the Law at all, that he need never think of it again, need never read it, need not be concerned about it to the slightest extent. I say unhesitatingly that that is grievous error. In what sense, then, is the Christian 'dead to the law'? Let me remind you that in this context, the Law means God's moral Law, God's moral demands upon mankind. We have a perfect summary of it in the Ten Commandments. Paul is not here talking about the ceremonial law, he is not saying that all who believe the gospel need no longer offer their burnt offerings and sacrifices. He is addressing Gentiles as well as Jews, as we have already noted in verse 1. He is talking about God's moral Law, God's moral demands upon mankind; and he says that we are dead to that law. But only in this sense, that we are no longer 'under the law'. That is the phrase used in chapter 6, verse 14: 'Sin shall not have dominion over you, for ye are not under the law, but under grace.' We are no longer 'under' it as a covenant of works. We are no longer in the position of trying to save ourselves, to justify ourselves, to sanctify ourselves and to make ourselves fit to stand in the presence of God by keeping the Law. That *was* our position; that is still the position common to the whole of mankind. God said to the Jews in particular, through Moses, 'Do this and thou shalt live', which means, If you keep this law you shall be justified. He told the whole human race when He made known His Law at the beginning, that if men kept it He would be satisfied. That is what is meant by being 'under the law'; it means the Law as a means or method of saving ourselves, of being justified before God, of being sanctified in the presence of God. The glory of the Christian gospel is that we are no longer in that position; we are now 'under grace'. We are no longer trying to justify ourselves by works, or by conformity to the Law. 'Christ is the end of the law for righteousness to every one that believeth', as Paul will say later in chapter 10, verse 4. It is in that sense, and in that sense only, that we are dead to the Law. It does not mean for a moment that we should have no interest at all in the moral Law of God and its demands. It should never be taken to mean that because we are Christians we may say, 'Ah, we are not now interested in what the Law says'. That is a most dangerous form of antinomianism, and it is utter contradition to the plain teaching of the Scripture. Indeed the whole purpose of salvation is to enable us to keep God's Law.

Both the Testaments are emphatic on this matter. Take, for instance, what we are told in Hebrews 8, quoting from Jeremiah 31, concerning the great characteristic of the new covenant that God has made with believers in Christ Jesus. God says, 'I will write my laws in their minds, and imprint them in their hearts'. 'Not according to the covenant that I made with their fathers in the day when I took them by the hand to lead them out of the land of Egypt. . . . For this is the covenant that I will make with the house of Israel after those days, saith the Lord; I will put my laws into their mind, and write them in their hearts; and I will be to them a God, and they shall be to me a people.' That is the new covenant. That is the covenant under which we are as Christians, and in which we rejoice. We find the same truth in chapter 10 of the same Epistle, where the statement is ascribed to our Lord Himself. 'Then said he, Lo, I come to do thy will, O God' (verse 9). That is why He came into the world – to do God's will. Yes, and to enable us to do it!

The Apostle Peter says in his First Epistle, 'Spend the time of your sojourning here in fear'. (1:17). Why? Because God has said, 'Be ye holy, for I am holy'. How am I to be holy? Read the Ten Commandments and you will discover the answer. Our Lord Himself said, 'Think not that I am come to destroy the law, or the prophets; I am not come to destroy but to fulfil. . . . Whosoever therefore shall break one of these least commandments, and shall teach men so, he shall be called the least in the kingdom of heaven; but whosoever shall do and teach them, the same shall be called great in the kingdom of heaven' (Matthew 5: 17–19). Similarly, take Ephesians 6, verses 1 and 2. Here Paul is writing to Christian families and this is what he says: 'Children, obey your parents in the Lord, for this is right. Honour thy father and mother; which is the first commandment with promise', the promise being 'That thy days may be extended in the earth'. The Christian must never say farewell to the Law. Thank God, we are no longer 'under' it as a way of salvation; but we are to keep it, we are to honour it, we are to practise it in our daily life. James in his Epistle says, 'If ye fulfil the royal law according to the scripture, Thou shalt love thy neighbour as thyself, ye do well'. (James 2: 8).

Now all this teaching is found in the chapter we are studying. Observe Paul's way of praising the Law. 'The law is holy, and the commandment holy, and just, and good'. Do not dismiss the Law, do not say that you have nothing to do with the Law. The Law of God is perfect, and we are to keep it. We are not 'under' it, there is no condemnation; it is not the way of salvation; but that does not mean that we have no interest in it.

But in the next chapter of our Epistle we have a still more clinching proof. Look at what the Apostle says in verse 3 of chapter 8: 'What the law could not do, in that it was weak through the flesh, God sending his own Son in the likeness of sinful flesh, and for sin, condemned sin in the flesh.' For what purpose? '(In order) that the righteousness of the law might be fulfilled in us, who walk not after the flesh, but after the Spirit.' Paul is not only referring to Christ's death for our sins; he is saying that the object of salvation is to enable us to carry out the righteousness of the Law. Finally, consider what he says in this Epistle in chapter 13, verses 8–10, and in doing so, remember that he is writing to Christian believers: 'Owe no man anything, but to love one another; for he that loveth another hath fulfilled the law. For this, Thou shalt not kill, Thou shalt not steal, Thou shalt not bear false witness, Thou shalt not covet, Thou shalt not commit adultery' – note that the Apostle is quoting the Ten Commandments – 'and if there be any other commandment, it is briefly comprehended in this saying, Thou shalt love thy neighbour as thyself. Love worketh no ill to his neighbour; therefore love is the fulfilling of the law.' That is how Christian people are to love! Therefore, as Christians, we must never say, foolishly and wrongly, 'I have nothing to do with the Law at all; you should never preach the Ten Commandments, I am under grace, I have finished with the Law'. The Apostle Paul preached the Ten Commandments to the Christian saints in Rome, and they are as applicable to us today as they were then. They are still a wonderful setting forth of the kind of life that you and I should be living. Beware of antinomianism. It is, in a sense, in order that we might be enabled to live according to the Law, and thereby bear fruit unto God, that Christ came and died for us and rose again. It is in order that we might do this that we are bound to Him, married to Him, found in Him, incorporated in Him. And His power working in us, and through us, enables us to fulfil the righteousness of the Law.

Having cleared that point we are now free to come to a positive exposition of the great liberating statement of the 4th verse.

Three

*

Wherefore, my brethren, ye also are become dead to the law by the body of Christ; that ye should be married to another, even to him who is raised from the dead, that we should bring forth fruit unto God.
                                                              Romans 7: 4

In this verse we come to the application of what the Apostle has been saying in the first three verses, and especially to the application of the illustration with respect to marriage which he is using in order to explain our relationship to the Law, and our standing before God in and through our Lord and Saviour Jesus Christ. It is, I suggest, one of those verses in which the Apostle delights to give a complete summary of the whole of the Christian life. He never seems to be content with stating just a part of the Truth. He so gloried in the Truth that he rejoiced in stating it all time and again. Here, then, we have, as it were, the gospel in a nutshell. It is one of the great basic definitions of what it means to be a Christian; and at the same time, and of necessity, it shows us the profound character of the Christian life. That is why it is worth our while to give it our undivided attention, and allow it to speak to us. One chief cause of our troubles, and a main explanation of the state of the whole Church today, is our failure to realize the full and the deep character of the Christian life. We are constantly defining it, thinking of it, and speaking of it in terms that fall hopelessly short of what we are taught here, and what, indeed, we are taught everywhere in the New Testament. Superficiality is one of the greatest curses that can befall the Christian. We have our little definitions, we take up certain aspects of the Christian life, and we miss its profundities, its true greatness and depth and largeness.

Let us then follow the Apostle as he expounds this glorious truth. There is a sense in which it is true to say that what he says

[29]

in this verse is really what he has already told us in chapter 6, verse 11, where he said, 'Likewise reckon ye also yourselves to be dead indeed unto sin, but alive unto God through Jesus Christ our Lord'. He has also said it in verse 17 of that chapter: 'But God be thanked, that ye were the servants of sin, but ye have obeyed from the heart that form of doctrine which was delivered you'. But as the Apostle repeats it we must repeat it, for we shall find that there are particular emphases which he brings out here which he has not brought out in exactly the same way in those previous summaries of the truth.

First, let us look at this verse as it gives us a general description and definition of the Christian life. It is here for us on the surface. It tells us immediately that to be a Christian means that we have an entirely new life. The Apostle speaks in terms of being 'dead' and 'alive'. To be Christian is nothing less than that. It involves a death and a rising. The difference, therefore, between the Christian and the non-Christian is obviously a radical one, and not merely something superficial. To become a Christian does not mean that you just modify your former life a little, or adjust it slightly, or make it look a little better, or 'brush it up' as it were. There are may who conceive of Christianity in those terms. To become a Christian, they think, means in the main that you stop doing certain things, and begin to do others. There is a slight adjustment in your life, a slight modification, some things are dropped, others added; there is some improvement, you live a better life than you lived before. All that, of course, is quite true, but that alone is not Christianity. Whatever our definition of Christianity is, it must include this idea of a death and a new life – nothing less than that. In other words, to be a Christian means to undergo the profoundest change that one can ever know. That is why the New Testament, in speaking of the way in which a person becomes a Christian, uses such terms as 'Ye must be born again', 'a new creation', a 'new creature'. It is nothing less than regeneration. Naturally, generation is fundamental; it is the giving of life and bringing into being. Becoming a Christian involves regeneration, and the spiritual far surpasses the natural. So here at once, and on the very surface, we are made to realize that to be a Christian is no small matter, and that the difference between the Christian and the non-Christian is not a slight one. It is the greatest difference possible between two human beings.

It is no other than the difference between life and death. That is why I say that the main trouble with most of us in the Church today is that our whole concept of the Christian life is much too small. We seem to have lost this idea, though we may pay lip-service to it, that it involves as radical a process and as deep-seated a change as is conceivable. That is the first truth.

The second truth is that the man who has become a Christian is in an entirely new relationship. That is what the Apostle is emphasizing here in particular. To be a Christian means that you are now in an entirely new relationship to God. Before, your relationship to God was one through the Law; it is now through the Lord Jesus Christ. What a change that is! My whole standing is different; my position, my status as I stand before God, is altogether different from what it was before. Here again is something which emphasizes the profound character of the Christian life. So as we talk about it we must always include this thought, that there has been an entire change in our relationship to God. We were 'under law', we are now 'under grace'.

The third truth is that as Christians we have an entirely new purpose in life, namely, 'to bring forth fruit unto God'. The man who is not a Christian knows nothing of that purpose; he lives for himself, he brings forth fruit unto himself. He lives to satisfy himself; he is self-centred, entirely egocentric. It matters not how good a man he appears to be; if he is not a Christian, he is always egocentric. He is proud of his morality, he is proud that he is not like other people, he looks at them with disdain. All along he is pleasing himself, coming up to his own standard, trusting his own efforts and endeavours. He revolves around himself. But the man who has become a Christian has an entirely new purpose, to 'bring forth fruit unto God'. These are basic definitions of what it means to be a Christian.

The fourth general truth which here lies on the surface is that the Christian is a man who has been provided with an entirely new ability, a new power and strength. Certain things have happened to him in order that he should 'bring forth fruit unto God'. He could not do that before; he can do so now. A new ability, a new power has entered into the life of this man.

There, I say, are four things which lie here on the very surface of this verse, and which are always true of the Christian. Therefore if we would know for certain whether or not we are

Christians we have four thorough tests that we can apply to ourselves. Can you say quite honestly, 'I am not the person I once was, I have been born again, I am a different person?' That is the first thing – new life. It does not mean of necessity that that evidence is always very strong or very powerful. You can be a 'babe in Christ', but even a babe has life. A babe is not as strong as a grown-up adult person, but he has life. The question therefore is: Are we aware of the fact that there is this 'new life' in us? It is not that we have done something, but that something has happened to us which causes us to be surprised at ourselves, and to wonder at ourselves that something is now true of us which was not true before.

For your encouragement and comfort – and especially for those who may feel that they are very weak, and doubtful about their position – let me suggest some few simple tests. What are the tests of 'life?' Here are some of them. The Apostle Peter writes, 'As new-born babes, desire the sincere milk of the word, that ye may grow thereby' (I Peter 2: 2). I put it to you in this way. Do you enjoy public meetings for worship? That is not true of the natural man, the non-Christian. Men and women of the world regard such meetings as the height of boredom; and they have no understanding of what is being said. They say, 'What is all that? What does it mean? What has it got to do with me?' And they would never want to hear it again. Does exposition of the Truth in preaching appeal to you? Do you like it? Do you enjoy it? Would you like to know more about it? If you can say 'Yes' to those questions you possess good presumptive evidence that you have new life in you. You may only be a 'babe'; but thank God, you are born again, you are 'in Christ'. Do not be misled by people who would apply the test of a mature, adult, fully-grown Christian to a new-born babe. 'The natural man receiveth not the things of the Spirit of God, for they are foolishness unto him; neither can he know them for they are spiritually discerned' (I Cor. 2: 14). If you therefore 'receive' these things, though you may be living an unworthy life, you are 'born again'. 'The natural mind is enmity against God, for it is not subject to the law of God, neither indeed can be.' If you can say honestly that your desire is to know God and to serve Him, you are a child of God. You may be imperfect, I am not excusing you – but you must be clear about this. If, because of your failures, you are made to feel, as I said earlier, that you are not a Christian at all, then your position is such that you have to go right back to the beginning once more. Therefore, I say, do not allow any legalist to cause you to doubt your position. The new-born babe desires the 'milk', 'the sincere milk of the word, that he may grow thereby'; he is interested in spiritual things. His understanding may be very small, and very immature; but if he has even a glimmer of light, and if he wants more of it – if he is drawn to the truth, and likes to be amongst God's people – then the statement that 'We know that we have passed from death unto life because we love the brethren' applies to him. Those are some of the tests which we can apply to ourselves. The Apostle's assertion is that you cannot be a Christian without a death and a new birth – a 'life'.

Then proceed to apply the other tests in exactly the same way. Can you say quite truthfully that when you think of God, and when you turn to God, you no longer do so with the slavish fear you once had; but that you have some consciousness within you that God is your Father, and that God loves you? Your assurance may not be a very clear one, but is there even that difference? Are you aware that, however incomplete it may be, there is some fundamental difference and change in your relationship to God? Before, you went before Him as a condemned criminal. Do you find that now you are able to go before Him as a child who feels very much ashamed of himself or herself? Are you conscious that you are now offending not so much against a law as against love? Are you aware of this filial, child relationship, rather than the old legal one?

Then go on to a third test. Can you say quite honestly and truthfully that you really have a new purpose in your life, that however unworthily you are carrying it out, your real purpose is to serve God? Are you concerned about this in a new way; no longer in that old, mechanical, legal way, but in this living, vital way because of your new relationship, and because of the love you have for God, however weak and imperfect it may be? Are you now governed by a new purpose as you face life and its responsibilities in this world? As you face these questions you will know exactly where you stand. The constant danger in this matter is to jump to details. Keep to these great principles. If you are aware of a new central purpose in your life, I say you are a child of God.

And do you know anything about a new ability, a new power? You may be very weak, you may experience much failure, but can you say, 'Well, even as I am, I am aware of something in me, something working in me which was not there before?' It may be largely negative, a mere counteraction against sin, an increasing dislike of sin, indeed nothing more, perhaps, than a growing desire to be delivered from sin. But it is indicative of this new power, this new ability, this new strength that is given to all who are truly Christian.

I am deliberately putting the evidences of new life at their lowest level; and I do so because one finds so frequently that the 'babes in Christ' are offended and caused to stumble and made miserable by legalists, who take it upon themselves to pronounce judgment when they are not in a position to do so, and who have not sufficient understanding to see that it is this essential difference of nature that is of prime importance. It is a very grievous thing to discourage babes in Christ; we are to encourage babes, and to help them. 'Ah but', you say, 'you are encouraging them to be Antinomians.' It is not so. If you really get them to see and to know what they are as babes in Christ, that above everything else will stimulate their growth and give them the desire to please God in all things. Read the New Testament epistles and you will see that that is how the babes are constantly dealt with. Certainly we can reprimand them. We have to train them, and teach them, and discipline them; but what we must never do is to discourage them. It is a grievous sin to suggest to them that they are not alive at all because they are only babes. That arises from sheer misunderstanding of the Scriptures.

Such, then, is the general truth about the Christian implied in this verse. I have indicated something of the things that must be in evidence. Whatever the degree, they must be there. And if it is so, then such a person is a Christian.

If these are the marks that characterize the Christian, how does one become a Christian? How is it possible for anyone to get into this position and condition which I have been describing? The Apostle deals with that also in a very clear manner. The first thing he tells us, as he tells us everywhere in his writings, it that it is altogether and entirely in and through our Lord and Saviour Jesus Christ – 'by the body of Christ'. Without Him there is no

Christianity. Salvation is in Him; it is in Him alone; and it is 'in Him' from the very beginning to the very end. Let me put that in this way. As you talk to other people whose whole position you may feel to be questionable, the first thing to do with them is to make them talk. Get them to talk about what they conceive a Christian to be; and if they regard themselves as Christians get them to state why they regard themselves as Christians. Encourage them to talk along those lines, and as they do so concentrate on one thing only – does the name of the Lord Jesus Christ come into it at all or not, or how much? You will find quite frequently that people will talk at great length without even mentioning His name. The test which I have always found to be crucial is to ask such a person this question, 'If you had to die tonight and to stand before God, what would you say? On what would you rely? What would your position be?' Put that question to them and you will find quite frequently that they will attempt to answer without even mentioning the name of the Lord Jesus Christ.

There is only one thing to say about such people, and that is that they are not Christians. 'Christianity is Christ.' He is central, He is vital, He is all in all. It does not matter how good a life may be, how moral it may appear to be, if it is not entirely dependent upon the Lord Jesus Christ and what He has done, it is not Christianity. It may be morality, it may be some other religion, but it is not Christianity. You can have religion without Christianity; you can have morality without Christianity; but the thing that makes Christianity Christian is the centrality, is the cruciality of our Lord and Saviour Jesus Christ. Hence, any claim that is made, if it does not directly relate everything to Him, and give the glory to Him, proves at once that it is not Christian at all. God forbid that any should be uncertain about this point. It is the very negation of Christianity to think that you are a Christian simply because you have been born in a particular country, or because you were baptised or christened when you were an infant, or because you were baptised when you were an adult, or because you were taken into church membership as an adolescent by a minister in consultation with your parents. If that is your idea of becoming a Christian you need to go back to the very beginning. If your position is not entirely dependent upon this blessed Person it is not Christianity at all; it is sham, it is counterfeit.

Notice that I am not putting it in terms of the life lived, I am putting it in terms of your relationship to Him.

The first thing the Apostle says, and I repeat, he says it everywhere, is that our Lord and Saviour Jesus Christ must be in the very centre, everything must focus upon Him. But this is a general statement, and before we can be clear as to how we become Christians we have to particularize; and the Apostle at once proceeds to do so. He singles out those things in the Lord Jesus Christ which are absolute essentials to our salvation. What are these? Here, of course, we come again into the realm of doctrine. Let us be clear about this: we must know as to how we are saved. The New Testament Scriptures have been given to us in order to teach us how we are saved. It is therefore wrong for a man to say, 'I am a Christian, but I cannot tell you how or why. I do not understand all about these doctrines and about theology; I am just a simple person.' A Christian does not speak in that way. A Christian should know how he is saved; and this one verse really tells us all that is essential. It is not enough simply to say, 'Yes, I believe in the Lord Jesus Christ'. We must know what we believe about the Lord Jesus Christ, what in particular we believe about Him.

The Apostle leads us to see what we must believe. We become Christians primarily because of certain things that have happened to Him. 'What do you mean?' asks someone. I am referring to His death, as does the Apostle. 'Wherefore, my brethren, you also have become dead to the law by the body of Christ.' Here is the first essential particular doctrine. How does the Lord Jesus Christ save me? Is it simply by His incarnation? No! I must believe in His incarnation, of course, because I am told here about His 'body'. 'God is spirit', and Christ is the Second Person in the blessed Godhead; but as Jesus of Nazareth He has a body, He is incarnate. I must believe that. I must believe in His coming from heaven to earth, that 'the Word was made flesh and dwelt among us'. But that is not the crucial fact according to Paul. He does not save me by His incarnation only; neither does He save me by His teaching. He taught the Sermon on the Mount. Does the Sermon on the Mount save me? Assuredly it does not; it condemns me. So He does not save me by His teaching. He did not come into the world simply to say 'This is how you ought to live. Do this and you will be Christians, and God will receive you and forgive you.' No! it was not by His teaching. Neither was it by His example. These are the things that are commonly taught, are they not? Incarnation – Teaching – Example – A fillip to our endeavour – an encouragement, and so on. No! says the Apostle; the crucial thing is His death. 'Wherefore my brethren, you also are become dead to the law'. Why this 'also'? Because Christ became dead to the Law. The Apostle is talking about His death. He could have used various words here to introduce the fact of death; but he deliberately chose the word for 'death' which is the most violent that he could have chosen. Why did he do so? To remind us of that violent death of the Son of God upon the Cross on Calvary's hill. Crucifixion was a cruel form, a violent form of death. He did not merely 'die'; He was 'put to death'. Paul has chosen this word to emphasize that He was put to a violent death, for he knows how prone we are to miss this, or to wander away from it. He even brings in the word 'body'; 'ye are become dead to the law by the body of Christ.' He is reminding us of the stark fact. We are not saved by an idea, but by something that was done to the Lord Jesus Christ in His body as He died there on the Cross on Calvary's hill. We are saved by historical facts and events, by things that happened to the Lord Jesus Christ.

What was it that happened? What was taking place there when the Lord Jesus Christ was dying upon the Cross? The Apostle makes it plain that whatever else might be included, something was happening that was quite directly connected with the Law. 'You also are become dead to the law by the body of Christ.' In other words, here we are face to face with the great doctrine of the Atonement. In this section, as we have already seen, the Apostle is concerned ultimately with a very practical matter, namely, our sanctification. But he cannot deal with sanctification apart from the doctrine of the Atonement.

Let me put it as a question. Why did the Son of God die upon the Cross? Why did the Lord Jesus Christ say that He could, if He willed, have called for more than 'twelve legions of angels' to carry Him up to heaven and so avoid death? Why did He not avoid death? Why did He die? This verse gives a complete answer. We have already met with it in chapter 3 in that vital section beginning at verse 24, but here it appears once more. Why did He die? He died because of the Law. Any view of the death of Christ which does not put it specifically and primarily in terms of the Law of God is a misinterpretation of His death. I am referring, of course, to the view which holds that His death was an 'accident', that it was merely the result of the jealousy and the cruelty of the Pharisees and Scribes, that it was no vital part of the process of salvation, but was the supreme tragedy of history, or may be but the death of a pacifist. The same applies to the sentimental view of His death which says that He was just showing the love of God. I rule out all these explanations of His death because they do not put themselves before us in terms of His relationship to the Law. There was only one reason why the Son of God died on the Cross on Calvary's hill; it was because of the Law of God. The Apostle says this in writing to the Galatians in chapter 4, verse 4; 'When the fulness of the time was come, God sent forth His Son, made of a woman' – yes, 'made under the law'. What for? 'To redeem them that were under the law'. Such was His purpose. He came to 'redeem' us from the Law, to redeem them that were 'under the law'.

This is the key to everything He did, and especially to His death upon the Cross. But you may say, 'How does it work?' I answer: the Law cannot be ignored; the Law cannot be set aside. The Law is God's Law, and therefore it is immutable. Everything that God does is also just. It is God who has promulgated the Law, and He cannot go back on that; otherwise He would be denying Himself. Every action of God is just, and righteous, and holy; and God's Law demands that the punishment for sin should be death. It is God who issued the Law who has also said, 'The soul that sinneth, it shall die'. Here, then, is the demand of the Law of God, which is an expression of the character of God. It is not something apart from God, it is God Himself manifesting, revealing His character. That is what He was doing when He gave the Law on Mount Sinai. 'The soul that sinneth, it shall die'.

Here, therefore, is the problem. We all have sinned, we are all under the condemnation of the Law, and that involves death. But the Lord Jesus Christ came into the world to deliver us from the condemnation of the Law; and this is how He has done it. He first put Himself under the Law – 'made of a woman, made under the law'. He had no need to be 'under the law'; He was without sin, He was born holy; but He puts Himself under the

Law. That is why He asked John the Baptist to baptize Him;
He was identifying Himself with sinners, with us. He kept the
Law, He honoured the Law in every detail. He went to the temple,
and did everything that people under the Law should do. Why
did He do all this? Because He came to act as our representative,
to act on our behalf. He has put Himself in our position, He has
taken our place. In His life He rendered a perfect, positive obedience to God's Law. But that alone could not save us. We have all
sinned; our sins condemn us, even as sins condemned those who
sinned before He ever came into the world. What can be done
about them? Here is the answer. We saw it all in chapter 3, verses
25, 26 and 27. He has taken our sins upon Himself. Peter puts
it, once and for ever, in his First Epistle, 2nd chapter, verse 24:
'Who his own self bear our sins in his own body' – there is the
same word again – 'in his own body on the tree, that we being
dead to sins should live unto righteousness.' He died as the result of bearing the punishment that the Law metes out upon our
sins. It was the only way whereby we could be delivered. I say it
with reverence God cannot play fast and loose with His own Law.
God cannot wink at sin, and pretend that He has not seen it.
Although He is love, He cannot simply say, 'I forgive you everything', because that would mean that He is no longer just. No,
says Paul in Romans, chapter 3, verse 26: 'God (must) be just,
and (at the same time) the justifier of him that believeth in Jesus.'
This is God's legal, righteous way of saving men. He does it
'by the body of Christ'. 'You also have become dead to the law
by (or through), the body of Christ.'

If that had not happened to the Lord Jesus Christ there would
be no Christianity, there would be no forgiveness or salvation
for anyone. But, 'He was delivered for our offences,' as we are
told in the last verse in the 4th chapter of the Epistle to the Romans. So when you are asked how a person becomes a Christian
you do not start talking about yourself and what you have done;
nor do you speak only about the Person of our Lord and His teaching and example. You say, first, that one becomes a Christian
solely because, at a given point in history, 'God sent forth His
own Son, made of a woman, made under the law'. Then, you go
on to say that He lived a perfect life of obedience to God's Law,
and honoured that Law in every respect. But He did not stop
at that, He put Himself 'under' its punishment, under its penal

aspect, He took our sins upon Himself; God laid them on Him; and then the Law delivered its judgment and He was smitten and slain. He died the death that we should have died; He died 'for our sins'. Salvation becomes possible to us through His broken body, His shed blood. The Law demanded that satisfaction, and He rendered it to the full. That is the first absolute essential.

But we do not leave it at that; the Apostle mentions one further essential truth. 'Wherefore my brethren, ye also are become dead to the law by the body of Christ, that ye should be married to another.' Then you would expect him to go on to say, 'even to the Lord Jesus Christ'. But this is what he actually says, 'that you should be married to another, even to him that is raised from the dead'. This is something further that had to happen. As the Apostle thinks of the coming of the Son of God into this world, and His going back again to heaven, he seems to say, 'From the standpoint of salvation these are the two crucial things – Death, resurrection. 'Even unto him that is raised from the dead.'

Clarity at this point is vital. The Apostle is referring to the literal, physical resurrection of the Lord Jesus Christ from the grave. He is not thinking, as do some moderns who claim to be teachers, of some spiritualistic phenomenon; the Apostle means literal, physical resurrection. He is talking about the literal physical body. The body that was crucified and buried was the body that rose. It was changed, it is true, but it was the same body. He rose in the body; there was an empty grave. Resurrection! That is what the Apostle means. He is repeating what he has already told us in the last verse of chapter 4, 'Who was delivered for our offences, and raised again for our justification'. This is also essential; the Apostle is therefore careful to add it. He is asserting that it was essential to our salvation that, in addition to the death of the Lord Jesus Christ, He should also have arisen from among the dead, and out of the grave, that He should have appeared among men, and have ascended to heaven, and should be at this moment in God's presence, seated at His right hand interceding for us and on our behalf.

Why is this essential to salvation? One answer is that it is the final proof that what He did in His life and death is sufficient, that He has answered the last demand of the Law, that He has conquered the last enemy, which is death. The last enemy must be conquered before we can be fully saved. And He has done it; He has risen again. He had to rise also to give us new life, in order that we might live by Him and in Him and on Him. He had to rise again in order to present us to God. The death alone does not do that. It makes the Atonement, and provides the necessary offering; but I also need to be 'presented' to God. It is He who does that. 'He died to bring us to God', says the Apostle Peter. His resurrection also guarantees that our ultimate salvation shall be complete and entire, that our bodies shall also rise and be glorified and be entirely delivered from sin in its every manifestation and in its every form.

How does one become a Christian? How is it possible for me ever to display the four characteristics of the Christian that we have noted? Thank God this is the first part of the answer – because of something that has happened to the Son of God! I do not start with myself. What has happened to me happens because of what happened to Him. We shall go on to deal with that. But what make us Christians is the fact that He died upon the tree, His body was broken for us, His blood was shed. But He rose again, and 'ever liveth to make intercession for us'; His presence at the right hand of God is the guarantee of our final and complete salvation.

We are thus left always looking to Him and at Him. These are the events, the facts, the historical happenings which are absolutely essential to our salvation. We are not saved by teaching, we are not saved by ideas; we are saved by the fact that the eternal Son of God came into this world, had a literal physical body, was born of the Virgin Mary, died upon the Cross, was buried in a grave, conquered death, bursting asunder its bands, rose triumphant, and ascended unto God, and is seated now at God's right hand. 'Thanks be unto God for his unspeakable gift.'

Four

*

Wherefore, my brethren, ye also are become dead to the law by the body of Christ, that ye should be married to another, even to him who is raised from the dead, that we should bring forth fruit unto God.
                                                                    Romans 7: 4

We continue our study of this remarkable definition of the Christian, and of the manner in which one becomes the possessor of such a life. We have seen that that could only happen, first, as the result of something that has happened to the Lord Jesus Christ Himself, and very specially, His death. It was through 'the death of his body' that this has come to us. But we also saw that the Apostle was very careful to go on and to add that Christ is also 'raised from the dead' and that 'He is alive for evermore'. Our whole position is based on these facts; and any desire on our part to rush past them is a very bad sign. A Christian who does not delight always to go back again and consider our Lord, and all that He did, how He came and died and rose again, is confessing that there is something seriously wrong with himself. We must never cease to marvel at the fact that God so loved the world that He sent His only begotten Son into it in the way He did, and that the Son endured and suffered and died and rose again. Even here, where the Apostle is concerned primarily with our relationship to the Law, and our sanctification, the Apostle brings it in, and we must always do the same. A subjective, sentimental Christianity which loses sight, to any extent, of the grand objective facts, is already seriously defective. That has been the chief trouble with the Christian Church during this century in particular.

We come now to the second factor, for as certain things had to happen to Him before we could have this life, in exactly the

[42]

same way, as we now go on to see, something has to happen also to us. It is something that is absolutely essential; and the Apostle therefore puts great emphasis upon it. We have looked at the great facts concerning Christ; but what is my relationship to them? Is it just a question of belief only, of accepting these propositions, of believing these statements of fact concerning the Son of God? Or is it that, plus a determination to follow Him and to imitate Him and to try to live life as He lived it? Does that make us Christians? The answer is that it does not. You can have an intellectual belief, you can accept the orthodox position with your mind, and still not be a Christian. You can live a good life, you can try to imitate Christ, and still not be a Christian. Those attitudes are essential, but they are not enough; something has to happen in addition to them. The Apostle teaches us, once more, that as Christians we are united to the Lord Jesus Christ. 'Wherefore, my brethren, ye also are become dead to the law by the body of Christ.' We have already considered this doctrine which the Apostle introduced in chapter 5, verse 10. He works it out in detail from verse 12 in that chapter and in chapter 6, especially in verses 1–7. It is implicit also in the remainder of chapter 6. As we were joined to Adam, we are now joined to the Lord Jesus Christ. That is the doctrine. The Apostle says that because that is true of us, '. . . yet also are become dead to the law by the body of Christ'. This is another statement of the doctrine which he worked out in detail at the beginning of chapter 6, verse 3. 'Know ye not', he says, 'that so many of us as were baptised into Jesus Christ were baptised into his death? Therefore we are buried with him by baptism into death; that like as Christ was raised up from the dead by the glory of the Father, even so we also should walk in newness of life. For if we have been planted together in the likeness of his death, we shall be also in the likeness of his resurrection.' Here, in verse 4 Paul is really saying that once again; but he does so in order to bring out an additional point. What he has established in chapter 6 is that we died with, and in the Lord Jesus Christ, to sin and to death. He is now concerned to show that we also died at the same time to the Law. That is the particular matter he demonstrates in this chapter.

Observe the way in which he puts it. The Authorised Version is rather weak at this point and indeed misleading – 'Wherefore my brethren', it says, 'you also are become dead to the law'.

A better translation is, 'You were made dead to the law'. Some would even say that it can be translated thus: 'You were put to death as regards your relationship to the law.' You have not 'become dead', you were 'made dead'. Again I have to emphasize that the Apostle deliberately uses a particular tense; and it is still – as we saw so often in chapter 6 – the aorist tense, which is not only past but final, and once and for all. It is not a process that goes on; it is one action, and it is an action that has taken place once and for ever; it cannot be repeated, it is absolutely final. 'Wherefore, my brethren, you also were made dead to the law, by the body of Christ.' Now that is just another way of saying that we died with Him. Though this is made so plain in chapter 6, people still stumble over it. Hence the Apostle repeats it, and we must do so. The position of the Christian is that he died with the Lord Jesus Christ once, once and for all, and for ever. When? When He died upon the Cross, when He died in that body which He had taken unto Himself. When He died on the Cross, we who are Christians died with Him. This is not something that happens to us subsequently; you cannot be a Christian at all without having died with Him. There are many who say, 'Ah yes, He died there; and we are justified by that event. Now we have got to die as well' – as if our dying is something subsequent. That is utterly unscriptural. We died with Him once and for all there. That is true of all who are Christians.

What the Apostle is saying therefore is, that when we died with Him there on the Cross we were dying to the Law as well as to sin and to death. In chapter 6 verses 9 and 10, we have seen that we died with Him unto death, 'Knowing that Christ being raised from the dead dieth no more; death hath no more dominion over him. For in that he died, he died unto sin once' – once and for all – 'but in that he liveth, he liveth unto God. Likewise reckon ye also yourselves to be dead unto sin.' Yes, and also in the same context showing our deliverance from death – 'but alive unto God through Jesus Christ our Lord'. The doctrine therefore is this, that when our Lord was there dying on the Cross He was dying to the Law – not only dying to sin, and to death, but also dying to the Law.

'How is that possible?' asks someone. In this way! Galatians 4, verse 4, tells us that 'When the fulness of the time was come, God sent forth his Son, made of a woman, made under the law'.

That is an amazing fact. In order to redeem us the Son of God was 'made under the law'. That does not mean that He was sinful – not at all. He never did sin; but He was subject to the Law. 'Made under the law' means that He put Himself under the Law, and became subject to it even as we are. He rendered a perfect obedience to it in His life. He kept its every precept; He never failed in anything. And in His death on the Cross He received the punishment that the Law metes out to sin for all for whom He died. It was the Law that demanded His death. The Law has done everything that it could to Him; but He has risen again, proving that He has finished with the Law. The moment He rose again He was no longer 'under the law'. That is why the Apostle emphasizes, and keeps on emphasizing, His resurrection. The Resurrection is the declaration that the Law has been completely fulfilled and satisfied, that He has finished with it, that He is no longer under the Law. He was only 'under the law' while He was here in this world. Now He is no longer 'under the law'; He is reigning in glory above it and beyond it; that is His position. So He has finished completely with the Law, and He will never be under it again. It has no more demands that it can make on Him. Every demand it could make on Him, it did make on Him; and He has satisfied them, every one. So He has finished with the Law for ever.

What the Apostle is asserting here is that the same is also true of us who are Christians, because of our union with Him, because we were baptised into His death, and died with Him. He has died to the Law; so have we! 'Wherefore my brethren, you were made dead to the law by the body of Christ.' This is one of the most glorious and liberating truths we can ever grasp. It is so important that this same Apostle states it frequently. There is a perfect statement of it in the Epistle to the Galatians in the 2nd chapter and the 19th verse, where he says, 'I through the law am dead to the law, that I might live unto God'. That is exactly the same as this statement here in this 4th verse of this 7th chapter of the Epistle to the Romans. What he means is this. The Law itself, in exacting its full penalty upon the Lord Jesus Christ in His death, has thereby set us Christians free from its penal claims. I 'through the law' am dead to the Law. In other words, the Law by putting Him to death and by making its demands upon Him as my representative – and He having fulfilled those

[45]

demands completely – the Law itself has set me free from the Law. It has no more demands that it can make on me. By what it did to Him it sets us free. 'I through the law am dead to the law, that I might live unto God.' That is the glorious statement which the Apostle makes here concerning our position in Christ Jesus. By the body of Christ crucified on Calvary's hill I am made dead to the Law. It has nothing to say to me. So far as the Law is concerned, it is as if I were indeed no longer alive.

Let us work that out. The Christian is dead to the Law therefore in the following respects. He is not merely a man who is forgiven. Of course he is forgiven, but much more than that belongs to salvation. Formerly we were all 'married to the law'; but we are no longer married to the Law. We have died out of that marriage; that contract no longer has any force or legal existence. Secondly, we can say that we are no longer under the ruling power of the Law. We took time to work out the Apostle's illustration and analogy about a woman who is married to her husband, how she is under the ruling power and dominion of that husband. Such was our relationship to the Law, but it is no longer our relationship to it. We were under the dominion and the reign and ruling power of the Law, but we are no longer in that position. That is not the power that reigns over us now; we are married to another Husband. The Law is no longer the main force or power in our lives. The Apostle will work this out in great detail in the remainder of the chapter; I just mention it as a principle at this point. Before we become Christians the Law is the ruling force and power in our lives. What that leads to we shall see later. But the moment we become Christian the Law is no longer the main force or power that is working within us. Then, thirdly, the Law can no longer condemn us. This is one of the most glorious facts of all. It must not be held in isolation; but it is a vital one. The Law has already done everything it can do to those of us who are in Christ Jesus, including our condemnation and punishment. The Apostle will assert that in the 1st verse of chapter 8: 'There is therefore now no condemnation to them that are in Christ Jesus.' The Law cannot point a finger at us, it cannot accuse us, it cannot condemn us. The fact is that as Christians we are entirely outside the jurisdiction of the Law. We have been made dead to it; we are in the position which Paul has already illustrated by his analogy concerning marriage.

I need scarcely say that the realization of all this is essential to true assurance of salvation, and to real liberty in the Christian life. It was because they had become confused about the matter that the Galatians had moved into a false position, which made it necessary for the Apostle to write to them in a truly severe manner. You cannot have a real sense of freedom and assurance in the Christian life until you realize that you are completely dead to the Law. We must not be afraid of being called Antinomian because we hold such a doctrine. The Apostle was charged with that error but he continues to assert the doctrine. He says that we are no longer 'under the law' because we have been made dead to the Law. The violent death which we died with Christ ended our relationship to the Law once and for ever.

> *The terrors of law and of God*
> *With me can have nothing to do;*
> *My Saviour's obedience and blood*
> *Hide all my transgressions from view.*

Christian people, do you know this truth? Have you realized its value? Are you rejoicing in it? Do you realize that in this sense you have nothing to do with the Law? That it has no jurisdiction over you? That it is no longer a power under which you are living?

We note then the categorical statement of the Apostle. Why is he so concerned to emphasize this and to say that we are no longer 'married to the law'? I answer: because this is not only essential to our justification; his whole point is that it is equally essential for our sanctification. And he goes on to work this out. We have to realize that we have finished with the Law in that relationship; otherwise, he says, our sanctification is in jeopardy.

Let us see how he proceeds to prove his assertions. Here are the steps. First, we are united to the Lord Jesus Christ. Secondly, we have died with Him, and are 'made dead' to the Law as the result of that death. Then we come to the third element, which is positive, namely, that we are married to the Lord Jesus Christ. 'Wherefore, my brethren, ye also are made dead to the law by the body of Christ, that (in order that) ye should be married to another, even to him who is raised from the dead.' The Apostle leaves out one step in his statement here; but as he has stated it so fully in chapter 6 he seems to feel that it was unnecessary to repeat it in detail at this point. You notice that he says 'we have died with Christ', and then proceeds immediately to say that we are married to Him. But something must have happened in between; namely, that we have risen with Him – 'planted together in the likeness of his death, we shall be also in the likeness of his resurrection' (chapter 6, verse 5). We do not remain dead; we have risen with Christ. We are alive, and being alive we are now in a position to be married to the Lord Jesus Christ. He emphasizes the death because obviously you cannot be married to the Lord Jesus Christ if you are still married to the Law. That, he says, is adultery; it is illegal and under Divine condemnation. 'If while her husband liveth she be joined to another man, she shall be called an adulteress.' So if we are to be married to the Lord Jesus Christ our marriage to the Law must be dissolved, and the only way to end it, he says, is by death. Hence he is very much concerned to say that we have died to the Law. We are out of that old marriage relationship because we have died with the Lord Jesus Christ; it is essential to the new relationship that the old relationship must first be broken and ended. That is why, in this 4th verse, in many senses the most important word is the little word 'that': 'Wherefore my brethren, ye also were made dead to the law by the body of Christ, that (in order that) you may be married to another, even to him who is raised from the dead, that (in order that) . . . '. Everything takes place 'in order that' some new thing may happen. In this way the great plan of redemption is worked out. As we look at it we cannot but marvel at its glory, at its wondrous character. We have died to the Law, and are no longer married to it, in order that we may regard ourselves as people who have made a second marriage – to the Lord Jesus Christ.

There is a point which I must emphasize in passing. The Apostle had great respect for the Law. 'Know ye not, brethren,' he has said in verse 1, 'how that the law hath dominion over a man as long as he liveth.' The Apostle Paul never makes light of the Law, he never disparages it. He will say some great things about the Law later in verse 12: 'Wherefore the law is holy, and the commandment holy, and just, and good'. A man who speaks disparagingly of the Law merely shows that he is a very defective and ignorant Christian. If your idea of Christianity is that it is something which 'dismisses' or 'makes light of' the Law, you

have never understood it. The Apostle was very sensitive on
this point. The Jews were constantly bringing it as a charge against
him; indeed that is why he wrote this particular chapter. They
were saying, 'This man is doing away with the Law; he is dismissing and deriding it'. But the Apostle resents and refutes the
charge. He has already told us in the last verse of chapter 3, 'Do
we then make void the law through faith?' And his answer is,
'God forbid. Yea, we establish the law'. What he means is that
everything God does is always legal. God never breaks His own
Law; He never countenances any breaking of the Law. Salvation
in Christ does not break the Law. As the Apostle says, 'it establishes the law'; and this verse shows us how it does so. That is the
way his illustration came in. You cannot play fast and loose with
marriage, he says. A woman who becomes joined to another
man while her husband is alive is an 'adulteress'. She is breaking
and violating the Law. But if her husband be dead and she becomes joined to another man in marriage she is no longer an
adulteress. Why? Because this second union is legal. She is no
longer bound to the first husband, and therefore she is free to be
married to this second husband. The second marriage is legal.
That is the point Paul is making, and he makes it because he is
concerned to show that our marriage to the Lord Jesus Christ
is absolutely legal and righteous. But you can only understand
this aright if you take the right view of the death of Christ upon
the Cross. If you say that Christ's death was just a wonderful
exhibition of God's love, or just the manifestation of the
cruelty of men, or hold one of the other sentimental notions
concerning it, there is no 'Law' involved at all. But the Apostle's
whole point is that God has released us from that old husband,
the Law, in a legal manner. The death of Christ is a legal transaction. On the Cross He is receiving the just and the full penalty
demanded by the Law. If you do not see Law being honoured on
the Cross of Calvary you have never seen the true meaning of the
death of Christ: it is essentially an honouring of the Law. Everything that God does is just and holy and righteous, and because
the Law has been honoured in that way we are now free to be
married to the Lord Jesus Christ.

We must be clear about the 'legal' aspect. We must never
give the impression that in the matter of our salvation the Law
is put on one side, and that God says, as it were, 'I am going

to make it easy for you'. That is a false and unbiblical representation of Christianity. The true doctrine honours the Law because the Law is God's Law, an expression of His eternal holy
character. Much 'Christianity' so-called is unethical and almost
immoral. We do not 'make void the law through faith, yea, we
establish the law'. God forbid that we should even attempt to do
anything else. But further, every one of us who is a Christian is
married to the Lord Jesus Christ. What are the consequences of
this? Let me start with an important negative. As married to
Christ you must never again allow yourself to feel as you felt
while you were 'under the law' and married to the Law. If you,
as married to Christ, ever feel as you used to feel when you were
married to that first husband, you are disloyal to your second
husband, that is, to the Lord Jesus Christ. Have you ever thought
of yourself and your life in these terms? Are you still afraid of the
Law? If you are, you are disloyal to your new husband, because
it means that you are still afraid of the old husband. That is a
great insult to the new husband. You must not be afraid of your
old husband, the Law. He is no longer there; and it is a very
grievous act of disloyalty to the new husband, who wants all
your thought and attention, and the fulness of your life.

It is even worse to feel condemned by the Law. I desire to
emphasize this. A Christian who continues to feel the condemnation of the Law is like a wife who still feels afraid of her first
husband from whom she has been separated by death. You
must never go back 'under the law'. You must really learn to say,
'There is therefore now no condemnation to them that are in
Christ Jesus'. 'But', you say, 'I feel that I am such a failure, I
feel that I am such a sinner, I feel I am so unworthy.' That may
well be true – I often feel the same, but I will never allow myself
to go back under condemnation. I may be unworthy of my new
husband, but that does not mean going back to being married
to the old husband. That is nonsense, that is confusion, that is
impossible. Whatever you may feel about yourself, and whatever you may know to be true about yourself, 'there is now no
condemnation to them that are in Christ Jesus'. None! You must
not think of yourself and your life in that way; you should now
think of it as your lack of faithfulness to the new husband. You
must think of it in terms of Christ, and never again in terms of
the Law, otherwise you are contradicting what you say you be-

lieve. You say that you have been separated legally from the
first husband, and yet you are putting yourself back into the old
relationship to him. Indeed, I do not hesitate to go so far as to
say that a Christian has no right to be miserable or unhappy.
If you are a miserable or unhappy Christian it is because you have
not understood this doctrine. You have not shaken yourself
and roused yourself spiritually and mentally; you have not
looked to the new husband and smiled in His face in spite of
your being what you are, and you have not seen Him smiling
upon you though you are what you are! As Christian people
we have no right to be miserable and mournful and unhappy.
Alternatively, look at the matter in this way. A Christian has no
right to be afraid of death and of the Judgment. If we realize
that we have been 'made dead to the law', what right have we to
fear death? What have we to fear in the Judgment? We should
all begin to feel as Augustus Toplady whose words I have already
quoted –

> *The terrors of law and of God*
> *With me can have nothing to do.*

'Foolhardiness!' says someone. No; that is faith, and nothing
but simple faith. It is an acceptance of the truth of God, it is
to believe God rather than to believe the devil or to believe my
own feelings. It is not because of anything in me, it is not because of anything I have done. I can use such words solely and
entirely because of my relationship to Him. These, then, are some
of the negatives, and it is our business to apply them. It is not
enough just to say, 'Ah, this is wonderful'. You must apply it;
and when you find yourself, or catch yourself being miserable,
or under a sense of condemnation, or fearful or afraid of death,
you must talk to yourself and say, 'This is wrong, I am being disloyal to my new husband!' 'That ye might be married to another,
even unto him who is raised from the dead.' I repeat: these are
some of the negative consequences of this marriage.

But let us turn to some positive consequences, for these are
amazing and extraordinary. I do not hesitate to assert that I am
about to say things which are the most wonderful things that
a human being can ever utter. I am about to tell you some of
the most marvellous and mysterious things that a human being
can ever hear. What is the nature of this union, our union with the

Lord Jesus Christ to whom we are married? It is a real union, it is a complete union. The Apostle Paul, fortunately, has put this for us very clearly in his Epistle to the Ephesians in chapter 5 beginning at verse 25: 'Husbands, love your wives, even as Christ also loved the church, and gave himself for it; that he might sanctify it.' But go on especially to verse 29: 'No man ever hated his own flesh; but nourisheth and cherisheth it, even as the Lord the church: For we are members of his body, of his flesh, and of his bones.' Then, 'For this cause shall a man leave his father and mother, and shall be joined unto his wife, and they two shall be one flesh. This is a great mystery: but I speak concerning Christ and the church.' What is my relationship to Christ as married to Him? We are 'one flesh'. What does that mean? says someone. The Apostle's answer is, 'This is a great mystery' – and if it was a mystery to him, it is certainly a mystery to me and to you, but it is true. The union implied in marriage is a mysterious thing, but the two are made 'one flesh'. That is what makes marriage marriage, there is this vital unity. And that is my relationship to Christ! 'One flesh'; 'members of his body, of his flesh, and of his bones'. There is no more intimate relationship than that; and that is our relationship to the Lord Jesus Christ. Shame on us, Christian people, that we do not live in the light of these things, that we do not live in the glory of these things! Shame on us that we do not live perpetually rejoicing in the contemplation and the realization of these things. Shame on us for our grumbles and complaints and groanings, our fears and our doubts – we who are 'one flesh' with the Son of God! It is a 'great mystery' but it is gloriously true.

The second thing about this union is that it means that we are to be entirely subject to Him. Our life used to be controlled by the first husband, the Law. The Law determined and controlled everything we did. Our position now is that we are subject unto the Lord Jesus Christ. As the Church is subject unto Christ, so the wife must be, argues the Apostle, to the husband. We must say these things to ourselves. When you get up tomorrow morning say to yourself, I am the wife of the Lord Jesus Christ. I take my position as His wife, subject to Him, to be guided by Him, to be led by Him, to be controlled by Him in all things. That is the relationship, and the realization of it transforms one's whole outlook and one's whole day. Think of a new bride entering into the

new relationship. She has left her father and mother, and she is
joined to this man. Her whole thinking becomes new. A woman
who marries a second husband does the same. She forgets the
first in order to be true and loyal to the second. She reminds herself of this. She must no longer think as she used to think; she
must think in a new way. Such is the second characteristic of
this union.

That brings us to the third, which is, the permanent character
of the relationship. The Apostle has taken great trouble to emphasize this. Yet there are foolish people who do not believe in
the permanency of this relationship and argue violently against
it. 'Know ye not, brethren', says the Apostle ('for I speak to them
that know the law), how that the law hath dominion over a
man as long as he liveth.' Nothing can terminate that but death.
Then to bring it right home he says, 'The woman which hath
an husband is bound by the law to her husband as long as he
liveth; but if the husband be dead, she is loosed from the law of
her husband.' Nothing but death can put an end to it – 'as long
as he liveth'. That is his illustration, and we must apply the
illustration to ourselves as we are married to the Lord Jesus
Christ. For how long am I married to Him? Is it only until
I fall into sin? Does my falling into sin mean I drop out of
the relationship and have to be married again to Him, and
then sin and drop out and be married again and again? What
utter nonsense! No, let us realize that the relationship is legal
and lasting. I am married to Him, and I remain married to
Him until one or the other of us dies; but neither the One or the
other of us can ever die! Says the Apostle in chapter 6: 9; 'Knowing that Christ being raised from the dead dieth no more; death
hath no more dominion over Him.' He cannot die again. There is
my Husband, He cannot die, and I am joined to Him.

But the Apostle has also reminded us that we cannot die
either. We have finished with death because we have finished with
Law, which alone has the power to prescribe death: 'The sting of
death is sin, and the strength of sin is the law.' It is the Law that
demands death; so as I am dead to the Law I am dead to death
– so I cannot die. The husband cannot die, and because He is the
'death of death and hell's destruction', the wife cannot die. It
is an indissoluble marriage, it will last throughout the countless
ages of eternity. Law is a tremendous and a majestic power;

nothing can put an end to its enactments and its prescriptions save death. But we are in a position in which we are above and beyond Law and death – we are married to Christ for ever. That is why the Apostle says at the end of chapter 8, when he sums up all this; 'For I am persuaded, that neither death, nor life, nor angels, nor principalities, nor powers, nor things present, nor things to come, nor height, nor depth, nor any other creature, shall be able to' – what? – 'to separate us from the love of God, which is in Christ Jesus our Lord.' We have been married to Christ eternally; He will never let us go; we are His for ever and for ever.

> *From Him who loves me now so well*
> *What power my soul shall sever?*
> *Shall life? or death? or earth? or hell?*
> *No! I am His for ever!*

That is the nature of the union. We shall next go on to consider something of the privileges of the union.

Five

*

Wherefore, my brethren, ye also are become dead to the law by the body of Christ; that ye should be married to another, even to him who is raised from the dead, that we should bring forth fruit unto God. Romans 7: 4

Having looked at some of the consequences of our being united with the Lord Jesus Christ in marriage we turn now to the privileges of that union. The very nature of the union makes it one of the most exalted comparisons that even this great Apostle ever used, and there is nothing that is so strengthening to faith, nothing so comforting, and especially so stimulating to sanctification, as to realize this particular truth. Our Lord, in the great High-Priestly prayer recorded in John 17, offers the petition, 'Sanctify them through thy truth', and then adds, 'Thy word is truth'. The means used in our sanctification is the truth, the Word. There is no aspect of the truth which is so stimulating to sanctification as this particular description of the Christian as one who is 'wedded', 'married' to the Lord Jesus Christ, and especially as we realize the privileges that become ours as Christians. Every Christian is married to Christ. You cannot be a Christian without being in that position. We are never detached. We are either married to the Law, or else we are married to Him. The privileges belong to all who are Christian.

The first privilege is that His name becomes our name. When a woman marries a man she gives up her own name and takes on the name of her husband. It is one of the most elementary facts about marriage. Scripture says that that is the position of the Christian – Christ's name becomes our name, His name is put upon us. We are called 'Christ-ians'. We are Christ's people, people who belong to Him, people who have changed their name. The 45th Psalm in its foreshadowing of this reminds us that we have left our home, and our parents, and that, being joined to Him, the old name no longer applies to us. This is a thought that baffles description and which no one can handle adequately. We are told that His name is a name which is 'above every other name'. There is no name in heaven or earth which is comparable to His. 'At the name of Jesus every knee shall bow, of things in heaven and things on earth, and things under the earth.' And this becomes our name! There is no greater title, there is no greater dignity that can ever come to a human being than this. Are you interested in honours? Are you interested in titles? Are you interested in names? Well, here is the highest rank of all, the name that is above every other name; and because we are married to Christ, it is our name.

Is there anything comparable to being a Christian? Shame on us Christian people for ever being apologetic, for ever being afraid that people should know that we are Christians, for ever being attracted by the world's 'pride of life'! Many of our troubles emanate from the fact that we fail to realize our position and our privileges. There is a sense in which Christians should be the proudest people in the world. I say 'a sense', because the Christian is not proud; but he should be proud of this name, he should be proud of his position. The Apostle tells us to glory in the Lord – 'he that glorieth, let him glory in the Lord' (I Cor. 1: 31). He means, 'Let him make his boast in the Lord'. People of the world are proud of their name, proud of the family name, proud of their titles, proud of the dignity that these things carry with them – so you and I should be! 'Children of the heavenly King, as ye journey sweetly sing.' Let us walk through this world, let us march through it, as realizing the dignity and the privilege and the magnificence and the glory of the name that is upon us. If we are not clear about this let us offer the petition:

Write Thy new name upon my heart,
Thy new best name of love.

But it *is* upon us! What the hymn-writer was asking for was that he might see it clearly, that he might be fully conscious of it. It has happened as a legal transaction, as we have already emphasized. This is not primarily a matter of experience – experience is the realization of it. It has happened, God has done this in a legal way. There has been a true union, and the documents have been signed in the books, the registers of heaven; and there is no power in heaven or earth that can query the marriage or ever dissolve it! Let us realize this and walk through this world as ever remembering it.

That brings us to the second privilege. Not only do we share His name, but also His standing. By that I mean what this Apostle tells the Corinthians in the 1st chapter of his First Epistle in verse 30, where he says, 'But of Him are ye in Christ Jesus, who of God is made unto us wisdom, and righteousness, and sanctification, and redemption'. It is a staggering thought, that His righteousness is put upon us. That is the teaching concerning justification by faith which we have seen so clearly in the early chapters of this Epistle; but let us remember that this is how it comes to us. Because we are married to Him, His wisdom, righteousness, sanctification and redemption are ours, and we are 'complete in Him'. It is His 'Robe of righteousness' that is put upon us. It is not our righteousness, it is His righteousness that is 'imputed' to us, and gradually imparted to us.

This is a most practical matter. The devil will come, as he does come, and point out to us our unworthiness and our failure and our sins. He will make us look inward, and he will depress us. He often succeeds in this because of our folly and our ignorance. Now there is only one effective way to counteract that, and that is, to realize that because we are married to Christ, His standing is also ours. We stand in the presence of God clothed with His righteousness. We are joined to Him, who, of God, has been made unto us these things, so that we stand before God, not looking at ourselves but at Him, and at what God has made Him to be for us and to us. This is the cure, the antidote, for all depression in the spiritual life – the realization that it is our relationship to Him that matters, and that it is God Himself who enables us to stand in this way.

> *Be Thou my shield and hiding-place,*
> *That, sheltered near Thy side,*
> *I may my fierce accuser face,*
> *And tell him Thou hast died.*

But then, because of this relationship, we share also and enjoy some of His privileges. This is what happens to a wife; any

privileges that the husband enjoys she enjoys. What are some of
these privileges? Writing to the Ephesians in the 2nd chapter,
verse 6, this Apostle reminds us that we are at this moment
'seated with him (Christ) in the heavenly places'. He does not
stop at saying that we have been 'quickened together with Christ',
and that we have been 'raised together' with Christ; he goes on
to say that we are 'seated in the heavenly places in Christ Jesus'.
We should never lose sight of the fact that we have this glorious
privilege even here and now. This is not a reference to something
future. Because of our relationship to Him we are already seated
with Him in the heavenly places. That is what made Augustus
Toplady say,

> *More happy, but not more secure*
> *The glorified spirits in heaven.*

But here is another wonderful fact. Because of our relationship
to Him we enjoy the privilege of access to His Father. We have
this access because we are the bride of His Son. There is no
greater privilege than to have a right of entry and of access into
the presence of the Heavenly Father. That is what the Scriptures
teach us. We are 'accepted in the beloved'. Work this out, think
it out, use your imagination. Think of this in practice in human
life as we know it, and especially if the father happens to be
some great and dignified and august person in whose presence
we would normally feel very nervous, and hesitate to ask for
an interview, and hesitate still more to put in a request or ask
for some favour. But we are the bride, the wife of the only-
begotten Son, the dearly-beloved Son of the Father; so we can
always be assured that He will never refuse us anything that
is for our good. He will refuse things that are harmful because
He loves us, because we are the bride of His Son, but He will
never refuse anything that is good for us. Go to Him with
confidence – 'accepted in the beloved'. You have a right of
entry and of access to the Father because of the relationship to
the Son.

Another very wonderful thing, and one which we tend to
forget, is that every Christian has and should enjoy the privilege
of the service of the angels. We notice in the Gospels that at
given points and at given times in our Lord's earthly life angels
came and ministered to Him, strengthening Him and helping

Him. Because we are married to Him this becomes equally true of us. This is not my fancy; we have it stated explicitly in the Epistle to the Hebrews in the 1st chapter, verses 13 and 14, 'But to which of the angels said he at any time, Sit on my right hand, until I make thine enemies thy footstool?' God has never spoken such words to an angel, says this author; He only spoke them to the Son. He has not said that to angels because – 'Are they not all ministering spirits, sent forth to minister for them who shall be heirs of salvation?' That refers to every one who is a Christian. The angels are sent forth to minister to all who are the heirs of salvation because they are 'joint-heirs with Christ'. Indeed our Lord had said the same thing Himself in Matthew 18: 10: 'I say unto you, That in heaven their angels do always behold the face of my Father which is in heaven'. We have also the great comfort, taught in the parable of Dives and Lazarus in Luke 16, of knowing that we shall be 'carried by angels into Abraham's bosom' when we die. Because we are Christians the angels of God are at our service; they are 'ministering spirits' sent forth by God to serve and to minister to you and to me. Though we are unconscious of this they are exercising this ministry. We are surrounded by them, they are unseen, but they are there, and they minister to us because we belong to Christ, because we are married to Him and are thereby 'the heirs of salvation'. We sadly neglect and forget the service of the angels; but if ever you feel lonely and bereft, and feel that you do not know what to do nor where to turn, remind yourself that your heavenly Father, the Father of the Lord Jesus Christ, has sent angels to minister to you as He did to Him in the hours of His greatest crises and His greatest agony.

We must realize also that a day is coming when we shall 'reign with Him'. It is almost incredible. Here in this world, as Christians, if we are worthy of the name, we are generally despised and derided and ignored; the world passes us by as if we were nobodies. It talks about its great privileges, its dignities and its honours, its possessions and its pomp. But we are the people who know something about real and lasting privileges and dignities. In I Corinthians 6: verses 2 and 3, the Apostle says: 'Do you not know that the saints shall judge the world?' He goes further, 'Know ye not that we shall judge angels'? That refers to us! We are destined to enjoy this privilege because of our relationship to the Son of God. We are married to the Son, we shall reign with Him and judge the world, and judge even angels. We are lifted to a position high above even that occupied by the angels, because of our relationship to the Son.

Those, then, are some of the privileges; there are many others. We must now look at the possessions which are ours because we are married to Him. Here, again, is something which the Apostle says in many places. One in particular sums it up very well: 'All things are yours' (I Cor. 3: 21–23). You cannot add to that. The Apostle was writing to those foolish Corinthian Christians who were glorying in men, and falling into party strife. He is astonished at them. 'Therefore let no man glory in men. For all things are yours; whether Paul, or Apollos, or Cephas, or the world, or life, or death, or things present, or things to come; all are yours: and you are Christ's; and Christ is God's.' 'All things are yours' because of your relationship to the Lord Jesus Christ. We are 'joint-heirs with him' – that is the position of a wife. 'Blessed are the meek,' says our Lord, 'for they shall inherit the earth.' Everything! 'All things are yours', life, death, everything! Again, in the Epistle to the Hebrews we find it stated wonderfully in the 2nd chapter in verse 5: 'For unto the angels hath he not put in subjection the world to come, whereof we speak.' To whom, then, has it been put in subjection? 'To us', he says; not to the angels – they are only the servants, our servants, 'ministering spirits' serving us. 'The world to come, whereof we speak' is not to be set in subjection unto them, but unto us; the inheritance is ours. That is the inheritance to which we look forward as 'heirs of God, and joint-heirs with Christ'; it belongs to us because we are married to the Son of God, the Heir of the whole universe.

Still further, we must realize that as married to the Lord Jesus Christ we are in a position to know His love in a way which no one else can do. It is to his bride that the bridegroom reveals and manifests his love. 'Therefore', says the Apostle Paul, 'husbands, love your wives'. How? 'even as Christ loved the church and gave himself for it'. That is how husbands are to love their wives. The words give us some indication of His love to us as Christian people. It is His peculiar, intimate love; it is a manifestation of His feelings, of His affections, which He shows to no one else. This is the peculiar treasure and privilege of the bride. Christian people, it is because we do not know our Scriptures that we live as we do; it is because we are ignorant of these Scriptures that we too often live as paupers instead of realizing that we are married to a Prince. The manifestation of His love! What do we know about that? A hymn reminds us that,

The love of Jesus, what it is,
None but His loved ones know.

The world knows nothing about that! It cannot know. It has never felt it; nor can it do so. What the world will know is 'the wrath of the Lamb'. Do you know the love of Christ? He has promised to show it. He said, 'I will manifest myself unto you'. He does not manifest Himself to any but the bride.

Has He spoken to you? Has He said to you, 'As the lily among thorns, so is my love among the daughters?' Has He ever said to you, whispered to you, 'My beloved is Mine?' Read the Song of Solomon and see how the bridegroom expresses his feeling to his bride, his love. How lightly we skip over these great statements so that we may argue about our pet ideas and theories! In one sense the whole object of being a Christian is that you may know the love of Jesus Christ, His personal love to you; that He may tell you in unmistakable language that He loves you, that He has given Himself for you, that He has loved you with 'an everlasting love'. He does this through the Holy Spirit; He 'seals' all His statements to you through the Spirit. 'The Spirit itself beareth witness with our spirits' (Romans 8: 16). He tells you directly. You believe it because it is in the Word; but there is more than that; He will tell you this directly as a great secret. The Spirit gives manifestations of the Son of God to His own, to His beloved, to those for whom He has gladly died and given Himself.

What do we know of these secret intimations? Read the lives of the saints throughout the centuries and you will find that they all know about this. They have known Him to come to them and speak to them, and love them, and tell them that He loves them. He embraces them and surrounds them, and lets them know, more certainly than they know anything else, that He loves them with all the intensity of His divine Being. It is because we are married to Him that He does this. 'The love of Jesus, what it is, None but His loved ones know.' But as 'loved

[61]

ones' do you know it as you should? Do you give Him an opportunity to tell you? Do you put everything on one side in order to look into His face and to listen to Him? Or is it that, when He comes to you, you are busy with other things? Or, like the bride depicted in the 5th chapter of the Song of Solomon, have you gone to bed and put off your clothes, and when you hear Him at the door you say to Him: 'I have put off my coat; how shall I put it on? I have washed my feet, how shall I defile them?' Then you suddenly realize how foolish you have been, and you get up and you open the door. But He has gone and you have nothing left but a smell of the myrrh that has been dropping from His fingers, and you do not know what to do with yourself; and you seek Him. If you would know the love of Jesus 'what it is', give Him opportunities of telling you. He will meet you in the Scriptures, and He will tell you. Give time, give place, give opportunity. Set other things aside, and say to other people, 'I cannot do what you ask me to do; I have another appointment, I know He is coming and I am waiting for Him'. Do you look for Him, are you expecting Him, do you allow Him, do you give Him opportunities to speak to you, and to let you know His love to you? We are married to Him. We know what the Law told us in the old life. There was no question about that – its threats, its condemnations. We have heard them, and we know them, and we paid attention to them. But we are no longer married to the Law and we must not listen to it. Turn your back on it and listen to Him. Look into His face, and hear what He has to tell you about His love for you.

Then, and resulting from this, there is His care and His protection. The Apostle writing to the Ephesians, in chapter 5, verse 29, tells them: 'No man ever yet hated his own flesh; but nourisheth and cherisheth it, even as the Lord the church.' Every husband knows about such matters; but multiply them by infinity and you have some idea of the care of the Lord Jesus Christ for every Christian who is married to Him. He thinks ahead for us, He plans for us, He protects us. It is He who commands the angels to look after us and shield us and guard us. There is nothing that He will not do for us; He knows all about us and the dangers of our position. He is separated from us, for the time being, in a physical sense, but He is caring for us and protecting us. We are reminded by Jude in his Epistle that He

is so strong that He is 'able to keep us from falling'. We are
walking and living in a world that is full of obstacles and things
that trip us up, and we fall and are led astray. But He 'is able to
keep you from falling'. That is a manifestation of His care and
His protection. He makes sure also that we have ample food,
He sees to it that we have supplies of the Spirit; everything we
need. Peter tells us in his Second Epistle, in the 1st chapter,
that 'All things that pertain to life and godliness' have been
provided for us by His virtue and His strength. We have no
complaint, we have no excuse for failure, He has given us
everything that we can ever stand in need of while we are passing
through this world. All is provided for us as the result of His
care and protection of His bride.

The last thing I would note under this heading is His desire
and His purpose for us. Let me go back to that great statement
in Jude's Epistle – 'Unto him that is able to keep you from
falling, and to present you faultless before the presence of his
glory with exceeding joy'. The metaphors break down, they are
not quite adequate. But what we are told there is that He takes
great pride in us, as it were, and that His great desire and purpose
is to present His bride to His Father. You can take Jude's
statement as a word-picture of a bridegroom taking his bride
home, and proudly showing her to the family. He will have made
us faultless by then, and so He will do it 'with exceeding joy'.
Or, to vary the imagery a little, I take you to the Book of Revelation where the same thing is really stated in chapter 19, verses
6–9.

'And I heard as it were the voice of a great multitude, and
as the voice of many waters, and as the voice of mighty thunderings,
saying, Alleluia: for the Lord God omnipotent reigneth. Let us
be glad and rejoice, and give honour to him: for the marriage
of the Lamb is come, and his wife hath made herself ready.'
(This refers to the whole Church.) 'And to her was granted
that she should be arrayed in fine linen, clean and white: for
the fine linen is the righteousness of saints. And he saith unto me,
Write, Blessed are they which are called unto the marriage
supper of the Lamb. And he saith unto me, These are the true
sayings of God'. We are married to Him now, but as yet we do
not realize it fully; then, we shall do so. When this great marriage
feast comes, and the bride is ready and attired and prepared,

everything will be perfect. All this refers to us who are Christian, those who are already married to Him. That great consummation will finally happen.

Those are some of the deductions which we draw with regard to the privileges that are ours because of our union with the Lord Jesus Christ.

We next turn to another aspect of the matter. If those are the privileges of the union, what is the purpose of the union? This is what the Apostle has particularly in his mind in this 4th verse. All the things we have mentioned are there, and we must draw them out. Is there some pedant who wants to say, 'After all, Paul is only concerned in this 4th verse with the purposes of the union, so why have you looked at all those other things?' I am tempted to say that I doubt whether such a person is a Christian. When you are studying the Scriptures and you find a comparison used, draw out its consequences. Never say, 'I will do that when I come to some other passage'; you may never come to another passage. As we are told here that we are married to Christ, draw out all the consequences. Certainly find them elsewhere in the Scripture also and gather them together. Remind yourselves of them.

But now we come to the purpose of the union, and this certainly was what was uppermost in the Apostle's mind, because of the particular argument that he is engaged in at this point. The purpose of this union, he tells us, is 'that (in order that) we should bring forth fruit unto God'. 'Fruit' means children, the fruit of the marriage, the offspring, the children that are to be born. You are married, he says, 'that you should bring forth fruit unto God'.

Notice, negatively, that this marriage of ours, this union between us and the Son of God, must never be regarded only from our standpoint. It is just there that we go wrong and miss so much. We start with ourselves and we end with ourselves, and ask 'What am I to get out of this?' A superficial evangelism often leads people to act thus; it tends to represent the Lord Jesus Christ as just an agency to bless us. It looks at it the wrong way round. What is the object of this marriage with the Son of God? It is not only forgiveness; it is not merely that I might have security. It is a very poor sort of bride who gets married merely

that she may have security. Such a woman says 'I shall not have
to work any more, my future is made certain, I shall be looked
after in my old age'. We all despise such an attitude, such a
mercenary view of marriage, even on the human level. But
what of people who believe in the Lord Jesus Christ for such
reasons? Thank God we are given forgiveness, and we are
guaranteed security; but you should not enter into the marriage
solely in order to have these blessings; that must not be the
motive. Neither is it to be happiness only, nor joy; nor that you
may have help, and may be able to share your problems and
have someone at hand always to help you. Neither is it to have
healing for your body only, nor to have experiences only. I have
mentioned the wonderful experiences of His love, but you do
not get married only for such experiences. Nor should our motive
be mainly to obtain victory over certain particular sins that
happen to be bothering us.

But is not that the approach of many? Something has been
'getting them down'. They have been trying their best, but
only to fail; and their one concern is, 'How am I to get rid of
this particular sin?' They meet people who say to them, 'Come
with me to a meeting, believe the message you will hear, and then
you will be delivered. You will be given help and you will get
rid of that sin, it will be taken from you.' That is all they want,
and having got it, they feel that all is well. But oh, what they
fail to realize! What they miss! All they wanted was to get rid
of the one sin. They have given no thought to knowing Him
and His love and all these other wonderful blessings; they are
interested in themselves alone and in their own problems. Their
approach is purely subjective; they know nothing about forgetting themselves in His love and in His presence. Thank God,
all these blessings come to us because of this marriage, and they
are all true. But what I am emphasizing is that they are not the
ultimate purpose and object of salvation, and they are not to be
our motive and main concern. I do not like such titles as *The
Christian's Secret of a Happy Life*. It should be, *The Christian's
life in Christ as His Bride*. Happiness is a by-product, it should never
be put in the centre; none of these things should be put in the
centre. People who write books with such titles emphasizing
happiness primarily, often end their lives in misery and unhappiness. The author of the book called *The Christian's Secret of a*

Happy Life spent the latter years of her life in great unhappiness. I am not surprised. If you put happiness first you will probably lose it. You may think you have it; you may get a kind of happiness temporarily, but you will not hold it. It is not happiness, but our Lord and our relationship to Him that matters; all else is a by-product.

What then is the true purpose of the marriage? Let me give it first as the Apostle puts it in Ephesians 5 : 25 and the following verses: 'Husbands, love your wives, even as Christ loved the church and gave himself for it, that (in order that) he might sanctify and cleanse it with the washing of water by the word, that he might present it to himself a glorious church, not having spot, or wrinkle, or any such thing; but that it should be holy and without blemish.' But you cannot improve on the way in which the Apostle puts it in this 7th chapter of Romans; 'that we should bring forth fruit' – bear fruit, bear progeny – 'unto God'. What is the fruit? The fruit is holiness. What is holiness? Holiness is to live to God's glory and to God's praise. Holiness is not a feeling; holiness is a life lived to the glory of God and to His eternal praise. The fruit is, 'the fruit of the Spirit – love, joy, peace, longsuffering, gentleness, goodness, meekness, faith and temperance'. We are married to Him in order that we may bring forth such fruit.

Let me put it plainly and clearly. The Apostle teaches here that it was essential we should be married to Him; because until we are married to Him we shall never bear this fruit. We were married to the Law, but the Law was impotent; it could not bring forth children (fruit) out of us. But we are now married to One who has the strength and the virility and the potency to produce children even out of us. It is His strength that matters. The Apostle puts it explicitly in the 3rd verse of the 8th chapter: 'For what the law could not do', he says, 'in that it was weak through the flesh, God sending his own Son in the likeness of sinful flesh' has done. What has He done? He has made it possible 'That the righteousness of the law might be fulfilled in us, who walk not after the flesh but after the Spirit'. Here is the real purpose of the marriage; we need One whose seed is so powerful, who can so impregnate us with His own holy nature that He will produce holiness even in us. That is why we are married to Him, in order that 'we should bring forth fruit unto God'. His strength is so great, His might is so potent, that even out of us He can bear this progeny of holiness.

This therefore is the Apostle's argument. He says in effect, You had to be delivered from your marriage to the Law before you could produce the fruit. You had to die to that Law, that old marriage had to be dissolved, in order that you might be married to this mighty One who can produce the fruit in you. And he says it has happened. The central object of salvation is holiness. I would not hesitate to assert that it is sinful to say that you can stop at justification even temporarily, or say that a man can be justified and not sanctified. It is impossible. 'Who of God is made unto us wisdom, righteousness, sanctification and redemption.' You cannot stop at justification; these things must never be separated. The whole object, the whole movement of salvation is to make us holy. So from the moment we are joined to Him the process begins. From the moment of the marriage and the union, the moment the two become 'one flesh', His power begins to work. The fruit may appear at times to be very small and weak and ailing and marasmic, it is nevertheless the life of God in the soul, and it is nevertheless true to say that we are 'partakers of the divine nature', and that we are already bringing forth something of this fruit, which is 'holiness unto God'.

Thank God for Romans 7: 4: 'Wherefore my brethren, ye also are become dead to the law by the body of Christ, in order that ye should be married to another, even to him who is raised from the dead, in order that we should bring forth fruit unto God.' Paul rejoiced in this and so should we. Do you?

Six

*

For when we were in the flesh, the motions of sins, which were by the law, did work in our members to bring forth fruit unto death. But now we are delivered from the law, that being dead wherein we were held; that we should serve in newness of spirit, and not in the oldness of the letter. Romans 7: 5, 6

These two verses go together and constitute one statement. Verse 5 gives the negative half of the statement; then in verse 6 we have the positive half. Obviously, here, in this statement, the Apostle is giving an explanation of something that he has already said. The 5th verse begins with the word 'For'. That at once lets us know that he is going to give an explanation, and it is the explanation of what he has just said in verse 4. He is going to explain why the marriage to Christ there mentioned was an absolute necessity, and why it was necessary, prior to that, that we should be dissolved from the marriage tie to the Law. This statement in these two verses is most important for this reason – that the remainder of this 7th chapter, from verse 7 to the end, and indeed chapter 8 to the end of verse 4 is nothing but an elaboration of this statement in verses 5 and 6. Clearly we are dealing with a vital and most crucial statement. Here he tells us in general why we had to die to our marriage to the Law, and be married to Christ. He states it as a whole. Then from verse 7 he goes on to consider objections to that statement, and furthermore, he works out what he says here in great detail, in order to establish his statement to the full and prove it beyond any doubt. This is his method, as we have seen so often. He makes a statement; then he takes it up and works it out in detail, and then sums it up at the end.

I assert again that this statement in verses 5 and 6 is the key to the understanding of the whole of this 7th chapter of this

Epistle. It is essential to an understanding of the Apostle's argument. There are many who get bewildered and lost in this 7th chapter. It is impossible to follow the Apostle's argument in detail unless we are clear in our minds as to the general proposition which he lays down here.

Secondly, this statement is absolutely essential to an understanding of the Apostle's doctrine concerning the Law. That, of course, is the central theme of this Epistle, as it is of the Epistle to the Galatians. The doctrine of justification by faith is always dealt with in this way. Here is the central, classic statement with regard to that matter.

Then, thirdly, the understanding of this statement is absolutely essential to the full doctrine of salvation, and in this particular context, to the doctrine of sanctification. The Apostle has already dealt with the Law in the matter of justification; here, he is concerned about the Law in the matter of sanctification. But it is right to say, I repeat, that we find here vital teaching as to the whole doctrine of salvation.

We look first at the actual terms the Apostle uses. The first is the expression 'in the flesh'. 'For', he says – or we can translate it 'Because' – when we were in the flesh certain things were true of us. What does he mean by saying that we were once 'in the flesh?' Here we find the first use in this Epistle of the term 'the flesh' in this particular sense. It is a term found frequently in the epistles of this Apostle. We shall find it repeatedly from here on in this Epistle; we find it also in the Epistle to the Galatians. There has been much discussion concerning the meaning of this term, 'the flesh'. Conflicting schools of theology have come into being simply because of different interpretations of this expression. It is therefore one of those important terms about which we must be quite clear.

In the Scriptures this term is used in a number of different ways. That is partly why the confusion has arisen. Paul himself, when he came to handle this particular subject, was hampered by the limitations of language. The same difficulty is a constant factor in the exposition of Christian truth. Our terminology, our language, is limited, so the same word may be used in a number of different ways and may carry a number of different meanings. Sometimes the word 'flesh' is used in the Scripture to mean the whole of mankind. 'All flesh shall see the salvation of God'; and again, 'All flesh is as grass, and all the goodliness of man as the flower of grass'. 'Flesh' in these instances simply means the whole of mankind. That is one possible meaning.

But then at other times the word 'flesh' is used to mean 'the body'. For instance, in the great statement in Galatians 2: 20 the Apostle says: 'I have been crucified with Christ; nevertheless I live; yet not I, but Christ liveth in me: and the life which I now live in the flesh I live by the faith of the Son of God, who loved me, and gave himself for me.' There, obviously, Paul is using the word 'flesh' to mean 'the body', the bodily part of our being.

In other places 'the flesh' obviously means 'the sensuous part of our nature'. You will find this, for instance, in Galatians 5: 17. 'The flesh lusteth against the Spirit, and the Spirit against the flesh.' There, Paul is not talking about the body, but about the sensuous or sensual part of our being, and obviously something which is still present in a believer. That is a third possible use.

The question that arises here is whether the word 'flesh' as it is used in our verse is to be explained in any one of these ways? I suggest that it is not. The Apostle is not referring to the whole of mankind, he is referring here, in particular, to Christian people. He is not making a general statement about the whole of mankind, he is saying that something was formerly true of Christians which is no longer true of them. Again, obviously, he is not referring to the body, because when he wrote he was still in the body; but he says 'when we were in the flesh'. As Christians are no longer 'in the flesh' it clearly cannot mean the body; so we have to exclude that meaning. In the same way we reach the conclusion, as we shall see later, that the third possible explanation, namely the sensuous part of our being and of our nature, also has to be excluded.

What, then, is the particular connotation of the term in this 5th verse? I maintain that here we have what is after all the commonest use of this particular term. The very context itself surely explains what it means. It means the opposite to life 'in the Spirit'. We were 'in the flesh', but we are no longer 'in the flesh'. What, then, is our state now? We are 'in the Spirit'. We were formerly in the realm of the flesh, whereas now we are in the realm of the Spirit. We shall find this explained more fully in chapter 8 from verse 4 onwards: 'That the righteousness of the law might be fulfilled in us, who walk not after the flesh, but after the Spirit.' And the Apostle continues: 'For they that are after the flesh do mind the things of the flesh; but they that are after the Spirit the things of the Spirit.' Again in verse 8 of that chapter, 'So then, they that are in the flesh cannot please God. But you are not in the flesh, but in the Spirit' (verse 9). I argue therefore that the obvious meaning of 'in the flesh' is that it is the opposite to being 'in the Spirit'. 'You are not in the flesh, but in the Spirit, if so be that the Spirit of God dwell in you. Now if any man have not the Spirit of Christ, he is none of his' (8: 9). That establishes the meaning here quite clearly; to be 'in the flesh' is the antithesis to being 'in the Spirit'.

This is a most important term therefore, a most important definition. Perhaps the clearest statement on this matter is to be found in our Lord's talk with Nicodemus recorded in the 3rd chapter of John's Gospel, and especially in the 6th verse: 'That which is born of the flesh is flesh; and that which is born of the Spirit is spirit.' Our Lord was telling Nicodemus that he 'must be born again'. Nicodemus could not understand the matter, simply because 'That which is born of the flesh is flesh'. 'All your questions are pointless', says our Lord, in effect, to Nicodemus; 'you are trying in your fleshly condition – "in the flesh" – with your natural mind, to understand what I am talking about. But you cannot do so, because "that which is born of the flesh is flesh". What I am talking about is spiritual.' So He goes on to say, 'Marvel not that I said unto thee, ye must be born again'. We can say, then, that to be 'in the flesh' is to be unregenerate. It is the natural state of man in sin, a state in which sin has dominion over him. It means that the evil principle of sin is controlling the whole of his life. It means that he has a corrupt nature – man unregenerate in sin under the dominion of sin – and is polluted at the centre of his being.

An alternative term to 'in the flesh' is the term 'carnal'. Again, there is a great deal of confusion concerning this term 'carnal'. It figures prominently in the various doctrines of sanctification. A common popular teaching tells us that man by nature is unregenerate; then he becomes converted, and at that stage he is only 'carnal'. Then he has a further experience and becomes 'spiritual'. But surely the 8th chapter of this Epistle makes it quite clear that that is a wrong use of the term 'carnal'. Consider the words again – 'That the righteousness of the law might be fulfilled in us, who walk not after the flesh, but after the Spirit. For they that are after the flesh do mind the things of the flesh' – the things in which they are interested – 'but they that are after the Spirit (mind), the things of the Spirit. For (because) to be carnally minded' – and that is obviously exactly the same as to be 'after the flesh', which leads to minding the things of the flesh – 'to be carnally minded is death; but to be spiritually minded is life and peace.' The opposites are 'spiritual' and 'carnal', 'spiritual' and 'flesh'. 'Carnal' and 'carnally minded' are identical and synonymous with being 'in the flesh', because, as the Apostle goes on to say, 'The carnal mind is enmity against God; for it is not subject to the law of God, neither indeed can be'. That obviously cannot refer to a Christian; to be 'carnally minded' means to be unregenerate. He goes on to say, 'So then they that are in the flesh' – in other words, they that are 'carnal' and are 'carnally minded' – 'cannot please God'. But Christians are not 'in the flesh', are not 'carnal', but 'in the Spirit', if so be that the Spirit of God dwells in them.

'Ah yes', says someone, 'that seems clear; but what about I Corinthians 3, where the Apostle starts by saying "And I, brethren, could not speak unto you as unto spiritual, but as unto carnal, even as unto babes in Christ" ' Then, in verse 3, 'For ye are yet carnal; for whereas there is among you envying and strife and divisions, are ye not carnal and walk as men'? What of that? There is only one thing to say about that. The Apostle is clearly teaching those Corinthians that because they were doing certain things they were behaving as if they were still carnal people. We do not suddenly see everything clearly and perfectly the moment we are converted. We are no longer 'in the flesh', we are no longer 'carnal'; we are already 'in the Spirit'; but our understanding is defective, and those Corinthians were still thinking of certain particular matters as if they were still unregenerate. Paul was simply telling the Corinthians that they were behaving still in the old way. The basic definition of 'carnal' is what we have in the 8th chapter of this Epistle to the Romans, and we must explain I Corinthians, chapter 3, in terms of this, rather than the other way round. In Romans 8 the Apostle uses the terms interchangeably, and this must be the basic definition.

Bearing that in mind we find that the Corinthian statement resolves itself quite simply. Paul is saying, 'You are babes, and because you are babes, in this matter you are still thinking as you used to think'.

Such, clearly, is the main meaning of 'in the flesh' in this verse. But it surely carries another meaning also; because the Apostle not only contrasts being 'in the flesh' with being 'in the Spirit', he also contrasts being 'under the law' with being 'in the Spirit'. Part of the answer to the meaning of 'the flesh' in verse 5 is given in verse 6: 'But now we are delivered from the law'. We were 'under the law', but we have been delivered from it. But when we were 'under the law' we were 'in the flesh'. So it carries the double meaning: being 'in the flesh' means also to be 'under the law'. The Apostle uses it in exactly the same way in Galatians 3: 3 – 'Having begun in the Spirit, are ye now made perfect by the flesh?' The trouble with the Galatians was that they had listened to the false Judaistic teachers who said, 'It is right to believe the gospel, but that does not put you right as Christians; you have to be circumcised also, you have got to carry out certain parts of the Law'. 'No,' says Paul, 'having started in the Spirit, are you now made perfect in the flesh?' 'In the flesh' there clearly means going back to the old rules and regulations which were under the Law. This term 'flesh' carries the dual meaning of our being not 'in the Spirit', and of our positively being 'under the law'.

There is a very clear statement of all this in Philippians 3: 3 where again the Apostle is dealing with this question of the Judaisers. He says, 'We are the circumcision'. The Philippians must not listen to the teachers who were trying to compel them to be circumcised. 'We are the circumcision, who worship God in the spirit, and rejoice in Christ Jesus, and have no confidence in the flesh.' What does he mean there by 'in the flesh?' Surely the two ideas we have found in the 5th verse of this 7th chapter of the Epistle to the Romans! He says: We have none of the self-confidence we had when we were in the flesh – confidence in birth, in race, in tribe, confidence in good religious works under the Law. 'Touching the righteousness which is in the law, blameless.' All that means 'having confidence in the flesh', confidence that by keeping the Law I can justify myself before God. Similarly in this 5th verse the Apostle is emphasizing both meanings of the term 'in the flesh': when we were in the flesh, we were not 'in the Spirit', and we were 'under the law'.

Furthermore, he says that that is universally true of the whole of mankind in its unregenerate state. However good people may be, however moral they may be, however religious they may be, if they are not 'in the Spirit' they are 'in the flesh'; and at the same time, as we saw in verse 4, they are 'under the law'. There are only two possible positions: all people in this world at this moment are in one of these two conditions; they are either 'in the flesh and under the law', or else they are 'in the Spirit and under grace'. The Apostle has already stated this truth in verse 14 of the 6th chapter: 'For sin shall not have dominion over you, for you are not under the law, but under grace.' These terms must be taken together. If we regard 'flesh' in this verse as meaning the body, and the sins of the body only, we shall confuse the entire issue, because there are certain people who are not guilty of these flagrant sins of the body, and therefore they could say that they are not 'in the flesh'. But they are in the flesh! The most moral man in the world who is not a Christian is 'in the flesh'. A verse that puts this distinction quite perfectly is found in the Epistle to the Ephesians, chapter 2, verse 3, where the Apostle uses the word 'flesh' in two different senses. 'Among whom also we all had our conversation in times past in the lusts of our flesh, fulfilling the desires of the flesh and of the mind.' The second use of 'flesh' there, where he talks about 'fulfilling the desires of the flesh and of the mind,' means the sensuous part of our nature. But 'the flesh' in the first instance, where he talks about 'the lusts of our flesh', is to be taken more generally. 'The lusts of the flesh' can be sub-divided into 'the lusts of the sensuous part of the nature' and 'the lusts of the mind'. There then we have a good illustration of the difference between the two particular meanings of the term.

To sum up on this point: We were, says the Apostle, 'in the flesh', we were unregenerate, we were dominated by an evil principle of sin; and at the same time we were under the 'dominion of the law'; for 'the strength of sin', as he tells the Corinthians (1 Cor. 15: 56) 'is the law'. What we are to glory in as Christians is that whereas we were 'in the flesh', thank God we are no longer in that state. We are now 'in the Spirit', we are 'under grace', we have been translated into an entirely new realm. So much for the first term!

The second term is 'the motions of sin'. This means passions, affections, 'sinful affections and lusting'. 'When we were in the flesh' says the Apostle, 'these passions, lustings, sinful affections . . . were within us.' They are in all of us by nature – every one of us. There has never been a human being since the Fall in whom these 'motions', 'passions' of sins were not found. That is the result of the Fall. Here, once more, I have to remind you of a very important distinction. When Paul talks about the passions or the 'motions' of sin he does not simply mean our natural bodies in and of themselves. Many Christians have gone astray at this point. The Apostle, in writing to Timothy for instance in the First Epistle, chapter 4, puts it like this, 'Now the Spirit speaketh expressly, that in the latter times some shall depart from the faith, giving heed to seducing spirits and doctrines of devils; speaking lies in hypocrisy; having their conscience seared with a hot iron; forbidding to marry, and commanding to abstain from meats, which God hath created to be received with thanksgiving of them which believe and know the truth' (verses 1–3). Here were people who claimed to be ultra-spiritual; they said that they were so spiritual that they could never think of getting married, for they regarded sex as sinful because it is a bodily appetite. For the same reason they did not eat meat. But the Apostle condemns such an attitude; and it should always be condemned utterly. All the natural appetites have been created by God, and given to us by God. That is apostolic teaching, as it is the teaching of the Bible throughout; so for us to regard the natural appetites as sinful in and of themselves is grievous error.

This truth needs to be constantly emphasized. Take, for instance, the Roman Catholic Church, with its so-called 'celibate priesthood'. Why do its priests not marry? Surely they have gone wrong at this point. That is a false asceticism which regards the body and its appetites as necessarily sinful. It is a plain denial of the Scriptural teaching, and it is a very serious misunderstanding. There is nothing wrong with the natural appetites in and of themselves. God put them in man for the purpose of procreation, for the filling of the world with people; and all the other instincts – the desire for food, for society, and so on –

are the gift of God for the well-being of man and for the enjoyment of life in this world.

What, then, does Paul mean by 'the passions of sins?' He means the natural appetites, which, though good in and of themselves, acquired an evil bias as the result of the Fall and of sin. God made man with certain natural appetites; and before man fell he kept them in their place; there was a balance in man's life. But the moment man sinned the balance was upset; and instead of man controlling his appetites the appetites began to control him. Such is Paul's meaning; and it is what is so evident in the world today. The natural appetites are a part of man; but they were never meant to be 'front page news' in the newspapers. Sex was created by God; but not as you see it flaunted in your newspapers. It has become the controlling, dominant factor in life. Today, men live to eat and to indulge in sex. That is where man has gone wrong. These things are lawful and good as long as they are kept in their place, and governed and controlled by the intellect, the understanding, and a sense of righteousness, and by our relationship to God; as long as they are used to the glory of God. But when man reverses that order, and is dominated by these 'drives', 'passions' and 'lusts', he is in a sinful state, he is 'in the flesh'. A term used in the Scriptures to express the same thing is 'inordinate affections'. Affections are natural and legitimate; but they must never become 'inordinate'; the moment they become 'inordinate' they are sinful. We can paraphrase the expression 'the passions of sin' by 'the feelings that prompt us to the commission of sins'. That is what is meant – any feeling that you have that drives you and prompts you and urges you to commit an act of sin.

We now look at the next term in the Apostle's statement – 'the motions, the passions of sin, which were 'by the law'. This is one of the most remarkable statements, in many ways, that this Apostle ever made; not the most glorious, but the most remarkable, and especially as coming from one who had been a 'Pharisee of the Pharisees' and an expert on the Law. He talks about 'the motions of sins which were by the law'. Be clear about that word 'by'; it means 'through' – 'through the law'. Is Paul then saying that it is the Law that has created the 'passions of sins'? No! he is not talking about their origin. He is saying that the Law 'stirs them up', arouses them, in a sense 'inflames' them. These 'motions of sins' are in us all as the result of the Fall; but the Law sets them to work, as the Apostle tells us: 'For when we were in the flesh the motions of sins, which were by the law, did work in our members'.

The word 'work', as used here, is a very interesting word which carries in it the notion of 'working powerfully'. You will find it also used in the Epistle to the Ephesians, where Paul writes, 'You hath he quickened, who were dead in trespasses and sins; wherein in time past ye walked according to the course of this world, according to the prince of the power of the air, the spirit that now *worketh* in the children of disobedience' (2: 2). It is the same word. This evil spirit which we do not see nevertheless controlled our lives. This 'spirit of iniquity' 'works'. And here Paul says that 'the motions of sins' work in exactly the same way in the unregenerate person. Take another illustration of the use of this word as found in Philippians 2: 12, 13: 'Work out your own salvation with fear and trembling', he says, 'for it is God that worketh in you, both to will and to do of his good pleasure.' What God works He works powerfully. God cannot work in any other way. 'It is God that worketh.' When he says 'Work out your own salvation' he does not use the same, but a much weaker word, because it is we who 'work it out'. But when he says that 'God worketh' he uses this powerful word.

But this word carries another meaning also, namely, that it works inwardly. Paul's description of man in sin is that of unregeneracy, man with these passions and affections and lusts of sin working powerfully and inwardly within him. How true it is! And he says that they work 'in our members'. We defined the meaning of that expression several times in chapter 6. We met it in verses 12 and 13: 'Let not sin therefore reign in your mortal body, neither yield ye your members as instruments . . .' We defined it as meaning all our faculties; not the body only, but the whole of our faculties – mind, imagination, interest, everything through which a man expresses himself and his personality. That is what is meant by 'members'. So what the Apostle means is that these sinful, lustful feelings were working within us and working on our natural powers and ways of expression, in order to 'bring forth fruit unto death'. Let us remember that such activity was not confined to outward actions.

Would to God it were! The 'members', as I have said, include
the mind, the imagination, as well as the body. A man may sin in
thought and in imagination as well as in the body. Our Lord has
stated that once and for ever in Matthew 5:28: 'Whosoever
looketh on a woman to lust after her hath committed adultery
with her already in his heart.' These 'motions', 'passions of sins'
were working in us and getting our members to act. We sinned
in mind, in imagination, in heart, in body.

What was the result of this? Paul says it was 'fruit unto death'.
Notice the contrast. At the end of verse 4 he says that we are
married to Christ in order that we should 'bring forth fruit
unto God'; but in the old life we spent our time in bringing
forth 'fruit unto death'. 'Death' is personified for the moment
in order to emphasize this. It is, of course, the simple truth that
all sinful actions lead always and only to death. That is the
terrible thing about the life of sin; it is a life of death. That is
why Philip Doddridge asks in a hymn, 'With ashes who would
grudge to part'? 'Ashes!' The life of the man of the world,
the sinful life, leads to 'ashes'. It burns out, and there is nothing
left at the end but the ashes; remnants, the ruins of a life – death!
The author of the Epistle to the Hebrews puts that clearly.
He is contrasting the 'blood of bulls and of goats, and the ashes
of an heifer' with 'the blood of Christ'; and in chapter 9, verse
14 he says: 'How much more shall the blood of Christ, who
through the eternal Spirit offered himself without spot to God,
purge your conscience from dead works to serve the living God.'
All sinful actions are dead, and they lead to nothing but death.
All who are not regenerate, and who are not 'in the Spirit', are
but existing, and using their faculties in a way that leads but to
death, to moral death, the death of the soul. They will get coarser
and coarser, duller and duller, and all that is fine in them will
become gradually extinguished. They will be left as exhausted
hulks or as heaps of ashes – moral death! Yes, and spiritual
death! All these activities mean the death of the spirit. When
man rebelled and sinned against God he died a spiritual death.
'You hath he quickened who were dead in trespasses and sins' –
spiritually dead. All the works of a 'dead' man are dead works.
But a state of sin also leads to physical death. I am simply
recapitulating what we found in chapter 6, verse 23: 'The wages
of sin is death' – and physical death is included there. Man

would never have died if he had not sinned. He was not meant for death; it was sin that produced his physical death.

And finally, and most serious of all, there is the 'second' death (Revelation 20: 6). All who are not 'in the Spirit', who are out of Christ, who die 'in the flesh', will not only die physically, they will be consigned to a 'second death' which will continue to all eternity. Those who are in Christ, those who are 'in the Spirit', will never experience 'the second death' which means final, eternal separation from God and His glorious presence and life.

We have now looked at the various terms used by the Apostle. Let me sum up the doctrine. What does this verse teach us? First, it teaches us the truth concerning the terrible nature of sin. What a terrible thing sin is! What a terrible power it is! The modern, popular, psychological view is, that sin is only negative, that it is only 'the absence of good qualities'. The popular psychologists do not like the term 'sin', they do not believe in it. They say that sin is not positive, that a man is not positively sinful; it is just the absence of certain good qualities. No, says Paul, 'the motions' of sin, 'the passions' of sin, exist. Other psychologists with greater insight and understanding talk about the 'drives' that are within us. The natural man is utterly helpless in their grip. They control him, they master him, they 'drive' him. The Apostle actually says that they are so powerful that they have the ability to frustrate, as it were, the Law of God. The power of sin in the unregenerate man is so strong that the Law of God cannot deliver him. Indeed it does the opposite, says Paul; it 'rouses sin,' it 'aggravates' the passions and the motions and the lusts. It makes them 'work in the members' more than before. He will work that out in great detail from verse 7 onwards; but he states it in principle here. There is nothing more fatal than a failure to realize the terrible power of sin. Sin is the greatest power next to God Himself. It is so powerful that even God's holy Law cannot deliver us.

The second lesson we learn from this verse is the limited scope and value of the teaching of morality. There is a great deal of moral teaching today and it looks as if we are going to have more and more. The authorities are going to reform the prisons, and they are going to treat the prisoners psychologically. Such a programme is based on a failure to realize the truth about sin, and to understand Romans 7: 5. They really believe that it is possible to solve the problems of crime and juvenile delinquency, and check all the sins that are multiplying so rapidly, simply by abolishing punishment, and speaking nicely, and persuading people, and encouraging them. The astonishing thing is that they are still saying such things in spite of all that is glaringly obvious in society today. They have largely abolished punishment in the schools, of course; and we are seeing the consequences. Punishment has all but been abolished in the family circle; and we are seeing the consequences of this also. We are witnessing an increasing lawlessness. But the authorities will not believe the facts; they are going to multiply the educational aspects of prison life, and so on. They believe that, if you are nice and kind, the condemned will respond. But they cannot respond, for 'the motions of sins' are too powerful for man's will and his systems. The most tender appeals of a father or a mother or a wife, or children, are not enough; the power of sin is greater than them all; yet the authorities go on relying on this kind of thing. To teach morality is, speaking generally, a sheer waste of time. The best it can ever do is to frighten certain timorous people against certain particular sins; it will do nothing more. It cannot change the heart, it cannot change the desires, it cannot change the man.

But the position is even worse still. According to the Apostle's teaching here, to teach morality may be a positive danger; for it tends to inflame the passions; it encourages them, it stimulates them. 'Unto the pure all things are pure, but unto them that are defiled and unbelieving is nothing pure, but even their mind and conscience is defiled' (Titus 1: 15). I have known many men who have said that they read certain books because they thought they would help them and strengthen them in the fight, the moral fight. They were honest enough, many of them, to admit and to confess that those books had done them great harm. A minister of religion once told me that the book that had done him the greatest amount of harm in his own personal life was a book entitled *The Mastery of Sex*. Avoid such books, for they will do more harm than good. The reason is that 'the motions of sins' are actually inflamed even by the Law of God. The very law that prohibits them encourages us to do them, because *we* are impure. So morality teaching can even be a positive danger. By teaching children about sex, and by warning them against the consequences of certain actions, what you are really doing is to introduce them to the whole subject. Naturally they will greatly enjoy it, their curiosity will be aroused, and they will desire to read further. It will do grievous harm.

I have made a strong statement; but I am ready to assert that the Victorian attitude towards sex, in actual practice, was more successful than the present-day method. I am not concerned to defend Victorianism, but to expound the Scriptures; and the Scripture says that moral teaching in and of itself can be dangerous. If we were all pure and innocent, then it would be safe; but we are not pure by nature, we are impure. These 'motions of sins' are there, and the more you tell people about these things, the more you will arouse a wrong interest and desire. The way to overcome sin is not to teach morality, it is to preach the gospel.

The third principle which we are taught here concerns the real function of law, and in particular the Law of Moses. It was never meant to save us. God did not give the Law to the children of Israel in order that they might save themselves by it. It was their misinterpretation of it that ever led them to think that. It could not save, because what it does is to aggravate 'the passions of sins'. Why, then, was it ever given? As we have seen at the end of chapter 5, 'The law entered that the offence might abound'. It was given to define sin, to bring it out in its real nature, and to show the need of a Saviour. The Jews, and the Pharisees in particular, had gone completely wrong at this point. The Law was never intended by God as a way of salvation; it was given simply to show 'the exceeding sinfulness of sin'.

That brings us to the last lesson. This verse, in a most amazing manner, and perhaps, from the negative side, more powerfully than any other verse in the whole of Scripture, shows the utter, absolute necessity of the Lord Jesus Christ and His work. Do you see it? Having seen the depth of sin, and the complete inability of the Law to deliver from it – indeed the fact that the Law even aggravates it, that even the giving of the Law of God cannot save a man – we ask, What then can save man? There is only one answer. It is the Lord Jesus Christ, and His perfect work on our behalf. It was because the whole of mankind was 'in the flesh', and because 'the motions of sins which were by the law' worked powerfully within us, in our members, to bring forth fruit unto death', that the Son of God left the courts of heaven and was born as a Babe at Bethlehem, gave perfect obedience to the Law, bore our sins in His own body on the tree, was dead and buried, and rose again. That is why He came. He had to come; there was no other way. This verse proves it. The condition of man was such that nothing else, no one else, could save him. 'Thou must save, and Thou alone' – and thank God, He does! He delivers us from 'the flesh' and puts us into 'the Spirit', and the Spirit into us; and thereby we are joined to Him and to the power of His might, which is more powerful even than 'the motions of sins'. Thank God for so great a salvation, which gives us so great a deliverance.

Seven

*

> *But now we are delivered from the law, that being dead wherein we were held; that we should serve in newness of spirit, and not in the oldness of the letter.*
> Romans 7: 6

This verse is the second half of the statement which is made by the Apostle in these two verses, 5 and 6. We have already considered the negative side in verse 5, and we now come to the positive side in this 6th verse. It is, in a sense, a repetition of the positive half of verse 4, which says 'that we should be married to another, even to him who is raised from the dead; that we should bring forth fruit unto God'. But the Apostle never simply repeats a statement; he always adds something to it, a further emphasis; and we shall find that he does so in this particular instance.

Here, once more, we have one of those great statements in which the Apostle seems to delight, in which he states the essence of the Christian gospel. He has just done that in verse 4, but he does it again, he so rejoiced in doing it. It is also one of those statements which gives us a definition of a Christian. There are many things you can say about a Christian; or you can say the one thing about him in many different ways. The latter is what the Apostle does here.

He starts with the two glorious words, 'But now'. If the expression 'But now' does not move you, I take leave to query whether you are a Christian. 'But now' introduces the whole Christian message. We have met it before in the 22nd verse of the previous chapter. Paul had been saying, 'For when ye were the servants of sin, ye were free from righteousness. What fruit had ye then in those things whereof ye are now ashamed? for the end of those things is death.' *'But now'* . . . There was another glorious example of it in the 3rd chapter, verse 21. The Apostle

[83]

had been working through his great argument from verse 18 in chapter 1, and he has wound it up in verse 20 in chapter 3 saying, 'Therefore by the deeds of the law shall no flesh be justified in his sight; for by the law is the knowledge of sin'. These words explain the hopelessness of our position by nature. Is it the end? Not at all! '*But now* the righteousness of God without the law (apart from the law) is manifested, being witnessed by the law and the prophets? This is how every Christian should think of himself or herself. This is our life, this is our position. 'We were' . . . 'But now'. So in verse 5 here we have: 'When we were in the flesh'. But, thank God, we are no longer there – '*But now*', verse 6. That is, I say, the test of whether we are Christians or not – Can I say 'I was . . .', '*But now*'? That tells us everything.

We shall be elaborating this, but at this point I emphasize that we are reminded of the completeness of the change. You are either a Christian or not a Christian; you cannot be partly Christian. You are either 'dead' or 'alive'; you are either 'born' or 'not born'. Becoming a Christian is not a gradual process; there is nothing indeterminate about it; we either are, or we are not Christian. We 'were' – We 'are'. '*But now*'. It is a complete change, something which, as Paul goes on to remind us, is entirely new.

The other matter I would emphasize at this stage is that what the Apostle says here is true of all Christians. He is not speaking only of some Christians; he is speaking of all Christians without exception. He is not speaking of certain Christians who have had some additional 'second blessing' which therefore puts them into a higher category; what he is saying is true of every Christian. Formerly we were, as was the whole of mankind, 'in the flesh'. '*But now*' we are delivered. That is to say, all who are Christians, every individual Christian. You cannot be a Christian at all without this being true of you.

The tremendous significance of this truth we shall see increasingly as we proceed with the exposition of the Epistle. Chapter 8, in a sense, is nothing but an exposition of this 6th verse of chapter 7. Hence it is essential and vital that we should be clear as to what Paul is saying here. Chapter 8 is not true of certain Christians only, it is true of every Christian. There are many who claim that the Christian who was 'in chapter 7' leaves chapter 7 and passes over into chapter 8. But every Christian is 'in' chapter 8, as every Christian is in this 6th verse of chapter 7.

What, then, is the truth about the Christian? The first thing the Apostle says is that we are 'delivered'. A better translation is, 'we have been delivered'. It is something that has happened once and for ever; 'we have been delivered from the law'. This is a very strong word. Some translate it as 'discharged', 'set at liberty', 'set free'. We are no longer under the Law; we have had a complete discharge from it, such as happens to a man who is discharged out of the army. In using that comparison, we can say that he can pass every tyrannizing sergeant-major without being at all afraid of him. He has no authority over him any longer; he has finished with him. Having obtained his discharge he can smile in that bully's face and tell him that he has no authority over him at all! The Apostle says that we have had our discharge. There was no real need for me to seek an illustration, for we have already met one in the 2nd verse of this chapter. 'The woman', says Paul, 'which hath an husband is bound by the law to her husband as long as he liveth, but if the husband be dead she is loosed from the law of her husband.' The word translated 'loosed' is the same word in the Greek; it carries the same meaning of 'being discharged', 'set free from'. In other words Paul is still working out his illustration of the woman who was married to one husband, and is now married to another. She has been separated from the first by means of death, and is now joined to the other. What he is emphasizing is that she is absolutely free from the control and the dominion and the power and the authority of that first husband. We have already been told in verse 4 that this has happened because of the death of the Lord Jesus Christ in His body on the Cross, and that because we are joined to Him we died with Him. That is how we have obtained the discharge, the deliverance from the old marriage, from the old contract.

In what sense has the Christian been delivered from the Law? The Apostle repeats this, and we must repeat it, though we have said it several times already. The Christian is delivered from the condemnation of the Law. Paul will say that again in the 1st verse of chapter 8: 'There is therefore now no condemnation to them that are in Christ Jesus.' We are also delivered from the inability of the Law to justify us. In some shape or form we were all trying to justify ourselves by the Law, 'by works'. We are freed from that misery. The Law which held us could not justify us, as we were told back in the 20th verse of the 3rd chapter. We are freed from that.

But the point about which the Apostle is most concerned here is that we are delivered from the inability of the Law to sanctify us. While we were under the Law we could never be sanctified. The Law can no more sanctify us than it can justify us. While we were held there we could not be joined to the One who can sanctify us as well as justify us. We had no freedom; but now we have been delivered. Now there is the possibility of sanctification. If I can but get out of the clutches, as it were, of that first husband, and be joined to another, there is hope for me. There was no hope while I was under Law; but now I am set free. I am delivered from my inability to experience sanctification. This is what the Apostle is particularly concerned to emphasize.

But he is particularly concerned also to emphasize something further, which he has touched on in verse 5, and which I have already explained, namely the work of the Law in aggravating and inflaming our sins. '*But now*', says the Apostle, you are set free from that aggravating effect of the Law of God upon our sinful nature.

That is a very strong statement; but it is the Apostle's. It is his main argument at this point. We have been set free from this tendency of the Law to aggravate our problem. That is the first statement of verse 6: '*But now*, we are delivered from the law.' Then an explanation follows: 'that being dead wherein we were held.' This translation as found in the Authorised Version is most unfortunate. There is nothing to be said in its favour. It is one of the few cases where the translators of 1611 really have done something which has no justification. Not only are the manuscripts against them, but the whole parallelism and argument of the chapter indicates that they are wrong. This is virtually agreed by all. The translation should not read 'that being dead wherein we were held', but 'we having died to that wherein we were held'. It is we who have died. Consider the parallel in verse 4, 'Wherefore, my brethren, ye also are dead to the law'. It looked as if his illustration in verses 2 and 3 would lead him to say that the Law, our first husband, had died; but he deliberately does not say so. He says, 'ye also are become dead to the law by the body of Christ'; and he is really saying the same thing here. We have now been delivered from the Law, 'having died to that wherein we were held', 'that' being the Law. In the end the meaning is very much the same, because if we have died to the Law, as far as we are concerned the Law is dead. But actually the Law is not dead; that is why Paul is so careful in his statement. It is we who have become dead to the Law wherein we were held. And of course it obviates having to say that the Law is dead – something which Scripture never says. But there have been people who have used such language, and have involved themselves in grievous heresies and in consequent trouble in their life and living.

But notice the Apostle's term; we were 'held' by it, we were 'ruled' by it. It is the same term exactly which he has used in the 1st verse – 'Know ye not, brethren, how that the law hath dominion over a man as long as he liveth' – where 'hath dominion' corresponds to the 'held' of verse 6. Whether we like it or not, that was the position. Every man until he becomes a Christian is in bondage under the Law; he is 'held' by it, he is dominated by it, he is married to it; it controls him and governs the whole of his activity. But, says the Apostle, that is no longer true of us; we have been delivered, we are dead to that which formerly had this dominion, this tyrannizing power and effect over us.

Why does the Apostle rejoice in all this? Why does it give him such happiness to say *'But now'*? The answer is found in the word 'that', the next word, which means 'in order that': 'in order that we should serve in newness of spirit'. I give the correct translation. There are some – for instance, the Revised Standard Version – who wish to translate it 'so that we serve'. But that is not what the Apostle is concerned to say. It is true to say that we do serve, but the Apostle is more concerned to emphasize the object and the intent and the purpose of that serving. We have been set free, he says, in order that we might serve.

Here, then, we come to the very nerve and centre of the Apostle's entire argument; this is what he is really concerned about. The great, grand object of salvation is our sanctification, our being made holy. The coming of the Son of God into this world, and all He did while He was here, His death upon the Cross, His burial, His resurrection, His ascension, and the sending of the Holy Spirit, has one grand end and object, 'that we should be holy and without blame before him in love' (Eph. 1: 4). That is the ultimate purpose of salvation. It is not forgivenesss only. We must never stop at that. It is not justification only; we must never stop at that. Indeed we cannot. God has done everything to bring us to holiness – 'This is the will of God, even your sanctification' (1 Thess. 4: 3).

There is nothing so wrong, therefore, as what was being said by the critics of the Apostle Paul. 'Ah', said they, 'this is dangerous preaching; he just says that all you have to do is to believe on the Lord Jesus Christ. This really means that we should continue in sin that grace might abound.' So they asked, 'What then? shall we sin because we are not under the law but under grace'. 'This is terrible teaching', they said, 'this is going to lead to chaos, this is going to lead to the complete breakdown of morality and of law; this is immoral; this is wrong teaching. Where is the Law, and where does righteous living come in?' The Apostle answers their charge in this passage as he does also in chapter 6. Salvation is from sin to holiness. It is completely wrong, therefore, to say that the preaching of the doctrine of grace leads to sin, because the whole point of the doctrine is to show us that God's end and object in doing all that He has done for us through His dear Son, by the Holy Spirit, is to sanctify us, and to make us 'holy and unblameable in his sight'. At the same time it is also true to say that there is nothing which is so wrong, and which so denies this truth, as antinomianism. That is the position of those who are so concerned about doctrine that they never trouble themselves about their practice. As long as their minds are clear about doctrine they do not care how they live. They are the people who think of salvation only theoretically, and never put it into practice, and who do not discipline themselves. Such antinomianism is always the greatest enemy of the doctrines of grace. It is a blank and a complete denial of them, because the whole object of the doctrine, the whole purpose of the salvation, is to deliver us from sin, as the Apostle goes on to show.

Consider Paul's argument in the following way. He says that nothing could enable us to 'bring forth fruit unto God' except our being delivered from the Law and its dominion and being joined to Christ. The advocates of the Law were really answering

themselves and contradicting themselves. They objected to the
Apostle's preaching of justification by faith only, because of their
concern for morality and right conduct. The advocates of
'morality' still bring that charge against the evangelical preaching
of the gospel. But they defeat their own end, as the Apostle
proves. His argument is that if you are really concerned about
morality and good behaviour, then the sooner you believe the
gospel the better; because as long as a man is under the Law,
not only can he not resist temptation to sin, but his very knowledge will even aggravate the position. While he is under the
power and the dominion of the Law he will sin more and more,
the offence will 'abound'. The Law, or his moral teaching,
will inflame his passions; it will work in his members and he will
get worse and worse. The very Law that tells him not to do a
thing makes him do it! So, if you are interested in morality
and conduct and behaviour, says the Apostle, the sooner you
are delivered from the clutches of the Law the better. That, he
says, is the glory of the Christian way of salvation. *'But now'*
a righteousness from God has come in, a way of salvation has
appeared, and this really can deliver us. We are no longer joined
to that which aggravates the position, we are now delivered from
it and joined to another and a greater Power.

But we must look again at the words 'in order that'. 'In order
that' – what? In order that 'we should serve in newness of spirit
and not in the oldness of the letter'. Notice the word 'serve'
which we have met with before. In chapter 6 we had to remind
ourselves that in the epistles the term 'servants' always means
'slaves'. For instance, in verse 16, 'Know ye not that to whom
ye yield yourselves servants (slaves) to obey, his servants (slaves)
ye are to whom ye obey; whether of sin unto death, or of obedience
unto righteousness? But God be thanked, that ye were the
servants (slaves) of sin, but ye have obeyed from the heart the
form of (sound) doctrine . . .' Then verse 20, 'But when ye were
the servants (slaves) of sin, ye were free from righteousness';
verse 22, 'But now, being made free from sin, and become
servants (slaves) to God'. Here Paul takes up that expression
again. This has happened to us, he says, that we may 'slave in
newness of spirit'. 'Serve' means 'to slave'. Paul rejoiced in
calling himself 'the bond-slave of Jesus Christ' whose service

is perfect freedom. There is nothing more wonderful than to be the slave of such a Master. The object of our being set free from the Law and its dominion is, that we might 'slave in newness of spirit and not in the oldness of the letter'. That is just another way of saying what he has said in verse 4, 'that ye should be married to another, even to him who is raised from the dead, that we should bring forth fruit unto God'. But take careful note of the extra meaning, for Paul is taking the argument a step, a stage further than he had done before.

We have now arrived at the vital point where the Apostle is going to emphasize the character of our service, the entirely new and different character of the service, the new 'slavery' in which the Christian lives. He contrasts it with the old way of living, and we must understand that he is contrasting here the life of the Christian, the man in Christ, with the life of the best possible type of moral man who is 'under the law' and 'in the flesh'. We must keep that contrast in our minds. There were men then, and there are men now, who read the Moral Law and say, 'That is right, that is good, I am going to live in that way; I am going to try to practise that very code'. And they do their utmost in the energy of their own flesh. The Apostle is contrasting that type of man with the man who has become a Christian. He is concerned, of course, to bring out the differences, the striking contrasts.

The Apostle first shows us the general differences between the two men, and then, in closer detail, the particular differences. The first broad difference is that between the old and the new. He says 'in newness of spirit, and not in the oldness of the letter'. Here are great New Testament words again – 'old' and 'new'. Once more he cannot refrain from emphasizing the tremendous contrast, the complete and entire difference between the Christian life and the non-Christian life. This is not peculiar to this Apostle; it is the teaching of the New Testament everywhere. I turn again for an illustration to our Lord's words to Nicodemus. Nicodemus thought that Christianity was something that you were to add on to what you had already. That was clearly the whole basis on which he sought the interview. 'Rabbi', he said, 'thou art a teacher come from God: for no man can do these miracles that thou doest, except God be with him'. But he was not allowed to go further. He was obviously about to add, 'Now I am a master of Israel, and I know much more than the people, but you clearly know more than I do, and have greater power; what must I do to get to where you are, how can I get this extra?' Suddenly our Lord cut across him, reading his mind. We have already been told at the end of chapter 2 of John's Gospel that He had no need for anyone to tell Him what was in man because 'he knew what was in man'; and He read Nicodemus as an open book. So He said to him, 'Verily, verily, I say unto thee, Except a man be born again, he cannot see the Kingdom of God' – he cannot even get a fleeting glimpse of it, he must be 'born from above'. This is no question of addition; this is regeneration, this is a new birth, this is literally starting *de novo*. 'Old' – 'New'. The old deadness – the new life.

Or take another way in which our Lord put the matter. People could not understand Him, so they came to Him and said, 'We do not quite follow you; the disciples of John the Baptist fast often, but your disciples do not seem to be fasting at all. You claim to be greater than John, you set yourself up as the Teacher; but you seem to behave quite differently from John. Answering them He said, 'New wine must be put into new bottles' (Matt. 9: 14–17). This is absolutely new. This is not just a superior brand or a better brand of what you used to have; it is absolutely new. New wine must have new bottles to suit it. Or it is like a piece of cloth. You do not take a new piece of cloth and put it into the old; for it will tear that and make the rent worse. It is not a matter of gradually passing from that to this; it is 'old – new'.

Or take the way in which this Apostle puts the same point in the Second Epistle to the Corinthians, chapter 5, verse 16. He says, 'Henceforth know we no man after the flesh'. Formerly he knew men 'after the flesh', but no longer so. As a preacher of the gospel, as an emissary and an ambassador of Christ, as one who preached because 'the love of Christ constrained him', he no longer knew any man 'after the flesh', in that old way. 'Yea', he says, 'though – even though – we have known Christ after the flesh, henceforth know we him (so) no more'. And he proceeds to say in verse 17, 'If any man be in Christ' – that is, if he is a Christian – 'he is a new creature (a new creation), old things are passed away (have gone), behold, all things are become new'. Now that is precisely what he is saying here in Romans chapter 7. Again I say, that if you do not thrill at this, you cannot be a Christian. No longer the 'old', but the 'new'! 'Not in the oldness of the letter, but in newness in the spirit'.

But let us look at the second contrast, the contrast between the Law and the spirit. 'That we should slave in newness of the spirit, and not in the oldness of the letter.' Now what is meant by 'the letter?' Here again is an interesting point. What the Apostle actually wrote was not 'letter' but 'writing'. He is referring, of course, to the written Moral Law that was given through Moses to the children of Israel. They referred to it as the 'writing' because God wrote it on the tables of stone which He gave to Moses. That was the explicit statement in writing of the Law which God had originally given to man, and of which Paul has reminded us in chapter 2 where he says that the law 'is written in the hearts' of all men, even the Gentiles who had never known the Law of Moses (Rom. 2: 14, 15). In the law of Moses that was made explicit, it was reduced to writing. God wrote it in order that it might be plain and clear. Now we are to serve, says the Apostle, not after, or according to that old way which called for conformity to that which was written. That was the position 'under the law'. We are no longer in that position; that was the old. What is the new? It is 'in newness of spirit'. The 'new' is a life lived 'in the Spirit', not 'under the law'.

Another question of translation arises here. The text does not mean simply that we are now trying to keep the Law in a new spirit. That does not bring out the true contrast. Paul means that we are now living in the sphere and the realm of the Holy Spirit of God, and not living under Law. It means living in and under the power of the Holy Spirit. 'Spirit' should be spelt with a capital S – 'that we should serve in newness of Spirit' – the Holy Spirit, the Spirit of God – 'and not in the oldness of the writing'. Here, the Apostle introduces the Holy Spirit. The last time he mentioned the Holy Spirit was in verse 5 of chapter 5. Again, I would remind you that the whole of chapter 8 is just an exposition of this 6th verse of this 7th chapter. Chapter 8 is concerned to describe this 'life in the Spirit'. It starts in verse 2, 'For the law of the Spirit of life in Christ Jesus hath made me free from the law of sin and death'. There, Paul takes up again what he says here in this 6th verse of chapter 7, so that he can work it out and elaborate it. Verses 7–25 of this chapter 7 are a digression in which he deals with objections and difficulties, and having done that, he takes up again in chapter 8 the very thing he is saying here. In other words, the Christian life is an entirely new life which is made possible because the Holy Spirit of God dwells in us as the result of our union to, and marriage with, the Lord Jesus Christ. The Christian life is essentially a life in the Spirit; and is therefore entirely different from the old life which was lived 'in the flesh' and 'under the law'.

There are several statements to this effect in the New Testament. Take for instance what the Apostle says in 2 Corinthians 3, verses 5 and 6. He is talking about himself and his ministry. 'Not that we are sufficient of ourselves to think anything as of ourselves; but our sufficiency is of God; who also', he says, 'hath made us able ministers of the new covenant.' We are ministers of a new covenant. But then he is not content with saying that positively, he has to say it negatively also – 'able ministers of the new covenant; not of the letter' – not of the writing again – 'but of the Spirit: for the letter killeth, but the Spirit giveth life'. 'I am a minister of the New Testament, of the New Covenant', he says. He means that his ministry is not 'of the writing', it is 'of the Spirit', the Spirit of the living God, to which he has referred in the 3rd verse of that chapter. Indeed the whole of the Christian life is 'life in the Spirit'.

I have already quoted the 2nd verse of chapter 8: 'The law of the Spirit of life in Christ Jesus hath made me free from the law of sin and death.' That is true of every Christian; everything he does is done 'in the Spirit'. Take also verses 5 and 6 of the 8th chapter. He says, 'They that are after the flesh do mind the things of the flesh' – they think of, and understand, and are interested in, the things of the flesh – 'but they that are after the Spirit (mind) the things of the Spirit'. The Christian has a new mind and is interested in new things – not in the old but in the new – and they are spiritual things. The difference between the Christian and the non-Christian is an absolute difference; they do not even think in the same way. 'For', says Paul, 'to be carnally minded is death, but to be spiritually minded is life and peace.' And the Christian worships God in a new way, as our Lord explained to the woman of Samaria (chapter 4 of John's Gospel). She was concerned about the question of whether worship should be 'in this mountain' or in Jerusalem. That was the big question – where should one worship? How should one worship? It is still the same – Vestments, and do you stand or kneel as you pray? That was that woman's idea of worship and of praying. But our Lord said to her: 'God is Spirit; and they that worship him must worship him in spirit and in truth'. That is the all-important matter.

Paul says the same as his Lord and Master in Philippians 3:3 – 'We are the circumcision which worship God in the spirit.' We do not have altars, we do not have signs, crucifixes and other supposed aids, we 'worship God in the Spirit'. We do not place our emphasis on particular buildings; we can use any building, or we can do equally well without them. We worship God 'in the Spirit', not as in the former temple. The burnt offerings and sacrifices are no more: all that is finished. 'We worship God in the Spirit, and rejoice in Christ Jesus, and have no confidence in the flesh.' Our worship is now entirely different.

Our praying is also different. Jude 20 speaks of 'praying in the Spirit'. In 1 Corinthians 14:15 we read, 'What is it then? I will pray with the spirit, and I will pray with the understanding also.' There is a purely spiritual prayer which cannot always find words for itself. 'The Spirit itself maketh intercession for us with groanings which cannot be uttered.' In the 4th verse of chapter 8 of this epistle Paul says, 'That the righteousness of the law might be fulfilled in us, who walk not after the flesh, but after the Spirit'. And he gives this exhortation to the Galatians in chapter 5:16: 'Walk in the Spirit, and ye shall not fulfil the desires of the flesh.' The Christian life is a complete contrast to the old unregenerate life at its very best. It is the difference between the new and the old, between life in the Spirit of God, and life under, and dominated by, the Law. Thank God we can say 'But now'. We are no longer what we were; we have been delivered from the Law which tyrannized over us and held us down, and are now free to slave in this new way in the power of the Spirit of God, and in the realm of the Spirit. It is no longer 'in the oldness of the letter', 'the writing'. All Christians should be rejoicing in this 'But now'. Do you know as you look at yourself that you are a 'new creature', that everything is changed, that 'old things are passed away; behold, all things are become new'? Is the sunshine new, are the flowers and the birds and all in nature new? Do you see something of the glory of God in them that you never did before? Can you say –

Something lives in every hue
Christless eyes have never seen?

Thank God for this control of the Spirit over mind, affections, will, indeed, over the whole man. The Christian life is a life in the Holy Spirit.

Eight

*

But now we are delivered from the law, that being dead wherein we were held; that we should serve in newness of Spirit, and not in the oldness of the letter.   Romans 7: 6

We continue to consider this 6th verse which is quite pivotal in the understanding of the Apostle's argument in this chapter, and particularly this point at which we have arrived. The Apostle gives here what we may describe as his final answer to the criticism that was so constantly brought against his preaching, namely, that it discounted the Law and could lead to nothing but immorality and antinomianism. He has dealt chiefly with the charge of antinomianism in chapter 6, and here in this chapter he specifically takes up the question of the relationship of the Christian to the Law. He is concerned to show that the Law, and any attempt to base life on the Law only, far from helping us to live the godly life actually is a hindrance. He has established that in verse 5. But now, he says, we are in a position to live the godly life because we have finished with that which held us down and which aggravated our problem; we have entered into an entirely new life. We are considering, therefore, at the moment, the contrast which the Apostle draws between this new life and the old life, and we have dealt so far with the general differences.

We come now to the particular differences which we must look at in detail. This is not something merely theoretical; it is essentially practical, because the charge brought against him was a practical charge, something like the following: 'Ah', they said, 'this preaching of grace and this preaching of justification by faith sounds very wonderful and of course it pleases people, but the question is, What does it lead to in practice? That is the test; what is it like in ordinary daily life and living?' The Apostle was prepared to meet them on their own ground, and to show that it is because this, and this alone, leads to the practical daily living of holiness that he is preaching it, and rejoicing in it. The big contrast between the old and the new is that we no longer 'slave' 'in the oldness of the writing, but in the newness of the Spirit'. The Apostle regards this distinction as most important, indeed vital; and it is emphasized frequently in the New Testament. We have seen it in the 3rd chapter of this Apostle's Second Epistle to the Corinthians. It is found also in the Epistle to the Hebrews in chapter 8, where the writer draws a contrast between the old covenant which God had made with the children of Israel through Moses, and the new covenant which He has made through Jesus Christ.

We have here, then, a crucial verse, which is vital in the Apostle's argument in this section, and indeed vital to the whole of his exposition of the Christian salvation in this Epistle. As I have suggested, the remainder of this chapter is but a digression to deal with difficulties that have arisen in people's minds. But verse 6 is the important, crucial statement.

What are the differences, in detail, between life lived 'in the Spirit' and the old way of living 'according to the writing' and 'under the law' and 'in the flesh?'. First, there is the difference between an external and an internal relationship to the Law of God, in other words, to morality. This difference is well described in the 3rd chapter of Second Corinthians, verse 3, where Paul says, 'Forasmuch as ye are manifestly declared to be the epistle of Christ, ministered by us, written not with ink, but with the Spirit of the living God'. Before, it was, as it were, a writing 'with ink', but it is no longer that, it is now a writing with the Spirit. But, further, 'not in tables of stone' – that is something outside you. Well, where is the writing now? In 'fleshy tables of the heart'. The old law was outside a man, written on stones, written with ink, something you looked at with your physical eyes. That is no longer the position. It is now engraven and written and implanted in the fleshy tables of the heart, in the very centre of the personality, in the deepest recesses of our being. We are no longer looking at something outside ourselves, we are considering something that is already within us, and working within us as a principle. The Epistle to the Hebrews states it in chapter 8. The author is quoting what Jeremiah had said in the 31st chapter of his prophecy. God says that He is going to make a new covenant

[97]

with the people – 'not the old covenant that I made with your fathers', but a 'new covenant'. What are the characteristics of the new covenant? 'I will put my laws into their mind, and write them in their hearts.' Before, He had put the laws on tables of stone which He handed to Moses, and Moses brought them down to the people. But in the new covenant He is going to 'put (his) laws into their minds, and (imprint) write them in their hearts'.

Here we meet with a fundamental distinction between the two covenants, the two ways of life. Before you become truly Christian you try to conform to a standard and a pattern outside yourself; but to be a Christian means that the standard is inside you. Of course, in one sense it is still outside, but the important fact is that it is now inside as well. You read it in the Word, but it is also in your mind and in your heart. You are not only looking at something external, you are also aware of that which is within. You do not have to be persuaded to look at that which is outside you; there is now a power within you calling your attention to it, a principle operating in the centre of your personality. The same truth is stated in the Epistle to the Philippians, chapter 2, verse 13: 'Work out your own salvation with fear and trembling. For it is God that worketh in you (inside you) both to will and to do of his good pleasure.' The Apostle rejoices that we have become dead to the Law, and that we are delivered from the Law which formerly held us because we can now serve 'in newness of Spirit, not in the oldness of the writing'. It is within us, in our minds and in our hearts.

Secondly – and the first point necessarily leads to this – this new life in the Spirit means that we have now an understanding which we had not got before. I mean an understanding of the Law and its purpose, and everything that is true of it in the economy of God. What was the trouble with the people under the old dispensation? The Apostle, in 2 Corinthians 3, says that 'a veil was upon their hearts' (verses 13–16). That is the trouble with people who are 'under the law', who are 'in the flesh'. Week by week, he says, they hear the reading of the Law of Moses; but they do not understand it because there is a veil over their hearts; their minds are blinded. So though they are studying it, and regard it as important, and though their teachers spend the whole of their lives in expounding it and making comments upon it, and forming those traditions of which we read so much in the Gospels, they are still ignorant of the real meaning of the Law, and lack true understanding. But, says the Apostle, 'when it shall turn to the Lord, the veil shall be taken away', and they will begin to understand. The trouble with the man who is not a Christian is that he lacks a fundamental understanding of this new life that God would have us live; he does not see why one should live it, nor what its purpose is. He has no conception of God's purpose with respect to man; he knows nothing about God's great scheme and plan and purpose of salvation. Those Jews were reading the Old Testament and yet they saw nothing of this at all. That was why they misinterpreted the Law, and thought that, if they but carried out certain commands as they understood them, they would satisfy God. They never saw the real meaning and purpose of the Law. They never realized that it was but to be 'our school-master to lead us to Christ.' They never saw that its main function was to bring out 'the exceeding sinfulness of sin'; they never understood that 'by the law is the knowledge of sin'. They thought that they could justify themselves by the Law. There was a veil over their hearts, their minds could not function truly. That was their condition under 'the oldness of the writing'. But the moment a man turns to the Lord, the veil is taken away, and he sees and understands; his whole position is revolutionized.

The third thing is, that a man begins to see now the vital distinction between observing the mere 'letter' of the law and being concerned about the 'spirit' of the law. That is a great distinction, which explains the whole problem of the Pharisees and scribes and doctors of the law. They were only interested in the 'letter' of the law, they never understood that what matters, essentially, in the Law is the spirit that is involved. The supreme commentary on that matter is the Sermon on the Mount, and especially the 5th chapter of the Gospel according to Matthew. The section from verse 17 to the end is devoted almost entirely to an exposure of this false attitude of the Jews and their teachers to the Law of God. They taught and believed that, if you do not actually murder a man in a physical sense, you are not guilty of murder. But our Lord shows very clearly that that is only observing the letter, whereas the Law is concerned about the spirit. If you say 'Raca' to your brother, or if you say 'Thou fool', you are guilty of murder. Likewise He works it out in terms of adultery and other matters, such as going the second mile, and throwing in the cloak also.

Ultimately it is a question of loving, He says. 'Love your enemies.' They never understood that principle; they had always regarded these matters in terms of the external letter only, and had never realized that the essential thing about the law is the principle, the spirit, that belongs to true obedience.

The Apostle Paul here and there admits that all this was once true of himself, as for instance, in this very chapter in verses 8 and 9. 'I was alive without the law once, but when the command-ment came sin revived and I died.' He says virtually the same thing in Philippians 3, in that piece of autobiography in verses 4 to 8. What he had never understood and grasped was that the Law says 'Thou shalt not covet'. It is not enough simply that you refrain from doing certain things; the question is, do you desire them? Do you sin in your imagination, in your mind and in your heart? Do you 'covet' them? Concupiscence – the desire for these things – in the sight of God is sin. 'God seeth the heart.' Our Lord said to the Pharisees, as recorded in Luke 16: 15: 'Ye are they which justify yourselves before men; but God seeth the heart: for that which is highly esteemed among men is abomina-tion in the sight of God.' God reads and is concerned about the heart. So these people came to our Lord one day and asked, 'Which is the great commandment in the law?' They thought that they would catch him with this question concerning all their 613 rules and regulations. But He exposed their utter ignorance and blindness by answering, 'Thou shalt love the Lord thy God with all thy heart, and all thy soul, and all thy mind, and all thy strength; this is the first and great commandment. And the second is like unto it, Thou shalt love thy neighbour as thyself.' 'Love is the fulfilling of the law' (Romans 13: 10). The Law is not merely a collection of rules and regulations; it is not a mere matter of the letter; it is the spirit that counts primarily.

The Jews had never seen that. But the moment a man comes into the realm of the Spirit he sees it at once, and he perceives that all his former morality is but as 'filthy rags', 'dung', refuse. That old righteousness of which he used to boast so much is now of no value at all. Once he realizes the spiritual character of the Law, its positive character, he sees the hopelessly mechanical and superficial nature of his former external correctness. The super-ficial outward performance still leaves a sink of iniquity; he now learns that it is of no value at all in the sight of God. But it is only the man who is 'in the Spirit' who sees this. The tragedy of the moralist, the merely 'good' man, is that his native blindness remains, as was the case with so many Jewish teachers. But the moment a man is in the realm of the Spirit he sees that he is utterly condemned, and he is forced to seek his salvation in the Lord Jesus Christ.

The fourth point of difference between the man living this new life 'in the Spirit', and the man formerly living his life 'in the writing', 'under the law' and 'in the flesh', is that the former has an entirely new factor in his life, a new motive for his good and righteous living. The old motive was fear of God. He tried to keep the Law because he was afraid of God. It is the essence of wisdom to try to please God; self-preservation and self-interest dictate such a course. There are many people today who are trying to live the good life simply because they are afraid of hell, afraid of God, and the Judgment. 'If only' God and the spiritual realm could be dismissed, 'if only' someone could prove that when a man dies that is the end, you would see a difference in their conduct. They are living a life of fear; self- preservation, self-interest are supreme. But even at its best and highest, even when the fear motive is not so prominent as is the case with many so-called intellectuals today – the people who say they have no interest in Christian dogma and doctrine, but are very interested in morality for the sake of morality – what is the motive? It is self-satisfaction. They desire to keep up their own standard, they want to satisfy their own conception of the moral code, they want to live on good terms with themselves. One of them put it recently thus: 'Morality is a man's responsibility for himself.' That is self-satisfaction; and that was the main trouble with the Jews. The Apostle says in the 10th chapter of this Epistle in verse 3, 'They, going about to establish their own righteousness, have not submitted themselves to the righteousness of God'. He says, 'I bear them record that they have a zeal of God, but not according to knowledge'. They were working very hard, they were trying to produce righteousness, but, he says, 'it is their own righteousness'. They were very proud of it; they were well pleased with themselves, as the Apostle Paul says in Philippians 3: 'As touching the righteousness which is of the law, blameless.' How proud he was of his righteousness and of his keeping of the Law as he had misunderstood it! He tells the Galatians that in this matter of zeal for the Law he was 'more exceeding zealous' than others. He was pleasing himself, and was altogether self-satisfied. That is always the case with the Pharisee.

Our Lord has given a graphic picture of all this in Luke 18 in His parable of the two men who went up to the temple to pray, one a publican, one a Pharisee. The Pharisee, he says, walked right to the front and said, 'God, I thank thee that I am not as other men are, extortioners, unjust, adulterers, or even as this publican. I fast twice in the week, I give tithes of all that I possess.' How supremely self-satisfied was this man! He does not ask God for pardon and forgiveness, or for any help or strength; he is self-contained, self-sufficient, self-satisfied. His whole motive was to please himself. That is the characteristic of the old life lived 'according to the law' and 'in the flesh.

But what a difference there is when you come to this new life 'in the Spirit'! As Christians we are anxious to live this godly, this holy life because we have within us a desire to please God and to please the Lord Jesus Christ; also because we are anxious to express our thanksgiving and our praise. We live the Christian life, not because we are afraid of hell any longer, nor to please ourselves, nor to attain a standard of our own, nor to contrast ourselves with others who are flagrant sinners and failures. We are no longer primarily concerned about self-preservation, because we know that we have been saved, and shall be kept and preserved until 'the day of Christ'. We live it because we know that it is the way to show our love to God, our gratitude, our thanksgiving, for all that He has done for us. The Apostle expresses this eloquently in the Second Epistle to the Corinthians in chapter 5, verses 14, 15: 'For the love of Christ', he says, 'constraineth us; because we thus judge, that if one died for all, then were all dead: And that he died for all, that (in order that) they which live should no longer live unto themselves, but unto him that died for them, and rose again.' These words supply the Christian's argument. He says, 'I was dead, and Christ died for me that I might have life. Did He die in order that I might go on living for myself as I did before? No, but that I might live for Him who gave Himself for me and rose again from the dead.' The motive for Christian living is not even to be holy, it is to please God and to glorify His Name. 'The chief end of man is to glorify God'; and a Christian is a man who has realized that high calling. The other man knows nothing of it; he lives for his own glory. The first thing that is true of a Christian is that he is now living unto God and for the glory of God, not for himself. His grand motive is to please God who in his infinite love and mercy and compassion and kindness sent His only begotten Son into this world, even to die for us.

Love so amazing, so divine,
Demands my soul, my life, my all.

That is the New Testament way of preaching holiness; that is the only true motive for being holy. We should not go to 'holiness meetings' because we have a problem or something we desire to be rid of. We should desire to be rid of our 'self'. And as preachers we should not appeal to people to come forward to 'receive' something, but rather face them with the demand of the crucified, dying Christ, who has given His life, whose body was broken, whose blood was shed, that we might be rescued and redeemed and become the children of God. The motive should be love, gratitude, praise, thanksgiving to Him who has given Himself for us. The Christian is a man who has an utterly, entirely new motive; it is this love to God and the desire to extol His matchless grace.

The fifth consequence follows directly from that. This man, with this new understanding, and this new motive, lives his life in an entirely new spirit. In the old life, as the Apostle reminds us in the next chapter in verse 15, he was held by a 'spirit of bondage'. 'For', he says, 'ye have not received the spirit of bondage again to fear, but ye have received the Spirit of adoption, whereby we cry, Abba, Father.' 'The spirit of bondage'! That old life, that life 'under the law' is a grievous bondage, a slavery of the worst type, a heavy burden. Any man who is living 'under the law' always has a sense of hopelessness and despair. He lives in that spirit; he is always under tension and stress and strain. Oh, the bondage of that old life 'under the law' and 'in the flesh'! 'But now' we are living with an entirely new spirit, and doing our work 'in the Spirit and not in the oldness of the letter'. There should be no bondage in the Christian life. 'Blessed are they that do hunger and thirst after righteousness.' The other man does not 'hunger and thirst after righteousness'; he is trying to live the good life because he is afraid of God, and afraid of God because he does not want to suffer, and because of his pride. But with the Christian it is entirely different. You cannot be a Christian without it being true of you that you 'hunger and thirst after righteousness'. Christians are 'blessed', happy, and they 'shall be filled'.

John, in his First Epistle, chapter 5, says, 'And his commandments are not grievous'. God's commandments were very grievous to the man before he became a Christian; they were a burden. Peter explained to the Council in Jerusalem (Acts 15) that they were 'a yoke and a bondage', too heavy to be borne. But John says that to the Christian 'His commandments are not grievous'. That is, partly, how we know that we are Christians; we love His commandments now, they are no longer a burden, no longer a terrible task. Our great desire now is to live in this way, so it is no longer grievous, it is not 'against the grain'. Paul adds to that in 2 Corinthians 3: 17 – 'The Lord is that Spirit; and where the Spirit of the Lord is, there is liberty'. Another translation is, 'Where the Spirit is Lord, there is liberty'. When you are in the realm of the Spirit, there is liberty. There is no liberty 'under the law'; the task-master is watching you and you are afraid. That was Luther's experience as a monk before his conversion, fasting and sweating in his cell. But when you become a Christian and enter the realm of the Spirit, 'there is liberty'. You are set free from the shackles of 'that wherein we were held'; you are dead to the Law, you are a free man able to use your powers. 'Where the Spirit of the Lord is, there is liberty.'

Think of the encouragements enjoyed by the Christian. There were no encouragements in that old life; that is why we were dis-spirited. But all has become wonderfully different. Start with the knowledge of sins forgiven. God said that in the New Covenant He was going to make, 'Their sins and their iniquities will I remember no more'. There is nothing so liberating as to know that all your past sins are forgiven; indeed that all your future sins are forgiven also. It is the most liberating thought one can ever have. If you are worried about forgiveness, and worried about your whole standing and position before God, you are of necessity depressed; and in that depressed state Satan has an advantage over you, and you go down still further. There is nothing more wonderful than to know that our sins are forgiven – and we do know it! 'There is therefore now no condemnation to them that are in Christ Jesus.'

But secondly, and summarizing what we have been saying since we began studying chapter 6, we are dead to sin, we are dead to the Law, we are dead to 'death'. In chapter 6, verses 9,10, we are reminded that 'Christ being raised from the dead dieth no more; death hath no more dominion over him. For in that he died, he died unto sin once; but in that he liveth, he liveth unto God. Likewise reckon ye also yourselves to be dead indeed unto sin, but alive unto God.' What is true of Him is true of us. He has died once and for all; He will never die again; 'death hath no more dominion over him'. And it has no dominion over us. This is part of the liberty of the children of God. As a Christian I am dead to the dominion of sin, I am dead to the dominion of the Law, I am dead even to the dominion of death. As a Christian I am simply going to 'fall on sleep'; I am 'in Christ', and therefore I shall never die, I shall never experience the 'second death'. I am out of the dominion of sin and of the Law and of death. That is the new spirit in which one lives; that is the liberty the children of God enjoy.

God has also said to us – it is a part of the New Covenant – 'I will be to them a God, and they shall be to me a people'. He has said, 'I will dwell in them and walk in them, and I will be their God and they shall be my people'. Can anything be more wonderful than that? Nelson said on the morning of the Battle of Trafalgar, 'England expects that every man this day will do his duty'. What a motive, what an encouragement! But God says to us, 'I am your God, and you are My people. Remember that and live in the light of it'. Could a Christian have any greater encouragement?

But God tells us further, of His great purpose with respect to us, and of all He has planned and purposed for us. 'This is the will of God, even your sanctification.'We have already met with this at its very highest in chapter 5, verse 10: 'For if, while we were enemies, we were reconciled to God by the death of his Son, much more, being reconciled, we shall be saved in his life.' He has put us into the life of His Son, and if we are in the life of His Son all else is certain, it is guaranteed. We shall be saved completely and entirely; nothing can stop it. Then think of our relationship to the Lord Jesus Christ. Let me remind you of what we have been told in verse 4 in this chapter, that the Lord Jesus Christ is our husband. 'That we might be married to another, even to him who is raised from the dead' –

> *'Jesus, my Husband, Shepherd, Friend . . .*
> *My Lord, my Life, my Way, my End . . .'*

He is everything, He is the 'All and in all'. What an encouragement! The man 'in the flesh' knows nothing of this.

Then think of the 'hope of glory' and the certainty of our getting there. 'Being therefore justified by faith, we have peace with God, through our Lord Jesus Christ; by whom also we have access by faith into this grace wherein we stand, and rejoice in hope of the glory of God' (chapter 5 : 1,2). There is no encouragement beyond that! 'Every man that hath this hope in him, purifieth himself, even as he is pure' (1 John 3 : 3). This is the way in which the new man, the Christian man, lives his life 'in the Spirit'. He faces all problems in a new spirit of liberty, rejoicing, hope, thanksgiving and praise.

That leads me to the sixth great difference between the new and the old man – the new ability and power which the former has, and of which he is aware. In the old life the man was left to himself. 'What the law could not do', says Paul in the 3rd verse of the next chapter, 'in that it was weak through the flesh'. God gave the Ten Commandments and said – as we loosely translate chapter 10, verse 5 of this Epistle – 'If you keep them, and continue to keep them, you will save yourselves by doing so'. But 'all have sinned and come short of the glory of God'; 'there is none righteous, no, not one'. Man, left to himself, could not keep the Law; he is too weak. But what of this new man 'in the Spirit'? He has new life; he is a 'partaker of the divine nature', he has received new life in Christ, he is born again of the Spirit. Remember Paul's words in 2 Corinthians 3, verse 6 – 'The letter killeth, but the Spirit giveth life'. That is what we need – life and vigour and power – and 'the Spirit giveth life'. Not only so; the Spirit continues to work within us. Go back to Philippians 2, verses 12 and 13 again: 'Work out your own salvation with fear and trembling'. How can I do it? Why impose such a task upon me? The thing is impossible. The Patriarchs have failed, the Children of Israel have failed. But there the word stands: 'Work out your own salvation with fear and trembling'. How can it be done? 'For it is God that worketh in you.' He is working in you 'both to will and to do of his good pleasure'. As the result of the Spirit within us, and the new nature on which He operates, we are able to do things that were unthinkable before.

Paul says in the next chapter of this Epistle, verse 13, 'If you through the Spirit do mortify the deeds of the body, you shall live'. Ask a man who has not got the Spirit within him to mortify the deeds of the body. To discover the result you have but to read the lives of many of the so-called 'Catholic saints' and others who had never seen the truth of 'justification by faith only', and who segregated themselves from society, put on camel-hair shirts and often half starved themselves. They were trying to 'mortify the deeds of the body' and the more they tried the more conscious they were of failure. You can go 'out of the world', but you take the deeds of the body with you, in your mind and imagination. You cannot get rid of the deeds of the body in that way; but 'through the Spirit' you can do so, because you are given new strength. The Apostle says to Timothy in the Second Epistle, chapter 1, verse 7, 'God hath not given us the spirit of fear; but of power, and of love, and of a sound mind'. Power: love: discipline: or as he has already said in chapter 6, verse 14 of this Epistle, 'Sin shall not have dominion over you'. John says the same thing in his First Epistle, chapter 4, verse 4: 'Greater is he that is in you, than he that is in the world.' Hence, do not be frightened by the devil though he is a powerful enemy. Do not be terrified, do not be alarmed; you now have power, you have strength, you are 'in the Spirit'; life 'in the Spirit' brings all blessing to you.

So we come to the seventh distinction which emphasizes the entirely different result of these two lives lived in these entirely different ways. 'When we were in the flesh, the motions of sin, which were by the law, did work in our members to bring forth fruit unto death.' Paul says in 2 Corinthians 3: 6 that 'The letter killeth'. It always does so. That old life is a life of constant struggle, and of constant failure, constant defeat. It becomes increasingly difficult. As you get older you find your powers waning, and the devil seems to become stronger. Your very physical condition leads to new temptations and sins; it gets worse and worse; you are less and less able to resist, and you feel utterly and completely hopeless. It is a kind of living death. But what of this new life in the Spirit? Turn to 2 Corinthians 3: 18. The Apostle has said already, 'The Lord is that Spirit, and where the Spirit is Lord there is liberty'. Then, praise God, he adds, 'But we all with open face beholding as in a glass the glory of the Lord are changed into the same image (into His image) from glory to glory, even as by the Spirit of the Lord'. I have quoted the translation found in the Authorised Version, but there is a better one – 'We all, with open face beholding as in a glass the glory of the Lord, are being changed'. We ourselves are not doing this, it is being done to us. As we behold in the glass the glory of the Lord – as we go on living this life 'in the Spirit', with this new understanding and insight and motive and love and power, and all that is so true – as we go on doing all this, we are being 'changed into the image of God's dear Son', and 'from glory to glory'. It is a progressive life; it gets better and better and higher and higher. We become more and more like the blessed Son of God. Do not believe those who say that a Christian on the verge of the grave is in exactly the same position as he was at the beginning. He is 'being changed from glory to glory', from one degree of glory to another, and on and on progressively.

> *Changed from glory into glory,*
> *Till in heaven we take our place,*
> *Till we cast our crowns before Him,*
> *Lost in wonder, love, and praise.*

This is the truth. Even in this life we can say, 'He which hath begun a good work in you will perform it until the day of Jesus Christ' (Phil. 1: 6). If you are in the hands of this great Potter; if God, through His Son, and by the Spirit, has begun a work in you, He will never give it up, He will never leave it incomplete; He will complete it, until on that great Day, as Ephesians 5: 27 reminds us so gloriously, we shall be 'without spot, or wrinkle, or any such thing; holy and without blemish.' What shall we say to these things? There is but one thing, I feel, that is fitting. Let us say with Jude, 'Now unto him that is able to keep us from falling, and to present us faultless before the presence of his glory with exceeding joy, to the only wise God our Saviour, be glory and majesty, dominion and power, both now and ever. Amen.'

Nine

What shall we say then? Is the law sin? God forbid. Nay, I had not known sin, but by the law: for I had not known lust, except the law had said, Thou shalt not covet.   Romans 7: 7

The history of the interpretation of this chapter, and especially from this point to the end, is a most interesting and fascinating one. As I have already been suggesting, I believe that much of the disagreement has been due solely to the fact that so many have not troubled to be guided by the context, but have just come to the chapter in and of itself, and especially this section, and doing so, have gone astray.

I would remind you once more, therefore, of the whole setting; and to do this we must go back to the end of chapter 5. As I am never tired of repeating, the key to the understanding of chapters 6 and 7 of this Epistle is chapter 5. If we are not clear about chapter 5 we cannot possibly understand chapters 6 and 7; and in my view these two chapters form a parenthesis with two parts, chapter 6 being one and chapter 7 the other. The Apostle introduced this parenthesis because of what he had been saying at the end of chapter 5, especially in verses 20 and 21: 'Moreover the law entered, that the offence might abound. But where sin abounded, grace did much more abound: that as sin hath reigned unto death, even so might grace reign through righteousness unto eternal life by Christ Jesus our Lord.' It is that 20th verse that really gives us the key. The Apostle, having been describing how the Christian believer is 'in Christ' – he was in Adam, but he is now in Christ – and what is bound to happen to him because he is 'in Christ', suddenly realizes that many might say, 'But surely all this is to put the Law on one side, which means that there will be no standard or canon for conduct and for behaviour. It is the Law that has always guaranteed holiness; but your

The Law

teaching seems to brush the Law aside, and therefore there is nothing to safeguard holy living.'

The Apostle therefore takes up this difficulty. In chapter 6, as we saw at length, he takes up the moral aspect and deals with it in terms of 'Shall we continue in sin, that grace may abound?'

Here, in chapter 7, he deals with the other question, namely, the place of the Law. In chapter 5, verse 20, he had remarked that 'The law came in by the side' as it were. Then in chapter 6, verse 14, he had made the statement, 'For sin shall not have dominion over you; for (because) you are not under the law, but under grace'; and he seems to rejoice in the fact that Christians are not 'under law'. But he realizes that there were people who would misinterpret those two statements as meaning that the gospel entirely dismisses the Law, and renders it valueless and pointless.

It is this subject that the Apostle takes up in this 7th chapter. It is the chapter of chapters concerning the Law and its function, and the relationship of the Christian to the Law. It is vitally important that we should be clear as to this particular relationship; so the Apostle expounds it in the body of this chapter, and step by step shows that sanctification by the Law is as impossible as was justification by the Law. In his first four chapters the Apostle is proving that 'no man can be justified by the deeds of the law'; he is now equally concerned to show that no man can be sanctified by the Law or by being 'under the law'.

That is the general theme of the entire chapter; but he divides it into three main sections. The first is verses 1–6, with which we have already dealt. It supplies a general statement to show that as Christians we are in an entirely new relationship to the Law, and that that is essential in order that 'we may bring forth fruit unto God', serving God in 'newness of Spirit, and not in the oldness of the letter'.

We now come to the second section. It is best to regard it as running from verse 7 to verse 12. Verse 13 then sums it up and also acts as a point of transition from this section to the next, which starts at verse 14 and goes on to the end of the chapter. In verses 7 to 12 the Apostle's purpose is to vindicate the Law, the Law in and of itself, the Law as such; and to prove that the Law must never be held responsible for our failure to keep it. It is a vindication of the character of the Law. He absolves it

The Apostle absolves the Law [110]

completely from every charge of involvement in our guilt. Verse 13, as I say, is a kind of summing up of that argument and an introduction to the next section, verses 14–25. In verse 14 to 25 he gives a demonstration in practice, and from the experimental standpoint, of what he has been saying in the second section. He clearly felt that this was necessary in order to show how the Law not only fails to deliver us, but actually aggravates our problem. He ends by showing that, though the Law leaves us in a state of complete hopelessness, there is nevertheless a hope. So we have the triumphant cry, 'I thank God through Jesus Christ our Lord'.

To recapitulate: the first section, verses 1–6, really says everything; and what Paul does in these two further sections is merely to elaborate what he has said there. His whole case in the first section, as we have already seen, is to say that we are no longer 'under the law', but joined to Christ, so that we can now 'serve in newness of Spirit, and not in the oldness of the letter'. These two sections, 7–13 and 14–25, are nothing but a working out in detail, and a demonstration of, that original contention, and a defence of it against possible misunderstanding.

What the Apostle is still doing, in an ultimate sense, is to establish what he said in verses 1 and 2 of chapter 5: 'Therefore being justified by faith, we have peace with God through our Lord Jesus Christ: by whom also we have access into this grace wherein we stand, and rejoice in hope of the glory of God.' The man who is justified is a man who is safe and secure, his position is certain. Paul states that once more in verse 10 of that 5th chapter: 'For if, when we were enemies, we were reconciled to God by the death of his Son, much more, being reconciled, we shall be saved in his life.' He repeats it again in verse 21: 'That as sin hath reigned unto death, even so might grace reign through righteousness unto eternal life by Jesus Christ our Lord'. Grace is going to be victorious, nothing can stop it; and nothing is more important than that we should be clear that our salvation is entirely in and of the Lord Jesus Christ. We must not bring in the Law again; if we do so we are ruining everything. So the Apostle takes time in this parenthesis to clear up the whole situation, and to define the position of the Christian with regard to his relationship to the Law.

We are now ready to start upon this second section beginning at verse 7, where we read 'What shall we say then? Is the law sin?' The Apostle has been making certain statements about the Law, and he imagines someone saying: 'Well, there is only one conclusion to draw from what you have been saying, and that is, that the Law, the Law that was given through Moses, is something evil, is something bad in and of itself.' He seems to imagine this objector saying, further, 'You had already made two statements which disturbed me. You had already insulted the Law by saying that it only "came in on the side"; and then you had gloried in the fact that we are not "under the law but under grace". But you have gone further now. You have said in verse 5, "When we were in the flesh, the motions of sins, which were by the law" – aggravated, produced by the Law – "did work in our members to bring forth fruit unto death". Surely you are saying therefore that the Law is sin? You rejoice in the fact that we are not "under law" in exactly the same way as you have rejoiced that we are not "under sin". Therefore sin and law must be synonymous; there is no difference between them. The Law is bad, sinful, harmful, something that leads only to our death. Is that what you are saying?'

At once the Apostle answers with his famous formula, translated in the Authorized Version as 'God forbid', but which should be translated as 'Far be it from our thoughts,' 'Let it be unthinkable'. That suggestion, he says, should never enter one's mind. He has already used the same formula in chapter 6, and before that in chapter 3. He said in chapter 6, 'Shall we continue in sin, that grace may abound? God forbid,' Here again he says that this is something that no one should ever entertain. He virtually says the following: 'As there are people who think such things, we must investigate, we must examine this, because if you really draw that conclusion from what I have been saying about the Law, the fact of the matter is that you have completely misunderstood my whole teaching.' So he has to introduce a subsidiary parenthesis – a parenthesis within a parenthesis – in order to make it plain.

I am labouring the point for this reason. In this section, and the one that follows, the Apostle puts his case in personal terms. That is what has caused all the argument and the disputation. It has been assumed that the Apostle's main purpose in this chapter is to relate his experience. In my view that is not the case at all. He would never have written what we have from verses 7 to 25 were it not for the likelihood of the misunderstanding of what he had said in verses 1 to 6, indeed of what he had already said at the end of chapter 5. In other words the Apostle's object in this chapter is not to give his experience but to make clear his teaching about the relationship of the Christian to the Law, and to show how the Law can never sanctify us any more than it could ever justify us.

So he says 'God forbid' to the suggestion that 'the law is sin'; it just means that the objector has misunderstood the entire purport of his teaching. But he does not leave it at a mere general statement. He goes on to say, 'Nay' – 'not only is that not right, but on the contrary.' Such is the force of the added expression. On the contrary, says the Apostle, the position is not merely that I am not teaching what your question suggests, I am teaching its exact opposite.

In what ways is the Apostle's teaching the very opposite of saying that 'the law is sin?' He gives us two answers. The first is, 'I had not known sin but by the law'. To understand this answer it is essential that we should again start with a negative statement, because this has been, and can be, misunderstood. Obviously the Apostle is not saying that he was once not aware of the fact of sin, of the fact that he had sinned and that others had sinned. He cannot mean that, because there are many non-Christians who are well aware that certain things are wrong, and who say that certain things are sinful. There is a kind of general knowledge of sin in all people, so the Apostle could not possibly say that he had no knowledge whatsoever of sin apart from the Law. His meaning is that he was not aware of the real nature of sin until the Law made it clear to him. It is the Law, he says, that brought him to a right understanding of the essential character and nature and meaning of sin. Now this is, in many ways, but to repeat what he had said in chapter 3, verse 20. 'Therefore by the deeds of the law shall no flesh be justified in his (God's) sight: for by the law is the knowledge of sin.' His point there was that the Law, far from justifying, can do no more than give us a knowledge of sin. He is saying the same thing here. It is the Law of God alone that really gives us a right conception of the true character and nature of sin.

This is a tremendous proposition. The real trouble with the unregenerate is that they do not know and understand the truth about sin. They have their moral code, they believe that certain things are right and certain things are wrong; but that is not to understand sin. The moment a man understands the true nature and character of sin he becomes troubled about his soul and seeks for a Saviour. So the trouble with people who are not seeking for a Saviour, and for salvation, is that they do not understand the true nature of sin. It is the peculiar function of the law to bring such an understanding to a man's mind and conscience. That is why great evangelical preachers three hundred years ago in the time of the Puritans, and two hundred years ago in the time of Whitefield and others, always engaged in what they called a preliminary 'law work'. In their preaching of the Gospel they generally started with a presentation of the Law. They knew that man would not understand salvation unless he understood the nature of sin. So they expounded the Law of God, showing its relevance, and by means of it they brought men and women to an understanding of what sin really means in the sight of God. Now nothing but the Law, says the Apostle, does that. 'Without the law' he had no real knowledge of sin. 'I had not known sin' – I would never have discovered what it really means – 'were it not for the law'. That is his first statement.

But he makes a second statement, which illustrates the first. 'I had not known sin, but by the law: for I had not known lust except the law had said, Thou shalt not covet.' Here the 'for', introduces an illustration. Says the Apostle, 'I can make plain to you what I mean when I say that apart from the law I would never have known the real character of sin. For instance, I would never have known the meaning of lust were it not that the law had said, Thou shalt not covet.'

Here, again, is a vitally important statement. What is the meaning of 'lust?' It means coveting, 'to covet'; it means what is called 'concupiscence' in verse 8. 'Sin, taking occasion by the commandment, wrought in me all manner of concupiscence.' The terms means 'desire after anything forbidden'. We have to be careful about the word 'lust'. It is actually a word that means in and of itself simply 'desire', 'a strong desire'. You remember how our Lord says to the disciples, 'With desire I have desired to eat this passover with you before I suffer' (Luke 22: 15). The word used there is actually the word 'lust'. So the word in and of itself is neutral, but the context will always make it clear as to whether it is to be taken in a neutral sense, or in a good sense, or in a bad sense. Usually the word 'lust' is employed in an evil sense. It means a desire, a craving for something forbidden by God. So the Apostle is saying, 'I would never have known what lust means were it not for the law which says, Thou shalt not covet, Thou shalt not desire in that way.'

As for the meaning of 'the law' here, Paul doubtless meant the Ten Commandments, as they are given in the book of Exodus, chapter 20, and particularly the tenth Commandment which says, 'Thou shalt not covet thy neighbour's house, thou shalt not covet thy neighbour's wife, nor his manservant, nor his maid-servant, nor his ox, nor his ass, nor anything that is thy neighbour's'. You must have noticed the difference between that tenth Commandment and the others. The others say, 'Thou shalt not kill; thou shalt not commit adultery; thou shalt not steal; thou shalt not bear false witness'. But here there is a change – 'Thou shalt not covet'. At once we are introduced to the distinction between an outward action and a happening within a man's inner being. But we must not over-press this, because the idea of coveting is implied in the others also.

The Apostle is really saying two separate things. The first is, 'I would not have known that lust was sin in and of itself if the law had not taught me so'. That was undoubtedly true of the Apostle before his conversion as it was true of all the Pharisees. They thought of sin only in terms of external actions. As long as a man did not perform an evil act, he was not guilty of sin. An evil desire, they said, is not sin; it only becomes sin when a man does the thing, carries out his desire; but desire in and of itself is not sinful. So the Apostle is saying, in the first place, that he would never have realized that desires, coveting, lusts, evil thoughts and imaginations, are sin, were it not that the Law had given him enlightenment.

Our Lord was at great pains to bring this point home to the Jews, and especially to the Pharisees in the Sermon on the Mount. In Matthew's Gospel, chapter 5, verse 21 to the end of the chapter, he deals with this one great matter. The Pharisees were teaching the people, and deceiving themselves also to think that as long as you did not actually murder a person you were not guilty of murder. But our Lord goes on to show them that if you say 'Raca', if you say to your brother 'Thou fool', you are already guilty of murder in your heart with respect to that person. And he says the same with the question of adultery. They said that as long as a man had not actually committed an act of adultery he was not guilty of adultery. But Christ replied to this: 'If you look upon a woman to lust after her you have committed adultery with her already in your heart, and you are therefore guilty of adultery.' They did not know that; they did not understand the real meaning of lust. They did not realize that lust is sinful in and of itself; so our Lord gave them these illustrations in order to show them that their fundamental conception of the Law was wrong, that the Law is essentially spiritual, that the Law is concerned about a man's heart.

On another occasion when He was asked about the Law, He said that the first, the great commandment is, 'Thou shalt love the Lord thy God with all thy heart, and with all thy soul, and with all thy mind, and with all thy strength. And the second is like unto it, Thou shalt love thy neighbour as thyself'. That is the Law, not just tithing mint, rue, anise and cummin, and all the little details and minutiae. The Law, Christ says, is spiritual, it is concerned with a man's heart and his ultimate attitude to God. That is the meaning of the Law. Now, says the Apostle, it was only when I really understood the meaning of the Law that I understood the truth about lust. I came to see that to covet is as reprehensible as to commit, that a desire is as damnable as a deed. He had never seen that before. It was the Law, the true understanding of the Law, that opened his eyes to this question of lust and of coveting.

But then the Apostle makes a second statement with respect to the matter: 'I had not known lust', he says, 'except the law had said, Thou shalt not covet.' The second meaning is something like this: 'I had never understood the power of lust and of desire within me until I was really enlightened by a true understanding of the law'. Take this word 'know'. Notice that he uses the word 'know' twice – at least it is here in the Authorized Version – 'I had not *known* sin, but by the law. I had not *known* lust, except the law had said . . .' Here it occurs twice; as also in most of the other translations. But in actual fact the Apostle used a different word the second time. and I am amazed that the translators have not concentrated on that. He does not use the same word in the Greek in the two places. The second 'know' is much stronger than the first. It means, 'to know absolutely'; it means 'to know as the result of reflection and experience'. The first indicates a kind of apprehension. Says the Apostle, 'I would never really have comprehended the meaning of sin but by the law'; but then he adds, 'I would never have understood and come to feel in the depth of my being, and have a full understanding and experience of the meaning of lust, and the part lust plays in a man's life, were it not that the law had said, Thou shalt not covet'. In other words, the Law had not only brought Paul to see that to lust was to sin, it had brought him to see the terrible power of lust in his own life. He certainly includes that second meaning as well as the first. So the Law had rendered this great service to him. He will show us this in greater detail in the verses which follow, but here he expresses it in a general way. He says in effect, I really had no true understanding of sin until the Law enlightened me. I had been oblivious of the power and the place of lust in my life until this command about coveting arrested me, and I suddenly began to realize the truth about myself.

Note then the Apostle's argument. You must not say that 'the law is sin', says Paul, because it is the Law that has brought me to see the meaning of sin, and my own sinful condition as the result of this power of lust within me. 'God forbid', he says, that anyone should think that I am teaching that the Law is something sinful or evil; I am saying the exact opposite. Do not misunderstand me, he says in effect, the fact that I say that the Law cannot sanctify a man does not mean to say that I am arguing that the Law is useless. The fact that I have said that the Law 'aggravates' sin does not mean that the Law is sinful. No, I am going to show you that it is this sinful principle that does just that; the Law itself is excellent, and I thank God for it. I would never have known, and had a true understanding and apprehension of sin, were it not for the Law. And, especially, I would never have understood this matter of lusting and the place of lusting in my life, were it not that this commandment had come and convicted me. Such is the Apostle's argument in verse 7. Obviously, he has not finished his explanation of his attitude to the Law; this is but the beginning of the matter. He will go on to work it out in greater detail.

But before we come to Paul's further explanations let us mark this great lesson and underline it. Are we clear in our minds that to lust after an evil thing is to sin? Are we, as the Apostle says was once his case, in the position of thinking that as long as we do not carry out an evil desire we have not been guilty of sin? There are many who teach that error. For instance, the Roman Catholic teaching is that as the result of being baptized by the Church you are cleansed from original sin, that there is no longer indwelling sin. Then they quite logically go on to teach that to lust is not to sin; it is only acts committed that constitute sin. That is a part of the whole error of that particular Church with regard to salvation.

But such teaching is not confined to Romanists; there have been certain Perfectionist Schools of thought which have really taught exactly the same thing. I refer to those who believe in the eradication of sin and who have to explain the difficulty concerning evil thoughts and desires. In the same manner as the Romanists, they do not regard inner desires as sin, and by this means they try to establish their position of entire sanctification. But the teaching of the Apostle here and elsewhere, and of the Lord Himself, is quite plain. To desire to sin is sin. You can sin in your imagination, in your thought. That is as much sin, says our Lord, as the act. Obviously there are differences in consequences, but in the sight of God the one is sin as much as the other. Our Lord's words are, 'he hath already committed adultery with her *in his heart*', and 'God seeth the heart'. Our Lord said to the Pharisees, 'Ye are they that justify yourselves before men, but God knoweth your hearts; for that which is highly esteemed among men is abomination in the sight of God' (Luke 16: 15). You Pharisees, who stand up at the corners of the street, and in the market-place, and say, Look at us. We have never committed murder, we have never committed adultery. God sees your hearts, and He knows that they are black, that they are full of sin. You have not done these things as acts but you have done them in your hearts, in your thoughts, and in your imaginations, and that is abomination in the sight of God.

This is obviously crucial teaching. It is an essential part of the Apostle's whole exposition of the great doctrine of salvation; and it is to the extent to which we are clear about this that we shall be able to follow his argument in the remainder of this particular chapter. The thing that awoke the Apostle to see his need of a Saviour from heaven was this question of lusting. There he was convicted; but only so when he saw the true character of the Law as essentially spiritual. Thereby he saw the true nature of sin. In other words, there is no better way of testing our understanding of the Christian doctrine of salvation than to examine our understanding of the true nature of sin and especially as regards this question of lust.

It is essential that we should be clear about the setting and the context of the argument of the Apostle here, because if we fail to carry this in our minds we shall inevitably go astray when we come to the later verses and their detailed teaching. The great principle is that Paul is showing that the Law is not sin. Thank God it is not! Thank God it does, and has done, what it was meant to do. It brought the Apostle to a knowledge of sin, and especially in terms of coveting. God grant that we all may be able to join him in saying the same thing, and in the offering of praise and thanksgiving to God for His holy Law, and for His work in us and upon us.

Ten

*

But sin, taking occasion by the commandment, wrought in me all manner of concupiscence, for without the law sin was dead.

Romans 7: 8

Here, in this 8th verse, the Apostle carries his argument a step further. He has made his fundamental positive statement about the character of the Law and what it does; then having done that he moves on. 'I had not known sin, but by the law: for I had not known lust, except the law had said, Thou shalt not covet. 'But' – and here comes the explanation; and it is a very profound explanation. Why has the Law had that effect of aggravating sin and lust in one's members? Oh, he says, the answer is because of the nature and the character of sin. The trouble arises not because of the Law, but because of sin. What, then, causes sin to do this? Here is the answer – 'Sin, taking occasion by the commandment, wrought in me all manner of concupiscence'.

What does that mean? Perhaps the best way of approaching this 8th verse is to take the various expressions one by one, starting with the word 'sin'. By 'sin' Paul does not merely mean acts of sin; he means sin as a principle and a power which works in fallen human nature.

Come to the next expression. 'Sin', he says, 'taking occasion'. Here we have a most fascinating expression. We shall find that he uses it again in verse 11, 'For sin, taking occasion by the commandment'. The root meaning of the word translated here 'taking occasion' is 'to make a start from a place'. It is a word used to describe a place from which you have set out on a journey, a starting point. 'Sin, having a starting point in the commandment'. But you can also think of it in terms of military operations, and in this sense it becomes a base in which you make your preparations, in which you train your troops and assemble your artillery and

[120]

your armaments, and from which you set out upon your campaign. So we have, 'Sin, making use of the commandment as a base of operations'. Or indeed, you can use yet another idea; and some of the translators have adopted it. It is a very interesting and picturesque one, which perhaps brings out the meaning even better than both the others. 'Sin, using the law as a fulcrum'. The meaning of the word 'fulcrum' is clear. If you are confronted by the problem of moving a great weight – a stone or some similar object – you find that in the ordinary way you cannot move it at all. You therefore proceed to get a long bar, the longer the better. Next you put a log of wood or something solid on which the bar can rest fairly near the object you want to move. You then place one end of the bar under the object, and by pressing on the other end and using the block of wood as a fulcrum you are able to lift and to move the weighty object which you are anxious to move. The word rendered here as 'taking occasion' was very frequently used in that way. So we can translate it like this: 'Sin, using the law as a fulcrum, was able to move our resistance and to produce the result that it was anxious to produce.' This wonderfully helps to bring out the idea that the Apostle has in mind.

Here, no doubt the Apostle is referring in particular to the Tenth Commandment with its whole idea of not coveting—'Thou shalt not covet'. Now, he says, what has happened is that sin has taken this commandment about coveting, this prohibition of coveting, and it has used it as a fulcrum, or a military base of operations. To do what? 'To bring to pass in me.' 'It wrought in me.' This word 'wrought', again, is very interesting and important; it is a very powerful word. It means 'to work powerfully', or 'to bring to a firm conclusion', to 'accomplish' something. It is not a mere attempt; it meets with success, it is a thoroughgoing operation. So we can translate it thus, 'Sin, taking occasion by the commandment, wrought powerfully in me'; 'wrought mightily in me', 'really did produce an end result in me in this respect'. It is important that we should give the full weight to that word 'wrought'.

What did it bring to pass? It wrought in me 'all manner of concupiscence'. What is 'concupiscence?' The same word as used by the Apostle in the previous verse, is translated 'lust'. 'For', he says, 'I had not known sin but by the law, for I had

not known lust except the law had said, Thou shalt not covet.'
Concupiscence means lust, desire, and particularly in an evil
sense. It means that whole state of the heart, and of the person,
in which evil desires, lusts and passions are in control.

There are two statements in the book of Genesis which put
this so perfectly that nothing is necessary but to quote them.
The first is in Genesis 6: 5, the description of the people before
the Flood. We are told that 'every imagination of the thoughts
of man's heart was only evil continually'. That was the characteristic of man in the antediluvian period. That is concupiscence!
Men were controlled and consumed by lusts and passions and
desires – they were full of them. Then there is a second description in Genesis 8: 21 which really says the same thing. 'For
the imagination of man's heart is evil from his youth.' That is
concupiscence! The inner being of man is in a state in which it
is controlled by these lustful, evil, unclean and unworthy desires.
So what the Apostle says is that sin, using the commandment as a
fulcrum, wrought mightily in him to produce all manner of such
lusts and evil desires. 'Concupiscence'! He is writing deliberately,
and he says 'all manner'; so we must interpret it as such; we must
not water it down. He says, I seemed to be filled with this kind of
thing, of all conceivable types. All manner of evil desires and lusts
were within my mind and heart; I seemed to be nothing but a
mass of corruption, and of evil thoughts, desires and imaginations; I seemed to be a cesspool of iniquity. That is what sin did
by the use it made of the Law. So we sum up his statement by
saying that sin used the Law as a base to produce such an effect.
The very prohibitions of the Law gave sin the very opportunity
it desired; it roused it, really gave it something to work on as a
fulcrum, and it moved in that terrible and terrifying manner.

So far we have the Apostle's general statement. But let us
examine it. The first thing it tells us is something about the nature
and the character of sin. How do you define sin, what is your
notion of it? Obviously, we must not say that sin is merely something negative. There are many who regard and describe sin in
that way. The biblical doctrine of sin is most unpopular today.
There are those who say that the old notion of sin ought to be
dismissed, that it has done much harm, that it made people condemn themselves and feel hopeless and pessimistic. They say that
sin should not be used as a term at all, that it is too negative, that

it is psychologically bad for us because it produces a kind of mournful person. I remember reading a sermon once by a well-known 'liberal' preacher. Most of the sermon was a denunciation of Charles Wesley's great hymn, 'Jesus, Lover of my soul', and particularly the verse which says:

> *Just and holy is Thy name,*
> *I am all unrighteousness;*
> *Vile and full of sin I am,*
> *Thou art full of truth and grace.*

He abominated the words. He felt it was a disgrace, and that it should be taken out of the hymn-book and never sung again. He tried to ridicule it by saying that when a man is applying for a post he does not go to his prospective employer and say, 'Vile and full of sin I am'. The answer to that, of course, is quite simple. The man does not say that to his prospective employer because he knows that the same thing is true of that prospective employer also. But when you are facing God, then the whole situation is entirely different. Such is the ridiculous position in which people land themselves when they deny biblical truth and doctrine.

But that is the common attitude today. They say that we must not talk about sin as something in and of itself; what we really mean is that there are certain things we would like to see in a man that are not there. In other words, we must not say that a man is a bad man, what we should say is that he is not a good man. We must not say man is positively evil; what we should say is that he has not yet developed to the extent he should have done. The concept is purely negative; it merely takes note of the absence of certain qualities, or, if they are there, they need to be drawn out. Education and culture and training will bring them out; but we must cease to say that people are positively evil and – to repeat Charles Wesley's term – 'vile'. What is called sin, if we want to use the term, is something which is entirely negative, mere deprivation as it were, rather than something that is essentially positive.

Clearly all that is something which the Apostle Paul would reject *in toto*, because his whole case depends upon this, that sin is a positive power that can use the lever, can put the pressure on the end of the bar, and use the fulcrum. You cannot move weights with negatives. You cannot lift weights with a mere absence of something. No, the whole concept, the whole picture, the very phraseology that he employs is designed to bring out the idea that sin is positive. And not only positive, but powerful in the extreme. It is something that can 'take occasion', that can have 'a base of operations', that can 'use a fulcrum', that can move great weights and obstacles – it can work powerfully.

And, of course, in saying that here, in this picturesque way, the Apostle is simply repeating what he has already been saying earlier in this Epistle in other language. In chapter 5 : 21 he says, 'Moreover the law entered, that the offence might abound. But where sin abounded, grace did much more abound. That as sin hath *reigned* unto death . . .' Sin is something so powerful that it can 'reign'; it is a monarch with tremendous power. It is an empire. Then Paul says the same thing in chapter 6 : 14 in the words, 'For sin shall not have *dominion* over you'. It has dominion over everyone else. Every man who is not a Christian is under the dominion of sin. Yet people say that sin is but a negative phase, just the absence of good qualities. It is positive, says Paul; it is so powerful that it can move men and throw them over. It knocked down all the patriarchs. He then uses even stronger language in chapter 6, verses 16, 17: 'Know ye not that to whom ye yield yourselves servants (slaves) to obey, his servants ye are to whom ye obey; whether of sin unto death, or of obedience unto righteousness? But God be thanked, that ye were the servants of sin, but ye have obeyed from the heart that form of sound doctrine which was delivered unto you.' Sin is a *slave-master,* sin is that which controls people absolutely.

There is nothing which is so foreign to the biblical teaching than this notion that sin is entirely negative. I will go further. Would you know how strong sin is? Well, Paul tells us here. Sin is as powerful as this, that it can even use God's own holy Law to its own ends. I do not know of a greater estimate of strength and of power than this. God gave His holy Law through Moses. Ah yes, says Paul, but sin was strong; it was as strong as this, it even used God's holy Law as a fulcrum to bring its own purposes to pass. And it succeeded. It wrought powerfully, it achieved, it accomplished what it wanted to do. Even God's holy Law could not resist it. Such is the measure of the positive character of sin, and the strength of sin. There is no doctrine, perhaps, which is more important in a practical sense in the life of this country and the world at this moment than just this doctrine.

How then does sin use the Law? How does it use the Law as a fulcrum, a base of operation, a starting point? The first part of the answer is this; it does so by arousing in us the element of rebellion that is in us. We are all born rebels, we are all born with an antagonism to God within us. That is a fundamental postulate of the Bible. Does anyone dispute it? If so, the answer is found in the next chapter – chapter 8, verse 7: 'Because the carnal mind is enmity against God; is not subject to the law of God, neither indeed can be.' He does not say merely that we occasionally do things that God has told us not to do. 'The carnal mind' – and that is sin in control – 'is enmity against God'. But many a modern man says – I have been told it many times – 'I have always believed in God, I have always tried to worship God'. But the God they have worshipped has not been God but rather a figment of their own imaginations. The Scripture says that the carnal mind, the natural mind, is enmity against God. The Apostle repeats the same statement in different words in the Epistle to the Ephesians, chapters 4 and 5, and elsewhere in such expressions as, 'being enemies', and 'alienated in your minds by wicked works'.

What happens is this. The Law comes and addresses a man, and at once the antagonism to God that is innate within him, and natural to him, the spirit of rebellion, is aroused and aggravated, and his self-assertiveness comes into play. This is because man 'in sin' desires to be autonomous; he is not prepared to bow to anyone. He is self-satisfied, he is self-contained, he is independent; and so he resents the idea of Law. That is why many people say that they do not believe in God. They resent the idea that there is anyone to whom they must bow the knee. They are men, twentieth-century men, who stand on their own feet! They boast of their abilities, their wisdom and knowledge. The natural man hates this notion that there is anyone, even God, before whom he has to bow down and submit himself. He is not going to be a suppliant to anyone, he wants to live his own life in his own way. Why shouldn't he? And so he says that the whole notion of God is nothing but a projection of the Victorian idea of a father. That is what the clever people, the psychologists and others are saying. The Victorian father, the stern Victorian father, repressed his children, he gave commandments, and his word was law. His children had to do what he said. Most people, they say, have projected that into infinity and say that that is God. Of course, it is something purely psychological! In saying all that, they are, of course, but showing this enmity, this hatred of God, this spirit of rebellion that is innate in us. So the great characteristic of an age like this, which does not believe in God, is lawlessness, dislike of discipline and order in any shape or form. People today have a rooted dislike of law and of sanctions and of punishment. We have almost reached the state in which they do not believe in punishing anyone; a murderer almost becomes a hero who engages public sympathy. The prisoner gets more sympathy than his victim. Thus the whole idea of right and wrong is rapidly disappearing from the human mind.

In essence, sin is lawlessness. It is the rooted objection to any law, any commandment, any prohibition, any notion of wrath and of punishment. This works itself out in endless ways. There is no longer discipline in the home or in the school. Children are not to be punished however much they misbehave themselves. If they are punished the parents will soon be demanding an interview with the head master or the teacher and protesting against their discipline. In New York City, I am told, it has reached the point that no one ever fails an examination in the schools; all are passed automatically. And for this reason, that the teachers, the head masters and others are afraid of the physical consequences to themselves if they fail a pupil or a candidate. There is soon to be an enquiry into this whole problem of these adolescents, these juvenile delinquents in New York City who are taking the law into their own hands. This attitude towards anything which savours of discipline and punishment is one of the ultimate ends of this lawlessness. The moment the natural man hears of the Law he reacts against it and resents it. What was already there is aggravated. And sin is the root cause. Sin was already present; the Law comes in with its prohibition, and sin uses it as a fulcrum and it presses down, with the result that there is greater sin than there was before. Thus the Law aggravates the situation because of this spirit of lawlessness that is in us, and it actually incites us to sin. Such is the condition of every person born into this world ever since the fall of man.

But there is another way in which sin works. When the Law comes to us with power, and especially when it puts this emphasis

upon not coveting and lusting, man in sin reacts also in another
way. He says, 'This is going too far, this is unfair. I am prepared
to agree that there are certain things that I should not do; and
that if I do them I am wrong. That is a matter of actions, and a
man is responsible for his actions. But now you tell me that the
Law says "Thou shalt not covet", that I am not even to desire;
that if I have within myself a longing for these things, a hankering
after them even though I do not actually engage in them, then I
am guilty of sin.' I am speaking here, of course, about that which
really comes out of the heart and not about a temptation from the
outside. I am taking the case of a man who enjoys sinning in his
mind, in his imagination and in his heart, but who feels that because he has not actually committed an outward act of sin all
is well with him. When the Law comes and says to the man 'Thou
shalt not covet', and tells him that to covet is sin, there is an immediate reaction. He says, 'Now this going too far, this is an
impossible standard, this is unfair to me. It is not unreasonable
as long as it stops at actions, but if it is going to examine my
thoughts and my innermost imaginations, why, this is a sheer
impossible position. I object to this. I am willing to go on living
a moral life, but my own inner life is my own, and no outside
authority shall come in there.' He hates the notion that a man's
innermost thoughts are open to God, and that evil thoughts are
as reprehensible in His sight as are outward deeds and actions.
And so when the Law comes in in that way, sin uses it as a fulcrum and it aggravates the situation. It puts a man into a bad
temper, he is annoyed, and he feels that he is being dealt with
unfairly and unjustly; and in that state he is going to sin more
than he ever did before.

Then there is a third way in which sin works; and this from
the practical standpoint is one of the most important of all.
'Sin (using the commandment as a fulcrum) wrought in me all
manner of concupiscence.' How? By putting ideas into my mind
which were not there before. The Law comes to me and tells
me not to do some particular thing; but in so doing it sets me
thinking about that thing. I was not thinking about it before,
but now I begin to do so. And as I begin to do so I begin to like
the idea; the thing appeals to me. Thus lust is kindled, I want to
do this, and I proceed to do it. The Law, by telling me not to do
it, brought it into my mind; the Law has introduced me to it.

And not only that, but it may introduce me to thoughts and ideas about which I was completely ignorant before. I may be reading a book which tells me certain things, for instance, about certain horrible perversions of which I had never heard and which had never bothered me, or ever tempted me because I was not aware of their existence. But I now read a book which warns me against these things, and the moment I begin to read, something stirs within me and my curiosity is aroused. I ask myself, 'Why do people do this? It must be pleasing, it must be attractive.' My curiosity then begins to work and I begin to see myself doing this. I am doing all this in my imagination and I am enjoying it. That is how sin works.

The classic statement of all this is found in the Epistle to Titus, chapter 1, verse 15: 'Unto the pure all things are pure: but unto them that are defiled and unbelieving is nothing pure; but even their mind and conscience is defiled.' If your mind is defiled, everything that comes into it is going to be defiled and twisted. Nothing will come in pure; it will have a particular angle on it, it will be coloured by the spectacles of your impure heart. Purity is not pure to the undefiled; the moment it makes contact it becomes impure – 'But even their mind and conscience is defiled'.

Paul's argument here is that because that is true of me, because it is true of every man born into this world since the Fall, the pure Law of God coming with its prohibitions and its restraints and its commandments, inflames our passions, rouses within us a desire to do the very things it prohibits, and introduces me to things I never knew of before. What is the result of this? 'It brought forth fruit unto death.' In other words the Apostle is here really giving us an explanation of what he said in verse 5 concerning 'the motions of sin'. Verse 8 throws light on verse 5. The Law of God is not sin; it is purity itself. But it reveals to us the nature of sin, it helps us to see that coveting is sin. What has happened then? Oh, the terrible truth about man by nature is that this powerful thing called sin is able even to use that pure Law of God as a fulcrum to produce all evil in me. It provides it with a base of operations, the enemy 'comes in as a flood', and I end by being worse than I was before. That is the explanation, says the Apostle.

Let us now apply this teaching, and draw some practical help from what the Apostle is saying here. First of all, if we are not clear as to the nature of sin we shall never really understand the teaching of the Bible. The whole of the biblical teaching concerning salvation is based upon a clear understanding of what sin really is. There is no hope of our understanding anything apart from this. We shall never see why we have to die to the Law if we do not understand the nature of sin. We shall never see why the Son of God had to come and die; we shall never see the necessity of regeneration and a rebirth. That is why so many people think that they can 'decide for Christ' as they are. How can they if this is true? This controls everything. Most of our troubles today are due to a failure to grasp and understand this biblical doctrine of sin. Here in this one verse we are given a view, and an exposure of it, such as you will scarcely find anywhere else with such clarity. It is this terrible power that can even use God's Law as a fulcrum to bring to pass its own nefarious ends.

In the second place, what the Apostle has said about sin, and the way in which it uses the Law as a fulcrum, proves to the hilt his double contention. The first was that no man can ever be sanctified by and through the Law. How can a man be sanctified by the Law when sin is reigning in him, and can even use that Law as a fulcrum? His second contention was that a man never can be sanctified until his old relationship to the Law has been abolished. He has to die to the Law and to be married to Another before he can be sanctified, and this too he proves. As long as sin is present, all the Law does is to provide a fulcrum to make things worse. How can we be sanctified, therefore, while we are 'under the law'? The Apostle reduces the whole thing to an absurdity. He is proving his contention; and he does so in a dual sense.

Then let me draw two more general and practical deductions and lessons. Is there anything that you know of, in the light of this teaching, which is more dangerous than the current ideas about sex and morality teaching? We are being exhorted constantly by all sorts of people to give instruction about sex and morality to our children. They say that the great trouble in the past has been that people omitted to do this; they made a bogey of sex. It was the unmentionable subject, it was always kept back; and the result was, they say, that all our forefathers were just a mass of complexes and repressions, they were all psychologically ill! All who lived until this generation arrived were more or less psychopaths because they never faced sex in an open, manly, free way. That is unhealthy, they say, and the thing to do is to bring it out and to talk to children about it. I saw recently that one man did grant fathers and mothers this concession, that it was perhaps better for them not to talk to their children, but to get an uncle or some other relation to do it, or a friend or outsider. The important thing is that it must be done; and if only we tell children about sex and give them the facts about life the moral problem will be solved.

What ignorance! Not only of human nature but of sin! They cannot see that what they are doing is simply to introduce the children to what will lead to sin. They tell them about sex and the more they tell them the more they will rouse in them an unhealthy curiosity. 'Unto the pure all things are pure'; but we are not pure by nature. Our children are not pure; we are not pure; and 'to the defiled is nothing pure'. When we realize the power of sin, and discover how it can even use God's Law as a fulcrum to create desires and lusts, because mind and heart are impure, we shall also realize that this modern teaching is pernicious and full of danger.

Finally I would say that this one verse is sufficient in and of itself to show the final and complete futility of what is being said so frequently today by many learned, well-meaning, moral men. They say to us, 'Ah yes, I was brought up in the Christian faith and religion; but of course I have developed since then; and have read a great deal. I still hold to the Christian ethic, but of course I had to say farewell to the doctrines.' I have referred to this earlier. Poor blind men! They know little about sin, and especially about the power of sin. The Christian ethic without the Christian doctrine is valueless; it is perhaps the most hopeless situation of all. For it does not provide us with power; and our greatest need is a power that is great enough to counteract this other power that can even use God's holy Law as a fulcrum, and a base of operations. Such power is to be obtained only through 'the precious blood of the Lamb'.

There is power, power, wonder-working power,
In the precious blood of the Lamb.

If I did not know that the Son of God had died for me and my sins, and had given me new life; if I did not believe that I am 'in Christ' and married to Him, I would be of all men most hopeless and miserable. I cannot live a truly good life, or practise any true morality or ethic, in my own strength and power, because of this terrible, devastating, awful power which is called sin.

So thank God for this 8th verse in Romans, chapter 7, which not only illuminates the doctrine of this particular chapter for us, but also helps us to understand something of why life is as it is today. Here alone are we able to see why we have this mounting problem of juvenile delinquency, increase in sex crimes and in crimes of robbery and violence, and why more and more men and women are objecting to discipline and the punishment of crime. Here is the explanation of it all. The modern man does not understand the biblical doctrine and teaching concerning sin. But as Christians we have been enlightened; the light of truth drives us to Christ, and makes us rejoice that we are in Him, married to Him, and that we no longer live 'in the oldness of the letter, but in the newness of the Spirit'.

Eleven

*

*For without the law sin was dead. For I was alive without the law
once; but when the commandment came, sin revived, and I died.*

Romans 7: 9

The Apostle, here, is obviously continuing what he has just
been saying. The word 'For' reminds us of that at once. He is
going to follow out the argument and give us a further exposition and explication of it. So far he has been stating facts, and
showing that what he has said about the Law in verses 1 to 6 of
this chapter does not mean or imply that the Law is sin and bad
and evil.

Having made those statements of fact he now comes to an
analysis of the facts. This is frequently the Apostle's method.
He makes a statement, he lays down his facts, and then proceeds
to analyse them. That is what he does here. It is a personal statement as to what was once upon a time true of him. It is a remarkable and very important statement because of the terminology
he uses, the way in which he puts it, and the expressions he employs. They clearly need careful handling. If they are taken at their
face value, as it were, and out of their context, we could easily
draw conclusions which would be the exact opposite of what the
Apostle desires us to draw. Indeed we might draw conclusions
which would lead us to say that the Apostle contradicts himself.
We must therefore look at his statement with extraordinary care.

Let us start with a general analysis of the statement. What he
is concerned to show is the difference that what he calls 'the coming of the law' made to him. He first tells us what the position
was before the Law 'came' to him; sin was dead, and he was alive.
But then the Law came, and what happened? There was a complete reversal – 'sin revived, and I died'. Such is the statement
we are examining – the position before the law 'came', and the

position after the Law 'came'. In between the two is 'the coming of the law' to the Apostle.

The best way of approach to this statement is to get clear in our minds what he means by 'without the law'. 'For', he says, 'without the law sin was dead'. Then he says, 'I was alive without the law once'. What does he mean by 'without the law?' It is just here that we have to be careful. Obviously he is using his words in a relative manner. He says, 'without the law sin was dead'. 'I myself was alive without the law.' 'Without' means 'apart from'. In Scotland they often use the expression 'out with', which comes to the same thing. It means 'in the absence of law'. 'In the absence of the law, sin is dead.' 'I myself, in the absence of law, was once alive.'

But what does Paul mean by saying that there was a time when he was 'without the law?' Obviously, it must be a relative statement, for this good reason, that there has never been a time in the history of the human race when it has been without law. There was even Law in the Garden of Eden, and ever since man sinned and fell he has always been 'under' that fundamental Law, the Law of God. The Apostle has proved that at length in chapter 5. He has pointed out, for instance, that that is the reason why 'death reigned from Adam to Moses'. It is the only possible explanation of that statement. We therefore assert that there has never been a time when there has been no law. But if that is true in general, it was particularly true of the Jews, and therefore true of the Apostle Paul himself. Every Jew was born under the Law of Moses, and yet, here, he seems to say that at one time he was alive 'without the law' and lived apart from the Law. Clearly, therefore, he must be using his terms in a relative manner. Indeed we shall find that he does so with all the terms that appear in this statement. What he is saying is, that as far as his experience was concerned, he was living without the Law, apart from the Law. In other words the Law was not really doing its work in him; he was virtually in a position as if there was no Law. There never was such a position, of course, but as far as his knowledge and his experience of the Law went, that was the position. As we look at the other terms this will become much clearer.

Let us move to the next term, which is, 'When the commandment came, sin revived and I died'. 'When the commandment came'! But the commandment had always been there! The Law had been given through Moses long centuries before Paul was ever born – fourteen centuries – and the basic fundamental law for all mankind was always there from the beginning. Yet he says, 'When the commandment came'. Again Paul is speaking relatively. He means that though the commandment was there it had never 'come' to him, it had never 'got' him. Let me give a very simple illustration of what that means. People sometimes come to a preacher at the end of a service and say, 'You know, I had never noticed that verse before', or they may say, 'You know, I have read that verse a thousand times and more, but I had never seen it'. What they really mean is that that statement had never really 'come' to them before. We have all had that experience as we read the Bible. You are reading a verse which you have read many, many times before, and which has said nothing to you; but suddenly it 'hits' you, suddenly it seems to be illuminated, and to stand out. What has happened? Well, it has 'come' to you. That is what the Apostle means by 'When the commandment came'. It was always there, as the Scripture was always there, but it did not 'get' him, it did not 'take hold of him', it did not really speak to him. It did not come, in other words, with power and conviction and understanding.

This is a most remarkable statement, and especially so as coming from the Apostle Paul. Not only was the Law of God always confronting him, but he, as a Pharisee, was a great expert in the Law. All his training had been directed to that end. He was teaching others about the Law; and he prided himself on his knowledge. But the truth was that he only had a knowledge of the 'letter', and he never understood the 'spirit'. That is why he writes frequently about that distinction. Take, for instance, the Second Epistle to the Corinthians, chapter 3, where he contrasts the letter and the spirit; he says that the whole trouble with the Jews was that they only knew the letter of the Law, and not its spirit. That is another way of saying the Law had not 'come' to them; it had not come with conviction, with enlightenment, with understanding. It was a bare dead letter, it had never 'found' them, it had never really 'spoken' to them, and come in a spiritual and powerful manner.

That is the key to the parallelism in this statement. He says in effect, 'Before the law came like that to me, this was the position'. What was it? The first thing he tells us is that before the Law had really come to him, and 'got' him, and 'found' him in that new way, 'sin was dead'. What does that mean? Again I must say that this is a relative statement. How can he say that sin was dead, if sin is in everyone? We are all 'born in sin, shapen in iniquity.' We are never without sin; it is in our very constitution. We are children of sin and it is active in all of us. But, here, the Apostle says that there was a time in his life and experience when sin was dead. There is only one explanation; what he is really saying is that sin was comparatively dead, that as far as his awareness was concerned it was dead. That is what he thought; that was his experience; that was his understanding of the situation at the time. Sin was 'lying dormant', as someone translates it. He was not conscious of it; it was as if sin had been dead.

Something our Lord said on one occasion throws light on this: 'A strong man armed keepeth his goods in peace' (Luke 11: 21). Here we have a perfect description of mankind in sin and under the dominion of the devil. Notice the terms. The devil 'keeps his goods in peace'. Everything seems to be very quiet; the tyranny is so great that in a sense they are not aware of it; there is a peaceful atmosphere. That is simply due to man's lack of realization of what the position really is. When I was 'without the law', says Paul, I was so dull and deluded that I thought sin was dead. Sin is never dead, sin has never been dead since the Fall of man; but, comparatively speaking, it appeared to be dead and lifeless.

A second illustration in modern terms will also help us to understand the matter. The Apostle has already told us that sin is a terrible power – so powerful that it can use even the Law of God as a fulcrum to bring to pass its own purposes. But Paul says that there was a time in his life and experience when he was not aware of that power. Let us think of it in terms of a powerful engine in a motor-car. The better, and the more powerful the engine, the more quietly it runs or 'ticks over' when you are not moving forward. You can be sitting in your car with its very powerful engine going; it is running but you can scarcely hear a sound. It has great power, but you are not aware of it because it is so silent. But then you put your foot on the accelerator and you become aware of power. Sin is like that engine. It was just 'ticking over' as it were. Paul was not aware that it was there and did not realize its tremendous power. Because it was not acting in a violent manner he thought nothing of it. As far as he was concerned, sin was dead. The power was there, of course, but he was not aware of it – 'Without the law sin was dead'.

Now let us look at another part of Paul's relative statement. Not only does he say that at that time sin was dead, he says also, 'I was alive'. That is the other part of the double statement – 'For I was alive without the law once'. Once more, of course, it is a relative statement. All who have read the first three chapters of this Epistle know that Paul has proved there beyond any doubt that none was alive, that 'all have sinned and come short of the glory of God', that 'there is none righteous, no, not one', and that the Jews were as hopeless and as condemned and as spiritually dead as the Gentiles. Yet, here he is, saying 'I was alive once'. So he cannot mean it in an absolute sense; everything here is relative.

The statement Paul makes in the first three verses of the 2nd chapter of the Epistle to the Ephesians proves this. 'You hath he quickened who were dead in trespasses and sins.' But not only was that true of the Gentiles, it was equally true of the Jews. 'Among whom also we all had our conversation in time past in the lusts of our flesh, fulfilling the desires of the flesh and of the mind, and were by nature the children of wrath, even as others.' All of us, born into this world, are born spiritually dead. Yet here the Apostle is saying that there was a time when he was 'alive once' apart from the Law.

Clearly, Paul means, that in the same way that he thought sin was dead as far as he was concerned, he also thought that he was alive. The moment he realized that sin was alive he died; but as long as he did not realize that sin was alive he thought that he himself was alive. It was all because he had not understood the Law. In that account he was not aware of the power of sin and of the truth about himself. He thought that sin was dead and that he was alive. He means that he felt well, he felt full of life, full of strength and of power. He patted himself on the back, he was self-satisfied, he was confident, he was congratulating himself on the wonderful way in which he was keeping the Law. He felt full of life and vigour and confidence and self-assurance and power; he was alive, thrilling with vitality. That is what he is saying.

The Apostle has said this same thing in other places in different words. For example, in the 3rd chapter of the Epistle to the Philippians, in a wonderful bit of autobiography, he says, 'Concerning zeal, persecuting the church; touching the righteousness which is in the law, blameless' (verse 6). 'Blameless!' He was alive; there was nothing wrong with him. He was a wonderful specimen of a godly, religious man; he was full of vigour and of strength in a moral sense. He says exactly the same thing in the 1st chapter of the Epistle to the Galatians, verse 14 – 'And I profited in the Jews' religion above many my equals in mine own nation, being more exceedingly zealous of the traditions of my fathers'. There was never a man who was more pleased with himself, more satisfied with himself, more full of life and power. He was indeed a typical Pharisee.

At the beginning of the 18th chapter of Luke's Gospel we meet with a similar statement in our Lord's parable of the Pharisee and the publican who went up to the temple to pray. No man could have been more full of the sort of life of which the Apostle is speaking than the Pharisee depicted there by our Lord. He starts by saying, 'God, I thank thee'. There is nothing to do but to thank God. He is such a fine fellow, he fasts twice in the week, and gives a tenth of his goods to the poor. He is not guilty of any sins. How he thanks God that he is not like that miserable wretch, that publican over there who is guilty of so many sins! He does not need to ask for anything, forgiveness or strength; and he did not ask for anything. Who that is brimming over with health and vigour and power asks for anything? The man is self-sufficient, autonomous, self-satisfied; so there is only one thing to do, and that is to thank God that he is as he is. He is alive – what a wonderful man, full of health and vigour and strength and power! Or take the case of the rich young ruler and his encounter with our Lord, and the Lord's handling of him. Our Lord said to him, 'You know the commandments—do not commit adultery, do not steal, do not bear false witness'. The young man replied, 'All these things have I kept from my youth up, what lack I yet?' (Matt. 19: 20) He was 'alive', he was aware of all that the Law required; and he had kept it all! There was no trouble, there was no difficulty; he was 'alive'.

The Apostle sums up the matter perfectly in the 3rd verse of the 10th chapter of this Epistle, where we have the last word about the whole contention of the Pharisees, and of Paul himself before his conversion: 'For they being ignorant of God's righteousness, and going about to establish their own righteousness, have not submitted themselves unto the righteousness of God.' That was the trouble. They were establishing their own righteousness, and so they thought they were 'alive' and that all was well; but they were not aware of the real meaning of righteousness in the sight of God and as revealed in the Law.

That, then, was Paul's position when he was 'without the law' – before the commandment came sin was dead, and he was alive. He was not aware of any real difficulty or problem, all seemed to be perfectly satisfactory: he was 'blameless'. But when the commandment 'came', this whole question of coveting was instantly illuminated. Suddenly he was arrested and apprehended by the realization of the spiritual character of the Law, and all that it was saying. It was a complete reversal of outlook. Sin which was dead before, now sprang to life; he who was alive before, now became dead. 'Sin revived', he says. He means that sin sprang to life again, it took on new life, it awoke to activity. In terms of our illustration of the powerful engine, it suddenly began to vibrate with power. The Law had put its foot on the accelerator!

This, at first sight, is a most surprising statement. We would have thought, naturally, that the effect of the coming of the Law would have been not to 'revive' sin, but to slay it; and, indeed, in an ultimate sense, that is what it does. But in experience it does the exact opposite – and he is writing here in an experimental manner. In other words, what happens is that the Law brings out the real strength and reveals the real nature and character of sin. The Law irritates sin, disturbs it, and by its prohibitions it arouses it; as I say, it puts its foot on the accelerator. Or, to use a different illustration, the Apostle is not using the picture of the fulcrum now, but rather a picture of the way in which a resistance always brings out a power. If you want to exercise your muscles, the best way to do so is to start lifting weights. There is always a certain amount of power in a muscle. It may be so little that you say that the person is an utter weakling, and has no strength at all. But even if small, it is there; and if you want to develop it, you have but to start picking up weights and increasing them continually. The greater the resistance against which you are working, the more your muscles will develop. You can accomplish the same result by pushing against an object; most exercises are based on this principle. The way to bring out the power is to increase the resistance; the more the resistance, the more it calls out your reserves of power, the innate strength that is there in your muscles. Something analogous to that took place when the Law 'came' to the Apostle. Without the 'resistance' provided by the Law he was not aware of the strength of sin; without this prohibition, without this antagonist, he had never known the real power of sin within himself. When the Law came powerfully and told him that he must not desire or covet what he could not rightfully have, he suddenly felt an overwhelming desire for such things.

What the Apostle teaches here is fundamental to the whole biblical teaching concerning sin. Take another statement which is a very close parallel to this, and which helps to throw light on it. In John's Gospel chapter 15, verses 22 and 24, our Lord says, 'If I had not come and spoken unto them, they had not had sin: but now they have no cloke for their sin', and 'If I had not done among them the works which none other man did, they had not had sin: but now have they both seen and hated both me and my Father'. Take it on its face value and our Lord seems to be saying, 'If I had not come into the world these people would not have had sin'. But we know that they were all sinners, all condemned, all 'dead in trespasses and sins'. He is actually saying exactly the same thing as Paul is saying here, namely, that the effect of His coming has been to expose the sins. Of course they were sinners before; but there was a sense in which they did not appear to be sinners; it was not obvious that they were so until He came. But the moment He began to speak, the moment He began to do works among them that no other man had ever done, or could do, then the malignity and the spite and the hatred and the malice that was latent in them became manifest and open.

Who would ever have understood the truth about the Pharisees if our Lord had not come and spoken to them? Look at them apart from Him. One would tend to say, 'They are very good men, they are wonderfully moral'. The Pharisee in our Lord's parable to which we have referred is not lying, he is speaking the truth. He did fast twice in the week, he did give a tenth of his goods to the poor. So looking at them apart from our Lord, you would have said, What noble, excellent men, what wonderful observers of the Law! It is only when you see their reaction to the Son of God that you really get to know the Pharisees. Look at their bitterness, their hatred; see their subtlety and their cleverness; watch them as they whisper together and conspire and weave a plot, and try to trip Him and to trap Him by putting their catch questions and their leading questions. What evil and sin there was inside the Pharisees! But we would never have known it if the Lord had not come and spoken to them. He drew it out, as it were, He convicted them of sin; it is their reaction to Him that shows what they really were. Once they came up against Him, all this suddenly came to light. You could now see it in their faces and in their whole demeanour and behaviour. It is a perfect illustration of what the Apostle says in this statement we are examining. 'When the commandment came', he says, 'and found me, sin sprang up to life again within me.'

But that in turn led to this other result – 'I died'. This man who was so much alive now dies. It is, as I have said, the same sort of relative terminology; but it is important that we should be clear as to what exactly he means when he says that he 'died' as the result of the coming of the Law. He does not mean here, primarily, that he was aware of his condemnation. That is true, of course; he died in the sense that he saw that the Law condemned him before God; but that is not what he is emphasizing here. Here he is dealing with his case in a much more experimental and practical way. What he means is, that he was now the opposite of what he was when he was 'alive'. Clearly the parallelism demands that. So we interpret 'I died' by 'I was alive'; and it means that he died in the sense in which we read of certain characters in the Bible that when they heard certain things it had a terrifying effect upon them. Of Nabal, for example, we read that when he heard a certain statement he 'became as one dead', even though he remained alive physically. We say 'I was petrified', or 'It almost killed me'. That is what Paul means – 'I became as a dead man'.

In other words he realized his weakness, his helplessness, and his hopelessness. The man who was so sure of himself before, felt as if he was dead. There was nothing there, self-confidence had gone, self-satisfaction disappeared, self-reliance had utterly vanished.

A good way of putting this is to say that he means, 'I became poor in spirit', as the first beatitude in the Sermon on the Mount puts it (Matthew 5: 3). A man who is poor in spirit is a lifeless man. The man who is 'alive' is a man who is full of spirit and of power and confidence. We say, 'there is a great spirit in that man'. But the true Christian becomes 'poor in spirit'; he says, 'Who am I and what can I do?' He is not only poor in spirit, he also mourns. He was not mourning before; he was boasting. But he is now mourning because of his sin; he is troubled and unhappy. He has now had such a view of the Law that he feels he can do nothing, he is exactly as if he were dead. He sees the holiness of God and the holiness of the Law; he also has a sight of the terrible, evil power that is within himself. He sees what it is doing to him, how it is breaking him down and defeating him; and so he begins to feel that he can do nothing whatsoever, that he is weak and helpless, that he is poor and blind, that he has nothing at all. He sees that he is utterly without strength and without vigour and life and power.

That is what the Apostle means by saying that he 'died'. The moment this illumination came in as to the Law and its spiritual character and its prohibitions, especially of coveting, that is what happened. He began to experience the terrible power of sin creating within him 'all manner of covetousness', and it knocked him down. He realized that he was an utter weakling – he who had been boasting of himself as being superior to all his contemporaries and so superior to them in his knowledge of the Law. He now saw that he had nothing at all, and that his righteousness was nothing but 'dung' and dross and refuse. He had been going about to establish his own righteousness, but when faced with the righteousness of God he found that he possessed nothing. That, he tells us, is what he realized about himself when the commandment really 'came' to him and found him and laid him low. He could not move; in a spiritual and moral sense, he was lying helpless on his back, as he had done in a physical sense on the road to Damascus. He was absolutely without strength. We have already been given the key to the understanding of this expression in the 5th chapter, verse 6: 'When we were yet without strength, in due time Christ died for the ungodly.' To be 'without strength' is to be like a dead man. There is no life, no vigour, no power; in fact nothing of value at all.

Here we come to the end of the Apostle's statement. What has he established, what has he proved? And what are our reactions? Our conclusions fall into two groups. The first is the particular conclusion that is essential to the Apostle's argument here. It is, that he has established once more that the Law can never justify a man, still less sanctify him. That is what he set out to prove – that no man can ever be sanctified by the deeds of the Law, can ever sanctify himself by performing the deeds of the Law. Indeed he is concerned to prove more than that. Not only can we not be sanctified by the Law, there is only one hope of our ever being sanctified, and that is, we must be set free altogether from the Law, in the same way as a woman is freed from her husband who has died. While we are 'under the law' it will simply produce more sin in us, and will reveal our deadness to us, our utter hopelessness. So our only hope of sanctification is to be set free from the Law. Paul has proved it once more. The Law cannot deliver us; the Law kills us, it makes us as dead men, for the reasons he has been giving.

That is the conclusion germane to the particular argument the Apostle is deploying in this section of the Epistle. But we must draw some further general conclusions which will be of value to us in our daily life and living, which will be indeed of supreme value to us in determining and discovering whether we are Christians or not. The first is that our spiritual health, our spiritual condition – in other words, on the negative side, our sinfulness – is never to be judged only in terms of actions but always in terms of our reactions to God's holiness and to God's Law. That, to me, is one of the fundamental postulates of the Christian faith. It should always be an essential preliminary in evangelism. A man's spiritual state and condition must not be determined in terms of actions only. To do so would mean that there is nothing wrong with the Pharisee, and that he does not need the gospel. He fasts twice in the week, he gives a tenth of his goods to the poor; he never committed adultery, and has never committed murder. He does not need forgiveness. That is why this type of good, moral man goes to an evangelistic meeting feeling that it has no message for him and that his duty is to pray for the conversion of the 'sinners' in the meeting. He does not feel guilty because he thinks of sin and sinners in terms of particular actions. Our churches are as they are because they contain so many people of this type, people who do not know that they are sinners because they judge sin only in terms of particular actions.

The way to judge and to estimate sin in yourself is to note your reaction to the biblical teaching about God in His holiness, and God as Judge eternal. Or think of it in this way – What is your reaction to the true preaching of the Cross? The message of that Cross is that we are all so damned and lost that nothing but that death could save us. 'What', says many a highly moral person, 'do you mean to say that I am in the same position as the prostitute or the drunkard or the murderer?' 'Precisely', says the message of the Cross, 'you need salvation as much as they do.' Hence 'the offence of the Cross'. In other words, What is your reaction to the Lord Jesus Christ? Is it the reaction of the Pharisee? He annoyed the Pharisees by telling them that He had come into the world because they needed to be saved as much as all others, that they could only be saved by His dying for them. They, the great teachers, they who were 'alive', they who had 'kept' the Law and had 'done all these things from their youth up' needed to be saved! And they hated Him accordingly. That is how you measure sin.

I repeat that there is nothing more misleading than to estimate sinfulness or our spiritual condition in terms of actions only. Actions are so varied. Go back again to my illustration. If you are going to judge the power of a motor car only by the silence of the engine when it is not moving you would be altogether wrong. That is not the way to test it. The way to test it is to confront it with a mountain or a gradient of one in three; then you will discover something of the power of your engine. The measure of our sinfulness is the measure of our resistance to the holiness of God, and the Ten Commandments and the Moral Law, the Sermon on the Mount and to the Person of the Lord Jesus Christ. In this way, and in no other, we begin to see the whole deceitful element in sin which we shall consider more clearly later.

The second principle is that there is no more complete misunderstanding of the Law, and of ethics and morality, than to think that 'obligation implies ability'. That is a very familiar argument. Most people today who think at all, and who reject the gospel of salvation, do so for this fundamental reason, that in their view obligation implies ability. They believe that God would never command us to do anything unless we were able to do it. So, they argue, the fact that God has given us the Ten Commandments and the Moral Law implies that we are able to carry them out and observe their dictates. And they further believe that they can obey them and that they are actually doing so. The final answer to such persons and claims is that the very Law that 'came' to Paul and said 'Thou shalt not covet', the very Law that reminded him of that obligation, was the very thing that proved to him that he could not perform it! 'Sin revived and I died' when 'the commandment came'. Far from the obligation implying ability in this realm, the exact opposite is true. The whole function of the Law is not to enable a man to justify himself, but to show him that he cannot do so; it is to bring out 'the exceeding sinfulness of sin', as the Apostle will tell us later. But that misunderstanding of the Law, and the ethical aspect of the gospel, is the popular view today. The moral man says, 'Ah yes, here are the ethical demands of the gospel. They address me; very well, I rise up and do them. The fact that they come to me means that I can carry them out.' But the whole function of the Law was the exact opposite of that; it was to 'kill' you, to show you that you cannot do it, to take the pride and self-confidence out of you, to take the 'life' out of you, to make you feel that you are weak and helpless and hopeless.

Our next conclusion is that there is no state which is more dangerous than to feel that we are not sinners, and that there is no sin in us. The Apostle John has said that very plainly, 'If we say that we have no sin we deceive ourselves, and the truth is not in us'. But there are many people who put forward such claims – I have met not a few. They have looked at me and said, 'I would be dishonest if I said that I felt I was a sinner'. They really mean what they say, and are quite genuine and sincere. They say, 'You keep on talking about sin, but I do not understand it, I do not really feel that I am a sinner. I have always lived a good life, I have always avoided these sins; and I have done as much good as I can. I cannot say honestly that I feel that I am a sinner.' Do you know why they feel and speak in that way? The commandment has not 'come' to them; they are as the Apostle Paul was before the commandment came to him. He was 'alive', he was not aware of the truth concerning himself.

I was talking to a preacher recently who told me that a lady had come to him at the close of a service and had said, 'You have been preaching about temptations, and have emphasized how terrible they are and their power. To be honest, I really do not know what you are talking about.' She was a good church member, and an active worker in the church. She said, 'I am not aware of being tempted in the way that you describe'. She was in the same condition as Paul before the commandment 'came' to him. He was not aware of all this 'concupiscence' and the terrible power that was within him; but when the commandment 'came' he was made aware of it. The Law stirred up sin in his heart, and he found that he was a mass of sin and evil, fit only for perdition, and utterly without strength and power. What a terrible condition to be in! Do we know that we are sinners? Do we know something about the horrible, terrible power of temptation? There is no more hopeless state to be in than to fail to realize that you are a sinner, a hopeless sinner.

The final principle can be put positively. The first sign of spiritual life is to feel that you are dead! 'When the commandment came sin revived and I died.' Thank God; the moment a man is 'dead' there is a possibility of his being resurrected. But a man who is 'alive' and on his feet cannot be resurrected. 'Sin revived, and I died.' If you feel utterly hopeless about yourself in a spiritual sense, I can assure you that you are spiritually alive. That is because you are aware of your spiritual barrenness and deadness. 'Blessed are the poor in spirit, for theirs is the Kingdom of God'; 'blessed are they that mourn, for they shall be comforted'. The modern Pharisees are those people in the churches, and often outside the churches also, who resent being made to feel uncomfortable by the preaching, who dislike feeling that they are sinners, who fight against the truth of God, and who fight against the Cross and 'the blood of Christ'. They resent gospel truth because they think they are 'alive' and that sin is 'dead'. What appalling ignorance, what a tragic condition to be in!

Has the Law come to you? Have you understood the meaning of coveting – 'Thou shalt not covet'? Do you know that 'the thoughts and intents of the heart' are as important in God's sight as our actions, and that evil desires and imaginations are sin? If they are within you, and if they are enjoyed and approved, it is sin, horrible sin. But above all, let us ever keep before us this central test – our reaction to the holiness and the glory and the majesty of God and His Law, the holiness and purity of His Son, the death of the Cross and its message about the holiness and the

justice and the righteousness of God! It is alarming, it is
appalling that there should be people prominent in the Church,
admired as Christians, who hate the Cross as a revelation of the
righteousness and justice and holiness of God, and see nothing
there but love. That is utter darkness and unbelief. It simply
indicates entire and complete spiritual death, spiritual blindness.
God grant that having looked at these statements we may be
able to say with the Apostle, 'The commandment has "come"
and I know that sin has revived within me, risen again to power,
and I have died'. Have we 'died' in this sense? If so we are truly
blessed.

Twelve

*

And the commandment, which was ordained to life, I found to be unto death. For sin, taking occasion by the commandment, deceived me, and by it slew me. Romans 7: 10, 11

In these words the Apostle Paul continues the tremendously important statement with regard to the character and the function and the purpose of the Law. As we have already seen, it is a subject which is in every way essential to a true understanding of the gospel; and not only before we become Christians, but equally so afterwards, for not only is there no justification by the Law, but also no sanctification by the Law.

In these verses 10 and 11, Paul sums up what he has been saying in detail in the previous verses where he has told us that he was 'alive' and that sin was apparently dead until the Law 'came', and how then sin revived and he 'died'. He does so by saying 'that the commandment which was ordained to life, I found to be unto death'.

Again, the terms used are to be carefully noted. Look first at the expression 'I found'. Paul does not mean that as the result of careful study and examination he reached a certain conclusion. It sounds as if he was saying that, but it is not so. What he is really saying is that 'the commandment, which was ordained to life, was found in my case to be unto death'. That is a better way of translating it. In other words, the 'finding' is not the result of his investigation; it was something he discovered as the result of the coming of the Law to him, and the consequences that followed.

Look next at the statement, 'The commandment which was ordained to life'. All careful students of Scripture must at once feel rather surprised at these words, for the Apostle has devoted the early chapters of this Epistle to proving that there is no such

[147]

thing as finding 'life' by the Law. For instance, he summed up his great argument in the 20th verse of chapter 3 by saying, 'Therefore by the deeds of the law shall no flesh be justified in his sight: for by the law is the knowledge of sin'. That means that no one can ever find life by the Law, that the whole tragedy and fallacy of the Jews was that they were seeking life by the Law. Yet here he seems to contradict himself completely by saying that the commandment 'was ordained to life'.

How do we face this problem? Let us first look at it in a very general way in the whole context of scriptural interpretation. We start by saying that obviously it cannot have its face meaning and value, otherwise it involves the Apostle in a blank contradiction of himself. Not only so, if it meant that, he would be undermining everything that he has been saying and establishing. So we cannot possibly read the words superficially. There we have a good principle which can always be applied. If the apparent meaning, the first meaning that suggests itself to you, is in obvious contradiction to some plain teaching of the Scripture it cannot be the truth and therefore you will have to seek for another explanation.

What, then, do the words mean? Clearly this, not that the commandment was given in order that people through it might obtain life, but that if men and women had kept the commandment, if it had been possible for anyone to do so, then it would have led to 'life'. This is so for the reason that the commandment, as Paul is about to tell us, is 'holy, and just, and good'. The commandment, after all, is the most perfect indication of the way of holiness and of happiness that has ever been given. When He gave the 'commandment', the Law, the Moral Law, God was outlining a way of life which would be well pleasing in His sight. It is the way of life, and that is what the Apostle says about it at this point. Here is God's Law which teaches us what the holy and the happy life really is, the life that is pleasing to God.

Let me show from other scriptures that that is the meaning. Take, for instance, what the Apostle says later in chapter 10, verse 5: 'Moses describeth the righteousness which is of the law (in this way), That the man which doeth those things shall live by them.' That means that when Moses gave the Law he said to the people in effect, 'If you keep this law you will have life, eternal life'. Yes, 'if' you do! Or take Exodus, chapter 19, verse

5. When God spoke to Moses about the giving of the Law to the people He said; 'Now therefore, if ye will obey my voice indeed, and keep my commandments, then ye shall be a peculiar treasure unto me above all people: for all the earth is mine: And ye shall be unto me a kingdom of priests, and an holy nation.' But we notice the 'if' again. The promise is conditional. Or take it as it is expressed in the Book of Leviticus, chapter 18, verse 5: 'Ye shall therefore keep my statutes, and my judgments: which if a man do, he shall live in them.' That is what Paul quotes in the 10th chapter of Romans, verse 5. Or read the same thing again in Deuteronomy 6: 25; 'And it shall be our righteousness', says Moses to the people, 'if we observe to do all these commandments before the Lord our God, as he hath commanded us.' But we have still higher authority for our interpretation, namely, our Lord Himself. In chapter 10 of the Gospel according to St. Luke there is an account of an interview between a certain lawyer and our Lord about how to inherit eternal life. Our Lord said to this man, 'What is written in the law? how readest thou'? 'And he answering said, Thou shalt love the Lord thy God with all thy heart, and with all thy soul, and with all thy strength, and with all thy mind; and thy neighbour as thyself.' And our Lord said to him, 'Thou hast answered right: this do, and thou shalt live'. There it is clearly! 'The commandment was ordained unto life.' But you notice again that the promise is conditioned upon performance – 'This do, and thou shalt live'.

There are, however, other statements which deal still more directly with the meaning of this phrase. The Apostle says quite explicitly in Galatians 3: 21: 'If there had been a law given which could have given life, verily righteousness should have been by the law.' That is enough in and of itself to show what the Apostle does not mean by this statement which we are examining.

What then is the truth about the Law? It is that the Law is the perfect expression of what it is necessary for a man to do if he is to obtain life in that way. But, as Paul will tell us again in chapter 8, verse 3: 'What the law could not do, in that it was weak through the flesh' – that is the explanation! – 'God sending his own Son in the likeness of sinful flesh, and for sin, condemned sin in the flesh: that the righteousness of the law might be fulfilled in us, who walk not after the flesh but after the Spirit.'

We need not stumble therefore over the particular phrase, 'the law which was ordained unto life'.

That brings us to the next statement. 'The commandment which was ordained to life, was found in my case to lead unto death.' We need not stay with this. In a sense we have already been dealing with it. It is just another way of saying that this is what happened when the commandment had really 'come' to him – 'When the commandment came, sin revived, and I died'. In other words, the Apostle says that the Law, far from giving life and happiness and holiness and joy, did the opposite. It condemned him, it showed him his failure and his evil nature, it inflamed sin within him, and therefore revealed to him his utter helplessness, and left him in a state of complete misery.

But why did it happen in the Apostle's case, that the Law which was ordained unto life was found to be unto death? The answer is – as he has been telling us already, and as he will tell us further in the next verse – that it was all because of sin, and because of what sin does with the Law, and did with the Law in his case, as in the case of the Pharisees and the Jews. We can sum it up by pointing to what he will say later in chapter 9, verses 31 and 32: 'But Israel, which followed after the law of righteousness, hath not attained to the law of righteousness. Wherefore? Because they sought it not by faith, but as it were by the works of the law. For they stumbled at that stumbling stone.' The trouble, the 'stumbling stone', was that they did not make the right use of the Law. Sin so affected them that, though this Law of God had been given to them, they made the wrong use of it; they used it as a 'way of righteousness'.

In his First Epistle to Timothy, chapter 1, verse 8, the Apostle makes a very illuminating statement which throws light on what he is saying here. 'We know', he says, that the law is good, if a man use it lawfully'. The Law is good on condition that you use it in the right way. The fact is, however, that because of sin we do not use it lawfully. And that is why he found in his case, as he says, that the commandment which was ordained unto life he found to be unto death.

The Apostle is virtually saying here what he says in 1 Corinthians 15: 56: 'The sting of death is sin, and the strength of sin is the law.' 'The sting of death', the thing that really kills in death, is sin. Sin makes death what it is, and that which puts power into the sting is the Law. We have already been considering some of the ways in which sin does just that. We saw how it increases lust and passion – concupiscence – and how it inflames the passions; and how, in addition, it leads to failure and misery and condemnation. So the Apostle will be fully justified when he comes to verse 2 in chapter 8, and sums up all that he has been saying in chapter 7 in the words: 'For the law of the Spirit of life in Christ Jesus hath made me free'. From what? From that law which he now describes as 'the law of sin and death'. The commandment which was ordained unto life, had become a commandment, a law 'of sin and death'. It aggravates sin and therefore leads to death still more certainly. There he actually refers to this Law of God as 'a law of sin and death', because that is exactly what it is to the whole of the human race as the result of sin and the Fall.

We now turn to verse 11 which is an explanation of verse 10. How careful Paul is in his method! 'For' – He throws out his statement first in a general way – 'the commandment which was ordained unto life, I found to be unto death'. But how? 'For' – here is the answer – 'For sin, taking occasion by the commandment, deceived me, and by it slew me'. Why does the Apostle continue to repeat his explanations? Why does he keep on saying the same thing in different ways? I can but repeat my previous answer, namely, that the biblical doctrine of sin is absolutely crucial to an understanding of the biblical doctrine of salvation. Whatever we may think, we cannot be right and clear about the way of salvation unless we are right and clear about sin. It is not surprising, therefore, that the Apostle is so much concerned about this foundation principle. Looking back across his own life he sees that the whole explanation of his condition was that he had been for so long in a state of blindness and ignorance about the Law and sin, and therefore about himself. And he knew that that appeared to be the case with some of those to whom he was writing, he knew that it was still the case with all the Jews. So he is much concerned to make this very clear.

So he says it once more – 'For sin . . . ' Sin is the trouble. He has already been showing something of what sin does. 'But sin', he said in verse 8, 'taking occasion by the commandment wrought in me all manner of concupiscence.' Here he says, 'For sin, taking occasion by the commandment, deceived me'. They are both statements as to what sin does in this terrible way. But it is not mere repetition; there is, as we shall see, an addition to the thought also.

Let me again emphasize the importance of the Apostle's repetition. This is still one of the greatest causes of trouble with regard to salvation. There are many outside the Kingdom of God solely for this reason, that they have never understood the meaning of the Law, and what sin does with the Law. It is one of the commonest stumbling-blocks still, standing between people and salvation. In the same way it still causes trouble in the Christian life. There are Christians in bondage, Christians who put themselves back 'under the law' as far as experience is concerned, and who spend their Christian life in 'shallows and in miseries' simply because they have never understood these things. So we must repeat the teaching. But not only that, this is the ultimate key, the only answer and solution to the greatest problem confronting this country and the world today, namely, the moral problem.

Here is some evidence of that problem. I read the following in a newspaper recently: 'Britain's standards of morality are bitterly attacked today by the National Association seeking to care for women discharged from jail. The Association criticizes the current situation in which downright dishonesty can be considered a clever fiddle, and vice is obviously exploited for commercial gain.' The report frankly gives warning that 'no amount of research into the causes of crime, or suggestions for combating it, are likely to achieve much progress while Christian standards of morality remain so widely disregarded'. Take also a similar disturbing report made by Mr Frank C. Foster, Director of the 'Borstal After-Care Division'. Mr Foster states that the year 1958 'marked the 50th Anniversary of the Borstal system as a statutory form of treatment'. He tells us that after fifty years, committals were higher than ever, and he shows that they were more than twice what they were three years earlier. 'I am more than convinced', writes Mr Foster, 'that the offenders we have been dealing with of recent years present more difficult problems than ever before. We know that they are in the main the product of homes and community groups having unsympathetic attitudes to education, work, recreation, social responsibility, and religion.' Then he adds, 'There is nothing new about this; but we seem now to be dealing with a generation that can best be described as having a low threshold of stress, and a low tolerance of frustration.'

My reason for quoting these words is that for fifty years and more, not only have we had the Borstal system, but the whole idea has been that we can solve these moral problems, problems of behaviour, by education, by teaching, by culture and by various refinements. We have been told we must punish less and less, and rely upon educational work. But the statistics show that there are more offenders than ever. Although we have multiplied agencies and institutions in order to diminish offences, these are the sheer facts as put before us by people whose livelihood and work it is to deal with these matters. When will they learn to read and to understand the teaching of this 7th chapter of the Epistle to the Romans? When will the authorities realize that the root problem is the problem of sin, sin as understood in biblical terms? Here is one of their own company who says that we are in a sense wasting our time by investigating and setting up research commissions to try to discover the cause, and to try to invent some new treatments.

There is only one explanation of the moral state of society, it is this terrible power which the Bible calls 'sin'. Men in their cleverness and sophistication no longer believe in sin. They have been trying to explain it away in terms of psychology, saying that it is non-existent. They have confidently claimed that they can easily train and teach people how to behave in a decent manner, and that they can deliver delinquents. And yet they are failing – failing so badly that their own servants are saying so in public. No, there is only one explanation; sin 'taking occasion', using even the Law of God, leave alone men's moral teaching, as a vantage point, as a military base of operations, as a fulcrum, is the cause of all the trouble. 'Sin, taking occasion' – Paul repeats the phrase he has already used in verse 8.

But now the Apostle adds something further. In verse 8 he told us that sin 'wrought' in him. There, as we saw, he was emphasizing the 'power' of sin. We have dwelt on that because it is, next to God, the greatest power in the universe. But here he is emphasizing another element in sin, its 'deceitfulness'. 'Sin, taking occasion by the commandment, deceived me.' This translation is not quite strong enough. The Apostle used a very emphatic word here. He said, 'Sin, taking occasion by the commandment, completely deceived me'. It 'took me in' completely. Not in a slight way, it took me in altogether, it deceived me absolutely. Such is the meaning of the word used by the Apostle. We must therefore realize that sin is not only terribly powerful, but at the same time terribly deceiving. How can anyone fail to see this? The Bible is full of this teaching.

Let me emphasize this point by some further quotations. I am taking no risks because people are so much influenced by what they read, and by the popular psychology. Even Christian people do not seem to believe the biblical doctrine concerning sin any longer. But not to believe it is ultimately to deny the whole Bible. I start with Genesis 3: 13; 'And the Lord God said unto the woman, What is this that thou hast done? And the woman said, The serpent beguiled me, and I did eat'. The first verse in that chapter has already said, 'The serpent was more subtle than all the beasts of the field'. The Apostle Paul in chapter 11, verse 3, of the Second Epistle to the Corinthians, takes it up and says: 'But I fear, lest by any means, as the serpent beguiled Eve through his subtlety, so your minds should be corrupted from the simplicity that is in Christ'. Again he says in chapter 4, verse 22 of his Epistle to the Ephesians; 'I exhort you that you put off concerning the former conversation the old man, which is corrupt through the deceitful lusts.' In chapter 3, verse 13 of the Epistle to the Hebrews we have: 'But exhort one another daily, while it is called today; lest any of you be hardened through the deceitfulness of sin.' Then a final quotation which puts it before us in a very staggering way; it concerns the 'antichrist'. There have already been 'many antichrists', but there is yet another great antichrist to come. We are told about him – that his 'coming is after the working of Satan, with all power and signs and lying wonders, and with all deceivableness of unrighteousness in them that perish' (2 Thess. 2: 7–10). Are we not witnessing something of this at the present time? I am not prophesying the end of the Age, but I say that we are witnessing something of what is prophesied. Never has this element of 'deceitfulness' been more manifest than at the present time.

These various scriptural quotations emphasize what the Apostle says here in chapter 7 of Romans, that sin is not only powerful

but subtle and deceitful, that it deludes us, beguiles us, and mis-
leads us. It is because this is true of sin that all of us sin. It explains why there is so much sin in the world, and why sin continues in the world. Sin continues in spite of the knowledge that
we have with regard to its effects and results. Men can read books
which show and prove the evil effects of alcohol, yet they go on
drinking it. People can read books which show the evil effects
of certain acts of immorality and uncleanness, yet men and women
still go on doing these things. They have the knowledge, but they
still go on in the practice of sin. Sin continues in spite of our
experience of remorse and sorrow and pain and suffering after
we have committed it. We still continue sinning, though the
whole record of history and of biography is there staring us in the
face showing us the consequences of sin. And, as I have already
said, in spite of all our morality teaching, in spite of all our
psychology and the multiplication of institutions and agencies
and educational schemes designed to produce better men and
women and better living.

In spite of it all sin continues, and sin abounds; and all because
it is its nature to deceive us. 'Sin taking occasion by the commandment, deceived me.' How did it do so? How does it still do so?
How does sin use the Law of God to deceive us? How is it that
'the strength of sin is the law'? I would classify the answers in
the following way. First, sin deceives us into mis-using the Law.
I take my statement from Paul in his First Epistle to Timothy
(1: 8): 'The law is good, if a man use it lawfully.' Ah yes, but sin
comes in and it makes us use it unlawfully. As I have previously
explained, one way in which it does so is that it persuades us that
nothing matters but actions, and that desires, imaginations and
so on do not count at all. It persuades us to believe that if we have
not performed an actual evil deed we remain free from sin.
Nothing matters except a man's actions. As long as I am not
committing those actions I am keeping the Law, and I am therefore justifying myself in the sight of God. 'Sin deceived me',
says Paul, and it did so in that way. Paul was quite convinced,
as we have seen in the Epistle to the Philippians, and in other
Epistles, that he was really keeping the Law, and that 'touching
the righteousness of the law, he was blameless'. He thought he
was doing really well, he was 'alive without the law once'. Sin
had deceived him by taking the commandment and saying, 'Ah

yes, the commandment means that as long as you do certain things and refrain from others you will be right with God'. And he believed the deceit and acted accordingly. Not a word about coveting, of course! And so sin deceived him into misusing the Law.

But sin also works in another way. When we fall into sin, and our consciences begin to speak strongly and to remind us of the Law and its dictates, then sin changes its tactics completely. It now comes to us and says, 'Yes, that is right; you have sinned, you have failed; remember that the "law of God is holy and just and good" and you have now broken it. You are in a completely hopeless position.' Then the next step is that we say to ourselves, 'Because I have failed and am hopeless there is no point in trying any further. Having sinned once I might as well sin again. I will be no worse, for I am already hopeless.' So we sin the second, and the third, and the tenth, and the thousandth time. That is how sin comes to us. Having depressed us, it persuades us that what we do no longer matters. That is a further misuse of the Law.

Another method used by sin – and this is one of the most terrible of all – is 'antinomianism'. I have made mention of it previously. It works in this way. We have sinned and we are conscious of having broken the Law. Then sin, coming as 'an angel of light', says, 'You have sinned and have broken the law, but don't be troubled. Realize that "where sin abounded, grace hath much more abounded". You have nothing to worry about at all. The more you are conscious of your sin, the more grace increases, and in a sense, the more you sin the more grace operates in your case. You are a saved man, you are "under grace", so what you do no longer matters.' Antinomianism is one of the most blinding curses that has ever afflicted the life of the Church. It troubled the early Church, and it has continued to do so ever since. Men, taking the letter of the doctrine of justification, and the 'letter of the law' twist them to say that our actions no longer matter because we are now under grace; we can continue in sin because we are no longer 'under the law' but 'under grace'. Thus the deceitfulness of sin makes us misuse and mishandle the Law.

Sin also deceives us by creating within us an antagonism to the Law; it makes us feel that God is against us. That is what the devil did with Eve. 'Hath God said?' 'Yes, He is against you'. The moment the Law begins to speak, sin always comes in at that point and says, 'Yes, that is exactly what it does say, and that is because God is what He is – He is against you, a stern, feelingless Lawgiver'.

But sin does not stop at that. It also makes us feel that the Law is unreasonable in its demands upon us, that it is unjust. It makes us feel that the sentiment expressed in the line of a well-known hymn is true. 'Always fast and vigil? Always watch and prayer?' The Law is made to appear narrow and cramped, prohibiting everything you like, and urging upon us things we do not like. The Law of God, says sin, is unjust, is impossible, is unfair; it asks of us something that no man can ever do. So sin persuades us to hate it; and because of our bitterness and hatred against it, when it tells us not to do something it creates within us the desire to do it.

Another manifestation of the subtlety of sin is the way in which it deceives us about ourselves. In a very subtle way sin comes to us and fawns upon us and praises us; it makes us think very highly of ourselves. It asks why we should be held down under the Law? As the devil put it to Eve, 'Has God said you are not to eat of that fruit?' In other words, 'Why did He set that limit? Why should you be deprived of what is desirable? Why should there be a limit to what you may do? It is an insult to your human nature. You were meant for freedom; God is against you. Assert yourself, live your own life; you are able to look after yourself and to govern your own life.' The devil still does that, and persuades us of our right to freedom and self-determination. He convinces man that he is autonomous, able to govern himself and his world, and does not need anything outside himself. O the subtle deceitfulness of it all!

Another expression of this subtlety is particularly common at the present time. The Law comes to us and prohibits certain things. 'Yes', says the devil, 'and that is where, again, it is obviously against you; because it is telling you not to use the powers and faculties that you have within you. You have certain instincts, you have certain impulses and drives within you. Obviously they are there for some good purpose, they are good in and of themselves. So why do you not use them?' That is the popular teaching today. We are told that we should never have a feeling ize

The Law

of guilt; that that is Victorianism and Biblicism, the Old Testament. We must never talk about sin, and never have a feeling of guilt because that violates our personality. One of the most popular manifestations of the modern mind is the cult of 'self-expression' which says, Let your instincts govern you, do what you feel like doing; give full expression to your innate powers. They are never to be repressed. That leads to unhealthiness and unhappiness. Many psychiatrists in treating their patients actually encourage them to do things which are prohibited in the Bible. They tell them that their trouble is due to the fact they have repressed their personality as the result of accepting the biblical doctrine of sin. Sin in its subtlety thus deceives people by praising them, and by getting them to express themselves and their innate evil powers.

Finally, sin deceives us about itself. It does so by making sin very attractive. We read that Eve 'saw that the tree was good for food, and that it was pleasant to the eyes' and she believed that it would make her wise if she took of it (Gen. 3: 6). How extraordinary it was that God should prohibit the eating of such pleasant, perfectly formed fruit, with its beautiful colour and all else. No doubt the taste would be equally wonderful. The finest fruit in the Garden; and yet God prohibits it! 'Sin deceived me', says Paul, and it still deceives by making sin very attractive. The Christian life is made to look very drab; but how wonderful the world looks! Look at the lights of London and of Paris and New York. Look at the smiling, laughing throngs, the beautiful dresses, the bright eyes. Of course you must not ask how all that is produced and to what it leads. You must not talk about the drugs or the alcohol such people have been taking, and all the heart-break after they go home or the next day. No, no! But look at it; does it not seem wonderful? A man comes up from the country, and seeing life in London he says, 'Why, I haven't been living, this is life, it is marvellous. How attractive, how beautiful, how pleasant to look upon, how good it must be!' He reads thrilling reports of it in the newspapers and hears people praising it and talking about it and recommending it. All are saying, 'This is real life; this is what the great and the famous and the illustrious people really do. How wonderful!' It all appears so attractive, so seductive, so interesting, so big, so noble, so free, by contrast with the godly, biblical, Christian life.

[158]

It deceives us further by discouraging any thoughts about consequences; it ridicules them. Do you remember what the devil said to Eve? 'Did God say that if you eat of this fruit you will certainly die?' Then he said, 'You will not surely die'. Note the dogmatism. Yet they did die. But the devil with the utmost dogmatism and assurance said, 'You will not surely die'. And Peter reminds us in his Second Epistle that the godless are always saying the same thing. 'Where is the promise of His coming?' You preachers are threatening retribution and punishment and disaster; but you have been doing it for centuries, and yet the world stands as it has always stood. 'Where is the promise of His coming?' (2 Peter 3: 1–11). Sin deceives us about results and ends; it assures us that nothing unpleasant is going to happen. It hates all punishment, it hates the very idea of retribution. The popular and prevailing teaching today says that you must never punish, that the purpose of prisons is solely to reform and rehabilitate. That is what leads to the present chaos in prison life, indeed in the whole of life. This is part of the seduction of sin, the deceivableness of sin which discourages any idea of justice and righteousness and of punishment; and, of course, supremely, any idea about hell.

Hell is just unthinkable to the modern mind. No intelligent person ever talks about hell, we are told; no decent person talks about hell. It is ridiculed and dismissed as being totally incompatible with a God of love. That is how sin speaks. Sin, as an angel of light, talks much about the love of God. It will talk about anything in order to get you to close your eyes to the consequences of your actions, and the end to which they lead, and especially to the death, the eternal death, in which they are going to issue.

To see the deceivableness and the deceitfulness of sin at its very zenith, listen to what it says about the Cross of Christ on Calvary's hill. Alas! how often is false doctrine heard in so-called Christian pulpits! Preachers say, 'What is the meaning of that death, that Cross? It is nothing but a great exhibition, a tableau, of the love of God. Do not talk about substitutionary atonement. Do not talk about the righteousness and the justice of God. Do not say that God was there punishing His Son in order that we might be freely forgiven. Do not talk about the wrath of God, do not talk about propitiation. It is all love; there is no punish-

ment. God is a God of love; so live as you like; all will go to
heaven at the end.' That is how sin talks in its deceivableness
and deceitfulness. Universalism! All are going to be saved;
there is no division of mankind into the 'saved' and the
'lost'. Even out of the Cross of Christ – the most glorious event
the world has ever seen, where God was revealing His eternal
justice and righteousness by punishing His own Son, and not
sparing Him anything – even out of that they take the glory in
order to deceive us about the whole function of the Law, and the
very character of God Himself. That is how sin deceives us by
giving us one side of the picture only.

Sin does this work, as Paul says in Ephesians 4: 17, by 'darken-
ing our understanding'. It prevents our thinking clearly, it mis-
represents everything; it gives us rose-tinted spectacles; it per-
verts everything, changes everything, transforms everything.
Even the devil, as Paul says, can transform himself into a veritable 'angel of light' (2 Corinthians 11: 14). So sin deceived Paul,
made use of the Law to deceive him, and by it knocked him down,
killed him, took the life out of him, made him to see he was
utterly helpless and hopeless and doomed and damned. Sin always does that. As James says in the 1st chapter of his Epistle
in verse 15, 'Then when lust hath conceived, it bringeth forth
sin; and sin, when it is finished, bringeth forth death'.

'The commandment, which was ordained unto life, I found to
be unto death. For sin, taking occasion by the commandment,
deceived me, and by it (the Law of God) slew me.'

Thirteen

*

Wherefore the law is holy, and the commandment holy, and just, and good.

Was then that which is good made death unto me? God forbid. But sin, that it might appear sin, working death in me by that which is good; that sin by the commandment might become exceeding sinful.   Romans 7: 12, 13

The Apostle here is obviously summing up, and bringing to a conclusion, the argument he has been developing in the previous verses. In a sense he has been stating, so far, what he had found in experience. His real purpose is to deal with the question put in verse 7: 'What shall we say then? Is the law sin?' He has to make clear that what he had previously said, especially in verse 5, does not mean that 'the law is sin'. It might look like that, he says, at first sight; but the moment you examine the situation it is clear that the trouble is not in the Law but in sin, and the use that sin has made even of the Law of God. He had ended by saying that what sin really does is to take advantage of the commandment, and to use it as a base of operations, and so it had deceived him, and as a result it 'slew' him.

Thus he has stated what he has discovered in his experience. That is the statement of verse 10. 'The commandment, which was ordained to life, was found by me to be, or, was found in my case to be, unto death.' That was his preliminary summing up, as it were. Verse 11 explains how that had happened, especially emphasizing the element of deceit. And now he brings it all to a head and says, 'Wherefore' – in the light of all I have been saying – 'the law itself is holy, and the commandment holy, and just, and good'. In other words, he is saying, 'This charge should never be proffered against me, that I am teaching that the Law is evil, that the Law is sin, because everything I have been saying really

[161]

asserts the exact opposite.' What he really believes about the Law is that it is 'holy', and the commandment 'holy, and just, and good'.

Notice that he refers to the 'law' and the 'commandment'. There has been much discussion as to why he does this. I find myself in agreement with those who say that he uses the variation in order to emphasize his point. He is really speaking about the whole Law. 'The commandment' may well mean the Tenth Commandment in particular – the commandment which says 'Thou shalt not covet' – but it is equally true, of course, of all the other commandments. So in effect he is saying that 'the law', and indeed every part of it, every individual detailed commandment, 'the law', general and particular, is 'holy, and just, and good'. The Apostle was obviously very much concerned to say this and to make it abundantly clear. After all, he was a Jew; and he had been brought up as a Pharisee. He had spent the whole of his life as a Pharisee in studying the Law. Not only that, he has a great burden in his heart, as he tells us in chapter 9, for his fellow-countrymen. The last thing he wants to do is to offend them, or to have any misunderstanding whatsoever with regard to his view of the Law. The Law is the Law of God, and therefore it is important that he should make perfectly clear what he really does think about it.

Now let us look at his terms. He says, 'the law is holy'. To be 'holy' means that it is the absolute antithesis of sin and evil. The charge brought against him is that he is saying that 'the law is sin'. So he says, 'Far from saying that the law is sin, I am saying the exact opposite, that it is holy.' Holiness means separation, and especially from sin and evil. So when he says that 'the law is holy' he is using the strongest term possible to show that it is as far removed as is conceivable from sin or evil.

Or look at the matter in the following way. 'The law is holy.' Of course it must be, it cannot help being so, for it is an expression of God's character. It is the function of the Law to give us a revelation of God, and His being and His character, in order that we may learn what we have to be, and to become, in order to have communion and fellowship with Him. Now the fundamental statement which the Bible makes everywhere about God is that 'God is holy'. So the commandment, the whole of the Law, can be summed up, in a sense, in this way, 'Be ye holy, for (because) I am holy'. The Law is a kind of transcript of the character of God; it is a perfect expression of His desire and of His will. The Law, therefore, is holy in the sense that it not only reveals to us the character of God, and what our character should therefore be, but it also holds us to that revelation. That, then, is Paul's first term, a most important term for us to remember.

Then, in the second place, Paul says that the Law is also 'just'. Here, again, is something to which we should pay the most diligent attention, because, as we have seen in our detailed examination of this section, sin in its deceitfulness is always trying to persuade us that the demands of the Law are unjust, unfair, and indeed impossible. As we have seen, that is one of the ways in which the deceitfulness of sin manifests itself. So Paul is concerned to emphasize that he had never said that the Law was unjust. His teaching is that the Law itself is absolutely just. It is just and right in what it demands of us; it makes no unfair demands of us whatsoever. There is nothing unfair to man in the Ten Commandments. It is all just, it is all perfectly fair. So the specious argument that was being brought forward cannot stand examination for a moment. The Law of God in all its demands is essentially righteous and absolutely just. Not only so; it is just in another sense. It is perfectly just, and justified, in the pronouncement and the sentence that it passes upon all sin or transgression, and on all failure to honour its requirements and to keep them. No man at the bar of final judgment will be able to say that any unjust demand was made of him, or that the Law is in any way unjust in punishing him. The Law has been given, and is plain and clear; it has told us what will happen if we do not obey it. So if we do not obey we must not grumble and complain when the Law exacts its penalty.

This is well illustrated in the case of Adam and Eve. They were given a law, and they were told exactly what would happen to them if they broke it. Then when they did break it, and sinned and rebelled against God, they had no right to complain when they were driven out of the Garden; for they had been warned that sin would have sad consequences. So the Law is perfectly just when it exacts its penalty. It is neither an excessive penalty, nor an unjust penalty; it is strictly just and righteous.

That bring us to the third term, 'the commandment is good' – it is just, it is holy, it is 'good'. Its 'goodness' extends to all its purposes, all its objects, indeed to all its effects. The Law is good for men, because amongst other things, as the Apostle has been arguing, it shows us what sin is. It not only does that, it shows us what we ought to be, how we ought to live, how we ought to conduct and comport ourselves. All that is very good for us. Indeed it is by the Law of God, supremely, that a man can learn what is good for him, what is best for him. There is no better life than a life lived in conformity with God's Law. Anyone who lived such a life would be living the best conceivable type of life. Our Lord lived such a life. We find very often in the Psalms that the Psalmist praises the Law of God; he says that he knows more than his teachers because of God's Law; it is by means of God's Law that he has understanding and insight; it is by knowing and learning about, and attempting to keep God's Law that he has had the greatest happiness and the greatest joy in his life. The 119th Psalm is, in a sense, devoted to that one theme – the goodness of the Law of God in and of itself. So the Apostle is justified in saying that the Law, and each individual commandment, is thoroughly good. Nothing can be better for us than the keeping of the Law. So the Apostle must never be charged with teaching that 'the law is sin'. His view of the Law is, he says, that it is 'holy, and just, and good', it is perfect. 'The law of the Lord is perfect, converting the soul', as Psalm 19 tells us.

But still Paul has not quite finished with the problem. There is a subsidiary problem. 'Was then that which is good made death unto me?' Notice how relentless man is in his opposition to God, and His Law, and His ways. We often meet this when handling people's difficulties. You appear to have answered the question fully and satisfactorily; but then they say, 'Yes, but' – there is still something troubling them. The fertility of the human mind and imagination in creating difficulties is almost endless; it is quite astonishing. But the Apostle is patient, and is ready to take the difficulties one by one. 'Was then that which is good' – 'You have just been saying that the law is holy, and just, and good; do you mean to say, therefore, that that which is good was made death unto me?' The question arises in this way. He has been emphasizing that the law killed him. 'When the commandment came, sin revived, and I died.' And again in verse 11, 'Sin, taking occasion by the commandment, deceived me, and by it slew me'. The law had killed him. The objector then sees a difficulty – 'Very well, I will agree that you have established beyond any doubt at all that the Law is not sin. But you have just said another thing which creates great difficulty in my mind. You say now that the Law killed you; are you saying, then, that that which is "holy, and just, and good" has killed you? How can that which is good kill you?' That is the further question which the Apostle takes up in the 13th verse.

In our general analysis of this section of this chapter we stated that this 13th verse is somewhat difficult to place. The question is, Does it belong to the section running from verse 7 to verse 12, or does it belong to the section that follows? Is it the introduction to the following section? There is a good deal to be said for both these views. It does not really matter ultimately from the standpoint of truth, but if you have an orderly mind you cannot help being interested in the problem. What would perhaps incline me to say that it belongs to the next section is the particular way in which Paul expresses himself. He began a section at verse 7 by saying, 'What shall we say then?' That is his usual way of introducing a new section. Then he puts his question, 'Is the law sin?' And he answers, 'God forbid'. He had adopted the same method at the beginning of chapter 6, 'What shall we say then? Shall we continue in sin, that grace may abound? God forbid.' And again he did it at verse 15 in chapter 6, 'Shall we sin, because we are not under the law, but under grace? God forbid.' He seems to be doing the same here again, 'Was then that which is good made death unto me? God forbid!' In many ways therefore he does seem to be introducing a new section.

At the same time it is clearly a continuation of what Paul has just been saying. The difficulty is occasioned by his saying that the Law is good but at the same time saying that it was made death to him. The solution seems to be to describe it as a transition verse which belongs partly to both sections. When we come to the next section I shall show that the whole of it, in a sense, is but an elaboration and an explanation of the theme of this section which we are now finishing. So this verse has a hook which connects it to the previous verse and also a hook linking it to what follows.

The question is: Granted that the Law is holy, and just, and good, nevertheless it does seem to have been the cause of the spiritual death to which the Apostle is giving such emphasis. Therefore the question follows, 'Is the Law then the cause of that death?' The answer is given immediately, 'God forbid!' – let it not even be mentioned, it is unthinkable. What then is the explanation of what he has been saying? Paul explains his answer in a most extraordinary statement, which is also difficult for one reason only, namely, that he left out the verb. This Apostle does that kind of thing from time to time – he was not a pedant, thank God. He often breaks the rules of grammar; and here he has actually left out the verb, which must be supplied in order to get at his meaning! What he is really saying is this: 'It is not the Law that killed me, but sin. God forbid that anyone should say that I am teaching that the Law was death unto me. It was not; it was not the Law that killed me, it was sin that killed me.' So we can translate it thus, 'Sin is the cause'; or 'Sin became death unto me'; or 'Sin was allowed to produce, and to lead to, this result of death to me'. That is patently the meaning of the statement, and it cannot carry any other meaning. The Apostle is saying that God in His infinite wisdom allowed sin to do this with the Law in order that certain results might follow. He has already said twice that 'Sin, taking occasion by' – making use of, setting out from there as a military base of operations, acting as a fulcrum – had done this. Now he says that God allowed sin to do that with the Law.

Here we meet with a great problem, of course. Why did the holy God allow sin to do this with His Law, which is 'holy, and just, and good'? The Apostle's answer is that this was allowed in order that sin might appear sin, which means, that sin might be 'shown up for what it really is'. The difficulty with sin is to recognize it for what it is. Sin is deceitful, sin is very clever, sin is like a fisherman who hides himself and conceals the bait. Sin has to be shown up in order that it might appear sin, that it might be 'shown' to be sin. What Paul is saying, therefore, is that it is the Law that really brings that about. Sin was not quite as clever as it thought it was! That is what the Bible says everywhere about the devil and sin. The devil is very clever and very subtle, but not quite as clever as he thinks he is. When the devil brought about, through men, the crucifixion and the death of the Lord Jesus Christ, he thought he was producing his final masterpiece; but ultimately that is what destroys him. The same is true of sin. Sin thought, cleverly, that it was going to use the Law, and it did so in the senses we have seen. But while it was doing so it was exposing itself.

That, he tells us, is the first reason why this was ever allowed to take place. It is in this way that sin, as sin, becomes clear and evident to us. Paul has already said this in an experimental sense earlier in the words, 'I had not known lust, except the law had said, Thou shalt not covet'. Also it was only when sin revived, when the Law came, that he was killed and realized the truth about himself and the truth about sin. That, then, is the first thing.

But there is here a second important statement about sin: 'That sin, by means of the commandment (or through the commandment) might become exceeding sinful.' It is only by the Law that the exceedingly sinful character of sin is demonstrated and brought out. In other words, the Apostle is concerned to show not only the power of sin, but the malignity of sin. This is the thing which we are so slow to learn; something of which all of us, by nature, know little if anything. It explains why, today, people object to this biblical doctrine of sin. They hate it; indeed, some clever, popular preachers ridicule it in terms of psychology. That is just the measure of their extreme, utter blindness. Nothing is so true of sin as its exceeding sinfulness, and nowhere do you see that exceeding sinfulness so clearly as just here – that it can even manipulate and use this holy, just, good Law of God, and by means of it kill us! It can twist and pervert and turn into an instrument that is opposed to us even God's holy Law which is for our good. 'Was then that which is good made death unto me?' No, it was not the Law itself, but sin which handled and abused it, sin which perverted it and used it deceitfully, that brought about that result. And by this deed we see sin's devilish character, its utter malignity, and its foulness. Nothing too strong can be said about it. It is all included in the expression 'exceeding sinful'. There is nothing worse to be said about sin than that.

This is clearly an important statement for us to grasp, not only because it shows us the exceeding sinful character and nature of sin, but because at the same time it instructs us with regard to the whole function and purpose of God's Law and the giving of the Law. That is, after all, the fundamental theme which the Apostle is handling.

Here I would interject a remark. The secret of expounding 'Romans seven' is to avoid becoming lost in the details. There is no chapter in the Bible in which it is so easy to 'miss the wood because of the trees' as in this 7th chapter of the Epistle to the Romans. It is essential, therefore, that we go on reminding ourselves as to the chapter's fundamental purpose, otherwise we shall become lost in the details. Its primary object, its fundamental theme is to deal with the place and the function of the Law in God's dealings with the human race. Every detail must be considered in the light of that purpose, and of nothing else. To start by thinking that the object of this chapter is that Paul should give us his experience is to miss the whole point. That is not his purpose at all. His fundamental object is to deal with the charge that the Jews and others were bringing against him by saying that his preaching meant that the Law of God was not only useless but actually evil, that it had no function or purpose at all, and that it would have been better if it had never been given. It was the charge that his preaching of justification by faith only, and by grace – salvation by grace – was really throwing the Law right out and dismissing it entirely.

Here, in this crucial verse, Paul shows the real function and purpose of the Law. It is to show 'the exceeding sinfulness of sin'. Of course, the Apostle has really said it before, not in these exact terms, but he has made the same general point in chapter 3, verse 20. Summing up the great argument about justification he says there, 'Therefore by the deeds of the law there shall no flesh be justified in his sight: for by the law is the knowledge of sin'. It is the Law that gives us an understanding of sin. It was never meant to justify a sinner. Here he is repeating that truth, but also saying something further.

There is a parallel statement in the Epistle to the Galatians, in chapter 3, and verse 19 in particular: 'Wherefore then serveth the law?' Paul answers, 'It was added because of transgressions, till the seed should come to whom the promise was made'. In other words, the Law was never intended to be a way of salvation. The fundamental error of the Jews was to think that it was so intended. That was exactly why they had gone so sadly astray. The Apostle says the same thing again in chapter 9 of this Epistle: 'Israel, which followed after the law of righteousness, hath not attained to the law of righteousness. Wherefore? Because they sought it not by faith, but as it were by the works of the law. For they stumbled at that stumbling-stone' (verses 31 and 32). That was their whole trouble. They would persist in thinking that God had given His Law to them in order that they might save themselves through it. But salvation is a matter of grace entirely. God had stated that away back in the Garden of Eden, and still more specifically in the covenant He made with Abraham. In Galatians, chapter 3, Paul says that what governs salvation is the covenant of God made with Abraham and his seed, and he reminds us that that was looking forward to Christ. And he argues that the Law, which only came in four hundred and thirty years after the covenant with Abraham, cannot disannual or affect that fundamental original covenant. It was never meant to do so. Why then was it brought in at all? Ah, says Paul, it was brought in afterwards in order that people might see their need of the Covenant of grace; it was brought in because of 'transgressions', till 'the seed should come to whom the promise was made'. So later he says that it was a kind of 'schoolmaster to bring us to Christ'. It does not save; it brings us to the Saviour. It is not the way of salvation; its purpose is to show us our need of salvation, and to give us some indication of how it is going to come.

Our understanding of this point is quite crucial. The Apostle is telling us that we must get rid once and for ever of the notion that the Law in any shape or form was meant to save us. The Law cannot justify us, the Law cannot sanctify us. And if you try to use it for either of these purposes you are attempting something which is impossible. Here the particular emphasis is upon the utter impossibility of ever being sanctified by the Law. Sin being what it is, in all its power and malignity, in all its subtlety and exceeding sinfulness, and we being what we are in our weakness on account of the Fall and the sin which is within us – render our sanctification by the Law an utter impossibility. The Apostle has been working out this argument from verse 7 to the end of this verse 13. But he is so anxious that we should be clear about the matter that he does not even stop at verse 13. In verse 14 and to the end of the chapter he proceeds still further to prove just this one point. He will do so by means of a psychological and spiritual analysis; but it is still the same point exactly. Verses 14 to the end of the chapter are an elaboration of just this one thing – that a man can never become sanctified by the deeds of the Law or by any attempt to work out for himself the commandments and the dictates of the Law.

Here, then, we have arrived at a point of transition, but before we begin to look at verse 14 we must give thought to one other question. It has to be faced because the Apostle, in a sense, makes us face it. It is this. Of whom has the Apostle been speaking in the previous verses? I am not for the moment going to discuss the identity of the person about whom Paul is speaking from verse 14 to the end, but the identity of the person of whom he has been speaking from verse 7 to verse 13. 'Nay', he says in verse 7, 'I had not known sin, but by the law; for I had not known lust, except the law had said . . .' 'I was alive without the law once: but when the commandment came, sin revived, and I died'. 'The commandment, which was ordained to life, I found to be unto death . . . and it slew me', and so on. The question is, Of whom is the Apostle speaking? There have been those who have said that the Apostle is not speaking of himself at all, but that he has been personifying in his own person the state and the condition of the Jews. They say that when he says 'I was alive without the law once' he is describing the condition of the Hebrews before the Law was given by God through Moses to them. The commandment came when God gave the Ten Commandments and the Moral Law. We need not stay with that, because there are very few, if any, today who still hold to this theory. If the Apostle meant that, why did he not say so? It would have been so much easier to say so. No, he is clearly and patently talking about himself and his own experience, because he puts it in terms of concupiscence. It is personal experience, something that happens to an individual.

But then there arises the question, What stage of his life, what stage in his human experience is the Apostle describing? Here again there are some who say that the Apostle is saying, 'I was alive without the Law once. From my birth until about the age of twelve, of course, I knew nothing about these things at all; but then at the age of twelve, like every other Jewish boy, I began to be instructed about the Law; and the moment I was given the teaching of the Law I began to understand about sin, and I saw that I was a sinner.' So they say that Paul's first statement is about himself until he became an adolescent; and that afterwards he is describing his experience as an adolescent. But I would reject this again out of hand, and for this good reason, that the piece of autobiography the Apostle gives us in the 3rd chapter of the Epistle to the Philippians excludes it completely. There he says in verse 6, 'Concerning zeal, persecuting the church; touching the righteousness which is in the law, blameless'. That was not when he was an infant, not when he was a boy, not until he became an adolescent, but right up to the time when he became a Christian. He was a typical Pharisee, and like all Pharisees he was very well pleased with himself. We have already interpreted verse 9, 'I was alive without the law once', as meaning 'I thought I was doing well, I was convinced I was keeping the Law'. That was because he had not understood about coveting, and had reduced the Law to a number of actions and particular sins. That was his condition as a Pharisee, and not merely until he reached the age of twelve. So we reject that interpretation.

Then there are those who would have us believe that Paul is referring here to his experience after his conversion. They say that no man can know what the Law really is until he is regenerated and converted. Paul says, 'The commandment came, sin revived, I died'. They teach that that came at conversion or subsequent to it. But, again, I would reject that for this reason, that the Apostle, surely, in this section is describing the condition of a man who is 'under the law'. Here is a man who is a victim of the Law, he is under the Law; everything he says describes a man in that condition.

But I have a yet more powerful argument. This section we have been looking at – verses 7 to 13 – is really an elaboration of verse 5, which reads, 'For when we were in the flesh, the motions of sins, which were by the law, did work in our members to bring forth fruit unto death'. That is the primary statement, and all we have been looking at is an elaboration of it – 'fruit unto death' – 'slew me'. Clearly he is describing a man 'under the law'. Sin takes advantage of the Law in order to kill him. He is describing a man who is 'in the flesh'; and a man who is 'in the flesh' is not a Christian. The Christian he describes in chapter 8, verse 9, thus: 'But you are not in the flesh, but in the Spirit, if so be that the Spirit of God dwell in you. Now if any man have not the Spirit of Christ, he is none of his.' So here we have a man who is 'in the flesh', and what he is dealing with here is not something that has happened subsequent to conversion.

We are left with this conclusion, that the experience described must have been before the Apostle's conversion. In that case the question arises, At what stage before his conversion? He has told us that he is 'in the flesh' still, and all the effects he describes are those which happen to a man 'in the flesh'; but he also tells us that he now has a spiritual understanding of the Law. The commandment has really 'come' to him with power; he sees its spiritual character; he has understood the meaning of 'Thou shalt not covet'.

We have therefore to put these things together. How can we do so? It seems to me that there is only one adequate solution. Here is a man who is 'under conviction of sin', but who has not yet understood the truth about salvation in Christ Jesus. He is deeply convicted of sin, he has been 'slain', he is 'dead', he realizes that he is not only guilty, but that he is helpless, and that he has sin within him; but as yet he does not understand anything further. The Apostle is describing something that was once true of himself; he is looking back. 'I had not known sin, but by the law; for I had not known lust, except the law had said, Thou shalt not covet'. 'Sin taking occasion by the commandment, wrought in me . . .' He is not saying that it is still doing so; it did so then. It is all in the past. 'I was alive without the law once, but when the commandment came, sin revived, and I died.' He is not still dying. He is looking back. It is all in the past. He is looking back across a past experience.

When did this happen? The Apostle does not tell us. Do you regret the absence of that fact? You should not do so. If it had been important for us to know exactly when this happened, he would have told us. As I keep on repeating, the Apostle is not primarily concerned here about his own experience or about himself; he is merely illustrating this tremendous point of his about the purpose and function of the Law. He is showing us the position of a man now awakened to the truth about the Law. And there he leaves it; he does not tell us any more about it. When was this? What I am going to say next is in a sense speculation; I am only putting ideas before you tentatively. There are different views, no one can establish any one of them. We cannot be certain because the Apostle has not chosen to tell us.

Did this happen to Paul before his experience on the road to Damascus? What exactly is the meaning of the phrase in Acts 9, verse 5, where our Lord, speaking to Saul of Tarsus on the road to Damascus, said, 'It is hard for thee to kick against the pricks', or 'to struggle against the goad'? Of course, the answer still is that we do not know. But it is not impossible that this man, Saul of Tarsus, was already convicted of sin. 'Ah but', you may say, 'if so, why did he go to Damascus "breathing out threatenings and slaughter" against the Lord Jesus Christ and all his followers?' Men convicted of sin have often done that in their misery and unhappiness. His self-righteousness as a Pharisee would make him hate this Teacher more than all others. It is not incompatible at all with his being under conviction. This is an interesting point from the experimental and practical standpoint. Take it as a word of encouragement. If you are concerned about some dear one whom you would like to see as a Christian, and for whom you are praying, remember that sometimes, just before they are converted, they become most violent against you and the Truth. It is an indication very often that something is going on. The violence is often a very good sign. Was it then the case that the Apostle was convicted of sin before he went on the journey to Damascus? I cannot exclude that possibility. But I am not saying that I believe it was actually so.

Take another possibility. Is Paul describing here what happened to him between the event on the road to Damascus and the coming of Ananias to him with the comfort of the gospel and the baptism of the Holy Ghost? Notice the very interesting things we are told in the narrative in Acts 9. Let me indicate those I regard as most important. In verse 6 we read, 'And he trembling and astonished said, Lord, what wilt thou have me to do? And the Lord said unto him, Arise, and go into the city, and it shall be told thee what thou must do.' In other words, our Lord did not really give him the full comfort of salvation there, if He gave it him at all. Here is Saul of Tarsus suddenly made to tremble and to be astonished. It was the sight of the Lord who was speaking to him, and the realization that it was Jesus that did this. At any rate, he came to realize there that he had

made a most terrible blunder about this Person, and he knew now
that He was the Son of God.

But then there is another statement of much interest in verse
9: 'And he was three days without sight, and neither did eat nor
drink.' This is not an account of a man rejoicing in his salvation
– 'trembling and astonished', 'amazed', 'blinded' physically,
and he did not eat nor drink for three days. Then we are told
in verse 19, 'And when he had received meat, he was strengthened'. He had become very weak. A three days' fast does not make
one as weak as the narrative indicates, but I can understand a
terrible conviction of sin doing so. Here was a man who was an
expert in the Law. Suddenly this light from heaven comes down
upon him, showing him that he had been utterly wrong; so I
suggest that in those three days he suddenly saw how completely
mistaken he had been about the Law. He saw its spiritual character, he understood the meaning of coveting. All hell was let
loose within him, and he saw his complete death, his wretched
failure, his utter inability. But the coming of Ananias was clearly
and obviously a great help to him. 'Brother Saul', said Ananias,
'the Lord, even Jesus, that appeared unto thee in the way as
thou camest, hath sent me, that thou mightest receive thy sight,
and be filled with the Holy Ghost.' And it was so. He not only
regained his sight, he now desires to eat; he is able to eat, and is
strengthened. For myself, I am content to believe that that
period is sufficient to account for all we have been looking at in
verses 7 to 13 of this 7th chapter of the Epistle.

There is only one other possibility – though I would exclude
it – and that is, that something of this went on during the three
years that he was in Arabia. I cannot accept that, because I cannot conceive that a man baptised with the Holy Ghost could go
through the experience which he describes in the verses we have
been considering. To me, therefore, it seems probable that he is
describing the period between the Damascus road experience
and the coming of Ananias; but I would not exclude the possibility that something had been happening even earlier.

But that is not the main issue here. It is not the Apostle's fundamental concern. All he is saying is that there was a time in his
life when he felt that he was 'alive' – self-satisfied, self-righteous,
self-confident – but that when he began to understand the spiritual character and nature and meaning of the Law, it killed him,

'knocked the life out of him'. He became as a dead man, completely hopeless, utterly and absolutely helpless. That is what he wants us to understand. When it happened really does not matter; but that it had happened is of extreme significance, as he will proceed to show us in the remaining verses of the chapter.

Fourteen

*

For we know that the law is spiritual, but I am carnal, sold under sin.
Romans 7: 14

In this verse we come to the beginning of this most interesting section in this 7th chapter of this Epistle; indeed we come to what is beyond any doubt the most famous and best-known section in the entire Epistle. There is no section, certainly, which has so frequently led to debate and disputation and, unfortunately, one must add, even wrangling and a display of a spirit far removed from that which is taught in the New Testament. This is a subject, therefore, which we approach, I trust, with a great deal of caution, and certainly with a maximum of humility.

The dispute has always centred round the question as to who this man is whom the Apostle is describing in this section. There have been three main views. First, there have been those who have said that the Apostle is here describing an unregenerate man, a man who is in the state of nature, not yet quickened and regenerated. The second view is that it is a description of a regenerate man, and not only a description of a regenerate man, but a description of a regenerate man always, even at his best; indeed, that the Apostle Paul was describing himself and his own experience at the very time he wrote these particular words. The third view maintains that it is an account of the regenerate man in his early stages, at the beginning of his Christian life, and before he has received a 'second blessing', or 'second experience', which takes him out of this state and puts him into the state of experience described in the 8th chapter. In other words they say that this is only a preliminary and temporary stage in the experience of the regenerate man.

The history of these three differing views is interesting, and it

[176]

is well that we should know something about them, because, whatever else it may do, I trust it will produce in us the desired humility to which I referred. Anyone who approaches this section without 'fear and trembling', and without humility, is not really fit to expound Scripture at all.

It is generally agreed that most of the Fathers of the Church, during the first three centuries, regarded these verses as being a description of the unregenerate man. That is just a fact of history. There were some exceptions, but speaking of them as a whole it is true to say that for the first three centuries the great doctors of the Church, the 'Patristic Fathers' so called, and others took this view, that this was an account of the unregenerate man. Then we come to the great figure whom we describe as Saint Augustine of Hippo, one of the greatest luminaries in the whole story of the Christian Church, who was active during the period 386– 430 A.D. His story with regard to this section is particularly interesting. He began by regarding it, as those who had gone before him had done in general, as a description of the unregenerate man. But Augustine was a very great man, and he gave proof of that by changing his mind on this question. I am not saying that he proved he was a great man by adopting the second view, I simply say that a mark of greatness is that he was big enough to change his mind. It is a small and narrow mind that is afraid to change; it is a sign of greatness that one is prepared to admit at times that one has been mistaken, and that therefore you have had to change your position. Augustine did so, and from teaching that Paul is describing here the unregenerate man, he then championed the exposition that it was clearly the regenerate man, and the regenerate man even at his best. So Augustine moved from the first position to the second.

The Protestant Reformers and the Puritans, and all who have followed them, have almost without exception followed that second exposition of Augustine; in other words, they have taught that this is a description of the regenerate man. We have two well-known examples of this in Charles Hodge and Robert Haldane whose commentaries I have so frequently recommended and praised. They both take the view that this is a description of the regenerate man: and the Reformed tradition of exposition has generally followed that course. On the other hand, those who have followed the different theological system commonly called the

Arminian, have generally taught that this is a description of the unregenerate man – the view that was taken by the Patristic Fathers. But then, during the last hundred years, there have been others who, while belonging to the general evangelical tradition in the main tenor and exposition of Scripture, have taken the third view, that it is not a description of the full-fledged regenerate man, the regenerate man at his best as long as he lives in this world, but the ill-taught and incomplete regenerate man who has not yet advanced to the position described in the 8th chapter of this Epistle.

This very brief summary of the history of the interpretation reminds us that we must approach this matter with care, and above all, with great humility. Nothing is quite so bad and reprehensible as a party spirit. Whatever party we belong to, or whatever views we may hold, a party spirit is always wrong. Our great concern should be the Truth. Of necessity, we all hold a particular point of view and adhere to some system of doctrine. We cannot avoid doing so. People who say that they do not hold to any particular system, and that they are 'just biblical', are simply confessing that they have never really understood the teaching of the Bible. But though we may find ourselves, in general, following a certain line of exposition, a particular school of thought and of teaching, a particular view of dogmatic theology, we must never allow that to turn into a party spirit. Though this is true of us, we must come to every particular statement of the Scripture with an open mind; we must try to discover what the Scripture is saying, because no system is perfect, and at particular points even the best system may have certain defects. No system worked out by man ever has been, or ever will be perfect. Therefore, though we are governed in general by certain views, that does not mean that we must slavishly follow in every detail what has generally been taught by that particular school of thought. We must always be honest, we must seek earnestly for 'the unction of the Holy Spirit', we must realize that no teachers in the Church have had a complete monopoly of Truth. We must realize that at certain points the best systems can be somewhat defective because they are human products. So we approach this section of Scripture with great humility, with great carefulness and concern, and yet without a prejudiced mind.

As we approach this problem we are confronted by two pos-

sible procedures. One is for me to outline immediately the view
I hold of this section, and then, as we come to the particular
statements, to proceed to prove that this is the correct view.
But I have rejected that way of approach because I believe there
is another method which is not only better in itself, but also
more Scriptural. It is the method we have hitherto adopted and
is as follows. First, let us look at the particular statements as if
we held no view with respect to the whole section; let us try to
discover what each statement says, and then, having arrived at
what seems to be the meaning of each particular part, let us gather
all together and try to arrive at a conclusion.

That is undoubtedly the better method, the method to be followed in any realm and department of thought. It is always right
to listen to the evidence before you give a verdict. He is a very
poor judge who starts with his verdict, and then proceeds to
turn down everything that opposes it, instead of listening first
to all the arguments, and giving them their full value. And any
ordinary fair-minded man would follow the same procedure.
As Christians, we should know the terrible danger of prejudice,
and how it has so often led to rancour, wrangling, a bitter
party spirit, and even cruelty and war, in the long history of the
Church. It behoves us, therefore, more than anyone to adopt this
second method. So we shall proceed to take this passage in the
way in which we have approached so many other passages of
Scripture. We shall adopt the inductive method and work up to a
conclusion.

We start then with a general analysis of the section, following
the exact order of the verses:

In verse 14 the Apostle makes a general statement about
the position and the condition of the man described – whoever
or whatever he may be. 'We know that the law is spiritual: but
I am carnal, sold under sin.'

Verse 15 describes that position and condition as shown in
practice and in daily life. 'For that which I do I allow not: for
what I would, that do I not; but what I hate, that do I.' These
words tell us how the man described in verse 14 behaves.

Verses 16 and 17 contain two inferences or deductions that
can be drawn about this man and his conduct. The first, 'If then
I do that which I would not, I consent unto the law that it is
good.' That is a fair deduction. But there is a second deduction.

'Now then it is no more I that do it, but sin that dwelleth in me.'

Verses 18–20 read: 'For I know that in me (that is, in my flesh), dwelleth no good thing: for to will is present with me; but how to perform that which is good I find not. For the good that I would I do not: but the evil which I would not, that I do. Now if I do that I would not, it is no more I that do it, but sin that dwelleth in me.' Here we have a fuller exposition and explanation of what has been said in verse 17 about this man. That is typical of the Apostle's method, as we have often seen.

Verse 21: Here we have another general statement, but at a somewhat deeper level. In effect Paul is almost taking up again the statement of verse 14; but in the light of what he has just been saying, he adds to it. 'I find then a law, that, when I would do good, evil is present with me.' It is, I repeat, another general statement about this man.

Verses 22 and 23 expound what has just been said in verse 21. 'For I delight in the law of God after the inward man: But I see another law in my members, warring against the law of my mind, and bringing me into captivity to the law of sin which is in my members.'

Verse 24: Here is the cry of despair, and at the same time, the cry for deliverance that results from the realization that he is in the terrible position which he has been describing.

Verse 25: This begins with an ejaculation of relief. I deliberately describe it in this way for reasons that will emerge later. The verse closes with a brief summing up of the statement he has been making about this man in the entire section.

Let us now take a somewhat closer view of the argument. What is the main thrust of the section? What is the Apostle really concerned to do here? We start with the word 'For', with which verse 14 opens. Never has this word been more important than at this point; because it tells us that Paul is not introducing an entirely new section here, not starting upon a new subject; he is continuing with the previous one. This section is an elaboration and a further and a deeper exposition of what he has already been saying. The next term settles that once and for ever. 'For', he says, 'we know'. What do we know? 'That the law is spiritual'. In other words, from verse 14 and onwards the Apostle is still dealing with the Law and its functions, as has been the case from the 1st verse of this chapter. That is still the theme; he has not finished with the Law, he has not finished with his exposition with regard to the Law and its function.

I am suggesting, therefore, that from this 14th verse to the end of the chapter Paul is still dealing with the same major theme that has occupied him from the beginning of the chapter. He is answering the charge brought against him with respect to his teaching concerning the Law. And we have seen that there were two main charges brought against his teaching, and two subsidiary charges. The general charge was that he was dismissing the Law altogether, and saying that the Law was of no value at all. That charge he answers in the first six verses. But in doing so he seems to be saying two things about the Law to which certain people objected. The first is conveyed in verse 7. 'What shall we say then? Is the law sin?' That arises because in verse 5 he seemed to say that the Law was sin – 'For when we were in the flesh, the motions of sins, which were by the law (energized by the law), did work in our members to bring forth fruit unto death'. And we have seen that from verse 7 to verse 12 Paul has been dealing with that charge and proving that the Law is not sin; it is sin itself that has so abused and twisted and misused the Law that it has produced, and led to, sin. But a second objector asks in verse 13, 'Was then that which is good made death unto me?' And Paul answers immediately, 'God forbid. But sin, that it might appear sin, working death in me by that which is good; that sin by the commandment might become exceeding sinful.' But he was not satisfied with that. This is always his method. In verse 7, having raised the question, 'What shall we say then? Is the law sin?' he replies, 'God forbid. Nay, I had not known sin, but by the law.' Then he proceeds to expound that in the following verses. He does precisely the same here. He asks the question, 'Was then that which is good made death unto me?' and answers immediately in the remainder of verse 13. But he does not stop at that; he goes on to expound it: and that is what we have in verses 14 to the end of the chapter.

Or we can put it positively and say that Paul is concerned here to show his actual view of the Law, to show what the Law is in and of itself, what it was meant to do, and especially what it was not meant to do. The Law is God's Law; it is 'holy, and just, and good'; it was meant to do certain things, but equally clearly it was not meant to do certain other things, and it cannot do them.

That is why we have to become 'dead to the law' before those things can happen. I suggest that he is still concerned with that theme; and that his fundamental object in particular is to show what the Law could not do. In other words, the Apostle in this section is not primarily concerned to 'give his experience'; he has not set out just to tell us something about himself. He is telling us and setting out before us his view of the Law – the nature of the Law, what it is meant to do, and what it is not meant to do, or the limits to the Law. In other words in this section he is, in particular, refuting the charge that he had taught in verse 5 that the Law is death or produces death. But at the same time he is showing how the Law, because of sin in man, becomes a minister of death. He had already shown this with respect to the charge that the Law is sin. He says that the Law is not sin, but because of the character of sin in man the Law aggravates sin, 'produces it', in a sense makes a man sin, and so brings out the 'exceeding sinfulness of sin'.

That is my suggestion as to the meaning and purpose of this section. May I offer a little proof of this at this point, before we proceed any further. Look at what the Apostle says in verses 2 and 3 of the next chapter. Verse 2: 'For the law of the Spirit of life in Christ Jesus hath made me free from the law of sin and death.' Here we find the same two thoughts again. The Law, because of sin in man, has become 'a law of sin', a law that aggravates sin. It has also become a Law that produces 'death', or leads to death – again because of sin. So he now calls it 'the law of sin and death'. That is the same Law of which he has been speaking since the beginning of chapter 7. He has proved that in terms of the relationship between husband and wife. Having said all he has said about it in chapter 7, in chapter 8, verse 2, he sums it up as 'the law of sin and death'. Then to make his point doubly sure he says in verses 3 and 4, 'For what the law could not do' – that is what he is concerned about – 'what the law could not do because it was weak through the flesh, God sending his own Son in the likeness of sinful flesh, and for sin, condemned sin in the flesh: (in order) that the righteousness of the law might be fulfilled in us, who walk not after the flesh, but after the Spirit'. In other words I suggest that in chapter 8, verses 2, 3 and 4, he is summing up all that he has been saying in chapter 7. He seems to say, 'Well now, there I have proved it to you; that is what I have been saying all along; that now "the law of the Spirit of life in Christ Jesus" hath set us free altogether from the Law which had become to us a law of "sin and death".' Above all, I repeat, his original intention is to prove that the Law was never given either to justify or to sanctify us, that indeed it has become an actual hindrance in both respects, and we have to be set free and delivered from it before we can be either justified or sanctified.

I suggest, then, that that is the theme of this section. It is about the Law, what it does do, what it does not do, what it cannot do. The Apostle is not primarily writing about himself or his experience, but about the Law and the truth about the Law.

There is one other general point which I must take up – the point that is so constantly made – that here the Apostle changes the tense in which he speaks. Hitherto he has been talking about the past. He has said 'I was alive without the law once, but when the commandment came, sin revived, and I died. And the commandment, which was ordained to life, I found to be unto death. For sin, taking occasion by the commandment, deceived me, and by it slew me.' He is talking about the past and we have agreed that he was talking about the past. But now, says someone, here he suddenly changes his tense and he says, 'We know that the law is spiritual: but I am carnal' – not 'I was carnal' – 'sold under sin'. And he goes on in the present tense, 'For that which I do' – not that which I did – 'that which I do I allow not: for that which I would, that do I not; but what I hate, that do I'. It is all, they say – and rightly – in the present tense. What do we say to this?

There are those who say that this settles the whole matter, and that when he says 'I am' he means 'I am', when he says 'I do' he means 'I do', and that clearly enough, he is describing his personal experience at the very time of writing. But that does not follow for a moment, and of itself does not prove anything whatsoever. If there were such a proof there would never have been the great discussion I have described, and a man like Augustine would never have changed from one position to the other. That the matter of tense does not settle the question, and that the matter cannot be disposed of so simply, can be stated in the following way. A form that is very often adopted in pleading a case, or in establishing a point, is to employ the method of speech known as the 'dramatic present.' This is done very often by preachers. I often use this method myself. I say to a man who puts a certain proposition to me, 'Well now, if that is so, the position you leave me in is this'. I am putting it in the present – I do this, I say that. I am dramatizing the argument, saying, 'Well now, this is the position in which you leave me'; and then I proceed to put it in terms of that position; 'This is how I find myself if what you are saying is right.' It is a very common way of establishing a point. So we are entitled to say that the Apostle here is putting this whole position in this personal and dramatic way in order to make it objective. He puts it in terms of a person and how that person finds himself, and what he finds in himself, in the light of this particular position.

In other words, all I am saying at the moment is that we must not be carried away by the notion that the mere change in the tense establishes the only possible interpretation of this particular section. And let me add that the great men who have taken the different points of view are on the whole ready to grant that what I have just been saying is a simple and well-known fact, namely, that this personalizing, this dramatic representation, is a form of expression frequently used in the Scriptures.

We can now begin to look at the statement of verse 14: 'We know that the law is spiritual.' There is no need to go over that again. He has already said that the Law is 'holy, and just, and good'; and has repeated that it is 'good'. This is something that can now be taken for granted. 'We know that the law is spiritual'; at least those to whom (to use Paul's own phrase) the Law 'has come' know that. The moment it has 'come' in that way a man knows that the Law is 'spiritual'. There is no need to debate the point. Once more he is not really saying anything new; he is just reminding us of what he has already said. It is a Law that has come from God, and hence it is holy, just, and good. God is Spirit, and therefore His Law is spiritual. But there is also a second meaning, namely, that the Law is not merely a matter of 'the letter'. There is a clear exposition of this distinction in 2 Corinthians 3: 6, where we find interesting contrast between the Law and the spirit. Paul says in verses 5 and 6, 'Not that we are sufficient of ourselves to think anything as of ourselves; but our sufficiency is of God; who also hath made us able ministers of the New Testament; not of the letter, but of the

spirit: for the letter killeth, but the spirit giveth life'. The Law
is spiritual in that sense. The mistake the Jews had made was to
regard the letter only; they took a carnal view of the Law.
That was the 'veil' that was still over their faces, as the Apostle
says later in the same chapter. But the Christian view is that the
Law is spiritual – not the letter but the spirit; spirit in contrast
to letter. The non-spiritual view of the Law regards it as concerned only with external actions. But the spiritual view of
the Law knows that it is as much concerned about motives,
desires, imaginations (that is, feelings) as it is about actions.
'Thou shalt not covet.' The moment a man realizes that the Law
so speaks, he has a spiritual view of the Law, and he realizes that
the Law is spiritual. Again, the Law is spiritual in its intent, its
concern is to lead to life. Paul has already stated that clearly in
verse 10: 'The commandment which was ordained to life'. If
only men had kept it, it would have led to life – 'Do this, and thou
shalt live'. That is a spiritual matter. The Law, if carried out,
leads to the life of God. We are reminded again of that
here.

But, alas, we know something else also – 'I am carnal, sold
under sin'. We have here what is, in many ways, the key statement of the whole of this section; and, as is his custom, the
Apostle puts it right at the beginning, so that we may be able to
understand throughout what he is saying. Here is the first fundamental and general statement. 'Carnal'! The word itself actually
means 'fleshy', 'pertaining to the flesh', 'fleshly'. We have already
met with it several times. It is a description of man as he is by
nature in contrast with the life of the spirit. The contrast is always
'flesh' and 'spirit'. It means man's life as organized and lived
apart from God and the power of the Holy Spirit in his life. It is
really present in verse 5: 'For when we were in the flesh, the
motions of sins, which were by the law, did work in our members
to bring forth fruit unto death.' You have it again in verse 6:
'But now we are delivered from the law, that being dead wherein
we were held; that we should serve in newness of spirit, and not
in the oldness of the letter.' We interpreted that as saying that 'the
oldness of the letter' is characteristic of being 'under the law',
which is the same as being 'in the flesh'. A man who is 'in the
flesh' is 'under the law'. So when he says here, 'I am carnal',
he does not mean that the flesh which remained in him was car-

nal, he does not say that there was something that was still within him which was carnal; he says that he himself is carnal – 'I am carnal'.

In Scripture the term 'carnal' is used in two main ways. The first is the one I have already been expounding, and which you find again, for instance, in the next chapter in verses 5–9. 'They that are after the flesh do mind the things of the flesh; but they that are after the Spirit' – mark the contrast – 'the things of the Spirit. For to be carnally minded is death; but to be spiritually minded is life and peace. Because the carnal mind is enmity against God: for it is not subject to the law of God, neither indeed can be. So then they that are in the flesh' – these carnal and carnally minded people – 'cannot please God. But ye are not in the flesh, but in the Spirit, if so be that the Spirit of God dwell in you. Now if any man have not the Spirit of Christ, he is none of his.' Such is the common use of the term.

But there is a second use of the term 'carnal'. We find it in the First Epistle to the Corinthians at the beginning of chapter 3. Notice how the Apostle puts it: 'And I, brethren, could not speak unto you as unto spiritual, but as unto carnal, even as unto babes in Christ. I have fed you with milk, and not with meat: for hitherto ye were not able to bear it, neither yet now are ye able. For ye are yet carnal: for whereas there is among you envying and strife, and divisions, are ye not carnal, and walk as men? For while one saith, I am of Paul; and another, I am of Apollos, are ye not carnal?' There Paul describes the 'carnal' person as one who is 'a babe in Christ', an immature Christian, a Christian who lacks fuller understanding. He says, 'I could not give you the fuller truth that I would have liked to have given you, because you are still carnal'. Obviously he means that though they were born again and had become Christians, they are still 'babes in Christ', and so much of their thinking is still that old type of thinking. In other words he says that they were behaving as if they were still 'carnal'. What else can be possibly mean? They are born again, and they are therefore 'in the Spirit'; and yet he says that they are 'carnal'. The Apostle can only mean that they are carnal in the sense that they go on thinking in the old way in which they used to think before they became spiritual.

Those are the only two uses of this word carnal that we find in the Scripture. What light does the first use throw on this statement, 'We know that the law is spiritual, but I am carnal?' Are we not already in a position to draw out an inference? This statement cannot possibly be about the mature Apostle Paul. He cannot say of himself as the Apostle who wrote this Epistle to the Romans 'I am carnal', if by 'carnal' you mean what he says it means in the next chapter, verses 5–9. But it cannot possibly carry the second use either, because that would mean that the Apostle is a mere 'babe in Christ', for in writing to the Corinthians he not only tells them that they are babes, and that he cannot give them the spiritual teaching which a spiritual man could give them, he also tells them in chapter 2 of that Epistle that there are other Christians of whom it can be said that they are 'spiritual', that they have the 'mind of Christ', and that 'he that is spiritual judgeth all things', etc. There is the type of Christian who can follow his exalted teaching; the Corinthians cannot do so because they are 'carnal', mere 'babes'. It is patently clear, therefore, that the Apostle cannot possibly be saying of himself, 'I am carnal', in that sense.

Whatever is being taught here, therefore, we can say that this is not a statement about a man who is unregenerate, neither is it a statement about a man who is as fully developed as a Christian as anyone can possibly be in this life, and in this world. The unregenerate do not know and cannot say that 'the law is spiritual'; and the Apostle who wrote this Epistle could not possibly be in the same condition as the Corinthians.

'But I' – who is this? He is someone who is 'carnal'. Look through your Bibles as to the meaning of the word carnal; try to find something over and above what I have put before you, and then face this question. Is this a description of the Apostle Paul when he wrote this Epistle? Is it a description of a Christian man who has matured as much as it is possible for a Christian to mature and to develop while he is alive in this world? For the moment do not go further than that. This is a preliminary and a key statement. We must not rush past it. 'I am carnal'. It is not the only thing that is true about this 'I'; there is something further which we shall go on to consider – 'sold under sin'. We have surely realized already that there is no glib or easy answer to the problem posed by this section. We must proceed cautiously and reverently, giving every word and statement its full value, and

[187]

above all, free from a desire to assert our particular point of view. May we all seek that 'unction' and 'anointing' from 'the holy One', for the matter with which we are dealing is beyond the realm of grammar and intellectual dexterity.

Fifteen

*

For we know that the law is spiritual, but I am carnal, sold under sin.
For that which I do I allow not: for what I would, that do I not; but what I hate, that do I. Romans 7: 14, 15

As we proceed with this difficult, much-discussed and controversial section of this 7th chapter of this Epistle we must gird up the loins of our minds, and make a real effort to understand. We must not give up because the subject matter is difficult. You will then find happening to you what is the almost universal experience of all raw students. When students first begin to listen to lectures on a subject they often feel on the first few occasions not only that they know nothing at all of what is being said, but that probably they will never be able to understand. There is only one thing to do at that point, and that is to go on listening. If you go on listening you will begin to find that more than you had ever realized is sinking and seeping in, and you will wake up one day and say, 'Ah, I now see what it is about, I am beginning to understand'. Do not be impatient with yourself when you are studying a difficult passage in Scripture; keep on, hold on, reading or listening; and suddenly you will find that not only do you know much more than you thought you knew, but you will be able to follow and to understand. It is necessary that one should say things like that from time to time, because the devil is ever at hand to say to us, 'This or that is of no use to you, you cannot follow it, leave it to the theologians'. Do not listen to him, but say 'I belong to the Christian family and I intend to listen and to read until I do understand it'. Do that, and you will not only defeat the enemy, but you will soon find that you have an understanding.

As we have already seen, the Apostle starts with a general proposition: 'We know that the law is spiritual.' Well, then, if the

Law is spiritual, where does the trouble lie? What is wrong? Why are things as they are? And he answers the question in the second half of the 14th verse. The trouble is that 'I am carnal'. But I am not only carnal, I am also sold under sin'. Here is the new phrase, here is a most remarkable statement. As far as I can make out, all the commentators are agreed that this is the most significant statement in the whole section, whatever view they may happen to take of it. This is the key phrase in many senses, and especially when taken with the previous one, 'I am carnal'. The two go together. 'I am carnal' – indeed, 'sold under sin'. The commentators who belong to the Reformed tradition and who generally take the view that this is a description of the re- generate man, indeed of Paul himself when writing, are honest enough, most of them, to admit that this statement is their major difficulty, the one they find most difficult to explain. Of course they then proceed to try to explain it. Whatever view you may take of this section, you will find yourself hard put to it at some point or another.

That is a great comfort to all of us. Whatever your view of this section there will be particular statements which will trouble you, and there comes the danger, the tendency just to twist things a little, or modify them, in order to make them fit in. We must try to avoid that. But all are in trouble. Those who take the view that this is a description of the regenerate man at his best, even as he will be until he dies, are in particular trouble with this phrase, 'sold under sin'. All are agreed that it is a very strong term. It means 'sold' or 'disposed of' 'into slavery'. There is no doubt about the meaning. 'Sold under sin' means that I am 'sold into a condition of slavery to sin', that I am 'a slave' to sin. Sin is the master and I am the slave. That is the plain meaning of the actual words used by the Apostle. He does not say that we have sold ourselves into this slavery; what he says is that we are in this condition of slavery. He is not concerned here to argue as to how we have arrived there. He has already explained that matter in chapter 5 from verse 12 to verse 21. But here he just makes the statement that we are slaves of sin, sold as slaves in the market unto, into the position of, and under, the governance of sin.

Another remark we must make about this statement is that it applies to the man, the whole man, and not merely a part of

the man, whoever he is, whom the Apostle is describing. He is
not saying 'The law is spiritual, but a part of me is carnal, a part of
me is a slave to sin'. What he says is, 'I am carnal, I am sold under
sin'. There is nothing here to suggest that he is only referring to
the sinful part of himself, or the old nature that still remains within him. It is a statement made about the man as a whole. That is a
most important point for us to grasp. What, then, is the meaning
of this statement? Surely this is a reference back to some statements he has already made in chapter 6. Take verse 16 for instance: 'Know ye not', he says, 'that to whom ye yield yourselves
servants to obey, his servants ye are to whom ye obey; whether
of sin unto death, or of obedience unto righteousness.' 'Servants' means 'slaves', being sold as slaves. Then in the 17th
verse we read: 'God be thanked, that ye were the slaves of sin',
and so on. Verse 18 mentions it again, putting it positively, 'Being then made free from sin, ye became the slaves of righteousness'. When you were taken out of that slavery to sin you became
the slaves of righteousness. Note also the 20th verse: 'For',
he says, 'when ye were the slaves of sin, ye were free from righteousness.' I suggest that he is still using the same picture here, the
same analogy, the same terms. 'I am carnal, the slave of sin.'

So we proceed to ask a question. We must ask these questions
as we go on in order that we may build up our evidence so as
to try to arrive at a conclusion. Of whom is such a statement
true? Who is it that can make such a statement about himself?
In the first place, I assert that no unregenerate person can make,
or ever has made, such a statement about himself. To me, this
verse alone is sufficient to put right out of consideration the suggestion that this passage describes an unregenerate person. I say
that for the following reasons. The unregenerate person does not
understand the nature of the Law. No unregenerate man knows
that the Law is spiritual. The Apostle has already told us so in
verse 7: 'What shall we say then? Is the law sin? God forbid!
Nay, I had not known sin but by the law, for I had not known
lust except the law had said, Thou shalt not covet.' That was his
whole trouble, as it was the trouble with all the Pharisees. He did
not understand the spiritual nature and character of the Law.
That is always the trouble with the unregenerate man. Not only
that, the unregenerate man does not realize that he is 'carnal',
and 'sold under sin'. The trouble with the unregenerate man, as

the Apostle tells us in verse 9, is this: 'I was alive without the law
once'. Far from thinking that he is carnal, or that he is a slave of
sin, he says that he is alive, that he was doing very well. This
results, as we have seen, from his complete misunderstanding of
the Law and its emphasis upon coveting; he regards the Law as
merely interested in actions. Now that is always the trouble with
the unregenerate man; he is wrong in his view of the Law, and
he is wrong in his view of himself. He is pleased with himself,
he thinks that he can justify himself by his works. He is totally
unaware of the sinful nature that is within him, that he is carnal,
and that he is 'sold under sin'. So I argue that this verse is enough
in and of itself to exclude the suggestion that this is a description
of an unregenerate man.

That leads to the next question. Is this, then, a description of
the regenerate man? Here again I have no hesitation in asserting
equally strongly that it is not, and that it cannot be so. I assert
that it is neither the unregenerate nor the regenerate. Why not
the regenerate? Because that would be to fly in the face of everything that the Apostle has been telling us from chapter 5, verse
20. Indeed, we could even go back to the beginning of chapter
5; but it becomes especially cogent in verse 20. 'Moreover', he
says, 'the law entered'. Now that is what we are dealing with in
this 7th chapter – the place and function of the Law. 'When the
law came, sin revived, and I died'. 'The law entered'. Why has
the Law entered? 'That the offence might abound.' Does that
mean that our situation is hopeless, worse than ever? No, says
Paul, 'Where sin abounded, grace did much more abound'.
That is his great theme and contention. Then he goes on, 'That
as sin hath reigned unto death, even so might grace reign through
righteousness unto eternal life by Jesus Christ our Lord'. That
was once our position; sin 'reigned' over us. From verse 12 until
verse 19 Paul has been describing what was true of us all, true
of all the seed of Adam. But the Apostle's whole contention is,
that we are no longer in Adam, we are in Christ; we are no longer
'under the law', we are under grace. We compared these two
reigns most carefully – the reign of sin and the reign of grace –
bringing out the 'much more' idea that he has used several times
in that famous section of chapter 5, 'Much more', 'More abundantly'. 'For as by one man's disobedience many were made
sinners, so by the obedience of one many shall be made righte-

ous.' 'Not as it was by one that sinned, so is the gift: for the judgment was by one to condemnation, but the free gift is of many offences unto justification.' Those are his phrases, and he used this word 'abundance' in verse 17 – 'which receive abundance of grace'. It is this superabounding' element that the Apostle is concerned about in that entire chapter. I say, therefore, that you cannot apply these words, 'I am carnal, sold under sin', to a man who is no longer 'under sin' but he is now 'under grace'. The 'much more' of the gospel has come in where the regenerate man is concerned. He is under 'the reign of grace'; so this statement cannot be true of the regenerate man.

Indeed we have an explicit statement again in the 2nd verse of chapter 6 where the Apostle takes up this point. Someone says, 'Very well, in the light of your teaching, what you are really saying is that we can sin as much as we like because grace will much more abound'. 'God forbid', says Paul, 'How shall we that died to sin' – we have done so, we have died to sin; it is the aorist tense – 'How shall we that died to sin, live any longer therein?' You recall his exposition of that truth, and how he proceeds to establish it, to work it out in detail, in terms of our 'union' with the Lord Jesus Christ. How, then, can you possibly say of such a man that he is 'carnal', that he is 'sold under sin'? He was in that condition once, but he is no longer there. And then you come to the great exhortation in verse 11 of chapter 6. 'Likewise reckon ye also yourselves to be dead indeed unto sin, but alive unto God.' That is your position now. 'Reckon' that, realize it, constantly realize it, take hold of it, hold it fast, keep on reminding yourself of it. You are dead to sin, you are alive unto God, your whole position is entirely different from what it used to be.

Then, on the basis of that, Paul goes on to make his exhortation in verse 12: 'Let not sin therefore . . .'. He says that we must not let sin reign, and need not let sin reign, even in our mortal bodies. But if the regenerate man is carnal, and 'sold under sin', how can that be reconciled with the exhortation to the regenerate, 'Let not sin reign in your mortal body'? Then there is the statement of verse 14 in that chapter, 'Sin shall not have dominion over you'. Why? 'Because you are no longer under law, but under grace.' Sin does not have 'dominion' over the man who is 'under grace' and no longer 'under law'. Indeed the whole chap-

ter seems to go on repeating the same thing. Verse 17 runs,
'God be thanked, ye were the servants of sin'; but you are so no
longer, because 'you have obeyed from the heart that form of
doctrine that was delivered you'. Then in verse 18: 'Being then
made free from sin, ye became the slaves of righteousness.'
I repeat these statements because the Apostle has repeated them,
and in so doing he has prepared the way for what he is saying
here in chapter 7. Yet so many seem to expound chapter 7 as if
they had never read chapter 6. Take again verse 20: 'For when ye
were slaves of sin, ye were free from righteousness.' Can you
still say that about a man who is regenerate? Can you say that he is
still the slave of sin, 'sold under sin'? And then finally, verse 22:
'But now being made free from sin, and become servants to God,
ye have your fruit unto holiness, and the end everlasting life.'
Those statements surely cannot be reconciled with the notion that
'I am carnal, sold under sin' is a description of a regenerate man
at any stage of development. That seems to me to be a denial of
everything the Apostle has been setting out to establish in
chapters 5 and 6.

But, indeed, Paul has already said the same thing even in this
chapter 7 itself. Look at that magnificent statement in the 4th
verse: 'Wherefore, my brethren, ye also are become dead to the
law by the body of Christ; that ye should be married to another,
even to him who is raised from the dead'. Why? 'That you should
bring forth fruit unto God.' We could not bring forth fruit unto
God while we were married to the Law. Thank God we are no
longer married to the Law, we are married to Christ in order that
we might bear offspring, 'bring forth fruit' to Him. We are no
longer 'under sin' but 'under grace', and that is why as Christians
we can and should bring forth fruit. Again we find the same
thing in verse 6. He puts it negatively in verse 5, saying, 'When
we were in the flesh' – far from bringing forth fruit unto God –
'the motions of sins, which were by the law, did work in our
members to bring forth fruit unto death. But now we are delivered from the law, that being dead wherein we were held',
or 'being dead to that wherein we were held' – 'that (in order
that) we should serve in newness of spirit and not in the oldness
of the letter.' The attempt at service in the 'oldness of the letter'
brings forth nothing but fruit unto death. But that is not our
position now. We are now in 'newness of spirit' in our service,

and we are going to 'bring forth fruit unto God'. I cannot re
concile the idea that verse 14 is a description of a regenerate man,
with verses 4 and 6 in this same 7th chapter. Then, when I go
to chapter 8, I am in still greater difficulty. 'There is therefore now
no condemnation to them that are in Christ Jesus', says verse 1.
Verses 2–4 state, 'For the law of the Spirit of life in Christ Jesus
hath made me free from the law of sin and death. For what the
law could not do, in that it was weak through the flesh, God
sending his own Son in the likeness of sinful flesh, and for sin,
condemned sin in the flesh; (in order) that the righteousness of
the law might be fulfilled in us, who walk not after the flesh, but
after the Spirit.'

We shall find, later, that those who hold that this is a description of a regenerate man have to add a footnote in which they
say, 'Of course, that is not the whole truth about the regenerate
man; what is said in chapter 8 is also true of the regenerate man'.
To which my reply is that these two things cannot be true at one
and the same time; I am either 'sold under sin' or I am not. Each
one of us is in one of two positions. I am either 'sold under sin'
or I am 'sold under Christ'. I am either a slave to sin or I am a
slave of grace and of God and of righteousness, as the Apostle
has put it so many times in chapter 6. In any case he is talking
about a whole man and not merely about a part of a man.
The word is 'I' – not 'a part of me'. He does not say this is
the partial truth about me; but 'I am carnal, sold under
sin'.

But let us go on to verse 15, because it will help us to see this
point still more clearly. In verse 15, as I indicated in the general
analysis, the Apostle goes on to describe the kind of life lived
by the person whom he has described in verse 14. 'For' – note the
continuation – 'For that which I do I allow not'. I, who am carnal
and sold under sin – this is true of me, 'I do what I allow not'.
Indeed, further: 'What I would, that do I not, but what I hate,
that do I.' Note well the description of this man, and observe,
once more, that the Apostle is not describing merely one part of
this man; he is describing the whole man. He is not only describing the sinful part of this man, because he cannot say of the sinful part of this man that it desires to keep the Law, but he says,
'That which I do, I allow not; for what I would, that do I not,
but what I hate that do I.' He is talking about the whole person,

and as I say, this connecting word 'For' surely proves and establishes that fact.

It is interesting to notice how those who take the view that the regenerate man is under consideration try to water down this statement. They must, of course, do so. So what they say is this, 'The Apostle, of course, was a most vehement kind of man, a man with powerful emotions, and now and again he gets carried away and uses hyperbole, he exaggerates, and he has been exaggerating here'. They say 'He is not as bad as he says he is; he puts it as a bald statement, but he does not really mean that that is true of the man'. Let me quote one of them who puts it thus: 'What is being expressed here is the Apostle's deep regret that his heart and life were not entirely spiritual, not perfectly in accordance with divine Law. What Paul is saying is that he felt "as if" he were the slave of a tyrant; not that he is, but "as if" he were the slave of a tyrant who employed him in work which he abhorred. His prevailing desire' – note the word 'prevailing' – 'was perfect conformity to a holy, just, and good law; yet he felt that much was wanting, much was wrong.' To me, that is a travesty of what the Apostle himself actually says here. He is not saying that his 'prevailing' mood is all right, but that 'much was wanting, much was wrong'. Look again to the words of the Apostle: 'I am carnal, sold under sin. For that which I do, I allow not; for what I would, that do I not; but what I hate, that do I.'

What, then, is Paul saying here? What is the meaning of this word 'allow' – 'That which I do I allow not'? The real meaning of the word is 'to know', as if he were saying 'that which I do, I really do not know why I am doing it'. In other words he means, 'I do not understand why I am doing it'. Indeed it means, 'I do not approve of what I am doing; that is not my understanding of these matters, so that when I do these things I do not understand myself, as it were. I am doing something which is the opposite of the view I hold.' That is the meaning of the word 'allow' – 'I don't know', 'I don't understand', 'I don't approve'.

The other word we must look at is the word 'hate', because again it is a very strong word. Paul is saying that he not merely disapproves of what he does, but he hates it, he abominates it. These are very significant statements.

Let us look closely at this 15th verse. It is a tremendous statement, a profound bit of analysis, a striking example of 'biblical psychology'. We must be clear that the Apostle is not saying that he is 'always doing evil' and that he 'never does any good at all'. That would be to ridicule the whole position. The Apostle is not saying so, but some have interpreted it in that way, as if the Apostle is saying, 'Everything I do is wrong, and I never do that which is right'. Obviously he is not saying that.

Secondly, while I assert that Paul is not saying that he always does wrong and never does right, at the same time we have no right to insinuate the word 'sometimes' or 'occasionally'. You will find that many commentators have recourse to these words. It is their only way out of the difficulty that arises for them because they think that a regenerate man is in view. So they express the case thus: 'That which I occasionally do, I allow not, for what I would, I occasionally do not, but what I hate, that I occasionally do.' I argue that it is as wrong to insinuate, to insert, the words 'occasionally' or 'sometimes', as it is to say that he 'always' did wrong and never did right.

My third comment has reference to the word 'do'. 'That which I do'. Have we any right to say that what Paul means by 'do' has no reference to actions but only to thought and imagination. You will find that some of the commentators who say that this was a regenerate man speak in that way. They say, 'You must not understand this as saying that Paul is actually doing these various things. No, no! Paul was such a spiritual man that if he thought of an action he said, "I have done it", or if he imagined it, he had "done it".' Of course, there is a sense in which that is true, as we have seen in expounding the previous section, but my question is: Have we the right to confine this word 'do' to thought and imagination only, and to exclude actions?

Fourthly, is it not obvious that this is a description, not so much of what is only occasionally or invariably true about this man, but of the man's life on balance, as a whole, looked at generally. Surely any unbiased reading must lead to that conclusion. 'We know that the law is spiritual; but I am carnal, sold under sin. What I do, I allow not, for what I would, that do I not, but what I hate, that do I' – not invariably, not occasionally; but looking at my life as a whole, looking at it on balance, this is what is true.

And if this be so, surely, then, we can take the next step. If this is what is true of my life, looked at as a whole and taken on balance, then it is a description of a life of frustration, defeat and failure. Am I going too far? If you think so, my answer is to refer you to verse 24, 'O wretched man that I am!' and so on, which is clearly a description of frustration, defeat, and failure.

So I ask once more, Who is being described here in the 15th verse? It is the same question as I asked in the 14th verse. I answer immediately that it is clearly not the unregenerate man, because he does not know the sort of conflict that is described in this verse; the unregenerate, as I have already reminded you, feels secure. I know that he gets an occasional twinge of conscience; but he never speaks in this way about himself. The whole trouble with the unregenerate man is that he feels he is alive; he is very healthy; he is in a good state and condition. Or, as he likes to put it – I am quoting the typical modern man – 'I don't say that I am a hundred per cent a saint, you know'. But he gives the impression that he possesses ninety-nine per cent of sainthood! He is quite pleased with himself, everything seems to go well. But the man depicted here is aware of frustration and of failure. The unregenerate never speaks in that way. Not only so, the unregenerate man never condemns sin in the way this man does who says, 'What I do, I do not allow; I do not approve of it'. The unregenerate man never uses such language. Neither does he ever say that he hates sin. He is very annoyed with himself sometimes, when he suffers the consequences of his sin; but that does not mean that he hates sin. He dislikes very much the consequences of sin, but if he could only have the sin without the consequences he would be happy in sin. In other words he does not realize anything about the nature of sin, and therefore he does not hate it. In his better moods he may be irritated by it at times, but here we have a man who hates sin – something which an unregenerate man has never done, and never can do.

Still further, the unregenerate man can never say, and never has said, 'What I would . . . ' He does not know the meaning of the Law, he has not understood it, and so he has not this desire to keep and to honour and to live according to God's Law. Let the Apostle say this for himself in the next chapter in verses 7 and 8. 'The carnal mind is enmity against God; for it is not subject to the law of God, neither indeed can be.' The carnal mind – the mind of the unregenerate – hates the Law when it really under-stands something about it; but, here, we have a man who tells us that he loves it, that he longs to keep it, and to be subject to it with the whole of his being. The carnal man, we are told, is not and cannot be subject to it and does not keep it. 'So then they that are in the flesh cannot please God'. So I repeat that this is obviously not a description of the unregenerate man.

What then of the regenerate? I answer carefully and guardedly. What is said here about this man's experience is true in a measure of the experience of the regenerate. I will go further. It is true of the experience of *all* regenerate persons in a measure. I do not believe in entire sanctification or sinless perfection. A man who says that he is entirely free from sin, that he never commits an act of sin, is a man who is guilty at some point or other of mis-understanding the meaning of sin. We do not believe in eradica-tion of sin or entire sanctification. As we indicated clearly in expounding chapter 6, the regenerate man still has sin left in his mortal body, in his members. He still has a fight to wage, that is why he is exhorted, as Paul exhorts him in verses 11, 12 and 13 of that chapter. But while I say that this is true in a measure, and only in a measure, of the regenerate, it is certainly not a description of the regenerate man as he is in general. It is not a description of the man to whom those exhortations are made, and to any of whom those glowing, wonderful statements have been made in chapters 5 and 6. The regenerate man, when he falls into sin, has to say that he has done something which he does not believe in doing; he is aware that he is not already per-fect; but he does not speak of himself as a man who lives a frus-trated, defeated life of failure. If so, he is not paying heed to the exhortation of the Apostle who says 'Let not sin reign in your mortal body'. And it cannot be a description of the Paul who could write, 'Brethren, be followers together of me, and mark them which walk so as ye have us for an ensample' (Philippians 3: 13–21.) So I reject the idea that this statement is about the regenerate man even at his best.

Therefore I end with this statement: Verse 15, we can safely say, is true of a man who has come to see the spiritual character of the Law. He sees that he should keep it. It is indeed a descrip-tion of a man who 'desires' to keep it, but who finds in practice that he cannot. He sees that the Law is spiritual; he admires it, he wants to keep it; but try as he will, he cannot keep it. I suggest that verse 15 says no more than that – that that is all the Apostle meant it to say at this point. Otherwise stated, this verse is nothing but an account of what is true in actual practice of the man described in verse 14. This is the truth about a man who is 'carnal, sold under sin', who nevertheless sees the spiritual character of the Law. He sees it but he cannot attain to it. The Law does not enable him to keep the Law. I end with a question. Does this verse say anything more than that?

We shall go on to consider the two inferences the Apostle draws from this striking statement, in verses 16 and 17.

Sixteen

*

If then I do that which I would not, I consent unto the law that it is good.
Now then it is no more I that do it, but sin that dwelleth in me.

Romans 7: 16-20

We continue our study of the closely reasoned argument which the Apostle develops and applies in this section of this 7th chapter. He is still telling us certain things about this 'man' whom he is describing. He has already told us that he is 'carnal', and under sin', and in consequence, that which he does, he does not allow, he does not understand, he does not approve of. Indeed he says that that which he wills to do, he does not do, but what he hates, that he does. Having said that about the man, and having described the kind of life which this man lives, he now proceeds to draw two deductions concerning his whole position. The first deduction is in verse 16, and the second in verse 17.

The first deduction is: 'If then I do that which I would not, I consent unto the law that it is good.' This is just an obvious and an inevitable piece of logic. The fact that he regrets his actions, and does not approve of them at all, means clearly that he agrees with what the Law says about them. And that, of course, in turn means that his view of the Law is that it is essentially good and right in all its demands and in all its condemnations. That is the first deduction.

The word 'consent' is an interesting one; its root meaning is 'I speak with'. Here is something or someone speaking; well, I 'speak with it', I am in agreement with it, I approve of it, I praise it. Here I am, says the Apostle, I am doing certain things which I do not want to do, which I do not approve of. But the Law, likewise, does not approve of them; it condemns them. Well then, he says, is it not obvious that I am in agreement with the Law', Am I not saying that the Law is good? The very fact that I condemn what I do, and thereby am condemning what the Law condemns, means that I am in agreement with the Law; in other words I am proclaiming that the Law of God is good, is excellent. He has already said that we know it is 'spiritual'; he now says that we also know that it is 'good'.

The question we have to ask at this point is, Why does the Apostle speak in this way? Why does he draw that deduction? He must have some reason for doing so. I answer: You can tell what a man is concerned about by the deductions which he draws; and, here, in these two verses the Apostle reminds us again of his real object in writing this paragraph. We see again that his object was not merely to state his experience – that is not what he is concerned to do at all – he is concerned to prove something concerning the Law. Firstly, he intends to show that the Law itself is in no way responsible for his failure in practice. 'Here is my position', he is virtually saying; ' "I do that which I would not"; well, clearly, the Law is not responsible for my sin. At heart, I am in agreement with the Law and regard it as good. It is obvious, then, that the Law is not responsible for the way in which I am living.' He was most concerned to say this, because he was being charged by some of his opponents as saying that 'the Law is sin'. He was also charged with saying that the Law 'was made death' unto him. He is answering these charges and saying that, whatever is responsible for his failure in practice, it is not the Law.

A related purpose is to show that his teaching concerning the Law does not involve any criticism of the Law in and of itself, still less a condemnation of the Law. That, again, was a charge that was being brought against him. There were various Jews who were saying that his preaching of what he called 'the doctrine of grace' was nothing but an attack upon the Law, a denouncing of the Law. His answer is, that the very fact that he denounces the things he does, that he does that which he would not, is proof positive that he consents to the Law 'that it is good'. His preaching of salvation by grace, and of justification by faith only, is not a criticism of the Law, for he regards the Law as 'good'. There is nothing wrong with the Law. His failure is not in any sense due to the Law. So, once more, the Apostle makes a statement which should keep us on the right lines in our exposition.

He is dealing with the Law, what the Law can do, what the Law cannot do – the place of the Law in God's economy and scheme and plan of salvation.

That brings us to the second deduction in verse 17. 'Now then', he says, 'it is no more I that do it, but sin that dwelleth in me.' How does he arrive at this deduction? He seems to say, 'What I have just been saying raises a problem. Here am I, saying that what I do I do not want to do, I do not will to do. I do not approve of it, and I am in agreement with the Law which condemns it.' The question then immediately and obviously arises, How does sin happen at all? Why does this man sin at all? It is clear that it is not the Law that does it. Well then, what does? 'Here is my problem', Paul seems to say, 'the Law is not responsible, and I myself do not want to do these things. I believe that they are wrong, I reprobate them; nevertheless I do them. What is responsible? How does this come to pass?' His answer is one of the most daring, and one of the most profound things that has ever been said; it is one of the most astonishing statements in the whole of the Bible. It must clearly be handled with great care. This is what he says: 'I agree with the Law and with what it says, and with what it prohibits. Therefore I hate sin; I do not desire to do it.' How, then, is sin committed, and why?, is the question that inevitably meets him, and he replies: 'It is no more I that do it, but sin that dwelleth in me.' It is a logical deduction, it is an inevitable deduction once more.

But what precisely is the Apostle saying here? This is not only one of the most daring sayings in the Scripture; it is at the same time one of the most difficult. Who is this 'I' to whom the Apostle is referring? In verse 16, 'If then I do that which I would not' – does the 'I' refer to the same person in both its uses? In my view, it cannot be so. The first 'I' refers to the whole personality, the man who is speaking, the man who is acting, the whole man. But the second 'I' obviously does not refer to the whole man. This is now no longer the whole personality; he is speaking now of a part of himself only. Which part? I answer: the part of him which has now been able to recognize the spiritual character of the Law. That is the second 'I'. This is where the exposition becomes difficult. The 'I' looks as if it is the same in both cases, but it cannot be. 'I do' – there is the man, the personality acting. Yes, but 'I would not' – there is a special part of the man, the part that agrees with the Law.

In other words, in verse 16 the Apostle introduces the division in the personality of this man whom he is describing. There is a kind of 'duality' here, and my contention is that this duality is introduced for the first time at this particular point, and it is certainly present here in verse 17. This is what he says therefore. 'Now then, it is no more I that do it, but sin that dwelleth in me.' This 'I' in verse 17 is certainly the 'I' to whom the Law has 'come' in the way he has previously described, the 'I' who is able to see that the Law is 'spiritual'.

We notice, then, that there is a duality in the man whom the Apostle is describing. He is able to say, 'There is that in me now' – and he wants to identify himself with this – 'that sees and agrees with the spiritual character of the Law, and therefore dislikes and disapproves the things I do'. This duality is never found in an unregenerate person. So, once more, we have a statement that helps us to solve our initial problem as to the identification of the one whom the Apostle is describing in this paragraph. This is sufficient to exclude the idea that this 'man' is an unregenerate person. The unregenerate person does not know this duality. The unregenerate person is 'one' in thought and in action. But someone may ask, 'Does not conscience trouble the unregenerate man?' It does, but there is all the difference in the world between an unregenerate man who has trouble with his conscience, and a man who is able to say 'It is no more I that do it, but sin that dwelleth in me'. In the case of the unregenerate man, the total personality of the man is 'aware' of the speaking of conscience, but he is united against his conscience. He loves sin, desires sin, and wills sin, and he wishes that he had not got a conscience. *He* does not 'condemn' what he is doing, he is simply aware that his conscience condemns it. He is worried about something, as it were, outside himself; hence he tries, by means of psychology and everything else he can lay hold of, to get rid of this voice of conscience. As a whole he is against this, but the man the Apostle is describing is a man who is divided in himself – 'It is no more *I* that do it'. Now this 'I', I maintain, is this aspect of the person that has come to realize that the Law of God is spiritual and good, and that what it prohibits should be prohibited. He agrees with that whole-heartedly. That is the 'I' he is describing here.

We look next at the second phrase which reads, 'sin that dwelleth in me'. Here again is a most profound statement about sin. Half the trouble that many have with this paragraph, and especially those who regard this as the unregenerate man, is that they fail to understand the biblical doctrine about sin. The Apostle here tells us two things about sin. The first is that sin is something that 'dwells' in us, takes up its home in us. In other words, we must not think of sin as something that is altogether outside us. There are many who think of sin in that way. Man they regard as more or less neutral; and sin is that which comes from the outside as a temptation to us. But here we learn that sin is in our very nature, sin is something that 'dwells', makes its home within us, takes up its abode, is a part of us. David expressed that well in the 51st Psalm where he says that we are 'born in sin'. It is in us from the very beginning; we do not 'acquire' it. It is something which we inherit; it is a part of our very make-up. The Apostle has been stating that at great length, of course, in chapter 5 in verses 12–21. Adam sinned, and thereafter everyone who has been born of Adam has had sin in his nature and in his constitution. We are all 'born in sin, and shapen in iniquity'. Sin is in us, it is a part of the warp and woof of our being; it is actually dwelling within us, it makes its home in us.

The other thing the Apostle emphasizes is sin's terrible power. 'Now then, it is no more I that do it, but sin that dwelleth in me.' In other words, the 'sin that dwelleth in me' is more powerful than a man's will-power: it is indeed even more powerful than the man who has actually come to see the spiritual character of the Law. This man says, 'As far as I am concerned I consent unto the Law that it is good, I agree with all it says, I agree in condemning what it condemns, I do not want to do that thing which I and the Law hate, yet I do it'; for this sin that dwelleth in me is more powerful than all my opposition to it. Though I know that certain things are wrong, not merely by conscience, not merely by the common consent of the morality of the world, but even as the result of the enlightenment I received when the Law 'came' to me and 'found' me and showed me its 'spiritual' nature – even all that is not enough to enable me to resist it.

This is one of the profoundest statements with respect to sin in the whole of the Bible. More and more I am convinced that all the trouble about morality in this country today, and in every other country, is due to the failure to understand this teaching. Is it not utterly ridiculous to suggest that a certain amount of moral teaching, more education with regard to sex and certain consequences that may follow certain actions, are going to solve the moral problem? That is what we are still being told. We must educate people for freedom, we must educate people for morality; all that is needed is that people should be taught. The answer to all that is to be found here. The Apostle says that even though you are enlightened as to the spiritual character of the Law of God, it is not enough. Knowledge alone can never solve this problem, it has already failed to do so. What man needs is not knowledge; it is power. The problem of sin is not a problem of knowledge, of instruction or of information. Here is a man who has it, says Paul, 'I do that which I would not'. 'I consent to the law that it is good' – I am in absolute agreement with it – yet here I am doing the exact opposite. What explains this? 'It is not I', says Paul, 'it is sin that dwelleth in me.' I say again that it is one of the profoundest statements that has ever been made with regard to the nature of sin, and the whole problem of sin.

But in order to see the matter still more clearly, let us glance at verses 18–20, because these verses are really nothing but an extended explanation of the statement in verse 17. In verse 17 Paul has made a startling claim and reached a staggering conclusion; so he feels it is necessary that it should be amplified. He proceeds to this in these three verses. First of all – 'For', connecting with what has just been said, 'For I know that in me (that is to say, in my flesh), dwelleth no good thing: for to will is present with me, but how to perform that which is good I find not. For the good that I would I do not; but the evil which I would not, that I do. Now if I do that I would not, it is no more I that do it, but sin that dwelleth in me.' In other words, at the end of verse 20 he is back to what he said in verse 17.

Here we see the extreme difficulty of expressing in human language the truth with which the Apostle is grappling. I say that once more in order to encourage those who may find all this very difficult. I assure you that I myself find it very difficult. This is one of the most difficult passages that one is ever called upon to handle; hence the various disagreements about it. I will go further. I believe that even the Apostle himself found this difficult. You may ask how I could ever make such a suggestion. It is because I find him inserting a statement in brackets. 'I know that in me (that is, in my flesh) dwelleth no good thing'. Why did he use these brackets and interject that particular qualifying statement? In my view it was because he knew well that when those Christians in Rome were listening to someone reading this Letter to them – remember that they did not have it in print as we have; someone would read out the Letter and they would listen – they might well find it difficult to follow the argument with this frequent use of 'I'. So he proceeds to help them and to clarify his meaning. The statement in verse 17, if you take trouble to understand it, is quite clear, but the Apostle was a very wise and loving teacher. He takes nothing for granted, and he wants to help us; so because of the difficulty of expressing in words this extraordinary, complicated character of man in sin, and especially after he is enlightened by the Law, the Apostle now explains briefly what he means. The qualifying phrase – '(that is to say, in my flesh)' – is introduced to prevent misunderstanding. He is working out the duality he has introduced in verses 16 and 17.

You may well feel for a moment that the Apostle is 'making confusion worse confounded'. But let none be so foolish as to complain about Paul's manner of writing. This subject is difficult because sin is difficult. One of the terrible things sin did when it came into the world was to introduce complications. Life in the Garden of Eden, in Paradise, was very simple until sin came in; but the moment sin entered complications arose. The first sin had to be covered, and they went and hid themselves. Then they began to lie, and so the process has continued ever since. Do not blame the Truth, do not blame God, do not blame the Law, do not blame the Apostle Paul; it is this foul sin that is in us that has produced these complications in man. It is all illustrated here most clearly. Let us take the phrases. 'For I know', he says, 'that in me dwelleth no good thing.' Which 'me' is this? This 'me' obviously is the same 'me' as the one of whom it can be said that 'sin dwelleth in me'. Here he calls it the 'flesh'. That is the same thing. There is a 'me' in whom sin dwells. That, he says, is the 'flesh', and the 'flesh' as we have seen many times before, is man as he is apart from the influence of the Holy Spirit upon him. That is the first 'me': 'For I know that in me'. The 'I' who knows this is again the whole personality. But the 'me' is not the whole personality; the 'me', this first 'me', is only a part of this 'personality', the 'I', who knows this. And what he knows about this 'me' that is in him is, that there is no good thing dwelling in him. Sin dwells in him, yes, but no good dwells in him. There is no good whatsoever in that part of this man's personality. That is the first 'me'.

Then let us go further with the Apostle. He says next, 'for to will is present with me'. Is this the same 'me' as the first? It cannot be. Why not? For the good reason that he has already told us about the first 'me' that there is no good in him at all; but about this 'me' he says that 'to will' is present with him. To will what? To will to keep the Law, to do good, and to please God. So it cannot be the same 'me' as the first one. 'To will is present with me', but there is no good at all in the other 'me'; there is a great deal of good in this 'me'. In other words, this second 'me' is the same as the 'I' in verse 17: 'Now then it is no more I that do it'. This is the 'I' that 'consents to the Law that it is good, that hates that which is wrong, but nevertheless does it, that delights in the Law of God. So we have different uses of 'me' in this verse.

Then Paul says further, ' for to will is present with me, but how to perform that which is good I find not'. Who is this 'I'? Is this 'I' the first 'me' or the second 'me'? The answer is, neither! Well, who is this 'I'? It is the man himself, it is the whole personality. This 'I' at the end of verse 18 is one who is able to speak about the two 'me's' that are in him.

This not only sounds complicated, but it is complicated; it is the complicated condition of a man who is enlightened by the Spirit of God and about the Law of God. This is what he discovers about himself. Have you not done so? Here I am, a personality, an entity, a being. I am myself, the man I am. But I can talk about the 'me' and the 'me' that are in me. There is a 'me' of whom I can say no good. I am personalizing the position, putting in terms of myself the statement made by the Apostle. I am aware within myself of a 'me', an entity as it were that has no good belonging to him at all. But I am also equally aware of another 'me' that desires to do good, that wills it, that consents to the Law of God, that agrees with it and wants to live the godly life.

This 'I', this person that I am, is able to look on at both and is aware of both. This is my predicament, to will is present with me (this second 'me'), but how to perform (in the presence of that first 'me' that is in me) I know not. There I am, I am paralysed and rendered incapable of action; how to perform that which is good (which one 'me' desires and wills) I know not. In other words, to will is present with one 'me', but the ability to perform is not present because of this other 'me'.

Such is the statement made in verse 18. You can test yourself as to where you stand by asking yourself one question. Do you know what the Apostle is talking about? Do you believe that it is true? If you do not I have but one thing to say – you are unregenerate. That can certainly be said. Does this mean, then, that Paul is describing the regenerate? No! that does not follow at all. But leave that for the moment. But it certainly excludes the unregenerate; and it is just there that the Reformed interpretation of this particular paragraph has been so essentially right. It is the failure to understand the character of sin in all men born into this world that accounts for the error of Pelagius and all his followers, and in a sense for the error of all the Arminians. But I admit at the same time that the Reformed interpretation has pressed its argument too far. However, it very rightly stresses that this passage cannot refer to the unregenerate man, because such a man knows nothing about the conflict described here. He has his occasional twinge of conscience, but that is not what is being described here. Here is a man who is aware of the 'me' and the 'me' within him at one and the same time, and there is this paralysis leading to 'How to perform that which is good, I find not'.

Verses 19 and 20 present no new problem because they are but repetitions of what Paul has already said. Verse 19 is practically an exact repetition of verse 15, 'For the good that I would, I do not; but the evil which I would not, that I do'. He repeats it surely for the reason that this subject is so difficult to state that you have to go on repeating it; and as you do so, at last people begin to grasp it. He is just working it out once more. As the result of this confusion within my total personality this is what happens, 'The good that I would, I do not; but the evil which I would not, that I do'. Not only so, he says in effect, But I am going to say again what I have said in verse 17: 'Now then, if I do that I would not, it is no more I that do it, but sin that dwelleth in me'. Here he is identifying himself with the second 'me' of verse 18, and of course one can well understand why he does so. The moment a man understands the spiritual character of the Law, and agrees with it, he says, 'That is where I stand, that is what I maintain'. He is identifying himself with this new understanding and therefore says that 'I' in that sense do not do these things, but, as I have already said, it is 'sin that dwelleth in me' that does them.

What, then, is the Apostle concerned to say in all this? Let me put it in the form of three conclusions. First, he is not disclaiming responsibility for his actions or even excusing himself. That is something that we must never do. But there have been people who have done so, and it has involved them in the most terrible and 'damnable heresies'. To what has it led? It has led to Antinomianism which has made them say, 'Ah, it is not I who am sinning, it is my flesh that is sinning; I am not responsible, I do not want to sin, therefore it is not I who am doing these things'. They use the language of the Apostle but in a very different way from the Apostle. They do it to excuse sin; they go on sinning and say that it does not matter what a man does. There was a teaching called 'Dualism' in the early Church, which said that sin belonged only to the body. It claimed that that was apostolic teaching; that the man himself was saved, it was only his body that was sinning, and as the body was going to die in any case, it did not really matter whether he sinned or not. 'I do not sin', they said, 'it is my body that is sinning'. They were even saying that our Lord's body was not a real body, for much the same reason. There is no more terrible and dangerous heresy. The early Church abominated it. There can be little doubt but that the Apostle John wrote his First Epistle very largely in order to counter that heresy. There is an old tradition that John was going into a public bath on one occasion but that when he heard that one of the teachers of this foul heresy was using the same bath-house he would not even enter the building. There is no more terrible perversion of the Christian teaching than this kind of thing. The Apostle Paul is not excusing the man he describes here, he is not disclaiming responsibility for himself; what he is doing is to make a confession. He is virtually saying: 'That is the truth about me, that is the weakness in which I find myself, that is the paralysis that I am aware of; that is my useless struggle.' He does not say, 'All is well, and it does not matter what I do'. No, he wants to get out of this condition, as he will tell us later when he says, 'O wretched man that I am! who shall deliver me?' It is the exact opposite of the foul teaching of Dualism, and the dangerous trap of Antinomianism.

Secondly, we conclude that what the Apostle is concerned to do here is to show the terrible power of sin. In other words, as I have indicated throughout, this section of chapter 7 is a commentary on verse 13. 'Was then that which is good made death unto me? God forbid! But sin, that it might appear sin, working death in me by that which is good; that sin by the commandment might become exceeding sinful.' Paul is showing us what a terribly foul thing is sin. It is in us, it is resident, it 'dwells' in us, and it has this awful power that paralyses us even when we have come to see the true nature of the Law and therefore the true nature of sin.

Our third and last conclusion is that Paul is showing us again the complete inability of the Law to deliver us even when we see clearly its spiritual character, that it is of God, that it is holy, and just, and good. Though we may see that with all clarity, it completely fails to deliver us. In other words, in all this complicated piece of psychology and self-analysis at its most brilliant, the Apostle is really not concerned about himself and his own experience as such. He is not even concerned about this bit of psychological analysis. What he is concerned to show is that the Law can never deliver us. Our only hope, as he has already said in verse 4 is, 'Wherefore, my brethren, ye also have become dead to the law by the body of Christ, that (in order that) you should be married to another, even to him who is raised from the dead, that we should bring forth fruit unto God'. While I am married to the Law, even though I see its spiritual character, I can never bring forth fruit. 'How to perform that which is good, I find not.' That is what Paul is emphasizing. It supplies the most overwhelming demonstration of the truth that even the 'holy', 'just', 'good' Law of God cannot deliver man from the thraldom and the tyranny of sin.

It is a wonderful statement. Whatever you and I may make of it in detail, Paul never forgot what he was setting out to do. He was not setting out just to talk about himself; but to demonstrate that he revered the Law of God. But though it is so essentially and altogether good it could not deliver man from sin, it was never given in order to do so. It was given that men might come to see 'the exceeding sinfulness of sin', and be led by it as a sort of pedagogue, a schoolmaster, to Christ. It was never meant to be an end, but a means to an end. Paul is showing what 'the Law could not do in that it was weak through the flesh'.

All along in his deductions, in his explanations, he keeps on reminding us that that is what he is concerned about. He is dealing the whole time with the Law, and all he says about this 'man' is simply to illustrate the truth about the Law, and how it is rendered null by the flesh, by 'the sin that dwelleth in me'.

Seventeen

*

I find then a law, that, when I would do good, evil is present with me.
For I delight in the law of God after the inward man:
But I see another law in my members, warring against the law of my mind, and bringing me into captivity to the law of sin which is in my members.   Romans 7: 21-23

Thus the Apostle continues the great argument of this section of the Epistle. He goes on from point to point, from step to step. He makes a statement and then proves it; then he takes up another and again demonstrates and proves it. All is focused, of course, on the place of the Law in the life of the Christian. That is his main concern. He is concerned to exonerate himself from various charges that were brought against him; but he is much more concerned to show the truth about the Law, to show what the Law was meant to do, and to show particularly what the Law was never meant to do, and what it most certainly cannot do. His point is, that in showing all this, he is not in any way derogating from the greatness of the Law.

We come then to this statement in verse 21, 'I find a law, that when I would do good, evil is present with me'. Obviously in this statement he is in a sense summing up what he has just been saying. The word 'then' tells us so. 'Very well', he seems to say, 'this is what I find, this is what I have discovered.' At the same time he is repeating one of the general statements he has already made, as found, for instance, in verses 14 and 15: 'For I know that the law is spiritual; but I am carnal, sold under sin.' But it is not just a repetition. The Apostle never merely repeats what he has been saying. He does re-emphasize, but generally you will find that there is a shade of difference, as is the case here. What he was concerned to show in the previous three verses, 18, 19 and 20, as we have seen, was why it is that he performs evil acts though he does not want to do so. In these verses 21–23, however, he shows why he fails to do what he wants to do. There are two things that are wrong about this man; he does what he does not want to do, and also fails to do what he wants to do. That is the dual aspect of his problem. In the previous verses he was mainly concerned with showing why it was that he does the evil that he would not do, and comes to the conclusion that it is no more he that is doing it, but sin that dwells in him.

The Apostle now takes up the other side. Why is it that he cannot do what he really wants to do? He begins: 'I find then a law'. Actually what he wrote was 'I find the law'. 'The' law, not 'a' law. What does he mean here by 'the law'? He has been talking about the Law of God before as we know. He says, 'We know that the law is spiritual; but I am carnal, sold under sin. If then I do that I would not, I consent unto the law that it is good.' Is he here talking about that same Law? Clearly he is not doing so. This is not a matter of opinion, but something that really can be proved. In verse 22 he says, 'For I delight in the law of God after the inward man'. Why does he call it there 'the law of God'? So far he has been referring to it as 'the law', and not as 'the law of God', because hitherto he has only been dealing with 'the law of God'. But here in verse 21 he is talking about another kind of law, some other law. So when he comes back to the Law of God he has to make it clear that that is what he is talking about. Therefore he says, 'For I delight in the law of God after the inward man' (v. 22). That is his way of telling us that in verse 21 he was not talking about the Law of God. This is a very important point for us to remember, because we shall find that he again uses this term 'law' in still another sense. But there should be no trouble about it if we only pay careful attention to the way in which the Apostle writes. The reference here then is not to 'the Law of God', neither is he referring to 'the law of sin' that dwells in him. I refer to the latter simply because Robert Haldane, in what is to me an inexplicable manner, says that that is what this word 'law' means here, that he finds the law of sin within himself which so works that 'when he would do good, evil is present with him'. I maintain that Paul is not saying that. He says that later; but he does not say it here.

What, then, is he saying here? He says in effect, 'This is my experience. There seems to be a principle working in me, indeed it is so constant that I can call it a veritable law. There seems to be a rule of action within me which works in such a definite manner that it is virtually a kind of law; and it seems to determine, to govern and to control what takes place within me. 'I find the law'. Or, we can look at the matter in the following way. Paul virtually says: 'What I find is this, that invariably when I would do good, evil is present with me. This is something which seems to operate in me much as laws operate in nature – as the night follows the day, as you get spring, summer, autumn, winter with such regularity. I find that, as certainly as I want to do good, equally certainly is evil there'. That is a law of the man's life and experience. It is so regular, so certain, he says, that it seems to be an absolute law.

Notice how he expresses the matter – 'evil', he says, 'is present with me'. That means 'always at hand', 'always lying near'. 'Whenever I will to do good, evil is always there, always asserting itself, jumping forward. The moment I act with this mind of mine, evil jumps in, persistent in its opposition, never absent. The moment I will to do good, evil is there.' I thus paraphrase what he is saying.

Verses 22 and 23 are simply an exposition of this theme. Just as we found that verses 18, 19 and 20 were an exposition of verse 17, so verses 22 and 23 are an exposition of verse 21. That is the Apostle's typical and characteristic method. One cannot imagine a better one. Proposition, then proof; and on he goes, advancing the whole argument.

Let us see what he has to say. 'For', he says – letting us know that he is going to explain what he has been saying; 'For' – this is what it comes to in practice – 'I delight in the law of God after the inward man'. Here is a very significant statement again. Take first of all the word 'delight'. Notice that there is a progression in the statements here made about the Law. Paul began in verse 14 by saying, 'We know that the law is spiritual'. In verse 16, 'I consent unto the law that it is good'. But now he goes beyond that, and says 'I delight in it'. He means by that, not merely that he 'agrees' with the Law, or that the Law is itself spiritual and good and carries his consent and his approbation. He speaks more strongly, and says, 'I rejoice, I exult in the law of God'.

It is a very strong statement. He undoubtedly had in mind here what the Psalmist tells us in the First Psalm about the good man whose 'delight is in the law of the Lord', 'the law of God'.

Then we come to a most important term, 'the inward man'. This expression plays a very great part in the discussion of the exact interpretation of this passage. Those who hold the traditional Reformed view have to lean very heavily upon it in their endeavour to prove that this is the regenerate man even at his very best. So they say that the 'inward man' means the new man, the new nature that is in this person. But it does not follow of necessity that this is a reference to the 'new man' that is in the believer, for it seems to me that the Apostle himself tells us what he means by the 'inward man' in the next verse. The verses read: 'For I delight in the law of God after the inward man: but I see another law in my members warring against the law of my mind'. The second part of the statement supplies an explanation of what is meant by the 'inward man' in the first part. The 'inward man' is surely synonymous with 'the mind'. 'I delight in the law of God after the inward man', 'the law of my mind' – 'the law that is in my mind'. Surely these are parallel statements. So the inward man, I deduce, is the mind, the understanding, the place of reason, the place where one is able to grasp truth. It does not mean the mind in the natural man, because, we have seen so constantly, and as we shall see here, this cannot be a description of the unregenerate man. It means a mind illuminated by the Holy Spirit. But I cannot see that we are entitled to claim more for this term than just that. The matter will become clearer when we see how Paul contrasts the 'inward man' with his 'members'.

What do the 'members' represent? We have already discussed that several times in chapter 6. The word 'members' stands for 'the bodily organs', that part of man through which he normally expresses himself and functions in his general life in this world. So the contrast is obvious. The parts of us with which we normally sin are the parts that we can see, the eye and various other parts, normally termed the organs of the body. That is the outward man. But the 'inward man' is the part of man that you cannot see. You cannot see a man thinking, you cannot see a man's mind. It is possible to see his brain but you cannot see his mind. That is why Paul calls it the 'inward man' as distinct from this outward man that is visible. The 'inward man' is described as the 'hidden man of the heart'; it is that part of man which is not visible. It includes the soul, of course. You cannot see the soul. This is as real, indeed much more real, than the things you can see; it goes on when the body is rotting in the grave. I say the 'inward man' stands for that invisible part of man, the most vital part of man – soul, spirit and so on – and including the 'mind', which is often used interchangeably with 'spirit'. Take, for instance, the way the Apostle puts the matter in 2 Corinthians 4: 16. He says, 'Though our outward man perish'. Here he is referring to his body. He suffered much from sickness and illness, he suffered from weariness of the body, his 'outward man' was decaying and dissolving. 'Though our outward man perish, yet the inward man is renewed day by day.' It is the same emphatic general contrast. It seems to me, therefore, that we have no right to press this term, the 'inward man', beyond this general reference to that part of man that can be illuminated by the Spirit; we must think in terms of the mind, the understanding, that part of man which eventually comes to see the truth as it is in Christ Jesus fully. We may take it, therefore, that Paul is here referring to the 'mind', as he calls it here in verse 23, as illuminated by the Spirit. In other words, what he is saying in effect is: 'I have now come to see the true meaning of the Law.' He has been saying that repeatedly since the 7th verse. There was a time when he was not illuminated, but now he has come to see the truth. The Holy Spirit has come upon him, the Law has 'come' and he has seen it – 'sin revived, and I died'. He sees that the Law is spiritual, that it is just, and right, and good, that it is holy; he even 'rejoices in it'.

So we pause once more and look at his statement. 'I delight in the law of God after the inward man'. This is an important statement for this reason, that, once again, it excludes definitely any idea that this refers to the unregenerate man. That is why I emphasize the word 'delight'. The unregenerate man is excluded for the reason that Paul gives us in the next chapter (verses 6 and 7): 'For to be carnally-minded is death, but to be spiritually minded is life and peace. Because the carnal mind is enmity against God, for it is not subject to the law of God, neither indeed can be.' Such is the unregenerate man. 'So then they that are in the flesh cannot please God.' No unregenerate man has ever said, or ever can say, that he *delights* in the law of God after the inward man'. So much for the idea that the unregenerate person is here described.

We have now reached this point. The Apostle finds that his daily constant experience is that the moment he wills to do good this other principle or 'law' is there, suggesting, arguing. The fact is, he says, 'I delight in the law of God after my mind, my understanding, what I really regard as myself (not my organs, not my body, not my flesh as it were, but this higher part of me); I delight in the law of God.' Why then does he not carry out the Law of God and live it and practise it? His answer is: 'I see another law in my members'. Here, again, we have a verse of crucial importance, as I remarked previously about verse 14. When we were dealing with verse 14, I emphasized that it seems to me to control its entire context. I say the same about this verse; so let us look at it very carefully. Paul says 'I find another law'. Now 'another' does not mean another in a numerical sense, as if he meant, 'I have already found one law in my mind but now I find a second'. No! What he means is a 'different law', not merely additional, but essentially different. He contrasts it with the law that is in his mind. There is a law in his 'mind', and there is a law in his 'members'. Obviously this latter is not 'the law of God', obviously it is not the law that operates in his mind now that he has come to see the real meaning of God's Law. No, this is yet another law. What he means is, that there is a permanent and controlling power and principle in his members that acts as a veritable law. It is not something that is there occasionally, and at other times absent; it is always there, it is a law, always present and always operating. That is why he calls it 'a law in his members'.

'Members' carries the same meaning, as we have seen, as 'members' in the whole of chapter 6. It is that which he contrasts with the mind. This is the way he looks at man at this point. There is in man his mind; and there is the rest of him – his bodily organs and appetites, and all the rest. Now there is a 'law' in the mind; and there is a 'law' in this other part also. What does this other law do? He tells us very plainly; in the first place it 'wars' against the law of his mind. This word 'warring' is a very interesting one. 'I find another law in my members, warring against . . .'. Its original meaning is 'to render service in a military campaign'.

It devives from the Greek word from which our word 'strategy' comes, and that is a very good way of looking at it. Here then is this man, with his mind delighting in the Law of God; but there is another law operating in his members which has a fiendish, devilish strategy. It is always watching the moves of the other law in his mind, and it is countering every move. It has a definite strategy and wages a kind of military campaign. What Paul means is, that as certainly as he delights in the Law of God with his mind, and wants to do it, then this other law that is in his members begins to urge the opposite, and puts its opposition in an attractive form, and strives to dictate to him what he should do. He wants with the mind to serve the Law of God; but this other power brings out all its forces and reserves to prevent his doing so, and to make him do the exact opposite. That is what the Apostle emphasizes here. In this same verse he later calls it 'the law of sin'. The 'law in his members' and 'the law of sin' are identical.

Such then, is the picture. The first thing this 'law in his members' does is to wage this war against the spiritual view of the Law, and his desire to keep it because he now delights in it. But unfortunately it does not stop at that. That would be bad enough, but it goes a stage further. It is not merely that the 'law in the members' is warring against the 'law of the mind', but Paul adds, 'it brings me into captivity to the law of sin which is in my members'.

The crucial statement is, 'brings me into captivity'. All commentators agreed that 'captivity' is a very strong word, and that it means, 'making and taking prisoner'. The original meaning of this word takes us back to a 'spear', so the picture is this. Here are two men who have been fighting. One beats the other, and the conqueror now points his spear at the body of the man he has conquered. He has taken him prisoner. But he has not merely taken him prisoner, he has his spear pointed at him, and he says, 'If you try to get away I shall push this spear through you. You are to walk from here to that door, go along.' And he follows him with the spear pointing at him. The defeated man is a complete captive, he is conquered, and he is absolutely helpless at the point of the spear. That is the kind of thing, says Paul, that I find. I see this other law in my members warring against the law of my mind, and bringing me into captivity – into a position in which I am a hopeless prisoner at the point of the spear.

My captor has 'got' me. Such is the meaning of the word 'captivity'.

Notice that Paul says, 'bringing *me* into captivity'. We are not looking now at either of the 'me's' we were considering earlier in verse 18; we are now looking at the man himself, the 'I'. This is the total personality. Paul is not merely saying that this 'law in the members' brings the sinful part of him into captivity, though some of the expositors tell us so. But the moment they do so, they are falling into the dangerous heresy of Dualism, in which they are saying, 'It is not I who am in captivity, it is only my sinful part; it is only my body, or something else within me'. That is a wrong division of man which says 'I am not sinning; it is only my body, or the sinful part of me, or the flesh. The law of sin in my members is sinning.' But the Apostle is not saying that at all. He says it brings *me*, my total personality, into captivity. 'I' am brought 'into captivity to the law of sin that is in my members'.

What then is the real meaning and purpose of this statement which, I repeat, is such a crucial one? Let us be clear first of all as to what Paul is not saying. Marcus Rainsford, a great commentator and godly preacher of the end of last century, says that the Apostle is 'referring to the fact of the presence, power and *tendency* of indwelling sin as warring against the law of his mind', and to nothing more. He italicizes the word 'tendency', and says that Paul is stating in very graphic language that there is this tendency for that part of him to 'war against the law that is in my mind'. To which I reply that Paul is saying no such thing. Paul is not merely describing a warfare. He does so at the beginning of the verse, but he says that the warfare leads to defeat, to captivity. He has himself been taken captive. He is not talking about a tendency to sin, he is talking about a captivity to sin.

But take also the exposition of Robert Haldane. Haldane was clearly in trouble here. He says, 'How far this captivity extends cannot be known from the figure'. I agree with him so far, but I regard it as significant that he should have had to make that comment. He says, 'If the evil principle of our nature prevails in exciting one evil thought, it has taken us captive. So far it has conquered, and so far we are defeated and made prisoners.' Then he goes on to say, 'But this is quite consistent with the supposition that, on the whole, we may have the victory over sin'. So what Paul is saying here is this: 'If you commit one sin you have been taken prisoner and made captive by sin, but on the whole you still have the victory over sin.' But listen to Paul again, 'I see another law in my members, warring against the law of my mind, and bringing me into captivity to the law of sin'. How can that possibly mean 'that on the whole we may have the victory over sin?' Surely that is the exact opposite of what Paul is saying. He is most certainly not saying that on the whole we may have the victory over sin, but that on the whole sin is having a victory over us! The Apostle, of course, is not saying that this man never has success – certainly not! There is no need for him to say that; but the Apostle is saying that, looking at his life on the whole, this is what this man 'finds', this is the law of his being, this is the regular state of his experience.

Marcus Rainsford refers to 2 Corinthians 10: 3–5; and he does so rightly because this word 'captivity' is also used there, where we read: 'For though we walk in the flesh, we do not war after the flesh: for the weapons of our warfare are not carnal, but mighty through God to the pulling down of strongholds: Casting down imaginations, and every high thing that exalteth itself against the knowledge of God, and bringing into *captivity* every thought to the obedience of Christ.' What is Marcus Rainsford's comment on that? 'Here', he says, 'in 2 Corinthians 10: 3–5 it is manifestly the aim and tendency of the warfare, not its invariable success, to which he alludes' – and he is right. Paul is not telling the Corinthians that every thought is always and invariably brought into captivity to the obedience of Christ. He could not say that, otherwise he would be sinless and perfect. But he is saying, as Marcus Rainsford points out, 'This is the tendency, this is my prevailing position now. Though I am in the flesh, I do not war after the flesh. No, I am warring after the Spirit, and this is the truth about me now, speaking generally, that I bring every thought into captivity to the obedience of Christ.' He may fail occasionally, but speaking generally, this is the tendency. But Marcus Rainsford seems to forget that if you say that so strongly about 2 Corinthians 10: 3–5, you must say the same about Romans 7: 23, and say that this man's general condition was one of defeat and captivity. In other words it is 'the general tendency' in both cases. Paul is saying that this is the general habit of this man's life, this is the law of his existence at that time. But that is the exact opposite of what Dr Marcus Rainsford says about Romans 7: 23. What the Apostle is asserting is that not merely is there a fight going on within the man (that is the first part of verse 23), he tells us about the result of the fight, the outcome of the fight. And the outcome of the fight is, as I am emphasizing, that he finds himself in captivity, he fails completely. The law that is in his members is too strong for the other law. 'I find then a law, that when I would do good, evil is present with me. Though I delight in this law of God after the inward man, this other law keeps on coming in and brings me into captivity to the law of sin which is in my members.'

Proof of the correctness of this exposition is found in verse 24. If Paul is saying here that on the whole this man is able to live the Christian life, and that on the whole he has victory over sin, why, in the name of all reason, does he go on to cry out in anguish, 'O wretched men that I am!'? That would be meaningless, senseless! His cry, 'O wretched man that I am!' is caused by the persistence of defeat, the feeling that he is down rather than up, that he meets with failure rather than success, that he is in captivity to sin. I cannot see how any other exposition of verse 23 can possibly lead us to verse 24. If, in verse 23, he is merely describing the fact that there is a conflict in the life of the believer, that would not lead to the cry 'O wretched man!' There is nothing that leads to that cry except defeat, failure. 'Wretched' is a cry of anguish and of hopelessness; there is a tinge of despair in it. The very word suggests this. All the Lexicons say so. 'Wretched' means 'exhausted as the result of hard labour'. Paul has been striving until he is weary and tired out and wailing; and so he cries out 'O wretched man that I am!' And then he cries out, 'Who shall deliver me?'

In a most amazing way, again, Robert Haldane says at this point that this 'shall' refers entirely to the future. He writes, 'At death Paul was to be entirely freed from the evil of his nature. The consolation of the Christian against the corruption of his nature is, that although he shall not get free from it in this world, he shall hereafter be entirely delivered.' In Haldane's view this is the Christian at his best. He knows that he will never be delivered while he is in this life and in this world; but he knows that at the end, in death, Christ will finally deliver him out of the body and its thraldom, and he will have a glorified body. 'Shall', he says, is entirely future. Such is the position in which you inevitably find yourself if you have started in the wrong way in your interpretation of this passage. This, surely, is not a reference to some remote distant future? Here is a man in anguish, in failure and exhaustion, who cries out, 'Who shall deliver me?' 'Who can deliver me?' He is not a man who is expressing a hope as to what is going to happen at death, he is crying out in despair for deliverance now.

The next expression to consider is, 'the body of death'. We need not linger over this. It is the same as 'the law of sin in my members', of which Paul has just been speaking. At the end of verse 23 he says, 'This is the trouble, that this other law in my members is bringing me into captivity to the law of sin that is in my members'. Then, 'Who shall deliver me from this law of sin that is in my members?', which he now calls 'this body of sin', 'this body of death'. He wants deliverance from this part of himself that is opposed to the 'inner man', to 'the law of the mind'. *He* wants to be delivered. In order to bring out the meaning I refer to Marcus Rainsford again, in order to bring out the positive exposition. He says 'that Paul was really saying "O wretched man that I am!" to have anything in me contrary to my God, contrary to His Christ, contrary to His Cross, contrary to His Spirit, contrary to His will'. In Rainsford's view, we see here the fully regenerate man, who finds intolerable the thought that there is in him anything contrary to God, and to all that pertains to God. To which my reply is this: Does a man who knows Christ as Saviour, who knows the glory of the Cross, and who knows about the Spirit, simply cry out saying 'Who shall deliver me?' Does he use this indefinite term 'Who'? No, the man of whom Paul is speaking is a man who does not yet know who can deliver him. All he knows is that he cannot deliver himself. His knowledge of the Law cannot help him; he 'delights' in it, but still it is of no value because this other 'law' is too strong for him. So he says, 'Who can? I cannot'. The man who knows Christ as Saviour, and the work and power of the Holy Spirit as a reality, can never cry out vaguely and indefinitely and desperately, 'Who can?' But this man asks and cries 'Who can?' He is in trouble, he is in a desperate plight. All these statements go together, and hang together, and each one comes out of the other. This man is wretched, conscious of complete failure, aware that there is this other power in his members that he cannot master but which is mastering him, and always taking him into captivity. He is a complete failure and hopeless, so he cries out in his anguish, 'O wretched man that I am! who shall deliver me?' He is not bemoaning the fact that there is still something in him 'contrary to his God, his Christ, the Cross, the Spirit'. On that other exposition all this has to be imported; but it is not present. It is present in the next chapter in great profusion, but not here. And yet we are concerned about the man who is described here, the man who is in a position in which he can simply cry out, 'Who shall, can, will deliver me?' There he is! What astounds me is that these great men, because of the controlling theory with which they began, could allow themselves to resort to these twists and turnings of exposition.

We still have to glance at the remaining statements; and then we shall gather up all this evidence we have been accumulating, and try to collate it all, and put it all together, and see the composite picture of the man that is depicted here by the Apostle. We have seen one thing very clearly, and that is, that here we are not looking at an unregenerate man. We have seen something else equally clearly; that it is the picture of a man who has come to see the spiritual nature and character of the Law.

Eighteen

*

I thank God through Jesus Christ our Lord. So then with the mind I myself serve the law of God, but with the flesh the law of sin.   Romans 7: 25

Here, we come to the last verse, the last statement in this most extraordinary complex statement. It is divided into two sections. The first statement is, 'I thank God through Jesus Christ our Lord'. I have described that earlier as a kind of ejaculation. The Apostle is suddenly carried away by what Charles Hodge describes so rightly as 'a strong and sudden emotion of gratitude'. We have had many occasions to observe and to emphasize the fact that the great Apostle was not over-punctilious in the matter of style. He was free and enjoyed the freedom of the Spirit. He was not a mere writer, not a mere literary man, not concerned, primarily, to produce some masterpiece of literature. He was much more concerned about what he said than the way in which he said it. The Apostle never cultivated 'art for art's sake', never attempted eloquence for the sake of eloquence. He shows this in these anacolutha, so called, these interruptions which frequently take the form of his bursting forth into praise and thanksgiving. He finds it difficult always, one gathers, to mention the Name of our Lord without uttering some kind of apostrophe. He interrupts what he is saying for the moment as he is carried away by the strength and the depth of his deep emotions. And here, it seems to me, that is what is happening. It occurred in this way. He had been saying, 'I delight in the law of God after the inward man; but I see another law in my members, warring against the law of my mind, and bringing me into captivity to the law of sin which is in my members. O wretched man that I am! who shall deliver me from the body of this death?' At that point he could not restrain himself so he cries out, 'I thank God through Jesus

Christ our Lord'. It is a sudden outburst, an ejaculation, and not an essential part of what he is arguing and saying.

We can prove that quite simply by looking at the rest of the verse where he goes on to say, 'So then with the mind I myself serve the law of God; but with the flesh the law of sin'. It proves my contention in this way, that if the expression 'I thank God through Jesus Christ our Lord' is an essential part of the argument it would mean that he is saying, 'I thank God through Jesus Christ our Lord for the fact that I myself with my mind serve the law of God, but with the flesh the law of sin'. Now that is something, surely, that the Apostle could never say. Charles Hodge is so right at this point. He says that that would be an 'unnatural combination' of statements. But this is actually a very striking under-statement on the part of Hodge. It would not only be an 'unnatural combination', it would be an impossible combination; because if you take them as being directly connected in that way it must mean that he thanks God in the Name of Jesus Christ for the fact that he is still in the condition he describes in the remainder of the verse. Surely that is quite impossible! The only commentator, as far as I am aware, who attempts to say that that is the order is Robert Haldane. He is quite consistent with himself right through. As I have suggested previously, he really went wrong in the 2nd verse of chapter 6 and has had to struggle to maintain consistency from that point. As we have already seen, he interprets 'Who shall deliver me?' in verse 24, as referring entirely to the future. So he says that the Apostle is saying, 'I thank God through Jesus Christ our Lord that I shall be delivered' – not in this world but in the next. While still in this world his position is, 'So then with the mind I myself serve the law of God; but with the flesh the law of sin'. But it seems to me that that is an impossible interpretation of these statements. The 'So then' in the second statement is a perfect summing up of what the Apostle has been saying from verse 14 to verse 24; a terse and concise statement about this duality. This, then, he says, is what it amounts to, 'With the mind I myself serve the law of God, but with the flesh the law of sin'.

There is only one difficulty, not a vital one, but more or less mechanical, in the interpretation here; it relates to the expression, 'I myself'. He is undoubtedly referring to himself, the person; but does the 'I myself' govern both the statements, the two parts of the one general statement? In other words, is he saying, 'So then with the mind I myself serve the law of God, but with the flesh I myself serve the law of sin?' It seems to me that, in the light of verse 23, we must so read the sentence. We cannot be certain about it. It could equally well be said that he is identifying himself, as he wants to do, with 'the mind', and that 'the mind' is the real 'I' now; as if it read: 'My real desire and will is to identify myself with the mind, but I find this other law in my members and so I have to admit that I serve the law of sin also.' In other words he is not disclaiming responsibility, as we saw before. It is he who sins and not only his flesh. Of course, he has told us, 'It is not I, but sin that dwelleth in me', but we have seen the explanation of that statement. He as a person is responsible for everything he does, but he is aware of these two 'me's' within him as we saw in verse 18. Notice that the word he uses is the word 'serve'. It means 'slave', 'to be a slave to' or 'a slave of', as we saw repeatedly in chapter 6. So he is saying, 'With the mind I myself am a slave to, or slave it to, the law of God'. He cannot say that he is only the slave of 'the law of God', for he finds also that he is a slave to 'the law of sin' because of his flesh. That is his trouble; that is the thing he has been telling us so frequently.

A question arises at this point which we shall have to consider when we come to our summing up – Is it possible for the fully regenerate man to make the statement of verse 25 in the light of chapter 6, verse 17, where he says, 'But God be thanked that ye were the slaves of sin, but ye have obeyed from the heart that form of doctrine to which you were delivered'? There he asserts very strongly that Christians are no longer slaves to sin. Indeed he goes on in the next verse to say, 'Being then made free from sin, ye became the slaves of righteousness'. We shall consider the matter later in greater detail.

We have now reached the end of our detailed verse-by-verse consideration of this most interesting and difficult passage which starts at verse 14. Let us now look at it again as a whole. First, let us try to have clearly in our minds the Apostle's main purpose. Leaving out the detail, what is his big statement concerning the man who is in view – whoever or whatever he may be – from verse 14 to the end of the chapter? We have seen very clearly that he is a man who is conscious of a duality within himself. The Apostle tells us so many times over. He is a man who has come to see that the Law of God is both spiritual and good; indeed he delights in it. But – and here is the problem – he cannot conform to it either positively or negatively. He desires to do the things it commands, but he finds that he cannot do so. He does not want to do the things it prohibits, but he finds that he does them. He sees clearly the character of the Law but he cannot keep it, the reason being that 'the law of sin' which is in his members is too strong for him.

The Apostle has stated all this quite clearly in the following verses: in verse 17, 'It is no more I that do it, but sin that dwelleth in me'. This power of sin within him is stronger than himself, so much so that he can make this kind of statement. In verse 20 again, 'Now if I do that I would not, it is no more I that do it, but sin that dwelleth in me'. Sin is too strong for him, it defeats him. But it is still more explicit in verse 23, 'I see another law in my members, warring against the law of my mind, and bringing me into captivity to the law of sin which is in my members'. Now these statements have only one meaning. The 'law of sin' which is in his members, that is to say, indwelling sin, is too strong for him, and brings him into a state of captivity. The final proof of that is the cry in verse 24. He is 'a wretched man', and he breaks out into the cry, 'Who shall deliver me from the body of this death?' And, finally, he sums it all up in the second part of verse 25, 'So then with the mind I myself serve the law of God, but with the flesh the law of sin'. There is only one conclusion that he can come to about himself; it is the confession he made at the beginning of the whole section – 'I am carnal; sold under sin'. In other words, the business of verses 15–25 is to expound that statement. As so often with this Apostle – and with many another New Testament and even Old Testament writer – he starts with his conclusion and then proves it and demonstrates it. He has told us at the beginning 'I am carnal; sold under sin'. That is the only conclusion at which this man can arrive about himself. Not only is there this duality within him, but he is made captive by the law of sin which is in his members. It is stronger than he is, it is defeating him, and he cries out, 'O wretched man that I am! who shall deliver me from the body of this death?' That is the essential statement, the vital statement, which is made in this most fascinating paragraph.

Are we now in a position to decide, to arrive at a verdict, as to the identity of the person whom the Apostle is describing? One thing we can say without difficulty or hesitation – we have said it often in working through the individual verses – this cannot possibly be the unregenerate man. The man's positive statements about his delighting in the Law, the loving of the Law, the appreciation of the spiritual character of the Law, make such an identification impossible. You cannot reconcile this passage, if that is the case, with verses 7–13, where Paul tells us that in the past when unregenerate he did not understand the Law, its meaning and purpose. That was his trouble in the old life; he was 'alive apart from the law once'; he thought all was well because he had not seen the real character of the Law. When the commandment 'came . . .' Ah yes! the man whom he describes here is a man to whom the commandment has 'come'; that is why he sees that it is spiritual and good; and that is why he delights in it. Not only so, but we have seen that the unregenerate man is incapable of recognizing this duality in himself and of conceiving of himself in the spiritual, psychological manner which we have seen to be characteristic of this particular section. We need spend no time, therefore, in considering the possibility that the Apostle, here, is describing an unregenerate man.

So we are left with the question, Is this, then, a description of the fully regenerate man? Is it true to say that the Apostle Paul was writing here about himself, and particularly about himself as he was at the time when he wrote the Epistle to the Romans? I mentioned previously the argument about the use of the present tense. Is it right to say that the regenerate man is always as here described, that he never rises at all above what is here described, and that it is indeed the Apostle Paul writing about himself at the height of his experience as an Apostle of our Lord and Saviour Jesus Christ? What of that exposition? It is a very good rule when you are dealing with a difficult passage of Scripture such as this not to be too anxious to arrive at a decision solely and exclusively on the evidence that is before you. Whenever you meet with such a passage, the first thing you should ask yourself is, Are there similar passages elsewhere in the Scripture? Can I find any light on this problem that is confronting me by referring to other parts of Scripture – other parts of Scripture written by this same Apostle, or parts of Scripture by other writers? There is no better rule than to compare Scripture with Scripture when you have a difficult passage to interpret. Heresies have arisen in the Church because people have founded a whole doctrine on one verse, or one section, and have omitted to consult other sections of Scripture which deal with the same point. Let us observe the rule ourselves.

Our next step, therefore, is this. There are certain passages of Scripture which, it is argued, say exactly the same thing as the Apostle is saying here in the 7th chapter of Romans. If that is so, it is a very important argument, because those who are not prepared to say that the Apostle is describing himself here, maintain that this is a unique statement without any parallel elsewhere in the Scripture. So let us look at some of the passages to which reference is made. They can be readily divided into two groups. There are passages which seem to be describing the same kind of struggle as is described by the Apostle in this 7th chapter of Romans. There is, for instance, the statement in the Epistle to the Galatians in chapter 5, verse 17, 'For the flesh lusteth against the Spirit, and the Spirit against the flesh; and these are contrary the one to the other; so that ye cannot do the things that ye would'. Let us admit at once that, at first sight, one is tempted to say 'That is the very thing the Apostle has been saying here in Romans 7'. There are these two sides, the 'flesh lusting against the Spirit', and 'the Spirit against the flesh, and these are contrary the one to the other'. Surely this is the same as saying that the mind on the one hand, and the law in the members on the other, are contrary the one to the other, with the result that you cannot do the things that you would. At first sight it seems to be an exact parallel, but the moment you examine it, and especially when you read the context, you will find that the two statements are indeed almost entirely different. Notice, for instance, that the Apostle introduces the statement in Galatians 5 : 17 by saying, in verse 16, 'This I say then, Walk in the Spirit, and ye shall not fulfil the lust of the flesh'. In a sense there is no need for us to go any further. The Apostle lays down a fundamental proposition: 'If you walk in the Spirit' (and I am commanding you to do so) you shall not fulfil the lust of the flesh'. But what we are told in Romans 7 is, that in spite of every resolution to keep the Law of God, the man remains captive to 'the law of sin which is in his members'. And again, notice that there is a factor in the passage in Galatians which is not present at all in Romans 7. It is the reference to the Holy Spirit. The Holy Spirit is not mentioned in Romans 7. The whole point of the passage in Galatians 5 is to emphasize the Spirit and His work. 'This I say then, Walk *in the Spirit* and you shall not fulfil the lust of the flesh.' The Apostle's object in Galatians 5 is to show the way of victory, and not only to show it, but to guarantee it because of this other factor – the Holy Spirit who is within us. But that is not mentioned in Romans 7. But there is also another point of difference. In verse 18 of Galatians 5 there is what at first sight seems a strange statement, 'But if you be led of the Spirit, you are not under the law'. This verse is an exact parallel with what the Apostle says in Romans 6: 14, which, as I have been emphasizing throughout, is as it were the key to the whole of Romans 7. Romans 7 is in a sense an exposition of Romans 6: 14 which says, 'Sin shall not have dominion over you', and for this reason, that 'you are not under the law, but under grace'. Paul is saying the same thing in Galatians 5: 18, though in a different way. He is showing, not only the possibility of victory, but the certainty of victory to those who realize this truth about themselves in Christ, and in 'the Spirit'. Then, to add still further proof, there is the statement in Galatians 5: 24, 'And they that are Christ's have crucified the flesh with the affections and lusts'. There is not a word about that in Romans 7 – not a word! But in Galatians he says that that is true of all Christians. Because they are Christ's they have done this; it has happened, they have crucified the flesh with the affections and lusts. The whole trouble with the man in Romans 7 is that he cannot do this. His problem is that the flesh is too much for him, and that he is being held captive all along to 'the law of sin which is in his members'.

We are entitled then to draw this conclusion, that Galatians 5, far from saying the same as Romans 7, not only says the exact opposite, but was designed to say the exact opposite. Romans 7 is concerned to show the state of failure of this man, who is trying, as it were, to sanctify himself by the Law. The whole point of Galatians 5 is to show us positively the success and the victory that attend the man who is sanctifying himself, and dealing with the problem within himself through the power of the Spirit. He is a man who is able to crucify the flesh with the affections and lusts and has no excuse for failure. There is not a word about that in Romans 7; but it will come in chapter 8.

Now take another statement. It is found in the First Epistle to the Corinthians, chapter 9, verses 26 and 27. The Apostle is describing men striving for mastery in a race – 'I therefore so run, not as uncertainly; so fight I, not as one that beateth the air: but I keep under my body, and bring it into subjection: lest that by any means, when I have preached to others, I myself should be a castaway.' This, again, is quoted because people feel that Paul is describing this same conflict within himself as is described in Romans 7. Now there is no question but that the Apostle was referring to himself, and to a present experience, when he· wrote 1 Corinthians 9: 27; but is that a parallel with Romans 7? In Romans 7 he says, 'I delight in the law of God after the inward man: but I see another law in my members warring against the law of my mind and bringing me into captivity to the law of sin which is in my members'. But in 1 Corinthians 9: 27 he says, 'I do keep my body under', 'I beat it black and blue'. That is what his words literally mean. 'I pummel it, I punch it, I keep it under, and bring it into subjection.' Again, it is the exact opposite of Romans 7. He does say, and we all must say, that the re-generate man is not yet perfect and does have a war to fight against sin. But the fact that he has a war to wage does not mean that he is defeated. But the man in Romans 7 is defeated, in captivity, sold under sin. In 1 Corinthians 9: 27 the Apostle says, 'There is a battle, there is this tendency, sin is there; it is always ready to take an opportunity; but' – I am putting these words into the mouth of the Apostle because this is what he is really saying – 'but I do not allow sin to reign in my mortal body'. He is in a position not to allow it to reign, in a position to 'keep it under'. 'I myself keep it under, I keep my body in subjection, I keep it in order. I am running this race and I do not intend to be robbed of my prize; I keep under my body, and I bring it into subjection.' The man of Romans 7 would have given the whole world if only he could have said that! But he could not say it; that was his problem, his tragedy. *He* was being brought into subjection by the law of sin that was in his members, in his body. It is the exact opposite of that depicted in 1 Corinthians 9: 27.

Another passage is sometimes quoted. I refer to it, even though I do not think that it has any plausibility. It is found in Chapter 6 of the Epistle to the Ephesians, from verse 12 onwards, 'We wrestle not against flesh and blood, but against principalities, against powers, against the rulers of the darkness of this world, against spiritual wickedness in high places'. Interpreters jump at the word 'wrestle', because it seems to suggest what we have in Romans 7; the fight is on! But there are two answers to this. In Ephesians 6 Paul is not talking about a struggle against that which is in the flesh. He says as much. 'We wrestle not against flesh and blood'. That is not the essence of the problem he is considering. Rather does he say, 'Our essential problem, in the last analysis, is not sin within us, but these evil forces, the devil and his cohorts that are outside us'. And even with respect to that he says, 'Finally, my brethren, be strong in the Lord, and in the power of his might'. As a Christian you can be strong, you can get a victory! 'Be strong in the Lord, and in the power of his might. Put on the whole armour of God, that you may be able to stand against the wiles of the devil', and defeat him. What would the man in Romans 7 give if he knew that, and could say that! But he did not know it; that was his whole trouble. Far from supporting the idea that the man of Romans 7 is regenerate, the whole point of Ephesians is to show that it is possible for the regenerate man to be victorious and to stand. 'Having done all things, to stand (in the evil day)'. He is a conqueror; he is not defeated.

These then are the passages that are so commonly quoted, because they seem to suggest the same kind of struggle as is described in Romans 7. I trust I have proved that they say the exact opposite.

We turn now to other passages that belong to a second group, and which seem to be similar to Romans 7 because they speak about 'mourning' and about 'groans'. From them it is deduced that the fully regenerate man 'groans' and 'mourns', so surely they establish that Romans 7 is a description of such a man. The first is in chapter 8 of this same Epistle to the Romans, verses 23 and 26 in particular: 'And not only they, but ourselves also, which have the firstfruits of the Spirit' (here is the fully regenerate man), 'even we ourselves groan within ourselves, waiting for the adoption, to wit, the redemption of our body.' Again: 'Likewise the Spirit also helpeth our infirmities: for we know not what we should pray for as we ought; but the Spirit himself maketh intercession for us with groanings which cannot be uttered.' There is a perfect parallel, it is claimed, between these verses and 'O wretched man that I am! who shall deliver me from the body of this death?'

But are they parallel statements? To start with, notice that in Romans 8: 23 there is this vital addition, which is absent from Romans 7 – 'We who have the firstfruits of the Spirit'. Not a word about that is to be found in Romans 7! But the argument does not depend upon that alone. The answer to this interpretation is simply this, that in the relevant section in Romans 8 the Apostle is not considering the struggle which a man has with sin within himself, but his struggle with sin in the world, sin in circumstances, sin in trials and troubles and tribulations that come to us in this life. Let me prove that. Go back to verse 17 in chapter 8; 'If children, then heirs; heirs of God, and joint-heirs with Christ, if so be that we suffer with him.' 'Suffer with Christ'! The words cannot mean suffering because of sin in the body, because Christ never did suffer in that way. In this context Paul in Romans 8: 17 onwards is dealing with 'suffering with him, that we may be also glorified together'. Observe what he goes on to say: 'For I reckon that the sufferings of this present time' (the sufferings in which we find ourselves in this world) 'are not worthy to be compared with the glory which shall be revealed in us.' And to make it doubly certain he says, 'For the earnest expectation of the creature' (the brute, the animal creation) 'waiteth for the manifestation of the sons of God. For the creature was made subject to vanity' – he means now, the animals and everything that is in the brute creation – 'not willingly, but by reason of him who hath subjected the same in hope. Because the creature itself also shall be delivered from the bondage of corruption.' Do these words indicate a fight against indwelling sin? Do the animals have to fight against indwelling sin? Of course they do not. What they have to fight is, 'nature red in tooth and claw'. The Apostle refers to the kind of 'agony' of the cosmos, the struggle in the whole of life that entered in because of the Fall, and because, when man sinned, God 'cursed the ground'. This struggle belongs to the whole of nature and creation; 'We know that the whole creation groaneth and travaileth in pain together until now. And not only they, but ourselves also, which have the firstfruits of the Spirit, even we ourselves groan within ourselves, waiting for the adoption, to wit, the redemption of our body.' In other words, though the Christian is redeemed and regenerate he is living in a world of sin, a world of sorrow, a world of pain, a world of suffering, a world of evil, ugliness, foulness; and he is subject to illnesses and diseases. This is the theme of Romans 8: 17-23. The Apostle does not even consider there the problem which is dealt with in Romans 7. But how frequently is this missed simply because he uses the word 'groaneth'.

'But what about 2 Corinthians 5?' asks someone. In verse 2 we read, 'For in this tabernacle we groan, earnestly desiring to be clothed upon with our house which is from heaven; if so be that being clothed we shall not be found naked'. Then again in verse 4, 'For we that are in this tabernacle do groan, being burdened: not for that we would be unclothed, but clothed upon, that mortality might be swallowed up of life'. Again it is claimed that this is a similar case to that of the 'wretched man' of Romans 7. It is argued that the burden is the load of sin, the 'sin that is in my members', this thing that is leading me into captivity. Here, it is claimed, the fully regenerate man is speaking, and we seem to be told that he is 'groaning' because of his burden of sin, and longing for his glorification.

What is the answer? Here again, however, I must point out that the Apostle is not speaking of the subject with which he is dealing in Romans 7. His theme is the same as that of Romans 8, verses 18 to 26. The context proves this. Paul begins on the theme of 2 Corinthians 5: 1-5 in the 7th verse of chapter 4 of that letter: 'We have this treasure in earthen vessels, that the excellency of the power may be of God, and not of us. We are troubled on every side, yet not distressed; we are perplexed, but not in despair; persecuted . . . ' He is dealing with things outside himself, not inside himself – 'persecuted, but not forsaken; cast down, but not destroyed; always bearing about in the body the dying of the Lord Jesus. We which live are alway delivered unto death for Jesus' sake.' This describes the kind of life Paul was living externally then. 'So death worketh in us, but life in you.' 'All things are for your sakes . . . For which cause we faint not; but though our outward man perish, yet the inward man is renewed day by day. Our light affliction' – that is to say, the things outside ourselves – 'which is but for a moment, worketh for us a far more exceeding and eternal weight of glory.' And to prove that they are outside, he says, 'While we look not at the things which are seen' (outside us), 'but at the things which are not seen'. And then follows the 1st verse in chapter 5, 'For we know that if our earthly house of this tabernacle were dissolved' – if they kill us, if they martyr us – 'we have a building of God, an house not made with hands, eternal in the heavens'. So in this Corinthian passage the Apostle is dealing with the trials and the tribulations, the persecutions and the sufferings of Christian people because they are Christians. It is not at all the same problem, the same question, as is dealt with in Romans 7.

But I have a further reason for speaking in this way. If you look for the word 'groaned' in the Scripture and say that every time you find a Christian man 'groaning' or 'being burdened' it describes of necessity the struggle against sin within, then you will find yourself saying that our Lord Himself had a struggle against sin within. The evidence is as follows. Isaiah reminds us in his 53rd chapter that the Saviour when He comes, will be 'a man of sorrows, acquainted with grief'. And when He came He was such. For example, we read in Mark 9: 19 that when He came down from the Mount of Transfiguration and saw His disciples arguing with the people in the presence of a man whose son was afflicted with terrible fits, He said, 'O faithless generation, how long shall I be with you? how long shall I suffer you?' Again, look at the account of our Lord at Bethany at the sepulchre of His friend Lazarus, in John's Gospel, chapter 11, verse 33 onwards, 'When he saw Mary weeping, and the Jews also weeping with her, he groaned in the spirit, and was troubled'. Indeed in verse 35 we read, 'Jesus wept'. He was burdened, He groaned in the depth of His spirit, He was troubled in His spirit and He wept. Look at Him some time later in the Garden of Gethsemane. This is what we find; 'And being in an agony he sweat as it were drops of blood'. Our Lord certainly 'groaned' when He was in this world. And we 'in this tabernacle', says Paul, 'we do groan, being burdened'. The Lord 'groaned in spirit' for the same reason. Not because of 'sin in the members', but because this is a world of sin, because of all that sin has done to God's world.

Why did Christ weep and groan at the grave of Lazarus? 'Oh, it was His natural human sympathy,' says someone. But that cannot be, because He knew that He was about to raise Lazarus and

restore him to his sisters. No, He wept because He was face to
face with this horrible thing called death that had come into the
world as the result of sin, and which was going to lead in a short
while to His own death and separation from the Father. That is
the meaning of 'Jesus wept', that is why He 'groaned and was
troubled in spirit', though He knew He was going to raise Lazarus.
He was looking at sin and its consequences in the world, looking
at sin objectively as Paul does in Romans 8: 18–23, and also in
2 Corinthians 5: 1–5. Indeed the Apostle puts this quite explicitly
in the Epistle to the Colossians in chapter 1, verse 24, where he
says, '(I) now rejoice in my sufferings for you, and fill up that
which is behind of the afflictions of Christ in my flesh for His
body's sake, which is the church'. That is exactly the same thing.
He has entered into such intimate communion with His Lord
and Saviour that he really feels something of what the Lord
Christ suffered when He was in this evil world. The sight of it
all, and the realization of it all, made him groan. 'In this tabernacle we do groan, being burdened.' Though we are saved, and
rejoicing in that salvation', the world is nevertheless a 'vale of
tears', a 'land of woe'. That is what the Apostle says in Romans
8 and also in 2 Corinthians, chapter 5.

We conclude therefore that the statements I have quoted
which, because they have this idea of burden and trouble and
tribulation and agony and groaning, appear on the surface to be
saying what Paul is saying in Romans 7, clearly and definitely
do not deal with the same subject at all, and therefore have no
relevance in the question of deciding who exactly is 'the man'
described in Romans 7, verses 14 to 25. We shall go on to show
that, if these verses are interpreted as applying to a fully regenerate man, that interpretation is incompatible with the plain
teaching of this Apostle elsewhere with regard to the regenerate
man. And after that we shall show that it is incompatible also
with the teaching of other New Testament writers concerning the
fully regenerate man. And even when that matter is resolved
we shall still be left with the suggestion that Romans, chapter 7,
is the description of an immature Christian who has not yet gone
on to receive the 'second blessing'. That is a very much simpler
question which can be disposed of much more easily.

Nineteen

*

Was then that which is good made death unto me? God forbid. But sin, that it might appear sin, working death in me by that which is good; that sin by the commandment might become exceeding sinful.

For we know that the law is spiritual: but I am carnal, sold under sin.

For that which I do I allow not: for what I would, that do I not; but what I hate, that do I.

If then I do that which I would not, I consent unto the law that it is good.

Now then it is no more I that do it, but sin that dwelleth in me.

For I know that in me (that is, in my flesh), dwelleth no good thing: for to will is present with me; but how to perform that which is good I find not.

For the good that I would I do not: but the evil which I would not, that I do.

Now if I do that I would not, it is no more I that do it, but sin that dwelleth in me.

I find then a law, that, when I would do good, evil is present with me.

For I delight in the law of God after the inward man:

But I see another law in my members, warring against the law of my mind, and bringing me into captivity to the law of sin which is in my members.

O wretched man that I am! who shall deliver me from the body of this death?

I thank God through Jesus Christ our Lord. So then with the mind I myself serve the law of God; but with the flesh the law of sin.

Romans 7: 13–25

We are engaged in the task of summing up our conclusions concerning the exact meaning of this famous portion of Scripture. We have gone through it in detail, verse by verse, and have also summed up the essential statement made by the Apostle. In attempting to decide whether the reference is to the unregenerate man or to a regenerate man – even Paul himself when he wrote the letter – or whether it is a description of an immature Christian, we felt that the best plan to adopt was to see whether we could find other passages in Scripture which would throw any light on the matter. We have found that passages which, on the surface, seem to describe the same conflict, and others which seem to describe the same 'groaning' and state of misery, do not really provide us with a parallel to what we find in this section.

The next step is to show that, if this passage is interpreted as describing Paul's experience at his best and highest, even as he was when he wrote this Epistle, then it is incompatible with his plain teaching elsewhere, indeed with plain teaching elsewhere in the Bible, not only by the Apostle Paul, but by other writers also concerning the nature of the regenerate man.

First, let us look at passages in the writings of the Apostle Paul himself, which, I suggest, exclude the possibility that he is describing his mature Christian experience in Romans 7. Take first the Apostle's other statements in this same Epistle. The evidence is abundant. I begin with chapter 5, verses 1 and 2, where he says, 'Therefore being justified by faith, we have peace with God through our Lord Jesus Christ: by whom also we have access by faith into this grace wherein we stand'. We emphasized there the 'standing' – not a crouching or a slouching or a lying down – we 'stand' in this grace, 'and rejoice in the hope of the glory of God'. Surely the man who could write that could not at the same time cry out, 'O wretched man that I am! who shall deliver me from the body of this death?' Furthermore, verses 12 to 21 in the same chapter emphasize 'the triumph of the reign of grace'. Though 'sin has abounded', 'grace has much more abounded'. The victory, the triumph, the certainty, the assurance of it all! This is the Apostle's central message, his main reason for writing the passage. 'Much more' he keeps on repeating – 'much more hath grace abounded'. It is always 'abounding' and 'superabounding'. There is no compatibility between emphasizing the 'superabounding' power and capacity of grace and crying out, 'O wretched man that I am! who shall deliver me from the body of this death?' The two things do not fit together in the same person.

When we come to chapter 6, we find that practically everything Paul says is incompatible with the interpretation I am opposing. In verse 2, for example, he replies to the question, 'Shall we continue in sin, that grace may abound?' by saying 'God forbid. How shall we that died to sin live any longer therein?' But here in this second section of chapter 7 is a man who is 'brought into captivity to the law of sin which is in his members'. But in chapter 6, verse 2, he says that this is impossible for the Christian. Having died to sin, it is impossible for him to continue in sin any longer. Paul says the same in verse 6: 'Knowing this, that our old man is crucified with him, that the body of sin might be destroyed (disannulled, brought to nothing) that henceforth we should not serve sin'. That is the whole object of salvation, and that is the cause of his rejoicing. In verse 7 he repeats the same truth: 'For he that is dead is freed from sin.' Then follows the great exhortation in verse 11, 'Likewise reckon ye yourselves to be dead indeed unto sin, but alive unto God through Jesus Christ our Lord'. What possible interpretation is there of that, if this section in chapter 7 is a description of the regenerate man at his very best? Similarly the exhortations in verses 12 and 13 would become quite meaningless. 'Let not sin therefore reign in your mortal body' – we must not allow it to reign there; there is no need for us to allow it to reign there – 'that ye should obey it in the lusts thereof'. 'Neither yield ye your members as instruments of unrighteousness unto sin'. There is *no need* for us to do so, we *can* stop doing so; we *must* stop doing so. But in Romans 7 we have a man who tells us that he cannot help himself, that he is brought into captivity constantly by this power which is greater than himself. Then there is the great asseveration of verse 14, 'For sin shall not have dominion over you; for ye are not under the law, but under grace'. It is the very antithesis of this particular interpretation of verses 13 to 25 of the 7th chapter.

But look once more at chapter 6. Take verse 17: 'But God be thanked, ye were the slaves of sin, but ye have obeyed from the heart that form of doctrine which was delivered you.' Then verse 18: 'Being then made free from sin, ye became the slaves of righteousness.' Verse 22, 'But now being made free from sin, and become servants to God, ye have your fruit unto holiness, and the end everlasting life'. Such words are not at all compatible with the statement 'I see another law in my members, warring against the law of my mind, and bringing me into captivity to the law of sin which is in my members. . . . For the good that I would I do not; but the evil that I would not, that I do'. The man cannot do what he wants to do, he does what he does not want to do. 'O wretched man that I am!' It is really astonishing that anyone who has worked carefully through chapter 6 could conceivably say that in chapter 7, verses 13–25 describe the regenerate man at the height of his experience. The appeal in the 19th verse of the 6th chapter would likewise be quite pointless, 'I speak after the manner of men because of the infirmity of your flesh; for as ye have yielded your members servants to uncleanness and to iniquity unto iniquity; even so now yield your members servants to righteousness unto holiness'. That appeal is obviously addressed to those who have the ability to respond, and not to helpless, hopeless, defeated captives of sin.

Look next at this very chapter in which this section comes. I argue that verses 4 and 6 are completely incompatible with that suggested view of verses 14 to 25. Verse 4 reads, 'Wherefore, my brethren, ye also died to the law by the body of Christ; that ye should be married to another, even to him who is raised from the dead, that we should bring forth fruit unto God.' Verse 6, 'But now we are delivered from the law, that being dead wherein we were held; that (in order that) we should serve in newness of spirit, and not in the oldness of the letter'. These great assertions make it quite impossible for us to interpret these later verses in the manner proposed.

Then move on to chapter 8, verses 1 and 2: 'There is therefore now no condemnation to them which are in Christ Jesus. For the law of the Spirit of life in Christ Jesus hath made me free from the law of sin and death.' In verses 13 to 25 of chapter 7 Paul says that the Law leads him constantly to 'sin' and to 'death'. But he says in verse 3 of chapter 8 that he has been set free. 'For what the law could not do, in that it was weak through the flesh, God sending his own Son in the likeness of sinful flesh and for sin' has done just that. He has 'condemned sin in the flesh, that (in order that) the righteousness of the law might be fulfilled in us'. Not that we should go on failing, but that 'it might be fulfilled in us, who walk not after the flesh, but after the Spirit'. Here Paul is describing the regenerate man; and his words cannot be reconciled with the interpretation of verses 14–25, chapter 7, which I oppose.

Again, look at verse 6 of chapter 8: 'For to be carnally minded is death, but to be spiritually minded is life and peace.' The man of Romans 7 has no peace. 'No', he says, 'I am always being led into captivity to the law of sin which is in my members. O wretched man that I am! who shall deliver me?' Is such a man enjoying peace? But the Apostle says that the great characteristic of the man who is spiritually minded, that is, the regenerate man, is that he has 'life and peace'. It is the exact opposite of this man who could not find peace, and who cries out in his agony 'O wretched man that I am! who shall deliver me?'

Then we move on to verse 13 and others in chapter 8 where Paul makes an appeal. He says, 'If ye live after the flesh, ye shall die; but if ye through the Spirit do mortify the deeds of the body, ye shall live'. The implication there, is that as Christians we can do what he enjoins, and therefore he tells us to do so. But the whole trouble with the man in Romans 7 is that he cannot do it. He has been trying, and he has failed completely, he is still in captivity; but in chapter 8 we see a man who has found a way of freedom and of life.

Then go on further to verses 14 and onwards: 'For as many as are led by the Spirit of God, they are the sons of God.' 'For you have not received the spirit of bondage again to fear'. Who is in bondage? The man who is 'in captivity' is in 'bondage'. Who is the man that is 'afraid?' He is the man who says, 'What is going to happen to me? What can I do? I try, I want to, but I cannot', and he cries out, 'O wretched man that I am! who shall deliver me?' But to the regenerate the Apostle says, 'Ye have not received the spirit of bondage again to fear; but you have received the Spirit of adoption, where by we cry, Abba, Father. The Spirit himself beareth witness with our spirits that we are the children of God: and if children, then heirs; heirs of God, and joint-heirs with Christ, if so be that we suffer with him, that we may be also glorified together.' If that is true of me, am I to go on to say 'O wretched man that I am! who shall deliver me from the body of this death?' These things are utter incompatibilities, they do not breathe the same atmosphere, they do not belong together at all. No, this man, the regenerate man, the Apostle Paul when he was writing, was not 'hopeless', not 'wretched'; he knows his position and 'rejoices in hope of the glory of God'.

Then go on to verses 29 and 30. 'For whom he did foreknow,

he also did predestinate to be conformed to the image of his Son, that he might be the firstborn among many brethren. Moreover whom he did predestinate, them he also called; and whom he called, them he also justified'. Now watch the leap – 'and whom he justified, them he also glorified.' A man who understands justification knows that, in a sense, he is already glorified. Can such a man cry out 'O wretched man that I am! who shall deliver me?' It is inconceivable, it is impossible. 'We know that all things work together for good to them that love God.' If I know that I am 'foreknown' and 'predestinated', I know that I shall be 'conformed to the image of his Son'. I do not cry out in despair, 'Who shall deliver me?', because I already know the answer. A wrong interpretation of chapter 7 renders the whole of this great 8th chapter quite impossible, and especially that leap from 'justification' to 'glorification'.

In chapter 12 there are further statements that I cannot reconcile with other interpretations. 'I beseech you therefore, brethren, by the mercies of God, that ye present your bodies even a living sacrifice, holy, acceptable unto God, which is your reasonable service. And be not conformed to this world; but be transformed by the renewing of your mind, that ye may prove what is that good, and acceptable, and perfect will of God.' That statement would be enough in itself, if we had nothing else, to yield a correct interpretation. In chapter 14: 17 Paul says, 'The kingdom of God (into which Christians have come) is not meat and drink'. It is not a matter of eating this and not eating that, and of observing days and various other punctilios; but the kingdom is 'righteousness and peace and joy in the Holy Ghost'. That is Christianity; the Christian is to know 'righteousness, and peace, and joy in the Holy Ghost'. Can a man have 'the joy of the Holy Ghost', and at the same time say, 'I am constantly being brought into captivity by the law of sin which is in my members. O wretched man that I am! who shall deliver me from the body of this death?' Surely the two conditions cannot possibly co-exist in the same person.

Thus far I have produced evidence from the Epistle to the Romans itself. Let us now turn to the evidence in the other writings of the Apostle Paul. I have already quoted 1 Corinthians 9: 27, where he says, 'I keep under my body'. But look at what appears to me to be the final answer to this particular argument in 2 Corinthians, chapter 3, which almost seems to have been written specially to deal with the very question we are considering. Look at what Paul says in verses 6 and 7 where his theme is Law and Gospel, death and life. Observe his negative – 'not of the letter, but of the spirit . . . the letter killeth'. The trouble with the man in Romans 7 is that he was being killed by the Law. He says in verse 10 of chapter 7, 'What was ordained unto life, I found to be unto death'. But Paul tells the Corinthians that 'The law killeth, but the Spirit giveth life'. Then take the phrase at the beginning of verse 7, 'the ministration of death'. Paul is writing about the Law of God, written and graven in stones', and is actually saying that God's holy Law given through Moses was nothing other than 'the ministration of death'; and for the very reason that is found in Romans 7 – 'That which was ordained unto life, I found to be unto death'. The trouble with the man in Romans 7 is that he is being killed by the Law. He is made to sin by it; he is killed by it. So here the Apostle actually uses this quite astonishing phrase, 'the ministration of death', for the Law of God. But look at the end of that chapter, verses 17 and 18. 'Now the Lord is that Spirit: and where the Spirit of the Lord is' – it can also be translated 'Where the Spirit is Lord' – 'there is liberty'. In other words, I am not 'brought into captivity to the law of sin which is in my members', I am no longer in the flesh; the Spirit is in me, and 'the Lord is that Spirit, and where the Spirit of the Lord is, there is liberty'.

But the Apostle is not content with saying that only; he adds to it in the 18th verse. 'But we all (the regenerate) with open face, beholding as in a glass the glory of the Lord . . .'. This is the regenerate man, not crying out 'Who shall deliver me?' but 'with open face, beholding as in a glass the glory of the Lord'. What happens? '(We) are changed into the same image (the Lord's image) from glory to glory'. We are progressing and developing; at the end of our lives and when we are approaching the topmost rung of the ladder of sainthood we do not say 'O wretched man that I am'. No; it is rather 'we are changed from glory to glory' – increasing, developing, advancing, going up – 'even as by the Spirit of the Lord'. You cannot equate that with what is said in Romans 7, 14–25; surely they are exact opposites!

Then turn to Galatians, chapter 2, verse 20: 'I have been

crucified with Christ'. This does not describe a second experience; it is what happens to every man who is regenerate. 'I have been crucified with Christ; nevertheless I live; yet not I, but Christ liveth in me'. That is how the regenerate man speaks. He does not say 'O wretched man that I am! who shall deliver me?'; he says, 'Christ liveth in me; and the life I now live in the flesh I live by the faith of the Son of God, who loved me, and gave himself for me'. Then in Galatians, chapter 4, 'Now I say, that the heir, as long as he is a child, differeth nothing from a servant, though he be lord of all'. We see here a man 'under the law'; but though a child of the family he resembles a servant. Indeed he may be tyrannized over by the servants, he may be having a very miserable time, though he is the heir. 'He is under tutors and governors until the time appointed of the father. Even so we, when we were children, were in bondage under the elements of the world. But when the fulness of the time was come, God sent forth his Son, made of a woman, made under the law, to redeem them that were under the law, that we might receive the adoption of sons.' And because we are sons, do we cry out saying, 'O wretched man that I am! who shall deliver me from the body of this death?' No! 'Because ye are sons, God hath sent forth the Spirit of his Son into your hearts, crying, Abba, Father. Wherefore thou art no more a servant, but a son; and if a son, then an heir of God through Christ'. You cannot reconcile these words with the statement in Romans 7: 14 to 25. Again in chapter 5, from verse 16 to the end of the chapter: 'Walk in the Spirit, and ye shall not fulfil the lust of the flesh . . . But if ye be led of the Spirit, ye are not under the law . . . They that are Christ's have crucified the flesh with the affections and lusts'. Such is the teaching concerning the regenerate in Galatians.

In Ephesians, chapter 1, verse 19, the Apostle tells the believers that he is praying for them, 'that the eyes of their understanding may be enlightened'. He wishes them to know 'what is the exceeding greatness of God's power to usward who believe'. He knew it himself; he prays that they may know it. Here is Paul the Apostle, who knows 'the exceeding greatness of God's power to usward that believe', the same power, the Apostle says, that God exercised 'in Christ when he raised him from the dead, and set him at his own right hand in the heavenly places, far above all principality and power, and might, and dominion, and every name that is named, not only in this world, but also in the world that is to come'. Then Paul adds: 'And hath put all things under his feet, and gave him to be the head over all things unto the church, which is his body, the fulness of him that filleth all in all'. Is it conceivable that a man who knows something about 'the exceeding greatness' of this power towards himself can cry out, saying 'O wretched man that I am! who shall deliver me from the body of this death?' – from this thing that is 'bringing me into captivity to the law of sin which is in my members'? Surely we are in a different world altogether; the whole situation is entirely changed.

At the end of Ephesians chapter 3, the Apostle prays again for these same regenerate people: 'That he would grant you, according to the riches of his glory, to be strengthened with might by his Spirit in the inner man; that Christ may dwell in your hearts by faith; that you, being rooted and grounded in love, may be able to comprehend with all saints what is the breadth and length and depth and height; and to know the love of Christ which passeth knowledge, that you might be filled with all the fulness of God'. And he continues, 'Now unto him that is able to do exceeding abundantly above all that we ask or think, according to the power that worketh in us, unto him be glory in the church by Christ Jesus throughout all ages'. Does the man who writes in that way say at another time, 'Ah yes, but it is equally true of me to say "O wretched man that I am! who shall deliver me from the body of this death?" ' Surely that is quite impossible! The same can be said of the remainder of the Epistle to the Ephesians, from chapter 4, verse 17 onwards.

But turn to Philippians, chapter 4, verse 4. What kind of people are Christians? Judge from the following words: 'Rejoice in the Lord alway; and again I say, Rejoice'. Can you 'rejoice in the Lord alway' if you are conscious that you are brought constantly into captivity to 'the law of sin that is in your members', and are crying out, 'O wretched man that I am! who shall deliver me?' These things do not belong together.

Then in the First Epistle to the Thessalonians – probably the first Epistle the Apostle ever wrote – chapter 1: 5; 'Our gospel came not unto you in word only, but also in power, and in the Holy Ghost, and in much assurance: as ye know what manner of men we were among you for your sake. And you became followers of us and of the Lord, having received the word in much affliction, with joy of the Holy Ghost; so that ye were ensamples to all that believe in Macedonia and Achaia.' Then in the 4th chapter, verse 3: 'For this is the will of God, even your sanctification.' And in chapter 5, verse 23: 'And the very God of peace sanctify you wholly; and I pray God your whole spirit and soul and body be preserved blameless unto the coming of our Lord Jesus Christ.' This is the Apostle's teaching.

I end this summary of Paul's teaching with a reference to the man himself. When he speaks of himself, this is his favourite phrase: 'Paul, the bond-slave of Jesus Christ'. You will find it generally at the beginning of his letters. Is it possible that a man who describes himself in that way should cry out at the same time, 'O wretched man that I am! who shall deliver me?' He has been bought, he belongs to the Lord; he is a 'bond-slave'. Listen to him as he writes to the Philippians: 'For me to live is Christ, and to die is gain' (1: 21). Or consider the astonishing things he says about himself later in the same Epistle: 'Brethren, I count not myself to have apprehended' – he is not perfect – 'but this one thing I do, forgetting those things which are behind, and reaching forth unto those things which are before, I press toward the mark for the prize of the high calling of God in Christ Jesus' (3: 13, 14). He is not constantly turning round in a circle and crying out for deliverance; he is 'pressing forward'. 'Let us therefore', he says, 'as many as be perfect, be thus minded: and if in any thing ye be otherwise minded, God shall reveal even this unto you. Nevertheless, whereunto we have already attained, let us walk by the same rule, let us mind the same thing. Brethren, be followers together of me' (vv. 15–17). Could a man who says of himself, 'O wretched man that I am! who shall deliver me?' have the effrontery to stand up and say 'Brethren, be ye followers of me, and mark them which walk so as ye have us for an ensample?' It seems to me quite incongruous. Then in the First Epistle to the Thessalonians; 'Ye are witnesses, and God also, how holily and justly and unblameably we behaved ourselves among you that believe' (2: 10). I cannot reconcile that with the condition of the man in Romans 7. Paul is not claiming that he is perfect; but he is certainly claiming that he is not in the position and condition described in Romans 7.

And that brings me to my last statement concerning this great man. We are told that Romans 7: 14 ff. describes Paul at his best, at his highest, nearing the end of his Christian life. But we find that at the end of his life he is able to write in a very different strain. In 2 Timothy 4: 6–8 he could say: 'I am ready to be offered, and the time of my departure is at hand. I have fought a good fight, I have finished my course, I have kept the faith: Henceforth there is laid up for me a crown of righteousness, which the Lord, the righteous Judge, shall give me at that day; and not to me only, but unto all them also that love his appearing.' Can a man who says that still say of himself, 'O wretched man that I am! who shall deliver me from the body of this death?' It is impossible, for the condition of the Apostle was as described by Witsius, the authority on the doctrine of the Covenants, in these words: 'The immense abundance of the Spirit inhabiting his noble breast, and the sparkling flames of the love of God kindled in his breast.' A man of whom that is true does not regard himself as a 'wretched man' who has to cry out in despair, 'Who shall deliver me?' It is a sheer impossibility. There, then, is the evidence for my contention from the writings of the Apostle Paul.

But let us turn to the writings of the Apostle John. The entire argument of his First Epistle, written to regenerate people, is the exact opposite of what is stated here. Why does John write his First Epistle? He supplies his own answer: 'These things write we unto you, that your joy may be full', and that 'you also may have fellowship with us; and truly our fellowship is with the Father, and with his Son Jesus Christ'. He and the other apostles were enjoying that fellowship and he wants all Christians to enjoy it. It is impossible to reconcile this with the statement in Romans 7. Then look at John's 3rd chapter and what he says in verse 9: 'Whosoever is born of God doth not commit sin (doth not go on committing sin), for his seed remaineth in him, and he cannot sin (continue committing sin) because he is born of God.' And verse 21; 'Beloved, if our heart condemn us not, then have we confidence toward God.' But the man in Romans 7 is utterly condemned by his heart. The same truth emerges in chapter 5, verses 4 and 5: 'Whatsoever is born of God overcometh the world; and this is the victory that overcometh the world, even our faith. Who is he that overcometh the world, but he that believeth that Jesus is the Son of God?' And then verse 18: 'We know that whosoever is born of God sinneth not' (does not go on living a life of sin and failure) 'but he that is begotten of God keepeth himself, and that wicked one toucheth him not. And we know that we are of God, and the whole world lieth in wickedness' (in the evil one). 'We know that the Son of God is come, and hath given us an understanding, that we may know him that is true, and we are in him that is true, even in his Son Jesus Christ. This is the true God, and eternal life.' Am I to add to that, 'O wretched man that I am! who shall deliver me from the body of this death?' Impossible!

The Apostle Peter teaches the same truth in his Second Epistle, chapter 1, verses 4–10: 'All things', he says, 'that pertain to life and godliness, have been given to us: Whereby are given unto us exceeding great and precious promises: that by these ye might be partakers of the divine nature, having escaped the corruption that is in the world through lust.' In the light of that, says Peter, this is what you have to do: 'Beside this, giving all diligence, add to your faith virtue, knowledge, temperance, patience, godliness, brotherly kindness, charity. For if these things be in you, and abound, they make you that ye shall neither be barren nor unfruitful in the knowledge of our Lord Jesus Christ.' The trouble with the man in Romans 7 was that he lacked that knowledge. 'He that lacketh these things is blind, and cannot see afar off, and hath forgotten that he was purged from his old sins. Wherefore the rather, brethren, give diligence to make your calling and election sure: for if ye do these things, ye shall never fail: For so an entrance shall be ministered unto you abundantly into the everlasting kingdom of our Lord and Saviour Jesus Christ.' These are descriptions of the Christian man, the regenerate man.

Finally, to confirm what I am saying, I would quote our Lord's own teaching. In Matthew 11: 28 he says: 'Come unto me, all ye that labour and are heavy laden, and I will give you rest.' He gives rest to the man who cries, 'O wretched man that I am! who shall deliver me?', and who is always being 'led into captivity by the law of sin which is in his members'. To such a labouring and heavy-laden and unhappy man our Lord says, 'Take my yoke upon you, and learn of me; for I am meek and lowly in heart; and ye shall find rest unto your souls. For my yoke is easy, and my burden is light.' It is the exact opposite of Romans 7. Then consider Luke 4 and the account of our Lord's reading of the Scriptures in the synagogue at Nazareth after his return from the Temptation in the Wilderness. He read out of Isaiah 61: 'The Spirit of the Lord is upon me, because he hath anointed me to preach the gospel to the poor; he hath sent me to heal the broken-hearted, to preach deliverance to the captives, and recovering of sight to the blind, to set at liberty them that are bruised, to preach the acceptable year of the Lord.' This being read, He closed the book, and gave it again to the minister, and sat down. And he began to say, 'This day is this Scripture fulfilled in your ears'. That is what He had come to do, and He claimed to be doing it. That is what He does to all who believe in Him. He delivers the 'captives' and those that are bruised; He gives sight to the blind. They are no longer 'wretched'.

Then there is the notable statement in John's Gospel, chapter 7, verses 37–39: 'In the last day, that great day of the feast, Jesus stood and cried, saying, If any man thirst' – if any man is longing and thirsting for righteousness, and the power to live according to the Law, if any man is wretched and unhappy and feels he is a captive to sin – 'If any man thirst, let him come unto me and drink. He that believeth on me, as the Scripture hath said, out of his belly shall flow rivers of living water.' The Christian believer is not only right in himself, he is able to send out these streams of blessing and of fructification to others. 'This spake he of the Spirit, which they that believe on him should receive; for the Holy Ghost was not yet given, because that Jesus was not yet glorified.'

Now take the 8th chapter, verse 12; 'I am the light of the world; he that followeth me shall not walk in darkness' – he shall not be groping in darkness and saying, 'O where can I find deliverance? Who shall deliver me?' – 'He that followeth me shall not walk in darkness, but shall have the light of life.' But look at the still more wonderful verses 34–36 in that same 8th chapter: 'Jesus answered them, Verily, verily, I say unto you, Whosoever committeth sin' – whosoever goes on living the defeated, failing life, a captive to the sin which is in his members – 'Whosoever committeth sin is the servant of sin.' That is precisely what the man in Romans 7 says about himself. Our Lord continues: 'And the servant abideth not in the house for ever; but the Son abideth ever. If the Son therefore shall make you free, ye shall be free indeed.' In other words, he will never say again, 'O wretched man that I am! who shall deliver me?' Our Lord says it again in chapter 10, verses 9 and 10: 'I am the door: by me if any man enter in, he shall be saved, and shall go in and out, and find pasture' – full satisfaction! 'The thief cometh not, but for to steal, and to kill, and to destroy; I am come that they might have life, and that they might have it more abundantly.' 'O wretched man! who shall deliver me from this bondage, this captivity, this body of death?' . . . 'Life – and that more abundantly.' What a complete contrast!

All the Scriptures in their accounts and descriptions of the regenerate man teach the exact opposite of what we find here in Romans 7. But we must go further. I suggest that to interpret Romans 7 in terms of the fully regenerate man – Paul at his best – is indeed to place the regenerate man at his best in an inferior position to the saints of God under Old Testament teaching. The man in Romans 7 is in a more desperate position even than David in Psalm 51. David had committed the terrible sin of adultery, and then murder on top of that. He knows what he has done, and he knows that he is guilty; but he does not cry out in despair, 'Who shall deliver me?' He wants a clean heart, and is amazed at himself that he could have done such things. 'Create in me a clean heart, and renew a right spirit within me.' His prayer is, 'Take not thy holy Spirit from me'. He was aware of an essential principle of righteousness. He has fallen, but he is not in despair about it; he is not in the position of the man in Romans 7. Psalm 119 also contains verses which make this faulty exposition quite impossible, as for example, verses 49–65, 97–104, 121, 165–168. We can all work the argument out for ourselves.

But look at the matter from still another angle. If Romans 7 is a description of the regenerate man at his best, then I say that the Old Testament prophecies concerning the Gospel have not been fulfilled. In Isaiah 35 we read that when the Messiah comes, when the Gospel age arrives, 'the lame man shall leap as an hart', 'the blind will see'. 'There shall be a way, an highway, it shall be called The way of holiness; the unrighteous man shall not walk upon it; but the wayfaring man, though a fool, shall not err therein'. Such words describe what the Gospel effects. But Romans

7 does not speak thus. Or listen to what the Gospel does, as described in Isaiah 61: 'To appoint unto them that mourn in Zion, to give unto them beauty for ashes, the oil of joy for mourning, the garment of praise for the spirit of heaviness'. In such words Isaiah had already answered Romans 7 nearly eight centuries beforehand. These are the blessings of the Gospel dispensation – beauty, joy, praise! It is the very antithesis of 'O wretched man that I am! who shall deliver me from the body of this death?'

Indeed, I do not hesitate to say that if you interpret Romans 7 as referring to the regenerate man you are really excluding the doctrine of sanctification altogether. Or if not that, it certainly excludes the possibility of any growth in sanctification. The argument is that the more a man advances in the Christian life the more he is aware of sin within him, and the more he therefore mourns. So it comes to this, that the more Christian a man becomes the more miserable he becomes, and the highest point he reaches will mark the greatest depth of his misery. Where then is 'growth in grace and in the knowledge of the Lord'? Where is progressive sanctification? That interpretation really amounts to this, that the main effect of the Gospel upon man is to increase his misery. The greater the awareness of sin the greater the misery; therefore the main effect of the Gospel is to increase misery; and the New Testament man must be more miserable than the Old Testament man. It is quite ridiculous, it is impossible.

In conclusion I would say this. The real clue to the understanding of this passage in Romans 7 is to notice that the Holy Spirit and the indwelling Christ are not mentioned; hence the trouble and the problem. The Holy Spirit, as the quotations have proved, is the great antagonist of the 'flesh' and of 'sin'. *He* gives the victory. But He is not mentioned here; and as the indwelling Christ and the Holy Spirit within are not mentioned, this cannot therefore be a full statement as to the condition and the experience of Paul at the time of writing. Here we have a man who is analysing himself, and the 'me' and the 'me' within him. It is a complete analysis. But when Paul analyses himself he says, 'Yet not I, but Christ that dwelleth in me'. This man does not mention Christ. It is clearly not an analysis of Paul at the time of writing, or of the Christian at his best. That is impossible, for such a man must mention the indwelling Christ and the indwelling Holy Spirit.

But it is said that it is simply one aspect of Paul. He is not speaking here, they say, of the whole of himself; you have to take chapter 8 with this chapter to have the whole Paul. But this man in Romans 7 is definitely and specifically talking about himself, and the whole of himself. He has analysed himself – the 'me' and the 'me' and the 'I'. It is the complete man. So that argument cannot prevail either. In my view, to say that Paul is describing only one aspect of himself here makes it incompatible with what he says about himself as a Christian in the first 17 verses of chapter 8.

'Ah but', says someone, 'why not the two at the same time?' I have already answered that objection. If a man already knows the answer, why does he cry out, 'Who shall deliver me?' If he knows that Christ does, and can, deliver him, why does he cry out 'Who shall deliver me?' It makes the position nonsensical. If Paul knows everything that he says in chapter 8 while he is describing himself in chapter 7, why does he give this description at all? Why does he not say that he is speaking of 'one aspect of my life, one part of me'? But he does not say this. He is giving a full description of a certain man, and it is quite incompatible with that of the regenerate man in chapter 8. The man in chapter 8 cannot use the expressions that Paul uses in verse 14 of chapter 7 where he says, 'I am carnal, sold under sin'. He cannot cry out in despair, 'O wretched man that I am! who shall deliver me from the body of this death?' This does not mean that I am asserting that the Christian man is perfect. Of course he is not perfect. He knows, and he knows better than anyone, that sin still remains in him, in his body. Accordingly he has to exercise restraint and care and watchfulness. He knows that he has to fight; he knows that he is liable to fall into sin; but when he does so he never speaks of himself as a wretched man. When the Christian, the regenerate man, falls into sin, he does not say 'This is terrible, I am filled with despair, O wretched man that I am! who shall deliver me?' He speaks of himself, as he should speak, in terms of the First Epistle of John: 'If we confess our sins, God is faithful and just to forgive us our sins, and to cleanse us from all unrighteousness' (1 John 1: 9). 'These things write I unto you, that ye sin not. And if any man sin, we have an advocate with the Father, Jesus Christ the righteous, and he is the propitiation for our sins' (1 John 2: 1–2). The Christian speaks in this way; he never cries out in despair.

The Christian knows that he has to fight sin; Paul has dealt with that matter in chapter 6. The Christian's fight with sin is described there, and in the first part of chapter 8, not in this section in chapter 7. But notice that the picture in chapter 6 is of a man who can be confident. Sin is present, it still remains in the body, and it is always ready to try to get the mastery. But the believer is reminded that he is now able to prevent it from doing so. He is not a despairing fighter; he is on top. In the Christian sin is not a master, and he its slave. Sin to the Christian is an annoyance, a nuisance; it is something that worries him, and sometimes trips him up; but it never drives him to despair. He should never go back 'under the law', never feel 'hopeless'. Not only do I assert that it is not a fully regenerate man speaking in Romans 7, I maintain that a Christian must never speak in that way. Indeed Paul's whole object in writing was to teach people that they should never speak in that way. And if that is his object in writing how can he possibly be writing about himself? The thing is ludicrous. No, this was not Paul's experience at the height of his saintliness.

Well, says someone, if that is not the case, why not say, then, that it is a picture of the incomplete Christian? Why not say that it is a regenerate man who has not yet had the 'second blessing', a man who is 'justified' but not yet 'sanctified'; in other words, that the man is an immature Christian? The simple answer to that is, that there is no indication whatsoever of that in the Apostle's words. He does not say that he is describing himself as he once was, and before he 'passed over' to Romans 8. If he were doing so, he would not be using the present tense; he would be using the past tense, and saying, I was like that once upon a time. He has written in that manner in verses 7–13 where he was describing a past experience.

No, that is not the answer. That view, of course, is based on the fallacy that a man can be justified without being sanctified. It is based on the false view which drives a wedge between the two and says that we can have the one without the other. But that is not the teaching of Paul. He teaches that if we are justified we are 'in Christ', we are married to Him, we are no longer 'under the law', His power is working in us. That is the entire teaching of chapter 6, and chapter 7: 1–6. He cannot go back on what he has already said; that is quite impossible. Furthermore, that view is based upon a further fallacy. However young a Christian a man may be, however immature, it is impossible for him to utter the cry of verse 24. Even the man who has the first glimmerings of an understanding and knowledge will never cry out, 'Who shall deliver me?' He has already believed that Christ is his Saviour, so he does not say 'Who?'; he turns to Christ. But that view, also, with its superficiality, imagines that, when you turn from chapter 7 to chapter 8, all your problems are solved, you never have any more difficulty and never any more struggle; whereas Paul in chapter 8, verse 13, says, 'But if through the Spirit ye do mortify the deeds of the body, ye shall live'. *You* have got to do that; it is not all done for you after you have had the 'second blessing', and have 'handed it all over to Christ'. No! 'If you, through the Spirit, do mortify the deeds of the body, ye shall live'. We shall work that out in greater detail when we expound chapter 8.

What, then, is the position? The Apostle is not describing his own experience here; but, as I have continued to repeat, he is concerned to tell us a number of things about the Law, and to show us that the Law cannot save in any respect; it cannot justify, it cannot sanctify. That is his one object in the whole of the passage. His interest is in the Law. In verse 5 he says that the Law makes us sin more than ever; in verse 13 he says 'the law kills me'. He knew he would be criticized and misunderstood over this, so he answers the objections. That is all he is doing; and he puts it in this dramatic form. He personalizes the whole argument. He says in effect, 'If you say that the Law was meant to save, and can save, the position you leave me in is this, that I know that the Law is spiritual. Yes, but I am carnal; what can I do? What is the point of knowing that the Law is spiritual? I approve it, I want to carry it out, but I cannot; I am paralysed. That is my position; you are leaving me there.'

What sort of man is Paul describing therefore? He is describing a man who is experiencing an intense conviction of sin, a man who has been given to see, by the Spirit, the holiness of the Law; and he feels utterly condemned. He is aware of his weakness for the first time, and his complete failure. But he does not know any more. He is trying to keep the Law in his own strength, and he finds that he cannot. He therefore feels condemned; he is under conviction. He does not know, he does not understand the truth about the Gospel, about salvation in and through the Lord Jesus Christ.

At the same time I have given abundant proof of the fact that the man is not unregenerate. 'But you seem to be saying', says someone, 'that he is not regenerate either.' How do we resolve the difficulty? This is the experience of large numbers of people, sometimes of people who have been reading a book on Revival, or the biography of some great saint. Suddenly they are brought under conviction of sin by the Holy Spirit. They see that the whole of their past is wrong, that it is loss. They see the meaning of the Law for the first time. They have lost their self-righteousness, they are 'dead', they are 'killed' by the Law; and they then try to put themselves right, but they cannot do so. They may remain like that for days and for weeks, even for years. Then the truth about Christ and His full salvation is revealed to them, and they find peace and joy and happiness and power. They glory in Christ and His Cross and offer up their praise. But for a time they are in this position, as it were, of being neither the one nor the other, neither unregenerate nor regenerate. All we can say for certain is that they are under deep conviction of sin. But they have not seen the truth clearly even about justification, leave alone about sanctification. This man is under the condemnation of the Law, and feeling his utter hopelessness, and helplessness, and spiritual death. He is 'under' what the Apostle calls 'the law of sin and death'.

Why did the Apostle write all that? He did so for two reasons; firstly, to answer the charge that was brought against him that he was dismissing the Law of God, and saying that it was evil. But he had a second and a much stronger reason which he has given us in the first six verses of the chapter. It was to show us that there is a way of sure deliverance in Christ; that which he had already said in verse 14 of chapter 6: 'Sin shall not have dominion over you; for ye are not under the law, but under grace.' Chapter 7 is an exposition and elaboration of that theme. 'All is well,' Paul seems to say, 'you are not under the law. You are like the woman whose husband is dead; you are dead to the law, and you are married to another, even to him that was raised from the dead, who is full of life and power, and will produce children out of you. He will impregnate you, he will put his life into you, and you shall bear fruit unto God. You will no longer be seeking to do this "under the law". You have been delivered from that in which you were held, and you will serve in newness of spirit and not in the oldness of the letter' (verses 1–6). Such is his great and glorious message; and in these verses from 7 to the end of the chapter we have nothing but two parentheses in which he deals with difficulties, and nothing else. He will go on in chapter 8 to give us his experience as a regenerate man in Christ Jesus, who has been 'made free from the law of sin and death' and who is now able to do what he could not do before because of the weakness of the flesh. This, then, is the position. This section is but a parenthesis to show us in a clear and dramatic way what the Law could not do because it was 'weak through the flesh'. Thank God, this is not the picture of the regenerate man! The regenerate man is the man I have been depicting and describing in the many quotations from this Epistle and the other Epistles, and the writings of other Apostles, and above all, in the words of the Lord of Glory Himself who said, 'If the Son shall make you free, ye shall be free indeed'.

Twenty

*

There is therefore now no condemnation to them which are in Christ Jesus, who walk not after the flesh but after the Spirit.

Romans 8: 1

Those who use modern translations of the New Testament will notice that the last statement in this verse as it is found in the Authorized Version (K.J.) of 1611 is omitted, namely, the phrase 'who walk not after the flesh, but after the Spirit'. The same phrase is found in the 4th verse, and the older and best manuscripts do not have it at this point in the 1st verse. Therefore, on grounds of textual criticism – not higher criticism but textual criticism – it is probably wise to omit this phrase at this particular point, and to read this verse thus, 'There is therefore now no condemnation to them which are in Christ Jesus'.

We come here to the great 8th chapter of this Epistle. There is general agreement about this chapter, not only from the standpoint of interpretation, but in saying that it is one of the greatest chapters in the Bible. There is a sense in which it is invidious to draw such distinctions, and yet we must agree that there are certain chapters and passages in the Scriptures which have always meant more to God's people than others. There is nothing wrong in that; it is simply that there are variations. As the Apostle says of the body that there are some parts which are more comely than others, so it is in this great body of Truth which we call the Scripture; and as long as that does not lead us to disparage other chapters and passages there is no harm done in saying that this is an outstanding chapter. I agree with those who say that it is one of the brightest gems of all. Someone has said that in the whole of the Scriptures the brightest and the most lustrous and flashing stone, or collection of stones, is this Epistle to the Romans, and that of these this is the brightest

[258]

gem in the cluster. Personally, if I were pressed for an opinion,
I would say that the most important chapter in this Epistle is
chapter 5, but in many senses the most moving is this chapter 8.
I would put them in that order; and my reason for doing so will
emerge as we proceed with our exposition.

The opening word, which immediately arrests attention, and
which is so important for us, is the word 'therefore'. Whenever
we start a fresh section, a fresh chapter, a fresh portion of Scripture, nothing is of greater importance than to be clear about its
connection with other portions. People who go wrong in their
interpretations of Scripture usually do so because they fail to pay
attention to the context. It is most unwise to pick out a verse, a
text, and interpret it apart from its context. In that way you can
make Scripture say almost anything you like. One way to safeguard against error is always to consider the context. Now if that
is true of individual verses, it is equally true of chapters; and it is
particularly true of this 8th chapter of the Epistle to the Romans.
What is its context? The word 'therefore' puts us immediately
on to the right track. It is a connecting link. The Apostle is drawing an inference, a deduction from something that has gone before, so we must first discover the exact reference of the term.
'There is *therefore* . . . ' In the light of what has been spoken already
by the Apostle, how are we to interpret the word?

Here is an interesting question. We need not spend much
time in pointing out that the connection is not with what he has
just been saying at the end of chapter 7. Here, fortunately, most
of the best commentators are in agreement. Charles Hodge, for
instance, says quite clearly that what Paul says here at the beginning of chapter 8 and what he goes on to say throughout the
chapter, is not an inference from chapter 7 and least of all an
inference from chapter 7, verses 14–25. You cannot deduce
from what Paul has just been saying that 'There is therefore now
no condemnation to them that are in Christ Jesus'. There is no
natural connection there. The only natural connection for this
statement, as I was at great pains to emphasize earlier, is found at
the end of chapter 5. There is no natural connection between this
statement and anything that Paul has been saying in chapters 6 and
7. But it does link up very naturally with what the Apostle was
saying at the end of chapter 5, indeed with the whole of chapter 5.

At the beginning of the 5th chapter there is another, a similar,

'Therefore'. 'Therefore being justified by faith, we have peace with God through our Lord Jesus Christ', and the further deduction, 'By whom also we have access by faith into this grace wherein we stand, and rejoice in hope of the glory of God'. In other words, having laid down the great doctrine of justification, and having met difficulties and objections, and having used the case of Abraham as a supreme illustration of it all, the Apostle says, 'Therefore being justified by faith, we have peace with God'. Now here at the beginning of chapter 8 he is really saying much the same thing again. 'There is therefore now no condemnation to them that are in Christ Jesus'. In other words we are at 'peace with God'; we are not under God's wrath; there is no condemnation upon us. I therefore argue that Paul is taking up here what he had been saying in chapter 5. He had worked out the original proposition of verses 1 and 2 of chapter 5 in the remainder of that chapter, leading up to the final statement, 'That as sin hath reigned unto death, even so might grace reign through righteousness unto eternal life by Jesus Christ our Lord'. We emphasized in dealing with chapter 5 that its great emphasis and teaching is the absolute certainty of the full and final salvation of all who are justified by faith. Once a man is justified by faith there is a sense in which he is already glorified – 'We rejoice in hope of the glory of God' (verse 2). Trials, troubles, tribulations cannot rob us of it, for our justification is the result of God's love for us.

Next the Apostle works out the same theme in still greater detail in the wonderful doctrine of our union with Christ which is dealt with particularly in verses 12–21 of the 5th chapter. Here in chapter 8, verse 1, I say, he comes back to that. Why do I put it like that? I do so in order to remind you once again that chapters 6 and 7 are really but a parenthesis; they are not a part of the great general argument. He could have left them out altogether, without depriving us of any vital aspect of his great message. But he turns aside, as we have seen in both those chapters, to deal with particular difficulties, to answer certain criticisms and objections that were being brought against his teaching. We must be clear about the main argument, the big principles. People go wrong over this great Epistle, and do such harm to themselves and their enjoyment of salvation because they fail to do this. In consequence they 'miss the wood because of the trees'; so we must look at the 'wood' again. Chapter 6 proves that our

sanctification is guaranteed because of our union with Christ,
which he had expounded in chapter 5, verses 12–21. Chapter 7
really proves exactly the same point in a different way. There, he
is concerned to prove that our sanctification is guaranteed because we have been set free from the Law and tied to, and married
to, the Lord Jesus Christ. Or, to put it in a different way, the
business of chapter 6 is to show positively what our union with
Christ does, and achieves, and will achieve. Chapter 7 is mainly
concerned to show what the Law cannot do, chapter 6 what
Christ can do. We have tried to show that that was the sole business of chapter 7, and nothing else at all. It was simply a digression,
a parenthesis to prove to those who were not clear about this,
that they really must stop thinking about the Law and its observance from the standpoint of either justification or sanctification.
Chapter 7, verses 14–25, does that in particular, leading to that
climax in which he shows the utter hopelessness of a man who
sees the spirituality of the Law but does not see how to be delivered from it. We said at the end of chapter 7 that the picture
in verses 14–25 is that of a man who realizes the condemnation of
the Law and no more. All his thinking is in terms of the Law and
his relationship to it. We argued that chapter 7 is nothing but a
hypothetical, imaginary picture painted by the Apostle of a man
who sees the complete hopelessness of salvation by the Law.
Or else we may say that it is the picture of a man who is actually
under a very deep conviction of sin. I would suggest that in John
Bunyan's *Grace Abounding* we have a picture which is very re-
miniscent of this. Bunyan spent eighteen months in an agony of
conviction of sin and repentance. He saw the sprituality of the
Law, but he had not seen the full message of the gospel. By the
work of the Holy Spirit within him he had seen the character of
the Law and the truth about himself, but he had not seen any
more; he had not seen the way of deliverance, the way of escape.
What is the position of such a man? My answer would be,
as I have said, that such a man has life in him. He could not
see the Law as spiritual if he had no life in him, and was but a
'natural' man. Regeneration is not a conscious experience. It
is something that happens in the realm of the unconscious. It is
the action of God in which He puts a seed of spiritual life in us;
and the first indication of the presence of that life is that there is
repentance. No man can repent apart from that act of God. The

natural man cannot repent, for these things are 'foolishness unto him' (I Corinthians 2: 14). But a man may remain in that condition of conviction of sin and condemnation for some time before he sees the way of salvation. But the exact relationship between repentance and faith is a difficult question.

I have quoted the example of John Bunyan, and those who are familiar with the accounts of the various Revivals in the history of the Church will have come across the same kind of thing frequently in them. Take for instance the great event at Kirk-of-Shotts in Scotland in 1630. As the result of the sermon preached by John Livingstone on that notable Monday morning there were many people who were in an agony of conviction as described perfectly in the second section of Romans chapter 7. Some remained in that state for hours, some for days, and some for weeks. They felt utterly lost. They saw the spirituality of the Law, they saw their own utter failure and the uselessness of all their own efforts. They could not find release and relief. There they were, groaning, some literally lying under the hedgerows, others knocking at the door of the minister in the early hours of the morning, crying for the relief which they could not find. That, it seems to me, is the position described so perfectly by the Apostle Paul in Romans 7: 13–25. It is a very early manifestation of spiritual life; but it is no more than that – conviction but not conversion.*

What the Apostle now proceeds to say in this 8th chapter seems to me to prove abundantly that what I have been suggesting is the only reasonable and adequate view of that section; because, here, he is now really going to show us how the Christian thinks about himself, what the Christian really does know to be true about himself. And what he is going to emphasize is that the Christian is not a man who talks about nothing but the Law of God. When the Christian talks about his sin and failure he does not talk about it primarily in terms of the Law; he talks about it in terms of love, about his failure to please the One who has died for him, and his failure to live to His glory. The Christian does not go on speaking in terms of the Law as the man in Romans 7 does. He is no longer 'under the law' but 'under grace'. Furthermore, as the Apostle will show us – indeed he announces it here already at the very beginning – the Christian must never

* See also Appendix, page 357.

[262]

allow himself to feel the condemnation of the Law. A Christian should chide himself for doing so. The whole object of this great 8th chapter is to emphasize that – 'No condemnation . . . no separation'. A Christian should never speak of himself in terms of chapter 7 verses 14–25. That is to be 'under the law' and 'under condemnation'. The Apostle says here in a most extraordinary and moving manner that 'There is therefore now no condemnation to them that are in Christ Jesus'. That is the glory of the gospel; he is writing his Epistle in order to show this. The very word 'therefore' with which he starts this chapter proves that he is going back and taking up again what he had been saying in chapter 5. This has nothing by way of a direct and immediate connection with, and is in no way a direct inference from the end of chapter 7. It is a further proof that we must regard chapters 6 and 7 as being nothing but a parenthesis in the Apostle's exposition of the Christian way of salvation. We can now go on to look at the further exposition of that salvation in this chapter.

Let us take a preliminary survey and look at in general. There are certain things we can say about it at once. My first statement may possibly startle some. There is little new in chapter 8; nothing essentially new. There is no new experience described in this chapter, no sudden change described here from what we were before. As I have said, the connection goes back to chapter 5; so the idea of your being 'in chapter 7' and then 'turning over to chapter 8' is not justified at all by the statements made by the Apostle. We are not suddenly introduced here to something we have not been told before. Everything in this chapter has already been hinted at. What we have here is the outworking, the exposition, the elaboration, of what he has already stated in germ and in embryo. That is why I say once more that chapter 5 is the great central chapter of this Epistle. Here, he takes up what he said in broad principle there, and works it out in greater detail. That is his method, as we have often seen. Chapter 5 sums up all that had gone before; and it introduces us to all that is going to follow. In this 8th chapter we shall find many moving statements; but there is no new truth. This is just sheer exposition. Let us, then, attempt a general analysis of the contents of the chapter.

I make bold to assert that the great theme of chapter 8 is not sanctification. Sanctification is only a part of it. The great theme is the security of the Christian, the absolute certainty of the 'final perseverance' of the saints, and of the ultimate, complete and entire salvation of every one who believes in the Lord Jesus Christ. But we have met that truth before. It is found in chapter 5. I used the same words in introducing chapter 5. 'Being justified by faith, we have peace with God through our Lord Jesus Christ; by whom also we have access by faith into this grace wherein we stand, and rejoice in hope of the glory of God.' It already refers to the end, to the glory to come; it supplies the assurance, the certainty, the absolute guarantee of the ultimate, final, complete salvation of the Christian; it shows that nothing can stop it, that nothing can frustrate it. Now that is the theme of chapter 8 as it was the theme of chapter 5.

In his handling of this theme, the Apostle again does what is very characteristic of him. The true hallmark of greatness is simplicity. It is little minds that are complicated and involved. This man's method is always the same, and it is essentially simple. In verse 1 he states his theme, and makes a general statement of what is true of the Christian: 'There is therefore now no condemnation to them that are in Christ Jesus.' The remaining thirty-eight verses of the chapter are just a working out of that opening assertion. He has already made the same claim in chapter 5: 'Moreover the law entered that the offence might abound. But where sin abounded, grace did much more abound. That as sin hath reigned unto death, even so might grace reign through righteousness unto eternal life by Jesus Christ' (vv. 20 and 21); and he would have gone on immediately from that to what he says in this 8th chapter were it not that he knew about the two major difficulties dealt with in chapters 6 and 7. The writing of those chapters, however, has not been a waste of time because they enable him to say again what he had already said, with greater force and power. He has got rid of the difficulty, so he can underline and emphasize the grand central statement concerning assurance more strongly than ever before. So we thank God for the digressions in chapters 6 and 7. We leave them, as they are, in their right place; but we now see exactly what they were meant to do.

The fundamental proposition is, 'There is therefore now no condemnation to them that are in Christ Jesus'. The Apostle is going to work that out, and to prove it. In verses 2–4 he proves

[264]

it in the following way. He says that it is true because we have been delivered from the Law altogether and are joined to Christ by the Holy Spirit. He works that out from step to step as if climbing up a ladder. The first thing is that there is 'no condemnation'. But 'What about the Law?' asks someone. 'We have no more to do with it', he replies, 'The law of the Spirit of life in Christ Jesus hath made me free from the law of sin and death'. Then he proceeds to say that what the Law could not do has been done in Christ. That is the first argument.

The second argument is found in verses 5–13. He has already mentioned the Holy Spirit in chapter 7, verse 6; and he now goes on to elaborate his statement. Our salvation is guaranteed, he says, because of the work of the Holy Spirit within us. He works in us two main things. The first is our sanctification, delivering us from sin and all its vestiges, and even delivering the body from it. In the digression in chapter 6 we have seen that sin remains in the body. Well, says Paul, even that will go: 'If the Spirit of him that raised up Jesus from the dead dwell in you, he that raised up Christ from the dead shall also quicken your mortal bodies by his Spirit that dwelleth in you' (v. 11).

The third argument is found in verses 14–17, where the Apostle again reminds us that the presence of the Spirit within us is a proof that we are children of God, sons of God. We are not merely left in a position in which God has forgiven us, but still continues to treat us as subjects 'under the law'. No, in this glorious salvation, says Paul, we are lifted out of that realm altogether. There is an 'adoption'. We have become the sons and the children of God, and because of that we are 'heirs of God, and joint-heirs with Christ'. We are to look at salvation in this way. We have to realize that we have become sons; and if God has done that to us and has changed our whole relationship, and made us sons and children, with all that that involves, how can our salvation possibly fail? That is the argument of verses 14–17.

The fourth argument is in verses 18–25, where Paul argues that, because we are sons, we are destined for an inheritance of glory, which God has not only promised us, but is even now preparing for us, and not only for us, but for the whole creation. That is a tremendous statement. The radical defect in so many of us is that we are so subjective and always thinking of our particular moods and states. The Apostle Paul reminds us that sin not only affects us and our fellow human beings, it has affected the whole creation – the animals, even inanimate nature, everything is affected. God's work, God's creation has been marred. Sin has come in, and evil has polluted it all. We are to look at salvation and ourselves as a part of the glorious scheme which is going to renovate the entire cosmos. And because God is going to do that to the whole cosmos he is going to do it to you!

In verses 26 and 27 the Apostle comes down to our level, becomes more directly practical, and reminds us that even while we are in this world with its difficulties and problems and struggles, God has seen to it that we are not left to ourselves. The Holy Spirit acts within us as an intercessor, praying, teaching us how to pray, stimulating prayer, showing us our need, reminding us of the supply that can satisfy it, and sometimes in a manner we cannot understand even praying within us, and leading us to utter sounds which we ourselves cannot understand always, but which God understands. Nothing can separate us from Him; we are in Christ Jesus; and this communion is going to be maintained always.

Then Paul moves on to the sixth argument, which is in verses 28-34. This is one of the greatest of all. Why can I say so confidently, and with such assurance, that the final and complete salvation of the Christian is guaranteed? The answer is that the very character of God is involved in it all; and that if this fails, if it fails with respect to any believer, the character of God has gone. I mean this; that God has told us quite plainly that He has a great plan and scheme and purpose of salvation. He formed it, He planned it, before the foundation of the world. There are steps and stages in it, and God has told us what they are. He set His heart upon us in eternity, and predestinated us. Then he calls us, and separates us, and goes on with His work within us through all the steps and stages from justification to final glorification. Such is God's announced plan and scheme of salvation. God purposed it in Himself before man had ever been created, leave alone before he had ever sinned. God has announced it and promulgated it. It cannot fail because God is God, and His purposes are ever sure.

But the Apostle tells us something further in this section. He not only tells us what God has purposed and planned, and has put into execution; he particularly emphasizes certain things that God has already done in connection with His plan. Here he says the most outstanding and astonishing thing of all. God, to bring to pass this great plan, did not even 'spare' His only begotten Son, but 'delivered him up for us all'. That, says the Apostle, is an absolute guarantee that the rest is going to follow. It is inconceivable that this immutable, eternal, holy, righteous God, who has all power, should even deliver His own Son up unto death for us and our salvation, and then allow anything to stop it or to frustrate it. It is inconceivable. We have not only God's character, God's Word, God's plan, but this action of God in sending His only begotten, beloved Son into this world deliberately to die, to be the sin-bearer, to be 'the Lamb of God'. That death was not an accident; it was not primarily the action of men; it was 'according to the determinate counsel and foreknowledge of God', as Peter declared in his sermon in Jerusalem on the day of Pentecost (Acts 2: 23), God planned the death of His own Son in order to save us. Is it conceivable that God would do that, and then allow anything to cause it to fail? It does not bear thought or analysis for a second. Our salvation is certain. As Paul puts it: 'Whom he did foreknow, he also did predestinate to be conformed to the image of his Son, that he might be the firstborn among many brethren. Moreover whom he did predestinate, them he also called; and whom he called, them he also justified; and whom he justified, them he also glorified.' Absolute certainty! 'What shall we then say to these things? If God be for us, who can be against us?' And so Paul works out his argument, bringing it to an end in verse 34.

All this having been said, the Apostle sums up everything in verses 35-39. 'Who shall separate us from the love of Christ?' He has already said in the first verse that no one and nothing can do so, that there is no condemnation, and never can be. Now he has proved it; so he concludes by asking, Who then shall or can separate us, conceivably, from the love of Christ? And he proceeds to show, in a mighty, moving climax, that nothing can do so, 'neither death, nor life, nor angels, nor principalities, nor powers, nor things present, nor things to come, nor height, nor depth, nor any other creature shall be able to separate us from the love of God which is in Christ Jesus our Lord'. That is the ultimate guarantee – not the greatness and the might and the power of God, not even His plan and His purpose; the final argument is the love of God. It is the love of God that has led to all the rest, for 'God is love'. And He is unchangeable, so nothing can ever 'make Him His purpose forego', or frustrate His glorious plan. Thus the Apostle in these verses from the 2nd verse to the 39th, proves, demonstrates and establishes what he lays down as a proposition in the first verse.

We now have to work this out step by step, statement by statement. The Apostle, I repeat, takes up again the great theme of chapter 5, namely, the absolute certainty of the ultimate glorification, the full, entire deliverance, emancipation, and salvation of any man who is justified by faith. You cannot make justification a terminus, and those who say that you 'take your justification, and halt or stop at that, and then later on decide to 'take your sanctification' are denying the central theme of the Epistle to the Romans. If you are 'justified', your final 'glorification' is guaranteed. Sanctification is one of the steps, but only one of them. Notice the place it has in chapter 8; it is one section only, and it is surrounded by the other sections. Thus in every way the Apostle demonstrates his contention that there is 'no condemnation to them that are in Christ Jesus'. As we take up these themes, and look at the particular statements, it will be easy to show that he is just elaborating what he has already said in germ and in essence in chapter 5.

Twenty-one

*

There is therefore now no condemnation to them which are in Christ Jesus.
For the law of the Spirit of life in Christ Jesus hath made me free from the law of sin and death. Romans 8: 1, 2

We now come to the detailed consideration of this chapter; we start with the first verse and its resounding statement, 'There is therefore now no condemnation to them which are in Christ Jesus'. This is one of the great statements of the Scripture, one of the most important for Christian experience and for the health and well-being of the Christian believer. This is, in a sense, the great good news of the gospel – that it is possible to announce a way of salvation in which there is no longer any condemnation. This is the greatest good news that has ever come into the world; it holds out the greatest possibility for man since the Fall. It is the heart and essence and soul of the Christian gospel. Not only that; as I have already indicated, this is the theme of the whole of this chapter. I would remind you that Paul is not making a new statement here; he has already said it, and particularly so in the 5th chapter of the Epistle. But he states it now in a new way.

Take verse 16 of chapter 5, for instance: 'And not as it was by one that sinned, so is the gift: for the judgment was by one (Adam) to condemnation, but the free gift is of many offences unto justification.' Then look at verse 18: 'Therefore as by the offence of one judgment came upon all men to condemnation; even so by the righteousness of one the free gift came upon all men unto justification of life.' Paul is now going to elaborate these great themes and to work them out in fresh detail. In other words, we shall expect to find in chapter 8 a repetition, in fresh terms, of the great doctrine of 'Justification by faith only'.

That is what we have here at the beginning of this 8th chapter. Certain Bibles which try to divide up the message of this Epistle in a mechanical manner into justification, sanctification, and so on, put this section under 'sanctification'. But it does not belong to that category, for the opposite of 'condemnation' is always 'justification', not sanctification. That readily appears in the two verses I have just quoted from chapter 5. Those who interpret the first four verses of this chapter in terms of sanctification, are not only going against everything the Apostle has been laying down, but furthermore falling into the Roman Catholic heresy of regarding sanctification as being the cause of our acceptance with God, that is to say, our justification. That is indeed a failure to understand the doctrine of justification by faith. Such interpreters have been so dominated by the erroneous teaching which misinterprets Romans 7, verses 7–25 and believes in some experimental 'going over from chapter 7 to chapter 8', that they must of necessity regard this as being sanctification. For this reason a true interpretation of Romans 7 is important not only in and of itself but especially from the standpoint of the development of the Apostle's central argument. As the opposite of 'condemnation' is 'justification', when Paul says 'There is therefore now no condemnation to them which are in Christ Jesus', he is teaching that those who are in Christ Jesus are justified. Or, to put it the other way round, the justified are in Christ Jesus.

In a sense, therefore, we can say that this first verse is a summary and summing up of the great argument about justification, the argument which began in the 1st chapter, and which is stated so clearly and dramatically in chapter 3, verses 21–31: 'But now a righteousness from God apart from the law . . .'. The theme is laid down in the 1st chapter in verses 16 and 17: 'I am not ashamed of the gospel of Christ for it is the power of God unto salvation to every one that believeth; to the Jew first, and also to the Greek. For therein is a righteousness from God revealed from faith to faith: as it is written, The just shall live by faith.' Here in chapter 8, verse 1, Paul is just coming back to that theme: such is his method, he keeps on coming back and repeating the great idea. And of course, when you have a truth like this what can you do but go on repeating it? The musical composer when he produces a good tune is never content with putting it once only into his composition, whatever its nature, he goes on repeating it. And we do not get tired of it; we are grateful to him for repeating it, and hope he will keep on repeating it. The Apostle does the same thing; and therefore he is very happy to say once more 'There is therefore now no condemnation'. He had already said it again in the first verse of chapter 5, 'Being justified by faith, we have peace with God' and it all follows from that.

'No condemnation'. 'There is therefore now no'. 'Therefore', 'now', 'no' – what important words they are! The words remind us of our position now as Christians. Look at that word 'no' – 'No condemnation'! What a statement! 'No' is a little word of two letters; but are we aware of its full meaning? It is entire, it is complete, it is absolute. In other words, Paul is saying that a Christian is a person who has been taken entirely outside the realm of any possible or conceivable condemnation. The Christian has finished with the realm of condemnation; he has been taken right out of it; he has nothing more to do with it. There is no condemnation to the Christian 'now' and never can be! Had you realized that? Not only is the Christian not in a state of condemnation now, he never can be; it is impossible.

There are many who misunderstand this. They seem to think of the Christian as a man who, if he confesses his sin and asks for forgiveness, is forgiven. At that moment he is not under condemnation. But then if he should sin again he is back once more under condemnation. Then he repents and confesses his sin again, and asks for pardon, and he is cleansed once more. So to them the Christian is a man who is constantly passing from one state to the other; back and forth; condemned, not condemned. Now that, according to the Apostle, is a wholly mistaken notion, and a complete failure to understand the position. The Christian is a man who can never be condemned; he can never come into a state of condemnation again. 'No condemnation'! The Apostle is not talking about his experience, but about his position, his standing, his status; he is in a position in which, being justified, he can never again come under condemnation. That is the meaning of this word 'no'. It means 'Never'.

Because this is true of him the Christian should never feel condemnation; he should never allow himself to feel it. The devil will try to make him feel it; but he must answer the devil. If the devil comes to you and tries to convict you, and to make you feel that you are condemned, stand up to him and say 'There is therefore now no condemnation to them which are in Christ Jesus'. Answer him with the Scripture, and he will 'flee from you'. This is a categorical statement; this is the truth about the Christian. The Apostle is asserting here that if we are Christians, your sins and mine – past sins, present sins, and future sins – have already been dealt with once and for ever! Had you realized that? Most of our troubles are due to our failure to realize the truth of this verse. 'There is therefore now no condemnation to them which are in Christ Jesus' is so often understood to mean nothing more than that past sins have been dealt with. Of course it means that; but it also means your present sins; even more, it means that any sin you may ever chance to commit has already been dealt with. You will never, you cannot ever, come under condemnation. This is what the Apostle is saying – nothing can ever bring the Christian again into a position of condemnation.

In other words, in this first verse he is already saying what he will further say in the last verse of the chapter, that there can be 'no separation from the love of God which is in Christ Jesus our Lord'. Many miss the point and teach that you start with 'no condemnation' and then, as the result of adopting certain teachings and receiving certain experiences, you finally arrive at 'no separation'. But the 'no separation' is here at the beginning; it is in the word 'no', indeed in the entire statement of verse 1: 'There is therefore now no condemnation to them which are in Christ Jesus.' Condemnation and separation are an utter impossibility for the Christian; a 'falling away from grace' cannot happen. The Christian can never be lost, the Christian can never come under condemnation. 'No condemnation' is an absolute word, and we must not detract from it. To do so is to contradict and to deny the Scripture. This is the Apostle's way, at this point, of teaching the doctrine of the 'Final perseverance of the saints'.

But why does the Apostle say this, and on what grounds does he say it? Is it not a dangerous thing to say? Will it not incite people to sin? If we tell Christians that their past sins, their present and their future sins have already been put away by God, are we not more or less telling them that they are free to go

out and sin? If you react in that way to my statements I am most
happy, for I am obviously a good and true interpreter of the
Apostle Paul. It was because he preached such things that people
said, 'What shall we say then? Shall we continue in sin that
grace may abound? (chapter 6: 1). That is the very charge they
were bringing against him, and if we do not preach and represent
this gospel in a way that sounds dangerous at first, we are not
preaching it truly. The true preaching of the gospel is always
liable to be misunderstood by people in that way. The Apostle
has already given the answer in chapters 6 and 7, proving that
there is no risk at all, but rather the opposite.

Let me show how he goes on to demonstrate this again. He
is summing up the argument of chapters 6 and 7 just in passing,
so that he can go on with his main argument. 'There is therefore
now no condemnation'. To whom? 'To them which are in
Christ Jesus'. Here is the explanation – 'in Christ Jesus'. In other
words, What is a Christian? The Christian, says someone, is a
man who has decided for Christ, the Christian is a man who has
decided to go in for the Christian life, decided to join a church;
he has believed in the Lord Jesus Christ, and so his sins are
forgiven. Of course those statement, looked at correctly, are
good and true; but that is not a true definition of the Christian.
The Christian essentially, says the Apostle, is one who is 'in
Christ Jesus'. Here is another little word – 'in'. How glibly we
say, 'in Christ Jesus'. It is the greatest statement of all; there is
nothing beyond being 'in Christ Jesus'. This again is not new,
we have already met it in chapter 5, as I am about to show.
Paul wants us to see that we are not only justified, but that if
we are justified we are 'in' Christ Jesus. The terms are not
identical. God 'justifies the ungodly'. He does not justify a man
because he is in Christ, He justifies him while he is still ungodly,
as is stated in chapter 4, verse 5. But God not only justifies him,
He puts him 'into' Christ. Once God starts a work He goes on
to complete it. We have to separate these things in our thinking
and understanding, but you cannot speak of these things
chronologically or be dogmatic in your view as to which comes
first.

God's act of justification is the basis of our final assurance, of
our absolute certainty that we can never again come under
condemnation, and that God will go on with His work in us

until we are glorified and entire and complete, 'without spot or blemish or any such thing'. 'In Christ Jesus'. If you are in Christ Jesus you will remain there, and nothing can ever take you out of Him. Nothing! That is the explanation of the 'no separation' at the close of the chapter.

But as I said, the Apostle is not introducing a new theme for the first time here; this is not a new idea. Where then does he introduce it? We find it in chapter 5, verse 10: 'For if, when we were enemies, we were reconciled to God by the death of his Son, much more, being reconciled, we shall be saved by his life.' That is the translation in the Authorized (K.J.) Version but we were able to show that the right translation runs, 'we shall be saved in his life' – 'in his life'! And as we saw further, the remainder of that chapter is simply a proof of the fact that we are 'in Christ Jesus'. As we were 'in Adam', we are now 'in Christ'. We were in that 'first man', and his sin led to certain consequences; so we are in the 'second man' now, and His death and life lead to certain consequences also in us. Then in answering the objection to his teaching which he puts in the 1st verse of chapter 6, the Apostle worked out in great detail the meaning of the phrase, 'in Christ Jesus'. That is the message of the first ten verses of chapter 6.

The same truth appears again in the 4th verse of chapter 7: 'Wherefore, my brethren, ye also are become dead to the law by the body of Christ; that ye should be married to another, even to him who is raised from the dead, that we should bring forth fruit unto God.' There Paul put our union with Christ in terms of the marriage bond and unity. The phrase, 'in Christ Jesus', is in many ways the great theme of the New Testament, and particularly of this Apostle. Consider it as it appears in 1 Corinthians 1: 30: 'But of him are ye in Christ Jesus, who of God is made unto us wisdom, and righteousness, and sanctification, and redemption'. We find it again in the Second Epistle to the Corinthians, chapter 5, verse 17: 'If any man be in Christ'. It is found also in the Epistle to the Ephesians.

'In Christ' means that we are united to Christ as we were united to Adam. We were 'in Adam'; we came out of Adam; and we come out of Christ, are born of Christ in the same way. The New Testament gives us certain illustrations to help us. Our Lord Himself gave the illustration of the Vine and the branches to show this intimate, organic, mystical union between Christ and

His people. But then there is the illustration of the body, and this was obviously the favourite illustration of the Apostle Paul. Christ is the Head and we are 'the body'; 'Ye are the body of Christ, and members in particular' (1 Corinthians 12: 27). He uses that illustration in several of his epistles, and he does so in order to bring out this truth of our union with Christ, of our being in Him, drawing life out of Him in the way that every part of my body is dependent upon my head. Such is our relationship to the Lord Jesus Christ.

The Apostle repeats it here again, he reminds us of it once more. 'There is therefore now no condemnation', no possibility of condemnation for us because we are 'in Christ'. How does that prove it? He has shown how, in detail, in chapter 6. If you are 'in Christ' you are in His death, you partook of His death, you shared in His death. 'Know ye not', he says, 'that so many of us as were baptised into Christ Jesus were baptised into his death.' We have died with Him, we have been 'buried with him'; but thank God we have also 'been raised' with Him. 'Therefore we are buried with him by baptism into death: that like as Christ was raised up from the dead by the glory of the Father, even so we also should walk in newness of life. For if we have been planted together in the likeness of his death, we shall be also in the likeness of his resurrection.' These are the inevitable consequences of being 'in Christ Jesus'. If I am in Christ what is His becomes mine. Because I am 'in him' I share in what He has done exactly in the same way as I shared in Adam and what he did. Adam committed that first sin, and we all sinned with him, and condemnation came upon us all. Thank God the other side is also true – When Christ died, I died; when Christ rose, I rose; Christ has ascended, I am seated with him in the heavenly places at this moment.

In chapter 7 in the first four verses, Paul puts the same truth in the context of the marriage relationship. The husband is dead, the woman is free, and can be married to another, joined to the other. So we have died unto the Law in which we were held, that we might be married to this Other, who dies; yes, but who is risen again. And we are risen with Him, and everything that belongs to the Bridegroom belongs to the Bride. The husband and the wife share everything in common because of this unity, this relationship. In the Epistle to the Ephesians, chapter 5, verse

30, the Apostle actually says, 'We are members of his body, of his flesh, and of his bones'. That fixes your relationship as a Christian to the Lord Jesus Christ; you are as much 'in him' as that. You are a part of Him, you are members of His body, 'of his flesh and of his bones'. Paul says that the mystical union between Christ and His Church is comparable to that between the husband and the wife.

All this is designed to show us that we are so intimately connected with Him that not only what is His is ours, but it always will be, nothing can ever remove us from it. That is why there is 'no condemnation'. The Apostle has argued thus in chapter 6, verses 8 and 9: 'Now if we be dead with Christ, we believe that we shall also live with him: knowing that Christ being raised from the dead dieth no more; death hath no more dominion over him.' He has finished with death, He has gone out of its realm to the other realm – 'For in that he died, he died unto sin once' – once and for ever – 'but in that he liveth, he liveth unto God'. The conclusion the Apostle draws is, 'Reckon ye also yourselves likewise to be dead indeed unto sin, but alive unto God through Jesus Christ our Lord'. 'Death hath no more dominion over him', and death hath no more dominion over us. It has not, it cannot have, it never will have dominion. I will go further. As Christ has risen to this new life with God in all His perfection, so my union with Him guarantees that I shall eventually be perfect, I shall be glorified, I shall be 'without spot or wrinkle or any such thing'; there will be no blemish in me. He will present me 'faultless before the presence of God and his glory with exceeding joy' (Jude 24, 25). Because I am 'in him' I am going to be as perfect as He is; I shall be glorified, even my very body, as He is. I am certain of this. Because I am joined to Him, because I am in Christ Jesus, nothing can prevent it. This is the guarantee of the ultimate and the final perfection and glorification of the saints.

For all these reasons the Apostle does not hesitate to make his categorical statement, 'There is therefore now no condemnation to them which are in Christ Jesus'. There is not, there never will be, there never can be condemnation. There is nothing more foolish than the notion that you can be 'in Christ' at one moment; then when you sin you are 'out of' Christ, then when you repent you are 'in Christ' again? How can that be reconciled with the illustration of the body? The very idea is ludicrous. No, if you are in Him, you are in Him for ever, you are in Him for all eternity. It is God who has put you 'in him', and no one and nothing can take you out – neither hell, nor Satan, nor any other power. If you are in, you are in. It is absolute. There is no condemnation, there never will be; it is impossible.

We must cease to think of ourselves merely as forgiven, merely as believers, merely as holding on to Christ. The truth about us as Christians is that God by the Holy Spirit has put us 'into Christ', 'implanted' us 'in him' – 'planted together' as we saw in chapter 6. So you do not go 'in and out' of that. You do not cease to be a Christian when you sin, you do not come under condemnation when you sin, you are not cast 'out of' Christ when you sin. No, you remain in Christ, and there is still no condemnation. You have sinned, of course, but you have sinned against love and not against Law. You may and you should feel ashamed, but you should not feel condemnation, because to do so is to put yourself back 'under the law'. If we are in this position, 'in Christ', we are there for ever; there is no condemnation, past, present or future.

Such then is this great fundamental statement which Paul makes here at the beginning of chapter 8. I have been carried away by this; but I do not apologize. If a man does not forget himself and his little plans and programmes when he is preaching on a theme like this he should not enter a pulpit. What has time to do with this? If you have got hold of this idea you will have discovered the most glorious truth you will ever know in your life. Most Christian people are miserable, most Christian people fail, and fall into sin, because they are depressed, because they allow the devil to depress them. 'Ah', they say, 'I have sinned, so how can I make these great statements?' Have you never heard of the word 'faith?' This verse is the answer of faith to all our troubles; this is what God tells us about ourselves; and He puts it in this absolute, complete, certain manner.

The next statement in verse 2 is just an elaboration of this; but this is the foundation of it all – 'in Christ Jesus'. He is the living Head; and I am joined to Him; I am a part of Him, a part of His life, sharing in His crucifixion, death, burial, resurrection, ascension to glory, and session at the right hand of God. We are seated with him in the heavenly places (Ephesians 2: 6).

If we are in Him all this must be true of us; and that is why we shall find the Apostle, later in this chapter, making the great leap from justification to glorification. That is implicit in this 1st verse of chapter 8. He states it here in order that he may go on to make other statements. He is reminding us again that we must be clear about this basic truth once and for ever. You who are Christians, even when you sin, do not go back 'under condemnation'. The reason is, as he tells us in the next verse, that you have finished with the Law. He has already told us that in the words 'Ye are not under law, but under grace'. You must never again feel 'under condemnation'.

We can put it in the form of an illustration. The difference between an unbeliever sinning and a Christian sinning is the difference between a man transgressing one of the laws of England or any other State, and a member of a family doing something that is displeasing to another member of the family. In the one case a man commits an offence against the State; in the other a husband, say, has done something that he should not do in his relationship with his wife. He is not breaking a law, he is wounding the heart of his wife. That is the difference. It is no longer a legal matter, it is a matter of personal relationship now, and that, a relationship of love. The man does not cease to be the husband of the woman, not the woman to be the wife of the husband. Law does not come into the matter at all; it lies outside that realm. In a sense it is now something much worse than a legal condemnation. I would rather offend against a law of the land objectively outside me, than hurt someone whom I love.

That is why there is no risk in the Apostle's statement. Being in this state and relationship as a Christian gives me a much higher standard, and makes sin much more offensive to me, much more hateful, something to be shunned. There is no risk here at all. The man who is in Christ Jesus, and who knows it, is a man who will fight sin and hate it and avoid it much more than the man who is 'under the law'. The Apostle will work that out in verses 2, 3 and 4; but it is all here implicit in this first statement. So we must get a firm hold of this great truth of 'no condemnation', because we are 'in Christ Jesus'. We are out of the realm of the Law, and of sin, and of death, because He was condemned for our sins. He is out of it, and so are we, because we are 'in him'. So, never allow yourself to go, even in thought, under condemnation again; that is to sin, because it is failure to believe the Word of God. Answer the accuser, the devil, with Romans 8. Tell him that you know what you have done, that you have grieved your Lord and disappointed Him; but that you also know that it has nothing to do with Law, and that therefore there is 'no condemnation'. You are like a child who has sinned against his parents, and you know what to do, and to whom to go. But it has nothing to do with Law. 'There is therefore now no condemnation to them which are in Christ Jesus.'

Twenty-two

*

For the law of the Spirit of life in Christ Jesus hath made me free from the law of sin and death.   Romans 8: 2

Having considered the first verse in which the Apostle lays down the theme for the whole of the chapter, and particularly the theme of the first four verses, we are now in a position to proceed to a consideration of his working out of that basic theme. The theme is the assurance of salvation, the final certainty of the ultimate glorification and entire deliverance in every respect of those who are in Christ Jesus. 'There is therefore now no condemnation to them which are in Christ Jesus.' The Apostle begins to expound it in verses 2, 3 and 4, the first subsidiary section of the chapter. This is his first particular reason for saying that there is now no condemnation to them which are in Christ Jesus. The first word of the 2nd verse makes that quite plain – the word 'For'. It is particularly important in this chapter that we should keep our eye on this word 'For'. Most wrong interpretations of this chapter result from ignoring the word 'For'. They have concentrated on the statement itself, but have not noticed the word 'For' at all. If they had noticed that it was introduced by the word 'For' they would not have produced the false interpretation we are going to examine. He says, 'There is no condemnation to them that are in Christ Jesus because . . .'. He is going to give us a reason for that. So the business of verse 2 is to help us to understand verse 1. Whatever we may make of it, it must always be in terms of an exposition and an explanation of verse 1. The 'For' reminds us that verse 1 is not a detached statement. There is a reason for, an explanation of what has just been said.

This is a most important verse, and especially concerning the question of sanctification. In the controversy over the question of sanctification there is, perhaps, no more important verse than this. As we shall see, it is because of the failure to interpret this verse in its context and setting that certain false teachings with regard to sanctification have gained currency. The key to its understanding is the phrase 'hath made us free'; with this therefore we start. The first thing we have to note is the tense. The King James (A.V.) 'hath made' is a bad translation. What the Apostle wrote was, 'The law of the Spirit of life in Christ Jesus freed me', or 'made me free'. The Apostle used once more, as so often, the aorist tense, which means that it has happened 'once and for ever'. In the exposition of chapter 6 we had to emphasize this constantly. In the 2nd verse there, for instance, where the Authorized Version reads, 'How shall we that are dead to sin?' we took great pains to show that that was quite misleading, and that it should read, 'How shall we that died to sin'. And the aorist tense is used here also. 'The law of the Spirit of life in Christ Jesus freed me' – 'made me free'. It is not 'hath made' but 'made'. It has already happened 'once and for ever'; it is completed; it belongs to the past.

But there is also another matter of translation here. The Authorized Version reads, 'has made me free'. But it is generally agreed that it should read, 'hath made *thee* free'. The word the Apostle used should be translated 'thee' or 'you'. He is writing about the Christian generally, and not about himself. Haldane in his Commentary makes quite a point of that 'me', and as to why Paul brings the 'me' back again. But Paul did not write 'me', he wrote 'thee' or 'you' – anyone who is a Christian.

Now we can turn to a consideration of the two main phrases; and the one to start with is 'the law of sin and death'. Something has 'freed' the Christian, anyone, everyone who is in Christ, 'from the law of sin and death'. It is just here that the whole question of sanctification is brought in – wrongly. There are those who say that the phrase 'the law of sin and death' carries the same meaning as the expression used by the Apostle in chapter 7, verse 23, where he says, 'I see another law in my members, warring against the law of my mind, and bringing me into captivity to the law of sin which is in my members'. They say that when he talks about being 'made free from the law of sin and death' he is referring to this principle of evil that is in his nature, and in everyone's nature by birth, the principle that brings us

[281]

into captivity and finally to death. Thus interpreting the phrase they say that the first phrase, 'The law of the Spirit of life in Christ Jesus', means the work of the Holy Spirit in the believer. They then proceed to assert that the operation of the Holy Spirit within us has delivered us from the 'law of sin and death' which was operating in our members. So, they say, the miserable, wretched man of Romans 7 turns over the page into Romans 8; the Spirit has now come, he has had a 'second blessing', a second experience, and he is set free entirely from that which was causing him so much trouble before, and getting him down, and making him cry out 'O wretched man that I am!' In this way they maintain that this verse teaches nothing but sanctification, and is a key verse in that connection. And, of course, if it is right to interpret the meaning of 'the law of sin and death 'in that way, they are quite logical in what they say.

Those who adopt this common and popular exposition of verse 2 do not hesitate to say, as the 'Scofield Bible' notes say, for instance, that the Apostle here introduces the Holy Spirit for the first time. The man in Romans 7 was the man without the Holy Spirit, but now the Holy Spirit comes in. He had received his 'justification' before, he now experiences his 'sanctification' – a second experience – and he is delivered from this Law 'which is in his members', warring against 'the law of his mind', and 'bringing him into captivity to the law of sin which is in his members'.

I shall endeavour to show that that interpretation is entirely wrong. I am not merely making a statement to that effect, I propose to reason it out. We must take these phrases and examine them one by one. Two main schools of teaching hold to this exposition. First, there are those who teach 'entire sanctification', and who claim this as their great proof. It is also taught by those who, while not teaching 'entire sanctification', do teach that a 'second experience' is possible for the Christian which introduces a 'principle of counteraction' to the element of sin that is still in him. This new principle is the Holy Spirit dwelling within him and enabling him to have the victory over sin. As long as he 'abides in Christ' the Spirit will thus give him victory from moment to moment. This verse is crucial for both those teachings with regard to sanctification.

Let us examine these teachings. My first comment is, that if that exposition is true, then the teaching of this verse would be that our being set 'free from condemnation' is the result of our sanctification, in fact that it depends upon it. Notice the connection, 'There is therefore now no condemnation to them which are in Christ Jesus, for (because) the law of the Spirit of life in Christ Jesus hath freed me from the law of sin and death'. There is no condemnation facing us because the Holy Spirit working in us has delivered us from that 'law of sin and death' that was in our members, that was getting us down, and keeping us in a state of defeat. In other words, we are no longer in a state of condemnation, because we are sanctified. Surely that, in and of itself, is quite enough to show the falsity of that particular exposition. As we have seen from the beginning of the Epistle, and as we have been constantly emphasizing, we must never say that the deliverance from condemnation in the Christian is the result of his 'sanctification'. Deliverance from condemnation is due always to his 'justification'. The opposite to condemnation is never sanctification, invariably it is justification. I would refer again to the two crucial verses in this connection, namely chapter 6, verses 16 and 18. There is not a single instance anywhere in the Bible where the opposite of condemnation is sanctification. Yet if you interpret 'the law of sin and death' in that way you are virtually saying, 'There is no condemnation to them which are in Christ Jesus because of their sanctification'. Our first reason for rejecting that exposition is that Paul is still dealing here with our 'justification', and all that that involves and implies.

Secondly, the Apostle is not describing here what can or may happen, or what is possible, to a Christian. Still less is he describing what happens only to certain Christians who seek and receive a further blessing. He is saying, Because you are Christians, in Christ Jesus, this has already happened to you. He is not saying, 'You have believed in Christ, you are justified and forgiven; but there is another blessing possible for you. You are having a struggle, and are failing and being defeated; but listen, there is a further experience open to you which will deliver you and turn defeat into victory.' As I have been explaining, there is nothing new here. The Apostle is repeating himself; he is summing up what he has already said, but putting it in a different way. This, he says, is something which has happened already in the past – aorist tense! – to all who are in Christ Jesus. In other words, if

[283]

you are in Christ Jesus at all, if you are a Christian at all, this has happened to you; you have been 'freed from the law of sin and death'. So how can this be offered as an additional experience to Christians? How can it be said to be true only of some Christians who have had this further blessing? The Apostle's whole case is that this is true of all who are in Christ Jesus. You cannot be a Christian without its being true of you.

Thirdly, it is quite wrong to say that the Holy Spirit is introduced here for the first time. We have found that the Holy Spirit was introduced in the 5th verse of chapter 5, where the Apostle introduces this great theme of the certainty of our salvation as Christians. 'Hope maketh not ashamed, because the love of God is shed abroad in our hearts by the Holy Ghost which is given unto us.' Not only so, but he has mentioned the work of the Holy Spirit in chapter 7, verse 6: 'But now' – and the context and statement are very similar – 'But now we are delivered from the law, that being dead wherein we were held; that (in order that) we should serve in newness of Spirit, and not in the oldness of the letter'. When we studied that verse I pointed out that the Apostle was anticipating there what he was going to take up and work out at the beginning of chapter 8. So it is incorrect to say that the Spirit is introduced here for the first time. The Apostle has been describing the Christian man and his position in the first six verses of chapter 7 and, indeed, in the whole of chapter 6. He does not go back on that in chapter 7, verses 14–25. That section indeed confirms the previous description of the Christian by contrast.

Fourthly, the faulty exposition of this phrase involves us, it seems to me, of necessity in a belief in the doctrine of 'entire sanctification', for the Apostle says, 'The law of the Spirit of life in Christ Jesus freed you from the law of sin and death'. If 'the law of sin and death' refers to sin remaining in the Christian believer, and to that law in my members that wars against the law of my mind, and which brings me into captivity to the law of sin which is in my members, then the Apostle's words mean that I am no longer in captivity to the law of sin which is in my members: I have been entirely delivered from it. This has happened to me; it is not progressively happening; it has happened. I repeat that Paul here uses the aorist tense. If that therefore has happened to me, if sin has been taken entirely out of me, then I am entirely sanctified. That exposition commits us inevitably to this conclusion, that not only is it possible for a Christian to be entirely sanctified, but that every Christian is already entirely sanctified. The fact that the aorist tense is used 'and that this is true of all who are in Christ Jesus makes that interpretation inevitable. I have been set free from everything that was getting me down, from the sin that was in my members, all that brought me into captivity. I have been entirely delivered. But such an interpretation is impossible; because, if it were true, the Apostle could not go on later in verses 12 and 13 of this 8th chapter to say, 'Therefore, brethren, we are debtors, not to the flesh, to live after the flesh. For if ye live after the flesh, ye shall die; but if ye through the Spirit do mortify the deeds of the body, ye shall live.' If entire sanctification has already happened, it would be wrong to say that; the Apostle would be contradicting himself. In other words that exposition ultimately proves too much, and contradicts its own theory.

So for these four reasons, without seeking any further, we must reject completely that interpretation of the phrase, 'the law of sin and death', which regards it as being synonymous with what he has said in chapter 7: 23 and the other parallel statements in that section. What then does 'the law of sin and death' mean? It means the moral Law of God, and especially the Law that God had given through Moses in the Ten Commandments. It is 'the law' about which he has been writing from the beginning of this Epistle. Why must it be this? Why must it be the Law of God given to men, written in the hearts of all men, and given explicitly through Moses to the children of Israel?

The first answer is that the Apostle is dealing here with condemnation; the basic statement is, 'There is therefore now no condemnation'. We have been set free from that condemnation. How? By being set free from the Law that causes our condemnation, 'For the law of the Spirit of life in Christ Jesus, freed you from the law of sin and death'. It is the Law that brings in and pronounces our condemnation. The Law that brings in condemnation is not 'the law of sin that is in my members' (chapter 7: 23) but God's holy Law (chapter 3: 31). To prove this I must quote statements which the Apostle has already made from chapter 1, verse 18 and onwards. Why does he exult and boast in the gospel of Christ? Why is he not ashamed of it? His answer is, 'Because the wrath of God is revealed from heaven against all ungodliness and unrighteousness of men who hold down the truth in unrighteousness'. But where has that wrath against sin been revealed? In the Law in particular. Paul demonstrates that from the 18th verse of the 1st chapter right on to the 20th verse of the 3rd chapter where he summarizes the argument by saying, 'Therefore by the deeds of the law there shall no flesh be justified in his sight, for by the law is the knowledge of sin'. What does the Law do? 'We know that what things soever the law saith, it saith to them that are under the law, that every mouth may be stopped and all the world may become guilty before God' (chapter 3: 19). But then, in verse 21, 'But now the righteousness of God without the law is manifested, being witnessed by the law and the prophets'. What is this? 'Even the righteousness of God which is by faith of Jesus Christ unto all and upon all them that believe . . . For all have sinned and come short of the glory of God.' The Law condemns; it gives 'the knowledge of sin', and that involves condemnation.

But the Apostle is not content to leave the matter there, he continues to say it time and again. Look at the 15th verse of the 4th chapter: 'The law worketh wrath: for where no law is, there is no transgression.' The Law always works wrath, it always produces condemnation. Then, again, in verses 20 and 21 of chapter 5: 'Moreover the law entered that the offence might abound'. The Law came in on the side 'that the offence might abound'. It was never meant to save; it was to cause the offence to stand out, and to condemn it. Such is the function of the Law. We find the same point again in the 13th verse of chapter 7: 'Was then that which is good made death unto me? God forbid. But sin, that it might appear sin, working death in me by what which is good.' Paul is referring to the Law, and what it does, 'that sin by the commandment might become exceeding sinful'. In other words the Law is always the great cause of condemnation. Therefore when the Apostle is concerned to remind us and to proclaim again that we are no longer under condemnation he obviously puts it in this way, that we have been freed from the Law which condemns us to death.

But turn to parallels elsewhere in the Apostle's letters. He says the same thing in 1 Corinthians 15: 56. 'The sting of death is sin and the strength of sin is the law.' It is the Law that ultimately produces death, sin is the subsidiary cause; but 'the strength of sin is the law'. The Law always leads to death. Or take 2 Corinthians 3, particularly verses 7 and 9, where Paul is talking about the Law as given through Moses. 'But if the ministration of death, written and engraven in stones, was glorious' . . . He is talking about the Law of God given to Moses, written on the two tables of stone that Moses brought down from the Mount. He calls it 'the ministration of death'. It is indeed 'the law of death'. In verse 9 he repeats his statement, 'For if the ministration of condemnation be glory'. The Law of God is 'the law of death', the Law 'of condemnation'. That is my first reason for suggesting that this phrase 'the law of sin and death' means 'the Law of God'.

But I pass on to a second reason. In chapter 7 from verse 7 to the end the Apostle took great pains to prove that, because of man's fallen condition, the Law of God inevitably and always produces two main results. The first is sin. The Law of God leads to sin; it aggravates it, it inflames the 'motions of sin that are in my members', as Paul puts it in verse 5. And he works that out in detail in verses 7–12. The second result of the Law – that it always produces death – he works out from verse 13 to the end of the chapter. Observe the way in which he opens both passages. Verse 7, 'What shall we say then? Is the law sin?' Then in verse 13, 'Was then that which is good made death unto me?' The answer is 'Yes'! but it is not the fault of the Law, it is our fault. In other words, in those two sub-sections of chapter 7 from verse 7 to verse 25 Paul has proved that the Law leads to sin and to death. So it is not at all surprising that here in verse 2 of this 8th chapter he should actually call it 'the law of sin and death'. He has proved that that is what it does, therefore he is entitled to call it that. He had, indeed, already hinted at this in verse 20 of chapter 5. He then worked it out in detail in chapter 7 in his long digression, and now he takes it up again. He is summing up in order that he may go on. So he says that it is the Law of 'sin and death'. Thank God that we have been delivered from it, set free from it. It is the Law of God that condemned us, and led us ever on to sin and even to death.

But consider a third reason. We have already seen that the false interpretation given to verse 2 must be rejected because it does not follow logically from verse 1. But our interpretation follows naturally from verse 1. 'There is therefore now no condemnation to them that are in Christ Jesus.' Why? 'For (because) the law of the Spirit of life in Christ Jesus freed me from the law of sin and death' (the law of God) which condemned me. If I have been freed from the Law which condemned me, there is 'no condemnation' to me now. So verse 2 does really explain and help me to understand verse 1.

But what is still more conclusive, and what finally clinches the argument, is that this exposition, and this exposition alone, leads on consistently to verse 3. There, again, we have another 'For'. 'For (because) what the law could not do, in that it was weak through the flesh, God sending His own Son in the likeness of sinful flesh, and for sin, condemned sin in the flesh.' Paul is telling us of what the Law could not do. All are agreed, and must be agreed, that the 'law' in verse 3 is the Law of God given through Moses. So if verse 3 is to follow naturally from verse 2 – as the 'For' insists – then it must be the same Law in both verses. He says we have been 'freed from the law of sin and death' by the salvation that is in Christ Jesus, because that old Law could not do this for the reasons given at great length in chapter 7. God has saved us in this other way. The Apostle is referring to and dealing with the Law of God all the time; he is not talking about 'the law of sin which is in my members', he is not continuing with, and referring to what he has been saying in chapter 7 in detail. That portion of chapter 7, I must repeat again, is nothing but a parenthesis, and must not be regarded as a part of the main statement of the gospel. Here, then, he is telling us once more that we are not under condemnation because we have been set free from the Law of God which was against us, and which condemned us, and which is 'the strength of sin' and which always leads to 'sin and death'. I argue, therefore, that if you interpret this phrase in verse 2 in any other way you have to take the verse right out of its connection with verse 1 and verse 3, and you have to dismiss the double use of the word 'for' which was obviously vital and crucial to the Apostle. You destroy his entire argument, and you end by making any clear exposition quite impossible. In any case the Apostle would never vary the meaning of the word 'law' in verses 2 and 3 without indicating that he is doing so.

The statement then is that we have been set entirely free from our old relationship to the Law of God. Is the Apostle saying something new here? The answer is that he said the same thing in chapter 6, verse 14, 'Sin shall not have dominion over you'. Why? 'For (because) you are not under the law, but under grace'. Then again in chapter 7, verse 4: 'Wherefore, my brethren, you also became dead to the law by the body of Christ; that you should be married to another, even to him who is raised from the dead, that we should bring forth fruit unto God.' He repeated it in verse 6: 'But now we are delivered from the law, that being dead wherein we were held; that we should serve in newness of Spirit, and not in the oldness of the letter.' So in this verse the Apostle is simply saying once more, as is his custom when there has been a digression, what he has said before. He is coming back to the main subject; he takes it up in order that he may follow on with his argument. And yet this verse has so often been taken right out of its context, and has been made the basis of the two defective theories of sanctification of which I have reminded you.

But we are still left with a question. What is it that has set me free from the Law? The answer is, 'The law of the Spirit of life in Christ Jesus'. What is the meaning of this strange phrase? We can say at once, and all will agree, that it is obviously the opposite of the Law of God to which we have been referring. We as Christians are no longer in the position in which we were before we became Christian; since we are 'in Christ Jesus' our whole position has been changed. What was our position before? We were 'under the law', we were under the rules and the reign and the power of the Law. But now, he says, we are in an entirely different position. So 'The law of the spirit of life in Christ Jesus' indicates the opposite of being 'under the law'.

What then does it mean? Is it a reference to the working of the Holy Spirit for sanctification in the believer? At once we have to answer, 'No'; it cannot be so. Paul is not saying that I have been set free from the Law of God because of the working of the Spirit in me; and for this reason, that nowhere are we taught that the working of the Spirit in us to produce sanctification justifies us, and delivers us from the Law. That would be to take us back again to that other teaching which says that we

[289]

are under no condemnation because we are sanctified, which, as we have seen, is never taught in the Scriptures. We are no longer under condemnation because we are 'justified'. It is the Roman Catholic teaching which says that we are under no condemnation because we are sanctified. That is why Romanists do not believe in and preach assurance of salvation, for according to their theory, until you are perfectly sanctified you cannot be sure of salvation. That is the error of Catholicism, which we must reject with the utmost vigour.

What then is the meaning of this phrase? It is just another way of describing the gospel, the good news of salvation. What has set me free from the Law of sin and death? It is the grace of God in Christ Jesus. Has not Paul told us so in verses 20 and 21 of chapter 5? 'Moreover the law entered, that the offence might abound. But where sin abounded (through the law) grace did much more abound'. The opposite of Law is grace. 'That as sin hath reigned unto death' – and it has done so through the Law – 'even so might grace reign through righteousness unto eternal life by Jesus Christ our Lord.' The Apostle is taking up again, and resuming the argument he interrupted at the end of chapter 5. So the opposite of 'law' is 'grace', and the Law of the Spirit of life in Christ Jesus means the 'rule of grace', the 'reign of grace'. It is the way of faith in Christ Jesus, as he has already explained.

But why the expression 'law' – 'the law of the Spirit of life?' How can the use of the term 'law' possibly mean that he is talking about the gospel, or the way of salvation by faith, as over against an attempt to justify ourselves by works under the Law? That can be answered quite simply. We do so by turning back to chapter 3, verses 26 and 27, where we read: 'To declare, I say, at this time his righteousness; that he might be just and the justifier of him which believeth in Jesus. Where is boasting then? It is excluded. By what law of works? Nay, but by the law of faith.' What is the meaning of 'the law of faith?' It is the new way of salvation in Christ mentioned in verses 23 ff., it is 'the righteousness of God which is by faith'. But notice with care that he calls it 'the *law* of faith'. He uses this term 'law' in the very context of the gospel, and he not only uses it there; he uses similar terms elsewhere. We have virtually the same idea in chapter 5, verses 20 and 21, where the opposite to the 'law' is 'grace', and 'the reign of grace' is contrasted with 'the reign of

sin'. Notice he calls it a 'reign' of grace, and a 'reign' and a 'law'
are the same. In chapter 6, verse 14, he expresses the same idea
by saying that we are not 'under' Law but 'under' grace. What
you are 'under' can be described as a 'law'. The principle is the
same. Chapter 7, verses 4 and 6, are also in agreement. While
her first husband was alive the woman there mentioned was
'under' the husband, but when the husband dies she is no longer
'under' him; and she can marry and be 'under' another.

In 2 Corinthians 3 this same idea is put very plainly and
explicitly in verses 6 and 8. 'Our sufficiency is of God, who also
hath made us ministers of a new testament' – a new covenant, a
new legal agreement. Everything God does is legal, it is a
'testament'. 'Not of the letter, but of the Spirit: for the letter
killeth, but the Spirit giveth life.' In verse 8 notice the contrast
with the 'ministration of death'. 'How shall not the ministration
of the Spirit be rather glorious?' 'The ministration of the Spirit'
is the same as 'the law of the Spirit'. We are no longer under
that old Law called 'the letter'; we are under the Law of the
Spirit now. There was once a 'ministry of condemnation and of
death,' it is now a 'ministry', as Paul describes it, 'of the Spirit'.
So here in Romans 8 : 2 he calls it 'the law of the Spirit of life
in Christ Jesus'. We find that James in the 1st chapter of his
Epistle, verse 25, has the same idea. 'Whosoever looketh into the
perfect law of liberty'. What a paradox! 'Law of liberty'! He
means 'a way', 'a reign'; it is 'the reign of grace' and that is a
reign or a law 'of liberty'.

So we can translate the verse we are considering in this way:
'For the principle, or the ministration, or the covenant of
the Spirit of life in Christ Jesus freed me from the law of sin
and death.' In other words the Apostle is saying that we are under
a new covenant now, under a new testament; there is a new
principle or power reigning over us and in us. The gospel has
set us free, we are under 'the law of liberty'. Instead of calling
it 'the law of faith' as he did in chapter 3 : 27, or 'the reign of
grace', as he does in chapter 5 : 20 and 21, he calls it here 'The
law of the Spirit of life in Christ Jesus'. He has already reminded
us in the first verse that we are 'in Christ'. One of the results of
that, he now says, is that the life of Christ is in us – 'life in Christ
Jesus'. As he argued in chapter 6, we have died with Him, we
have been buried with Him, we have also risen with Him. Or

as he puts it in Ephesians 2, we have been 'quickened together with him', we have been 'raised with him'. In 1 Corinthians 15: 45 we read, 'The first man Adam was made a living soul; the last Adam was made a quickening spirit', a life-giving spirit. Because we are 'in Christ Jesus' there is new life in us; and it is the life of Christ.

How does that life of Christ come into us? The answer is, 'by the Holy Spirit'. The Spirit that was in Christ is the same Spirit that is in us. Indeed, as he tells us in 1 Corinthians 12: 13, it is the Spirit that 'baptises' us into Christ: 'For by one Spirit have we all been baptised into Christ, whether we are Jews or Gentiles.' It is by this one Spirit that we have all been incorporated into Christ, been put into Christ. Another way, therefore, of explaining all this, is to say that the life of Christ passes into us through the Spirit. At the end of 2 Corinthians 3 the Apostle seems to be using the terms 'The Spirit' and 'Christ' interchangeably. He even writes, 'if the Spirit of Christ dwell in you'. He will use that expression in the 9th verse of this 8th chapter. It is difficult to maintain clear distinctions in these matters, but that is the best way of looking at it. The life of Christ comes into us through the Spirit, and it is the Spirit who energizes us, and leads us on. Who sets us free from the condemnation of the Law? It is the Lord Jesus Christ, as we shall see clearly in verses 3 and 4; but, indirectly, and as the result of that, it is the Spirit. That is why Paul says in 2 Corinthians 3: 17, 'Where the Spirit is Lord, there is liberty'. The Jews were blind, he has been saying; they read their Scriptures but they could not 'see' the truth; they needed the Spirit to enlighten them.

These truths mean nothing to the unregenerate, to the natural man, but 'God hath revealed them unto us by his Spirit'. That is what Paul is saying here. The gospel has freed us, and the gospel frees us through the Spirit. The work of salvation planned by God the Father and carried out by the Son, is applied to us by the Holy Spirit. We are not justified by or in the Spirit but in the Son. He sums that up in a phrase by saying, 'The Spirit of life which is in Christ Jesus'. Before, it was the 'power of the law' that was the chief power in us, and it led us to sin and to captivity, to defeat and to death. Now, we have been set free and delivered from all that; we are in a new realm, we are in Christ Jesus, living a life in the Spirit, energized by Him. We are not 'under law', we are 'under grace'. That is why there is, and can be, 'no condemnation to those who are in Christ Jesus'. We are not only forgiven, we have been moved into a new realm, we are 'in Christ'. We have nothing to do with the Law from the standpoint of salvation now; we have finished with it; we are dead to it. 'That by which we were held' has been removed, has died; we are in the life of Christ; we are in the realm and the reign of Christ, and the reign and the realm of the Spirit. The Apostle uses all these glorious terms interchangeably.

I would emphasize again that the Apostle is not describing some Christians only, who have had an additional blessing; he is stating what is true of every Christian, all Christians. But why does he mention the Spirit in this way and put emphasis upon it? I answer, that he has already drawn out the result of justification in terms of our relationship to God and His love in chapter 5. What he is concerned to do here is to show the same thing in terms of our being 'in Christ', and to work that out. To do so he has of necessity to bring in the work of the Holy Spirit.

In this chapter Paul shows us the work of the Spirit in sanctification, in adoption, and in our prayer life; but the main theme is our being 'in Christ'. One of the chief results of our being 'in Christ' is that the Spirit is in us; and the Spirit does certain things in us and to us. But the Apostle does not take that up until the end of verse 4: 'The law of the Spirit of life in Christ Jesus freed me from the law of sin and death. For what the law could not do, in that it was weak through the flesh, God sending his own Son in the likeness of sinful flesh and for sin, condemned sin in the flesh'. This refers to 'the Cross' and our 'justification'; not to 'sanctification'. But he continues, 'That the righteousness of the law might be fulfilled in us'. Now, there, he comes to sanctification – 'who walk not after the flesh, but after the Spirit'. He then works that out. This is his typical method. He first of all introduces an idea; then he works out the first half of the idea; then he takes up the second half, and works that out. In verse 2 he puts it all together; and then, after he has worked out the first part about the Atonement he takes up the second part which is the specific operation of the Spirit. He mentions this at the end of verse 4, and then proceeds to work it out in terms of sanctification up to verse 13; in terms of adoption and sonship until verse 17, in terms of prayer in verses 25 and 26, and then shows how it is all a part of God's eternal plan which cannot fail in any detail.

Verse 2 is a crucial verse. The Apostle is recapitulating and summarizing his message and argument. He wants us to be absolutely assured of our salvation, he wants every one of us to know that there is 'no condemnation' for us any longer, nor ever can be; he assures us that we have been freed for ever from the Law which condemned us, and which became to us 'the law of sin and death'. We have been freed from that by this new ministration, 'the ministration of grace', 'the ministration of the Spirit', 'the ministration of glory' as he calls it also; and all because we are 'in Christ Jesus'. 'The law of the Spirit of life in Christ Jesus hath made me free from the law of sin and death.'

Twenty-three

*

*For what the law could not do, in that it was weak through the
flesh, God sending his own Son in the likeness of sinful flesh, and
for sin, condemned sin in the flesh:*
*That the righteousness of the law might be fulfilled in us, who walk
not after the flesh, but after the Spirit.*   Romans 8: 3, 4

Here we look at one of the grandest and most important statements in this Epistle. And it is particularly important that we
should understand it as we work our way through the argument
the Apostle is working out at this point. Notice that I am taking
two verses together, and I do so because they constitute one
statement. There are two subsidiary elements in the statement,
but the two verses together constitute one statement; and it
is impossible to understand one part without the other.

What exactly is the Apostle saying in these two verses? At
once we are struck by the first word, 'For'. We met with it at
the beginning of verse 2 and again at the beginning of verse 3.
It indicates that the Apostle is continuing with his argument,
and this gives us a key to the understanding of the particular
statement in verse 3. He is supplying us with an explanation of
what he had been saying in verse 2. There, as we have seen, he
says in a different way what he had already said in verse 14 of
chapter 6, that we are 'not under the law, but under grace'. We
have been delivered from the Law, by the grace of the gospel,
which he here calls 'the law of the Spirit of life in Christ Jesus'.
The 'life' of Christ is in us, 'the law of the Spirit of life'. As
Christians we are 'in Christ', as he said in verse 1. In other words,
each one of these steps follows from the previous one. The
fundamental statement is, 'There is therefore now no condemnation to them which are in Christ Jesus', and that means that not
only have we been justified, and delivered from the guilt of our

[295]

sins, but that we are 'in Christ', and furthermore, that we are under the influence of, and in the realm of His blessed Holy Spirit. It is only as we understand this that we shall rejoice as we ought in the certainty, the assurance of our salvation.

I am not saying that, if you have not got assurance of salvation, you are not a Christian. You can be a Christian without assurance; but as a Christian you should have assurance, and enjoy it. The Apostle shows us here how to have and to enjoy this blessed assurance. We should all be enjoying it, and the way to obtain it is to see that, if we are justified, then our final position must be secure. Your final position can be safe without your knowing it. There are many who go to their graves without enjoying assurance; but whether they enjoy it or not, they are safe, and the end is certain. If you are 'in Christ' it must be so. But the fact that it is so does not mean of necessity that you know it and that you are enjoying it. You may be robbing yourself of your joy and happiness by your ignorance; and these epistles have been written in order to enlighten us, and to give us the full joy of salvation. As the Apostle has already said in verse 2 of chapter 5, we should be 'rejoicing in hope of the glory of God'. We come to that position by realizing that we have been delivered from the Law and are now living this new life which is to be found in Christ Jesus by the Spirit.

But now the Apostle goes further and explains to us why it was necessary for us ever to be delivered from the Law. He tells us how we have been set free, and he also tells us the result in our experience. That is what we find in verses 3 and 4. Observe how logical the Apostle is. We have been set free from the Law, but why emphasize this? He gives us the reason, he tells us how it happened, and points to the result to which it leads.

Before we come to examine these verses in detail I must point out once more – and it is vital from the standpoint of exposition that this should be clear – that the Apostle is not going to tell us anything new. He is taking up the theme which he left off at the end of chapter 5, and he is doing so in the light of what he has proved and established in chapters 6 and 7. The fundamental statement is found in chapter 5, verse 10, 'For if, when we were enemies, we were reconciled to God by the death of his Son'. He says that again here in verse 3 in this way, 'God, sending his own Son in the likeness of sinful flesh, and for sin, condemned sin in the flesh'. The remainder of verse 10, chapter 5 is, 'much more, being reconciled (having been reconciled), we shall be saved in his life'. Here, he puts that in this form, 'That the righteousness of the law might be fulfilled in us, who walk not after the flesh, but after the Spirit'. He had said it also in chapter 5, in verses 20 and 21, and also in chapter 6, verse 14, which is, in many ways, the key verse: 'For sin shall not have dominion over you, for you are not under the law, but under grace'. That is what he is saying again here – 'sin shall not have dominion over you' – in the words that 'The righteousness of God shall be fulfilled in you', the reason being that you are no longer under Law. You have been taken out of that position in the way he explains, and you are 'under grace'. You are no longer walking 'after the flesh', but 'after the Spirit'. So verses 3 and 4 of chapter 8 are just an exposition of chapter 6, verse 14. At the same time it is particularly true to say of these two verses that they are an exposition of what he has said so plainly in chapter 7 in verses 4 and 6. Verse 4, 'Wherefore, my brethren, ye also are become dead to the law by the body of Christ; that ye should be married to another, even to him who is raised from the dead, that we should bring forth fruit unto God'. Verse 6, 'But now we are delivered from the law, that being dead wherein we were held' (or being dead to that in which we were held) 'that we should serve in newness of Spirit, and not in the oldness of the letter'. We are now going to look at his exposition of those statements, a developing and an opening out of them.

The carefulness of this Apostle's exposition and argumentation is most fascinating and thrilling. Quite apart from the glory of the truth expounded one cannot but be captivated by the brilliance of the method. Let me show what I mean. Look again at verses 4 and 6 in chapter 7. They say the same thing, and they both say it in a double statement. There are two statements in verse 4, and there are two statements in verse 6; and they are virtually the same statement. Verse 4: 'Wherefore, my brethren, you also are become dead to the law by the body of Christ'. Then take the first half of verse 6, 'But now we are delivered from the law, that being dead in which we were held'. It is the same thing, is it not? Now look at the second half of verse 4. Why is he concerned to prove to them that they had become dead to the Law by the body of Christ? It is for this reason – 'That we should be married to another, even to him who is raised from the dead, in order that we should bring forth fruit unto God'. Then look at the second half of verse 6. Why was he concerned to say again that we were delivered from the Law, being dead to that in which we were held? 'That' – in order that – 'we should serve in newness of Spirit, and not in the oldness of the letter'. It is the same truth put in a slightly different manner.

Now compare the two halves of those two statements in chapter 7, with verses 3 and 4 in chapter 8. Verse 3 is a repetition of the first half of verse 4, and also of the first half of verse 6 in chapter 7. It says, 'What the law could not do, in that it was weak through the flesh, God sending his own Son in the likeness of sinful flesh, and for sin, condemned sin in the flesh'. That is just another way of saying that we have 'become dead to the law, by the body of Christ'. The fact is that verse 3 of chapter 8 is a repetition of chapter 7: 4a and 6a. And verse 4 in chapter 8 is a repetition and an elaboration of chapter 7: 4b and 6b.

All this proves my contention that verses 7 to 25 of chapter 7 are nothing but a parenthesis. He was only concerned to do one thing there, namely, to deal with the objections which people were constantly bringing against what he had to say about the Law. So here at the beginning of chapter 8 he reviews the assertion he made in the first six verses of chapter 7, which were themselves an explanation of what he had said at the end of chapter 5 in verses 20 and 21. Surely this ought to convince us finally as to the interpretation of chapter 7 verses 7 to 25. Verses 3 and 4 of chapter 8 repeat almost exactly what he had already laid down as his fundamental proposition in chapter 7 in verses 4 and 6.

The Apostle starts by telling us what the Law 'could not do'. He then tells us why it could not do it. Thirdly, he tells us how God has done what the Law could not do. And fourthly, he tells us the result of it all in us.

We commence then with the first point: what exactly is it that the Law 'could not do'? Various other translations have been suggested. Some people say that it should read thus: 'For the impossible thing of the law'. Others say, 'What is impossible to the law'. But these do not seem to be an improvement on the Authorized Version (K.J.) translation here. 'What the law could not do'. This is the key phrase, and it is crucial to any exposition of this portion, and to an understanding of the Apostle's teaching. What exactly is it that the Law could not do? As I see things, the wrong exposition says that there is no difficulty about that, that you have simply to take the statement as if it read, 'What the law could not do, in that it was weak through the flesh, God did'. Well, what did God do? He 'condemned sin in the flesh'. So those holding this view argue that what the Law could not do was to condemn sin in the flesh. But God did so in Christ; and there is no need to say any more. They argue in the following way. The Apostle had been telling us toward the end of chapter 7 about the 'wretched man' who could not get victory in his Christian life over 'the law of sin that was in his members'. They interpret the end of verse 2 in that way. 'The law of sin and death', they say, is what he talked about in verse 23, 'I see another law in my members, warring against the law of my mind and bringing me into captivity to the law of sin which is in my members'. So they maintain that what Paul is saying here is, first, that the Law could not deliver a man – and they have to agree, of course, that here the Law means the Moral Law of God, especially as given through Moses. They reject that interpretation in verse 2, but now they have to change and to say that here it is the Law of Moses. The Law, they say, could not give a man victory over this 'law in his members' that is always dragging him down to sin; but thank God it has been done in Christ. In short, they say that the Apostle is making a statement to the effect that the Lord Jesus Christ, when He came in the flesh, condemned sin in the flesh by living His perfect life; and therefore those who belong to Him, and who are in Him, are enabled to have the same victory through the Spirit.

Why cannot we accept that exposition? For this reason, that it treats the word 'condemned' as meaning 'delivered from' or 'destroyed'. But it does not mean that! 'Condemned sin in the flesh' is the same word as 'no condemnation' in verse 1, and it means 'to punish'. It never means to destroy. This word is not used in the Scripture in the sense of 'destroying' or 'doing away with' something; it always means 'to punish', and it means nothing else. So on that interpretation the word here is used in a different sense from its use in verse 1; and not only so, but you have to use it in a different sense from the way in which it is used everywhere in the Scripture. That is a fatal objection in and of itself.

But further, it is simply not true to say that the Law could not condemn sin in the flesh, for that is precisely what it was sent to do. That has been the Apostle's argument from the beginning of his Epistle. He says in effect, The Law cannot justify you, and was never meant to do so. He puts it in verse 20 of chapter 3 thus: 'Therefore by the deeds of the law shall no flesh be justified in his sight, for by the law is the knowledge of sin.' The business of the Law is to expose sin and to condemn sin. He has said it still more plainly in chapter 4, verses 14 and 15: 'For if they which are of the law be heirs, faith is made void, and the promise made of none effect: because the law worketh wrath: for where no law is, there is no transgression.' The whole business of the law is to condemn sin; and that is exactly what it does. And yet this exposition which I am now opposing would have us believe that the Law could not do that. The Law does nothing else, says Paul. He says it again in chapter 5, verse 20: 'Moreover the law entered, that the offence might abound.' The Law makes 'the offence to abound', it fixes the transgression, it pin-points it, it shows it up, and it condemns it. That is the whole purpose of the Law. And, indeed, in the whole parenthesis in chapter 7, verses 7–25, it is the one thing the Apostle has been proving – that the Law does nothing but condemn us and our sin in the flesh, and make us cry out, 'O wretched man that I am! who shall deliver me?' It works death in us, it leads to sin. And yet we are asked to believe that 'what the law could not do, because it is weak through the flesh', is to condemn sin in the flesh! The answer is, I say, that that is the only thing the Law can do. It does it very thoroughly, but it can do nothing further.

But there is a third and a final reason for rejecting this faulty exposition. It is found in the little phrase 'and for sin'. 'What the law could not do, in that it was weak through the flesh, God sending his own Son in the likeness of sinful flesh, and for sin . . .'. 'For sin' means as 'a sacrifice for sin'. It does not merely mean 'concerning sin', as I will prove by abundant evidence. The expression 'for sin' carries in it the notion of 'a sacrifice for sin', which is the central teaching of the Apostle everywhere. This is the gospel in which he rejoices, that God has established this way of salvation for us by what He has done in the sacrifice of His Son, the One whom He has 'set forth to be a propitiation', as he has already told us in chapter 3, verses 25 and 26. The faulty exposition does not bring this truth in at all here; it makes of the phrase something that is done by the sinless life of Christ only, and that which He enables us to do through the Spirit. It really leaves out of account the true meaning of the phrase 'and for sin'.

If then we reject that exposition, we need to ask afresh, What is it that the Law could not do? The answer is given at the beginning of verse 4. What the Law 'could not do' was to see to it that the righteousness which it demanded 'should be fulfilled in us'. In other words we should read the statement in this way, 'What the law could not do, in that it was weak through the flesh, God has done'. And he has accomplished it by 'sending his own Son in the likeness of sinful flesh, and for sin, and condemning sin in the flesh'. Why has He done that? 'That (in order that)' – this tells us the purpose and the object. This, then, is what the Law could not do, but which God has done in that way. The objective is 'to fulfil the righteousness of the law in us', in those who are believers. Do not look at the second half of verse 4 for the moment, because that is just a description of the believer. Here we have God's purpose.

So, we reject totally, and still more now as we see the positive exposition, that other explanation. That mistaken view arises because of over-concentration on the phrase, 'condemned sin in the flesh'. That is only a part of what God has done in Christ, in order to lead to this ultimate object expressed in verse 4. The ultimate object is, not condemning sin in the flesh, but the fulfilling in man of the righteousness of the Law. The Apostle says that the Law could not do that 'because it was weak through the flesh', but God has done it in and through all He did in the Lord Jesus Christ. And what He did in Him above all else was that He punished sin. As a result the Law is satisfied, and is therefore put on one side, and we are justified in the sight of God.

What the Law could not do, then, was to secure that the righteousness which it demanded was fulfilled in us. That leaves us with the question, What does this mean? Here, again, I find myself in the unhappy position of having to disagree with Dr Charles Hodge, who seems to me once more to be quite consistent and logical, but to say only half of what should be said, only half of what the Apostle is saying. Dr Charles Hodge confines this entirely and solely to the question of our deliverance from the 'guilt' of sin. He says it means this – that the righteousness, or the justice, of the Law might be established as far as we are concerned. In other words, the Law exacted its penalty as far as we are concerned when it exacted it in the Person, in the body of the Lord Jesus Christ. But he does not go beyond that. The Law in justice has punished sin, therefore it has been fulfilled; it has been carried out as far as we are concerned who believe in Christ, and he leaves the matter there.

But surely that is quite inadequate. Let me produce some reasons for saying so. It is to look, it seems to me, at only one side of justification, in other words, at one side only of the purpose and the object of the Law. The ultimate object of the Law is not merely, not only, to condemn; there is another side to it. The Law has two objects, the first and foremost being to provide a representation of God's demand of righteousness from man. Secondarily, it punished and condemns. As the Apostle has already reminded us in the argument in chapter 7, the Law was meant for good. As he says, 'Was then that which is good made death unto me?' (verse 13). He says also and equally plainly that it 'was ordained to life (verse 10). The Law itself is good, and that is why he delights in it. 'The law is holy and the commandment holy and just and good.' The Law indicates a way of life; but it completely fails to produce it in practice. We must never forget the two aspects of the purpose of the Law; it is to indicate the way of righteousness, the way of life, to remind us of the life God demands of man, as well as to condemn. Indeed our condemnation arises out of our failure to live according to the Law.

Hold that in your mind, and then realize that there are, in the same way exactly, two aspects to salvation. The first aspect of salvation that we stand in need of is the need to be delivered from condemnation, from guilt, from punishment. In our experience the second aspect of the Law confronts us first. The first thing we realize is that we are guilty before God, and we want to know how we can be delivered from guilt and from punishment. But salvation does not stop there; that only gives me forgiveness and saves me from hell. I need something further. I need a positive righteousness. I cannot stand in the presence of God by means of the forgiveness of sins only; I need a positive righteousness, the righteousness that the Law postulates. The second element in salvation, therefore, is that I am clothed with the righteousness of Jesus Christ. And I need the second as much as the first. My contention, as against Hodge, is that the Apostle is emphasizing here that the two things happen 'in Christ'. The Law could do neither of them. The Law could not deliver me from guilt and justify me; neither could it give me a positive righteousness, or give me life and the ability to stand in the presence of God. But what God has done in Christ accomplishes both. In verse 3 the Apostle tells us how God delivers us from the guilt of sin; in verse 4 how He gives us the positive righteousness, and how He will go on doing this increasingly through the work of the Spirit in sanctification until we are ultimately glorified, and free from sin altogether.

I next adduce some further reasons for saying this. I maintain that the word 'in' in verse 4 proves my assertion. Paul says, 'That the righteousness of the law might be fulfilled in us'. Now if the Apostle meant 'with respect to us', as Dr Hodge suggests, he would have used the word 'peri' and not the word 'en' here. Dr Hodge tells us that the righteousness of the Law in punishing sin has been exacted, and the justice of the Law has been fulfilled as far as we are concerned, because Christ has borne our punishment and therefore we have borne it. I suggest that the Apostle would not have said 'in' if he meant no more than Hodge states; he would have said 'as far as we are concerned', or 'with respect to us'. But he goes out of his way to say 'in us'. Not only so; I believe that the remainder of verse 4 makes our exposition absolutely essential. Paul says, 'That the righteousness of the law might be fulfilled in us'. If Dr Hodge were right Paul would have stopped there. But Paul goes on to say, 'in us, who walk not after the flesh but after the Spirit'. Why does he add this? Because he is talking now about this 'walk' of ours, he is talking about our new life in Christ, he is going on to talk about the way in which we live. He will develop that from the beginning of the 5th verse and continue with it to the end of the chapter. He is not thinking of justification only, of forgiveness and deliverance from the guilt of sin only, he goes on to deal with the whole future of the Christian.

The fact is that what Paul says here is the same as he will say very definitely and explicitly in verse 29 of this chapter, 'For whom he did foreknow, he also did predestinate to be conformed to the image of his Son'. That is 'righteousness', that is 'the fulfilment of the righteousness of the law'; it is to be conformed to the image of the Son of God. It is not only the negative aspect of the Law, it is this positive aspect also. This happens to us in all its fulness 'in Christ' as we 'walk in the Spirit' and not 'after the flesh'. That is what the Apostle has in view.

In other words, the righteousness of the Law is fulfilled in us in two ways. The righteousness of Christ is 'imputed' to us; but, thank God, the righteousness of Christ is also 'imparted' to us. The second is the process of sanctification which the Apostle begins to deal with in verse 5. There, we shall be considering the progressive growth of believers 'in grace and in the knowledge of the Lord', their increasing sanctification, until finally we shall be 'glorified', without 'spot or wrinkle or any such thing'. We shall finally be completely righteous, as righteous as Adam was before the Fall, and even more so. There is the imparted as well as the imputed righteousness. We have to insist upon this exposition, as against Dr Hodge, because of the immediate context.

But to clinch this matter finally, is not this what the Apostle has really been saying from the very beginning of this Epistle? Look at the 17th verse of the 1st chapter. Why is he not ashamed of the Gospel of Christ? Having said in verse 16 that it is because 'it is the power of God unto salvation to every one that believeth', he goes on to say in verse 17, 'For therein a righteousness from God is revealed from faith to faith'. What is revealed? Not merely forgiveness, not merely deliverance from guilt. The great thing, he says, about this gospel, is that it reveals the way for man to be righteous before God. That is the great message of the gospel; and he glories in it. He repeats that matter in chapter 3 in verses 20 and following: 'Therefore by the deeds of the law there shall no flesh be justified in his sight: for by the law is the knowledge of sin. But now the righteousness of God apart from the law is manifested' – a way of righteousness, a way of making men righteous – 'being witnessed by the law and the prophets.' What is it? It is 'The righteousness of God which is by faith of Jesus Christ unto all and upon all them that believe: for there is no difference'. That is exactly the same thing. Then he comes

back to it once more in the 5th chapter. Take it for instance in
veres 17: 'For if by one man's offence death reigned by one;
much more they which receive abundance of grace and of the
gift of righteousness shall reign in life by one, Jesus Christ.'
Verse 18, 'Therefore as by the offence of one judgment came
upon all men to condemnation; even so by the righteousness of
one the free gift come upon all men to justification of life'. But
verse 19 particularly, 'For as by one man's disobedience many
were made sinners, so by the obedience of one shall many be
made righteous'. It is the same thing everywhere. Verse 21,
'As sin hath reigned unto death, even so might grace reign'.
How does it do it? 'Through righteousness unto eternal life by
Jesus Christ our Lord.' Again in chapter 6, verse 13: 'Neither
yield your members as instruments of unrighteousness unto
sin; but yield yourselves unto God, as those that are alive from
the dead, and your members as instruments of righteousness unto
God.' That means positive, righteous, holy living; not only
forgiveness. In verse 18 of chapter 6, we read: 'Being then made
free from sin, ye became the servants of righteousness.' That is
not just being delivered from guilt, it is positive – 'servants of
righteousness'; it means righteous, holy living, in the way the
Law defines righteousness. We are servants to that now in this
new way. Paul says it all again in verse 19 of chapter 6, 'I speak
after the manner of men because of the infirmity of your flesh;
for as you have yielded your members servants to uncleanness
and to iniquity unto iniquity, even so now yield your members
as servants to righteousness unto holiness'. That again is positive.
Then in verse 20 of chapter 6 and again in chapter 7, 4b and 6b,
this is what he glories in, that 'We have died to the law'. Why?
'That we should be married to another, even to him that is raised
from the dead'. Why is it so important that we should be married
to Christ? For this reason: 'That we should bring forth fruit
unto God'. It is not merely that we are no longer guilty, as Dr
Hodge suggests. The Apostle rejoices that we are now able to
bring forth fruit unto God – that is, positive righteousness.
Again in chapter 7, 6b; 'That we may serve in newness of spirit'.
'Serve'. Serve what? Serve this righteousness of God, and serve
God, but 'in newness of spirit and not in the oldness of the letter'.

This is indeed Paul's argument everywhere. Take the great
statement in 1 Corinthians 1: 30: 'But of him are ye in Christ

Jesus, who of God is made unto us wisdom, even righteousness, and sanctification and redemption'. It is all in Him. See it also in Galatians 3, first of all in verses 13 and 14: 'Christ hath redeemed us from the curse of the law, being made a curse for us: for it is written, Cursed is every one that hangeth on a tree.' That is the same as we have in verse 3 here,'. . . and for sin, condemned sin in the flesh'. But now look at verse 14 of Galatians 3, 'That (in order that) the blessing of Abraham might come on the Gentiles through Jesus Christ, that we might receive the promise of the Spirit'. This is the positive aspect. It is not only that we are no longer under the curse, there is the positive element in addition; we are made heirs and inheritors.

But it is all in one verse in the 21st verse of that 3rd chapter of Galatians, 'Is the law then against the promises of God? God forbid: for if there had been a law given which could have given'. What? Forgiveness, deliverance from the curse, the negative aspect of justification only? No! 'If there had been a law given which could have given life . . .' That is what the Law could not do; it could not give 'life'. If the Law could have given life, then 'righteousness would have been by the law'. Righteousness and life are interchangeable terms. We must not confine righteousness, therefore, to the matter of deliverance from punishment only. It includes deliverance from guilt; but 'the righteousness of the law' is ultimately 'life'. It is that alone which can enable us to live with God eternally. The 'righteousness of the law' means 'eternal life', which is essential before a man can live with God. So I argue that the Apostle is saying here that the Law could not only not deliver me from the guilt and condemnation that it pronounced upon me; but still more important, that it could not give me positive righteousness, it could not give me 'life'. But thank God 'the law of the Spirit of life in Christ Jesus' has given it me. I am 'in Christ' and because of that I walk 'not after the flesh', but 'after the Spirit'. I am no longer walking under the Law, I am no longer 'under the law', I am 'under grace'.

So far, we have but attempted to deal with the first question only – what it was that the Law could not do. We shall go on to consider the further matters involved – why it is that the Law could not do this, how God has done what the Law could not do, and thirdly, the result in us. It was essential that we should engage in that pure bit of exposition and the working out of these arguments. Having done so we shall now be able to study the glorious positive statements which the Apostle makes here, as he shows us all that has been made possible for us by God in Jesus Christ. We shall be looking directly at the gospel and glorying and rejoicing in it. Remember that the Apostle argues as he does in order that he may establish the fundamental verities of the gospel, and give assurance and certainty and joy to all who are in Christ Jesus.

Twenty-four

*

For what the law could not do, in that it was weak through the
flesh, God sending his own Son in the likeness of sinful flesh,
and for sin, condemned sin in the flesh:
That the righteousness of the law might be fulfilled in us, who walk
not after the flesh, but after the Spirit.   Romans 8: 3, 4

As we proceed with out study of these verses it is well to keep
certain other verses in our minds. There is the 2nd verse in
chapter 6, 'How shall we, that are dead to sin (or died to sin),
live any longer therein?' It is impossible that we continue in sin
because we are 'in Christ' and under grace. Or take what Paul
says in the 6th verse of that chapter where it is still more explicit,
'Knowing this, that our old man was crucified with him, in order
that' – Why?'That the body of sin might be destroyed, disannulled'.
That is the great object of our dying with Him, that is what
results from our old man being crucified with Him – 'That the
body of sin might be destroyed, that henceforth we should not
serve sin'. The Christian should not 'serve' sin. The whole object
of his redemption is to produce that result. So it seems to me to
be very wrong to exclude that notion from the interpretation
which we put on the phrase, 'That the righteousness of the law
might be fulfilled in us'. We saw the same in the 4th and 6th
verses in chapter 7. The Apostle rejoices in this new position
because we are now married to Another, 'even to him that is
raised from the dead, in order that we should bring forth fruit
unto God'. It is not merely that we are forgiven and declared
just, we are bringing forth fruit, and we are going to do so, he
says in verse 6, 'in newness of Spirit and not in the oldness of the
letter.'

This is important for this reason, that it is the Apostle's great
point in this section of the Epistle. He was being charged, of

[308]

course, with the exact opposite, with teaching antinomianism. His preaching of justification by faith, it was alleged, told people that it mattered not how much they sinned – all was well. Paul resents and rejects that by showing that salvation in Christ leads to a 'newness of life', and does away with 'the body of sin', that we should no longer serve sin. In Christ we are now living, 'according to the Spirit', a new life in which we triumph over sin. That is the argument. So if that truth is not a vital part of our interpretation of this important phrase at the beginning of verse 4, we are failing to emphasize the very thing that the Apostle has been concerned to emphasize in chapters 6 and 7, and in the summary of that argument in the first four verses of this 8th chapter.

This is also an essential part of his proof of the fact that there is no condemnation now to them that are in Christ Jesus. His proof is based on the assertion that we are delivered from the Law, and from the realm and the rule and the reign of sin, 'that as sin hath reigned unto death, even so might grace reign through righteousness unto eternal life through Jesus Christ our Lord'. In other words, it comes to this – the moment we become Christians we are under the rule and reign and power of grace and we are living a new life, in Christ, 'in the Spirit'. The moment we become Christians, therefore, this process of sanctification, the imparting of the righteousness of Christ, commences in us. That is one of the essential points Paul is making in these four verses. You can be certain, he says, that there is no condemnation, and never will be, or ever can be, because we are now under this rule and reign of grace. 'Sin shall not have dominion over you, because you are not under law, but under grace.' Grace achieves what 'the law could not do'.

But why could the law not do that? The Apostle's answer is, 'in that it was weak through the flesh'. Here is another phrase that can be misunderstood. Notice that he does not say that 'the law' was weak. Read superficially it sounds like that; but he is not saying that the Law itself was weak; but that because the Law, of necessity, had to work through us, in us and by means of us, it was bound to fail. The Law does not work automatically; the Law for the purpose of carrying out its righteousness was dependent upon us and upon our efforts. So the weakness was not in the Law, the weakness was in us – 'in that it was weak through the flesh'. In other words the failure of the Law was due to the fact that it had to work through our flesh.

I once heard an old preacher using an excellent illustration to bring out this point. He was preaching in a country district and addressing people who had gardens. He said to them, 'You go out in the spring and dig your gardens. You have a spade and a fork and you begin to dig. But suddenly there is a bit of hard ground; and you have to put great pressure on the spade, with the result that the handle of the shovel breaks. The handle is made of wood whereas the shovel itself is made of iron. The trouble was that the handle was not strong enough because it was only made of wood. That does not mean there is anything wrong with the spade itself, but it does mean that there is something wrong with the handle. It is a good illustration. The weakness was not in the spade as such, which was made of iron, it was in the handle – 'in that it was weak through the flesh'. But you cannot use the spade without using the wooden handle. Now that was the position of the Law. The Law had to be carried out by us; and because of our weakness the Law could not produce the required righteousness. The Law depends on us.

We must work this out. The Apostle has already done so for us in chapter 7; that was the whole purpose of that chapter, as I must remind you once more. In the 5th verse of that chapter he says, 'When we were in the flesh, the motions of sins, which were by the law, did work in our members to bring forth fruit unto death'. Then in verses 7–25 he has only one object in view, namely, to show what the Law could not do. That is the theme of that entire section – what the Law could not do. Now here he is summing that up again. This is pure repetition, recapitulation, reminding us again of what 'the law could not do, in that it was weak through the flesh'. The Law, in other words, could never make us righteous; indeed, for the reasons given, it even increases our problem.

What then is our great need? Our fundamental need is to be delivered from sin. But in the light of all the Apostle has said we need first to be delivered from the Law. And he now tells us how that has happened. He has already rejoiced in it in verse 2, 'The law of the Spirit of life in Christ Jesus hath made me free (has freed me already) from the law of sin and death'. That must happen first. We need to be delivered from the Law, not only as it condemns us and our guilt, but also as it affects us by increasing the power of sin within us. A verse which throws great light on this is 1 Corinthians 15 : 56, which we have quoted earlier: 'The sting of death is sin, and the strength of sin is the law.' It shows clearly that if you intend to deal with the problem of sin you have to start with the Law, because it is the 'strength of sin'.

The problem of redemption, the problem of man in sin, can be stated in this way. Man needs to be delivered from the tyranny and the rule and the reign and the serfdom of sin, which is kept going by the Law. The Apostle uses these terms interchangeably – 'dead to sin', 'dead to the law'. You can use them interchangeably because 'the law' is the 'strength of sin'. To be 'under sin', and to be 'under the law' are the same thing, and we need to be delivered from sin as we need to be delivered from the Law. So the Law cannot help us; it holds us down in this terrible position, condemned, and in bondage; indeed the whole situation becomes aggravated. So we see clearly that our first need, from the practical standpoint, is to be delivered from the Law.

That brings us to our third subject: How has God done for us what the Law could not do? This introduces the glorious theme of the gospel of salvation and redemption. God has done for us something which neither we nor the Law could ever do. This is the heart of the gospel; this is what made Paul rejoice as he says in chapter 1, verses 16 and 17: 'I am not ashamed of the gospel of Christ, for it is the power of God unto salvation to every one that believeth, for therein is a righteousness from God revealed from faith to faith: as it is written, The just shall live by faith.' This is the great theme of the Epistle. But let us follow him as he tells us here how God has done this: 'What the law could not do, in that it was weak through the flesh, God sending his own Son . . .'. It is possible to translate it, 'God having sent His own Son . . .'.

We must first emphasize the great word 'God'. Salvation is God's salvation; it is the result of God's action. Salvation is altogether and entirely of God. It is what God has done, not man. 'But God'. 'God sending his own Son'. It is His plan, it is His purpose. Man was completely helpless. The Bible is full of that teaching, as are our best hymns. 'When all was sin and shame', says one of them. That was man's condition – sin and shame, failure; man was completely helpless, totally incapable, able to do nothing at all. 'God sent his own Son'. Yes, and the Bible makes it very clear that this was not a divine 'after-thought'. It was planned 'before the foundation of the world'. Our names are written, we are told, 'in the book of life of the Lamb slain before the foundation of the world'. Whether that means that the names were written in the book before the foundation of the world, or that in this mystical sense the Lamb was slain before the foundation of the world, does not matter. What matters is that the whole plan and purpose was conceived 'before the foundation of the world'. God was not taken by surprise when man sinned; salvation was planned before man and the world were ever brought into being.

Notice that here, as everywhere, the Apostle mentions the names of the Three Persons of the blessed Holy Trinity. 'God sending his own Son', and the end of the statement is, 'We walk not after the flesh, but after the Spirit' – Father, Son, Holy Spirit. The real explanation of the trouble in most Christian lives is the fact that believers start thinking about salvation in terms of themselves, and not in terms of God, the Holy Trinity, and what God has planned and purposed before time. They start by looking into themselves, and they spend their lives doing so. If they but looked at Him, looked out and saw it all there, then they would humble themselves and be filled with praise to God for ever having brought them into relationship with His great and glorious plan. That is the way to look at salvation: 'God sending his own Son in the likeness of sinful flesh, and for sin, condemned sin in the flesh, that . . .'. Work that out, I say! Let us spend the rest of our lives in looking at that, and in working it out.

The whole of the Apostle's argument here, and in this entire chapter, rests on the truth that I am emphasizing at this precise point. He starts with the triumphant declaration 'There is therefore now no condemnation to them which are in Christ Jesus' – that grand absolute which says that we are safe for all eternity. How can he be so certain of this? The answer is that we are included in a salvation which is God's salvation, God's action from beginning to end. If this salvation depended at any point upon us, he, the Apostle could never have said that 'there is therefore now no condemnation to them which are in Christ Jesus', because if it were left to us at any point it would fail.

We would be certain to fall out of it either as the result of acts of sin or of sin in our minds. If it depended in any sense upon us it would be a failure. But it does not. It is all of God. Man cannot save himself, and the Law of God cannot save him, because it is weak through the flesh, our flesh. And even if the salvation planned and prepared by God Himself had to depend upon our flesh – my faith, my holding on, my abiding, or anything else – it would fail. But, thank God, it does not depend upon us at any point; it is altogether from God: it is God's action from beginning to end. The God who saves is the God who keeps. He keeps us, we are in His hands, it is God's action.

This is vital to the whole argument of the Apostle. You cannot have assurance of salvation, you cannot have certainty of your final glorification unless you realize that salvation is altogether of God. That is why we shall discover as we go further into this chapter that the Apostle keeps on repeating this same truth: I am referring to statements such as, 'And we know that all things work together for good to them that love God . . . for whom he did foreknow he also did predestinate to be conformed to the image of his Son, that he might be the firstborn among many brethren. Moreover whom he did predestinate, them he also called; and whom he called, them he also justified; and whom he justified, them he also glorified. What shall we then say to these things? If God be for us, who can be against us?' (verses 28–31). It is all based on 'God sending his own Son'. It is entirely of God. That is why every teaching about justification or sanctification which puts emphasis upon man or his 'decision' or his 'abiding' at any point is a denial of the Apostle's teaching. We are not saved because we decide to go in for salvation, either justification or sanctification; it is God that justifies and sanctifies; it is His purpose, it is His power, it is His working – this is His great and eternal plan.

But come to the second phrase – 'God sending his own Son'. What a phrase! Salvation is in and through the Lord Jesus Christ, and exclusively so. There is no salvation apart from 'his own Son'. People may talk about believing in God, and serving God, and not mention the Lord Jesus Christ. They are but deluding themselves. There is no knowledge of God apart from Him, there is no reconciliation with God except through Him. All is done through Him. This is the way in which God gives salvation; and if the Son is not there at the very centre it is not salvation – it is a figment of the imagination, it is a delusion of Satan. Christianity is all and entirely about the Lord Jesus Christ and about what God has done in Him and through Him. Paul says, in writing his Second Epistle to the Corinthians, in chapter 5: 'We are ambassadors for Christ'. What is our message? It is: 'That God was in Christ, reconciling the world unto himself'. It is 'in Christ' that He has done it.

But let us look still more carefully at the phrase, because it is a statement which we shall fail to appreciate fully if we skim lightly over it. Why does Paul trouble to say 'God sending his own Son?' Why did he not simply say 'God sending his Son'? I answer: because he wished to define exactly who this Son is. There are others who are described as 'sons of God' in the Scriptures. There are statements about the angels in which they are referred to as 'the sons of God'. But this One is not a 'son of God' in the sense that the angels are sons of God. They are all created beings; they have not been generated by the Father, they have been created by the Father; they are not 'his own Son'. The term suggests a generation, a coming out of the Father, a reproduction of the Father. There are others who can be called 'sons', but 'son' is a title that is given to them; they are but created beings. But Christ is 'his own Son'. We who are Christians are referred to sometimes as 'the sons of God', and 'children of God'. But the One of whom Paul speaks in this verse is not a Son in the same way as you and I are sons of God. You and I are not 'his own' sons; we are sons by 'adoption'; there was a time when we were not sons. But of this One that cannot be said. He is 'God's own Son'. He always was, He always will be eternally the Son of God, not adopted. So by expressing it in this way as 'his own Son', the Apostle emphasizes the uniqueness. One of the creeds speaks of the Son as 'Begotten, not created'. They put the truth in those carefully chosen words because there were people in the Church who were teaching that Jesus Christ had been created like all others. There was a heresy in the early Church which taught that the Lord Jesus Christ was a created being. It was called Arianism. The answer to that is, 'Begotten, not created', 'his own Son'. We must contend for this, even unto death if necessary.

Consider the way in which the Apostle John puts the matter

in the prologue to the first chapter of his Gospel, in verse 18, 'No man hath seen God at any time; the only begotten Son, which is in the bosom of the Father, he hath declared him'. How glibly we repeat John 3: 16: 'God so loved the world, that he gave his only begotten Son, that whosoever believeth in him should not perish, but have everlasting life'! Never forget that God 'gave his only begotten Son'. That is the measure of the love of God. Then, at the beginning of the Epistle to the Hebrews the author goes out of his way to emphasize the same thing. He does so because the people to whom he was writing were beginning to be shaken in their belief in Christ. 'God, who at sundry times and in divers manners spake in time past unto the fathers by the prophets, hath in these last days spoken unto us by his Son' – or as it should be, 'in his Son' – 'whom he hath appointed heir of all things, by whom also he made the worlds'. Then the writer adds, 'who being the brightness of his glory, and the express image of his person'. Language cannot go beyond that. That is another way of saying 'begotten of the Father,' coming out of the Father, the eternal generation of the Son of the Father. 'His own Son' in this unique sense! The expression is a way of emphasizing the great doctrine of the 'eternal generation of the Son', that which enabled Him to say 'I and the Father are One'. It is an assertion that they are one in essence, one in glory, co-equal, co-eternal. But it is also concerned to emphasize that the Lord Jesus Christ did not 'become' the Son of God when He was born into this world. That is another heresy that has been taught. He always was 'the Son'. How important it is to pay attention to every word in the Scripture! He did not 'become' the Son when He was born as a Babe in Bethlehem. No, what happened there was that He 'became flesh', became man. The only begotten of the Father, God's own Son, who was ever the Son, the eternal Son, became man. His Sonship had existed from all eternity.

Neither did Christ become the Son, as some have thought, at the Resurrection. We read in the 4th verse of chapter 1 of this Epistle: 'And declared to be the Son of God with power, according to the spirit of holiness, by the resurrection from the dead'. There are those who say that it was there that He became the Son. But that is not what the Apostle is saying. He tells us that it was declared by the resurrection; it was announced, it was made perfectly plain and clear, it was promulgated that this is true of Him. But that was a declaration of something that had already been true, and true from all eternity. The truth is stated by this Apostle in another way in the First Epistle to the Corinthians, chapter 15, verse 47: 'The first man is of the earth, earthy: the second man is the Lord from heaven'. The first man Adam was created, and made, in the image and likeness of God; nevertheless he was 'of the earth, earthy'. The second Man was not created in the image and the likeness of God; He is God the Son, the everlasting, eternal Son, begotten, not created, He is 'the Lord from heaven'. That is the difference; and that is what the Apostle reminds us of here – 'God sending his own Son.'

All this is of vast importance for us because, for one thing, it is that which, above everything else, gives us an insight into the love of God. You are concerned about salvation? Well, remember this – we are saved because of the love of God. How do I know that? Because it is the only explanation. Here is man a rebel, a sinner, a vile person, in a world of sin; but God's love was so great that He sent his own Son into the world – 'God sending his own Son'. That is the measure of the love of God, the measure of the love of God to you. He so loved you, that He sent His own Son, His only begotten Son, into the world for you.

There is a second thing I would emphasize. The Apostle, as I am reminding you, is dealing here with the great problem of assurance, and of certainty of salvation. Now the Sonship of Christ is one of the most wonderful guarantees of that. It is not only that it is God who is doing all this to you; but look at this Person in whom He is doing it. He does not save us through any mere man, He does not save us by creating a second man like Adam. God has now committed Himself to this extent, that He has sent 'his own Son'. In other words, God Himself is involved in our salvation. And it is for that reason that we can be sure and assured that there will be no failure, that there will never be a repetition of what happened in the case of the first man Adam. The first man was made in the image and likeness of God, he was perfect, and everything 'was good'. But he sinned and dragged down his posterity and the whole world with him, as we have seen in chapter 5 of the Epistle. That is not going to happen again. There is a second Man now, a second humanity, a new race of men. But, asks someone, what guarantee have we that there will not be failure the second time as there was the first time? The answer is – it is 'his own Son' whom God has sent this time. Not a created being, not even a perfect created being, but 'his own Son'! In other words our salvation is as sure as this, it is guaranteed by the character and the glory of God. There is a double guarantee; it is God's plan, and it is being worked out in and by One who is 'God's own Son', His eternal Son. It cannot fail, and it most certainly will not fail.

These truths we have been considering are absolutely essential to the understanding of God's work for us and in us. Salvation is in and through the Lord of Glory, the everlasting Son. What God has done is to send Him to save us. He gave the Law, but He never gave the Law in order to save man. It was not designed for that. God knew that it could not save man. There was only one way whereby man could be saved, and that was that the eternal Son of God should become man. And He became man, and it was as man that He fought the foe, died the death, rose in resurrection power, and ascended to heaven and took His seat at the right hand of God. It was the only way. It is the way that God planned and devised in His infinite and eternal wisdom and love. Let us meditate, and continue to meditate, upon this astounding declaration. Our salvation is guaranteed and safe and sure, therefore, until we are finally glorified and presented by Christ to His Father 'without spot or wrinkle or any such thing'. We are 'in Christ' and Christ is 'God's own Son', the 'only begotten of the Father', eternally generated, with God from all eternity, co-equal and co-eternal. It is because God sent Him from heaven into this world as the Babe of Bethlehem and the Man Jesus that your salvation and mine is safe and sure. It is sure in spite of ourselves, in spite of man, in spite of 'the world, the flesh, and the devil', in spite of hell. It is God in the flesh, the God-Man, the One who took unto Himself human nature, and who in that human nature is now making intercession for us in the presence of God, who guarantees it all. It is all accomplished through God the Father's 'own Son' and mediated to us through God the Holy Spirit.

Twenty-five

*

*For what the law could not do, in that it was weak through the
flesh, God sending his own Son in the likeness of sinful flesh, and
for sin, condemned sin in the flesh:
That the righteousness of the law might be fulfilled in us, who walk
not after the flesh, but after the Spirit.*   Romans 8: 3, 4

We now move on to consider the next aspect of what God has
done to effect our salvation. He has sent His Son into the world,
and the Apostle tells us that the Son came 'in the likeness of sinful
flesh'.

This statement is of extreme importance in connection with the
whole doctrine of the Person of the Lord Jesus Christ, and the
Incarnation. The Babe of Bethlehem is the Son of God; Jesus of
Nazareth is the eternal Son of God. He came to live in this world
though He is eternally God's only Son. Nothing is more important,
obviously, than that we should realize the truth concerning Him
and His Person; and this phrase is one of the most important
in the whole of Scripture with regard to just that question of the
Incarnation and the Person of our Lord. It is so because it defines
our Lord's Person more closely, more in detail than perhaps any
other. There are certain general statements about the Incarnation
and the Person of the Lord Jesus Christ, such as for instance,
John 1: 14, where we are told 'The Word was made flesh,
and dwelt among us'. But that is more general than this one,
for here we read that He 'came in the likeness of sinful flesh'. It is
more particular. Or take another general statement, as in Galatians
4: 4: 'When the fulness of the time was come, God sent forth his
Son, made of a woman, made under the law'. That, again, does not
tell us as much as this passage in Romans tells us. Take also
Philippians 2: 7: where we have, 'He made himself of no reputa-
tion, and was made in the likeness of men'. Still, it is not as specific

and not as detailed as the phrase we are examining. Then there is the statement in the First Epistle to Timothy, chapter 3, verse 16: 'Great is the mystery of godliness: God was manifest in the flesh, justified in the Spirit, seen of angels, preached unto the Gentiles, believed on in the world, received up into glory.' God was 'manifest' in the flesh. Again, it is general and not as particular and as detailed as the statement here. Or take Hebrews 2 : 14: 'Forasmuch then as the children are partakers of flesh and blood, he also himself likewise took part of the same.' Again a most wonderful statement, but not as detailed as here.' Or, finally, Hebrews, chapter 10 and verse 5: 'Wherefore when he cometh into the world, he saith, Sacrifice and offering thou wouldest not, but a body hast thou prepared me'. Now all those statements remind us of the fact of the Incarnation, that the eternal Son of God was in this world as a man; but clearly that is not enough, and this phrase in Romans 8 : 3 tells us more about it, defines it still further, and clarifies those more general statements.

The first thing it does is to remind us that the Incarnation was a fact; it was a true Incarnation. The Son of God did not merely take unto Him an 'appearance' of a body; He did not come with a mere appearance of flesh. No, He literally had a human body and a human soul. The Incarnation is a fact and a reality. We emphasize that because in the very early days of the Church this matter led to a great deal of confusion. Certain false teachers arose in the Christian Church who taught that Jesus of Nazareth, the Son of God, did not have a true body – it was but an appearance, a phantom body; the Incarnation was not real. He 'appeared' as a man, but was never really man; the Word was not truly 'made flesh'. That is a terrible heresy; and the New Testament is at great pains to tell us so. Indeed it can be said that the First Epistle of John was probably written primarily to counter that seriously erroneous teaching. Notice that John starts that Epistle by saying, 'That which was from the beginning, which we have heard, which we have seen with our eyes, which we have looked upon, and our hands have handled, of the Word of life'. He is dealing with those people who were saying that in a sense you could not 'see' and 'handle with your hands'; he is nailing that heresy which said that our Lord's body was a mere appearance. Those false teachers went on to say that He came into this body at the baptism, and went out of it on the Cross;

so that the Son of God did not really die, He left this phantom body, and all that was on the Cross was a mere phantom. The First Epistle of John counters that heresy.

John was so deeply concerned about the matter, that in the 4th chapter of his Epistle, and in the first three verses, he says, 'Beloved, believe not every spirit, but try the spirits whether they are of God: because many false prophets are gone out into the world. Hereby (in this way) know ye the Spirit of God: Every spirit that confesseth that Jesus Christ is come in the flesh is of God: And every spirit that confesseth not that Jesus Christ is come in the flesh is not of God: and this is that spirit of anti-christ, whereof ye have heard that it should come; and even now already is it in the world'. Now that is ultimately the test of whether we have the true doctrine concerning our Lord. There were preachers going about who appeared to have great spiritual powers. They are not to be judged by their performances, says John, but by their doctrine. The test is: Do they confess that Jesus Christ is truly come in the flesh? Though they may appear to do wonderful works, if they deny the reality of the Incarnation they are not 'of God', but are anti-christ. In other words, the touch-stone by which we should always judge any preacher, or any one who claims to have spiritual power and authority, is his view of the Lord Jesus Christ – His Person, and especially the reality of the Incarnation.

We find similar treatment of the subject in many other places. For example the Apostle Peter writes: 'Who his own self bare our sins in his own body on the tree' (1 Peter 2: 24). He was in the body truly, and He bore our sins in that body on the tree. But perhaps the most conclusive argument of all is this, that the name our Lord most frequently applied to Himself was 'the Son of Man'. He used this name in order to emphasize the fact that He was truly man and did not merely appear to be a man. It was not a theophany – an appearance of God in human form – He was truly a man, and He had a literal physical body as we all have, not a phantom.

Secondly, the Apostle does not merely say here that God sent His Son 'in the flesh'. That is not enough. Those other statements have said that; but this statement goes further. Notice another matter. The Apostle goes out of his way to say that He did not come 'in sinful flesh', but 'in the likeness of sinful flesh'.

This is an important point because it corrects another heresy. Was the body, the flesh, of the Lord Jesus Christ sinful, or was it not? There were people in the early Church, as there are people in the Church today, who said that our Lord's human nature was sinful, as ours is, that He was 'born of a woman' and therefore inherited from her her sinful nature. Their teaching is, that though His human nature was sinful He was able not to sin; He rose above it, He mastered it and conquered it; but His nature, His human nature was actually sinful. They regard His Saviour-hood as a consequence of the fact that He overcame the sin that is in the whole of humanity; and that if we look at Him and seek His help, and His aid, He will enable us to do the same. That is how He saves us.

It is most important that we should be clear about this, as it is being taught commonly at the present time. The most famous theologian of this century is probably Karl Barth. His view of our Lord's human nature is that it was sinful; and it is the view held by his followers in this and in every other country. If that teaching were true the Apostle would have said here, 'God sending his Son in sinful flesh, and for sin, condemned sin in the flesh'. But he goes out of his way not to say that, but to say 'in the *likeness* of sinful flesh'. Clearly he wants us to realize that our Lord's human nature was not sinful.

And this is not an isolated statement! There are similar statements. Take the account of the archangel Gabriel announcing the birth of our Lord to Mary. I call attention particularly to Luke 1, verse 35. The entire context is important. Mary, having been told about this wonderful Son whom she is to bear, could not understand the matter, and said to the angel, 'How shall this be, seeing I know not a man?' This is impossible, said Mary; I am a virgin, how can I bear a son? I have never known a man. Then comes verse 35: 'The angel answered and said unto her, The Holy Ghost shall come upon thee, and the power of the Highest shall overshadow thee: therefore also that holy thing which shall be born of thee shall be called the Son of God.' What a description of our Lord! What a description of the Babe – 'that holy thing'! The archangel describes Him in that way because He is holy. Because there was no sin in Him, He is unlike every other babe that has been born into this world. Here is the only Babe of whom you can say that he is holy. 'That holy thing' –

entirely free from sin, altogether different from all others. Other biblical statements confirm this.

The doctrine of the Virgin Birth is, of course, involved at this point also. His birth was unique, and we are told that His conception was unique. Though Mary had never known a man she is going to bear a child. How is the child to be conceived? 'The power of the Highest shall overshadow thee', is the answer. This is not only stated in Luke's Gospel; it is also in the gospel according to Matthew, chapter 1: 18: 'Now the birth of Jesus Christ was on this wise: when as his mother Mary was espoused to Joseph, before they came together, she was found with child of the Holy Ghost.' Joseph is not the father; they had not come together; she is found to be with child 'of the Holy Ghost'. And in verse 20 Joseph is reprimanded. He had thought to 'put her away', but he is told this: 'Joseph, thou son of David, fear not to take unto thee Mary thy wife: for that which is conceived in her is of the Holy Ghost.' In those two verses we are told specifically that Jesus was conceived of the Holy Ghost – the Holy Ghost supplied the germ of life. This is something that had never happened before, and has never happened since. Here is a unique birth, something altogether in a category of its own.

The Scriptures would not take the trouble to supply us with these statements unless they were of great doctrinal importance. For further confirmation take the Apostle Paul's statement in 2 Corinthians 5: 21: 'He hath made him to be sin for us, who knew no sin; that we might be made the righteousness of God in him'. Christ 'knew no sin'. He not only did not commit sin, there was no sin in His nature. He not only never knew it in an experimental sense, He never knew it in the sense of having it in His nature as a pollution. Again: Hebrews 4: 15: 'For we have not an High Priest which cannot be touched with the feeling of our infirmities; but was tempted in all points like as we are, yet without sin'. The translation given in the Authorized Version is almost misleading. It should be translated, 'Tempted in all points according to our likeness, apart from sin'. In Romans 8: 3 we read, 'In the likeness of sinful flesh', that is, 'according to our likeness, apart from sin', which means that He is like us apart from the sin; in other words, He is 'in the *likeness* of sinful flesh'. His flesh was not sinful, it was 'apart from sin'; but it is in the likeness of that.

Then there is another statement of the matter in Hebrews 7:26: 'For such an High Priest became us, who is holy, harmless, undefiled, separate from sinners, and made higher than the heavens.' In other words, He is perfect, He is without sin, there is no blemish in Him in any respect at all. And again, in the 9th chapter of Hebrews, in verse 14, we read: 'How much more shall the blood of Christ, who through the eternal Spirit offered himself without spot to God' – 'without spot' – 'purge your conscience from dead works to serve the living God'. That links up with what Peter says in his First Epistle, chapter 1, verse 19. He says that we are saved, not with silver or gold, but 'with the precious blood of Christ, as of a lamb without blemish and without spot'. And in the Old Testament you will find the regulations laid down about the lamb that was to be taken and to be sacrificed as an offering; and the point is always made that there must be no blemish in him. Why had that to be true of the type? Because it was true of the great Anti-type, 'the lamb of God'. They could not take a lamb which had a blemish, it had to be a lamb which as far as they could tell was perfect, without any blemish whatsoever. This was to foretell the truth that, when 'the Lamb of God who taketh away the sin of the world' appeared, He would have no blemish at all. A sinful nature implies blemish and pollution.

All these statements combine together to substantiate the claim which is made in Romans 8: 3 that our Lord's human nature was not sinful, but was 'like' our sinful nature.

What then is the doctrine? It is this: Our Lord in the Incarnation 'took unto him' human nature that had been rendered free from sin. The Roman Catholics at this point are not only right, but in their anxiety to be right, they go so far as to say something that is wrong. In their great anxiety to safeguard the fact that our Lord's human nature was not sinful, they go too far and say that the human nature of the Virgin Mary also was not sinful. That is what they call the doctrine of the 'Immaculate Conception'. People often think that the doctrine of the 'Immaculate Conception' is simply a statement of the fact that our Lord's nature was free from sin. But that is not its meaning. The 'Immaculate Conception' as taught by the Church of Rome says that the human nature of Mary was sinless. But there is not an iota of evidence in the whole of Scripture to support the claim. Mary was human like all others, her human nature was definitely sinful. She was a descendant of Adam like every other member of the human race, and she inherited the polluted fallen human nature that everyone born into this world has received as the result of Adam's transgression. The Apostle has proved that in chapter 5 of this Epistle.

What is taught in Scripture is not that Mary had been either born or made sinless, but that that portion of Mary, that cell out of Mary that was to be developed into the body of the Son of God was cleansed from sin; and that only. So Mary remained sinful, but this portion that she transmits to her Son has been delivered, set free from sin; and it is to that that the Son of God is joined. That is the human nature He takes unto Himself. It is a miracle, of course; and we are told specifically that it is a miracle. It was because she did not realize that a miracle was to happen that Mary stumbled at the announcement of the archangel Gabriel, and his reply to her is, 'Do not try to understand this, The power of the Highest shall overshadow you, the Holy Ghost will come upon you, you are going to conceive "of the Holy Ghost" who has power to work this cleansing so that the body of the human nature of the Son of God who is to be born of you shall be entirely free from sin'. So we reject the so-called doctrine of the 'Immaculate Conception'; but we assert with all our power the doctrine that the human nature of the Son of God was entirely free from sin.

But why should any ever want to doubt this? Why should they say that the Lord's human nature was sinful? Their reply is that they cannot see how He could be truly tempted unless this was true of Him. They feel that it is essential in order that He should have been liable and subject to temptation 'like as we are'. The reply to that is in Hebrews 4: 15: 'Tempted in all points like as we are, apart from sin'. He was tempted to sin; but there was no sin in Him. Not only so, it is an entire fallacy to say that we cannot be tempted unless there is something within us that responds to it. After all, when Adam was tempted his nature was not sinful. When Adam was tempted he had a perfect human nature; Adam and Eve were tempted in a state of perfection. So obviously temptation can have force and power though the nature of the tempted one is not evil. That really is a sufficient answer in and of itself. I would not hesitate to assert that our

Lord knew the power of temptation in a way that no human being has ever known it. The devil brought out all his reserves, all his subtlety against Him. We see that in the three temptations in the wilderness; but he undoubtedly came back many another time and brought all his power of deception to bear upon Him. Though our Lord did not fall, He felt the power of temptation. He experienced the subtlety and the power of the devil, and of sin and evil and temptation to a degree that you and I can never know.

But there is a further answer to the suggestion that our Lord's human nature was sinful. Can you conceive of the Godhead combining in one person with sin, with sinful human nature? It is inconceivable. How can the divine, eternal nature possibly combine in one person with a sinful human nature? Then add to that this final argument. Our Lord, according to the teaching of the Scripture, did not come into the world simply to cleanse that first humanity that had been created in Adam; He came to bring in a new humanity. That is why Paul in 1 Corinthians 15 puts the matter in this way: 'The first man is of the earth, earthy; the second man is the Lord from heaven'. What God has done in 'his own Son' is to start a new race, a new humanity. It has its link with the old humanity in that portion that was taken from Mary which was rendered free from sin. In that sense you can say it is still the old humanity, but it has been so cleansed that it can be the seed of a new humanity. So Jesus Christ is the 'Second Man'. Adam was the first man, Adam was the head of a human race. Jesus Christ is the Head of a human race, the Second Man. He is the 'firstborn among many brethren' (Romans 8: 29). In Him God starts a new pattern, a new race of men, a new humanity. It has that link with the old, as it must have because we belong to it, but it is something essentially new. As we bear that in mind we see how utterly important it is that we should realize that His human nature was not sinful.

When God made the first man He made him perfect. Adam's human nature was not a sinful human nature. The first man that God brought into being was entirely free from sin in every respect. So it was also with the second. If you say that Christ's human nature was sinful, you are in a sense making Him an inferior man to the first man – less perfect, less complete – which is again unthinkable. Not only so, you have also to look at the matter as it relates to the following. What makes our salvation so certain and sure, as we have seen, is that it cannot fail; and it cannot fail because sin does not enter in at all at any stage. Christ was born with a sinless human nature, and sin could not enter in, because He is the eternal Son of God. He remained spotless and perfect, without ever falling, and without any trace of sin in any connection to the end.

So the Apostle emphasizes here that He did not come in sinful flesh; but he goes out of his way to say that He came 'in the likeness of sinful flesh'. There is a positive element in this statement and this positive element is a very valuable one. He had true flesh, He was truly human. His human nature was not an appearance, it was a reality; He had a rational soul like every one of us has, but it was not sinful in any way at all. But it was 'like' our sinful human nature in certain respects.

In what respects did Christ come 'in the likeness of sinful flesh'? The answer seems to be, inevitably, that though His human nature was not in itself sinful, it did have some of the characteristics that belong to our human nature as the result of sin. Sin not only polluted human nature, it brought into it certain infirmities. Adam, before he fell, had no infirmities, he was perfect, he did not know fatigue, he could not have been ill, he was innocent, and he was without sin. But as the result of his sin and fall he not only became sinful and perverted in his nature, but certain weaknesses entered into his life; and they have been transmitted to his progeny ever since. The New Testament shows clearly that our Lord had some of these infirmities. Now infirmities are not sinful in and of themselves. Think of fatigue, tiredness, weariness, pain, sorrow, grief, disappointment, the capacity to weep. All those were seen in our Lord's earthly life. Let us look at the evidences of this.

We read in Luke 2: 40: 'And the child grew, and waxed strong in spirit, filled with wisdom: and the grace of God was upon him'. Verse 52: 'And Jesus increased in wisdom and stature, and in favour with God and man'. As we have seen in Hebrews 4: 15, He was now subject to temptation. James tells us in his Epistle that God not only does not tempt, but cannot be tempted; so if our Lord had not become truly human, if He had not really become a man, He could not have been tempted. But He was subject to temptation because He came 'in the likeness of sinful

flesh'. Then take several other remarkable statements concerning
Him in the Epistle to the Hebrews, chapter 5: 1–2: 'Every high
priest taken from among men is ordained for men in things
pertaining to God, that he may offer both gifts and sacrifices
for sins: who can have compassion on the ignorant, and on them
that are out of the way; for that he himself also is compassed
with infirmity.' That was true of Jesus the Son of God. 'We
have not an High Priest which cannot be touched with a feeling
of our infirmities', for He knew these infirmities Himself; He
knew what it was to be compassed about with them. Take, for
instance, what we are told about Him in connection with the
incident of the barren fig tree. He obviously did not know that
it had not got fruit on it. He tells us about the exact day of His
Second Coming that He does not know it (Mark 13: 32). These
are all indications of infirmity. He appeared to be frail; He was
tired and weary at times. In connection with the incident of the
Woman of Samaria, we read that when the disciples had gone to
buy provisions He sat by the side of the well because He was
'wearied with the journey' (John 4: 6). He seems to have been
more tired than the disciples. Now that is infirmity. He came
'in the likeness of sinful flesh'. His flesh was not sinful but it
was like sinful flesh in these particular respects.

But why was this essential? Why did He have to come in this
particular way? Why did God send His Son into the world 'in the
likeness of sinful flesh?' The answer is that God sent His Son
to save man. And in order to save man the Son had to become
man. This is put most clearly in the 2nd chapter of the Epistle to
the Hebrews, first in verse 9: 'We do not see yet all things put
under him, but we see Jesus, who was made a little lower than
the angels for the suffering of death, crowned with glory and
honour; that he by the grace of God should taste death for every
man.' Then take verse 11: 'For both he that sanctifieth and they
who are sanctified are all of one: for which cause he is not ashamed
to call them brethren'. Then the 10th verse: 'It became him, for
whom are all things, and by whom are all things, in bringing
many sons unto glory, to make the captain of their salvation' –
the Leader of their salvation, Jesus Christ – 'perfect through
sufferings.' We learn here that Christ must have the same human
nature as His people have. Then go on to verse 14: 'Forasmuch
then as the children are partakers of flesh and blood, he also

himself likewise took part of the same, that through death he
might destroy him that had the power of death, that is, the devil'.
Because you and I have flesh and blood, in order to save us He
has to take on Him 'flesh and blood'. That is the argument.
Then verses 16 and 17: 'For verily he took not on him the nature
of angels; but he took on him the seed of Abraham. Wherefore
in all things it behoved him to be made like unto his brethren,
that he might be a merciful and faithful high priest in things
pertaining to God, to make reconciliation for the sins of the
people. For in that he himself hath suffered being tempted, he
is able to succour them that are tempted.'

I must expound these words. Why did Christ have to come
in the likeness of sinful flesh? First, because He had to keep,
and to honour, the Law. Man is 'under the law'; and he has
broken it, and therefore the Law condemns him. Before man can
be reconciled to God he must keep the Law – he must bear its
punishment, and he must actively obey it. Jesus Christ came into
the world to be our representative, to do these things for us.
Man cannot do it, man had failed to do it – 'There is none righteous,
no, not one; all have sinned and come short of the glory of God'.
'The whole world lieth guilty before God'. Man therefore cannot
render this essential obedience; nor can the Law enable him to
do it – 'What the law could not do'! So God 'sends his own
Son', to be our representative. As our representative He has to
honour the Law. So He must be born 'under it'. That means
that He has to become man, He has to take on human nature.
He could not keep and honour the Law for us unless He had done
this.

In the second place, our guilt has to be borne; and how can
Christ bear that guilt unless He is 'like unto us'. So in order to
take our sins and our guilt upon Him and to bear their punishment He had to take on human nature. He had to become
Incarnate, He had to be a partaker of flesh and blood as we are;
He must be a man to be man's representative, and to be the start
of a 'new humanity'. As sin had been committed in the body, so
it must be punished in the body. That is the next phrase here,
'in the likeness of sinful flesh, and for sin, condemned sin in the
flesh'. Sin was not condemned in theory but in the body of
God's own Son.

Thirdly, before Christ can save us He must not only do all

that I have mentioned, but He must also give us a new nature. We are to be made 'partakers of the divine nature' (2 Peter 1 : 4); and the only way in which that becomes possible is that He should take human nature unto Himself and then give it to us. If He had not become Incarnate we could never have been made 'partakers of the divine nature', and become 'the sons of God'.

Fourthly, as it is argued out so wonderfully in Hebrews, chapters 4 and 5, Christ's taking our nature is the only way whereby He could become our 'sympathetic high priest'. If He had not done this we would not be able to pray. Who are we to ascend into the hill of God? Who are we to go into the presence of the eternal God, who is a 'consuming fire'? There is only one way whereby I can pray, and go into the presence of God with confidence; it is revealed in the words, 'We have not an high priest which cannot be touched with the feeling of our infirmities'. No, He has come 'in the likeness of sinful flesh', He was 'made flesh', He was truly man, He has lived in this world, He knows its evil and the power of temptation; so He can bear with us, He can sympathize with us, He can strengthen us, He is a sympathetic High Priest. Because He came 'in the likeness of sinful flesh'; He knows what it is to be weary and tired, hungry and thirsty. He knows what it is to be disappointed in His friends, He knows what it is to feel grief and sorrow, He knows what it is to weep. Thank God He came 'in the likeness of sinful flesh', for it makes Him our 'sympathetic high priest'. Still more, if He had not come in this way He could never have conquered death for us. Before death can be conquered human nature must be able to go through it and come out on its farther side. He has done so! He is 'the firstborn among many brethren', or as the Apostle Paul put it in preaching before Agrippa and Festus, 'He is the first that should rise from the dead' (Acts 26 : 23). Here is a Man that has conquered death and left it behind for ever. 'He dieth no more', as Paul has told us in chapter 6 verse 10 of this Epistle. Yes, and because He has done so we can be sure of our resurrection. In 1 Corinthians 15 : 21 he states it in this way: 'For since by man came death, by man came also resurrection from the dead'. If it is man who has gone down to death, it is a man who must rise; therefore the Son of God had to become man. That is the argument.

Our last argument claims that this doctrine is the only way to silence the devil to all eternity. Ever since the fall of man the devil has been taunting God saying, 'You made man in your own image; but look at him; I have mastered him. What can you do about him? Your great plan has gone wrong.' Now if God had saved man by any other means or method save the one He has adopted, the devil could never have been silenced. If a great spiritual power had acted from heaven the devil would have said, 'That is not fair; it is not man. If your saviour came down on earth he could not stand, I would tempt him and I would defeat him as I defeated Adam.'

So God sent His own Son in 'the likeness of sinful flesh'; He made Him 'under the law' – 'made of a woman, made under the law'. He was subject to temptation; the devil was given a full opportunity; but he failed. There stood before him One whom he regarded as a man only; but he 'could find nothing in him'. He failed to trip Him, to ensnare Him, to drag Him down. He was completely defeated. It is argued, therefore, in Hebrews 2: 'Forasmuch as the children are partakers of flesh and blood, he also himself likewise took part of the same, that through death he might destroy him that had the power of death, that is, the devil'. The devil is silenced once and for ever. Man 'in Christ' is restored into the image of God and will be made finally perfect and complete. Paul has argued already in chapter 3, verse 26 of this Epistle, 'Whom God hath set forth to be a propitiation through faith in his blood; to declare his righteousness for the remission of sins that are past, through the forbearance of God: to declare, I say, at this time his righteousness, that he might be just and the justifier of him who believeth in Jesus'. That means that the devil has nothing to say. It was man that sinned; it is man that must be punished. Man sinned in the flesh; sin must therefore be punished 'in the flesh'. And God has so acted. Jesus Christ was truly Man; our sins were laid upon Him, and they were dealt with in His body. The devil is silenced, he has nothing to say. God has been vindicated; God is just, but at the same time He can now 'justify all who believe in Jesus'. But if it had been done in any way except this way – which is that Christ has been sent 'in the likeness of sinful flesh' – the devil could still be objecting that it had not been done in the flesh, in human nature. But he cannot say that now; because sin has been dealt with in human nature. So there is no condemnation for the believer and the devil is silenced.

So later on in this chapter Paul is able to ask triumphantly, 'Who shall lay anything to the charge of God's elect?' Who can bring any charge against us? No one! There is no one anywhere, in heaven or in hell, or anywhere else, that can bring any charge whatsoever against us. For this is *God's* work. 'It is God that justifieth, who is he that condemneth? It is Christ that died, yea rather, that is risen again, who is even at the right hand of God, who also maketh intercession for us' (verses 33–34). God sent 'his own Son in the likeness of sinful flesh' for those reasons. And the greatest of all is the last – God's glory is vindicated, God's honour, God's justice, God's righteousness are revealed, manifested, glorified for all eternity. Because His Son came 'in the likeness of sinful flesh', as man, for man, He did the work, and He did it perfectly, and God is 'just and the justifier of him that believeth in Jesus.' Hallelujah!

Twenty-six

*

For what the law could not do, in that it was weak through the flesh, God sending his own Son in the likeness of sinful flesh, and for sin, condemned sin in the flesh:

That the righteousness of the law might be fulfilled in us, who walk not after the flesh, but after the Spirit.   Romans 8: 3, 4

We are studying this great statement phrase by phrase because of the extraordinary riches which are presented to us by it. We are also doing so because it is only as we understand these doctrines that we can hope to live the Christian life. There is an indissoluble association between doctrine and life. So many foolishly say that what they want is to be able to live the life, and that they are not concerned about doctrine. To which the simple answer is that it is only the people who really know and understand the doctrine who can live the life. This is God's way of sanctifying us. Our Lord prayed, 'Sanctify them through, or by, thy truth: thy word is truth' (John 17: 17). There is no short cut to holiness. Holiness is developed in us chiefly as the result of our understanding of these great truths. That is why the Apostle keeps on repeating them, and he does so because it is only as we grasp these doctrines that we can hope to become a sanctified people 'separated unto good works', and unto God.

So we come now to look at the next step in this statement. Why did the Lord Jesus Christ come into this world 'in the likeness of sinful flesh'? It was 'for sin'. These two short words are a vital part of the Apostle's teaching. There are those who say that the expression just means 'concerning sin', or 'with respect to sin', or 'in connection with sin'. And of course they do mean that; but these two words tell us much more. The simplest way of approaching this matter is to look at the various translations which are offered us. I have quoted the Authorized Version, but in its marginal references there is an alternative translation – 'by a sacrifice for sin'. In the Revised Version you find, 'in the likeness of sinful flesh, and as an offering for sin'. In the Revised Standard Version the translation is as in the Authorized Version – 'for sin'. But there is a footnote saying, 'Or, and as a sin offering'. They give the alternative. The 'Scofield Bible' in the same way puts the alternative in the margin, indicating that what is really meant is that it is a sin offering – 'as an offering for sin'.

How have these translators arrived at this conclusion? The answer is not at all difficult to find. If you take the Septuagint – the Greek translation of the Old Testament – which was in current use at the time when our Lord and the Apostle Paul were in this world, you will find this interesting fact, that when those seventy translators came across the expression 'sin offering' in the Old Testament in the Hebrew, they often translated it by just these two words 'for sin', and no more. Let a few instances of this suffice. For example, in the Book of Leviticus, chapter 4, verse 3, you have, 'If the priest that is anointed sin according to the sin of the people, then let him bring for his sin, which he hath sinned, a young bullock without blemish unto the Lord for a sin offering'. But in the Septuagint translation you will not find 'for a sin offering' but simply 'for sin'. You will find the same in the Book of Numbers, chapter 8, verse 8; and again in Psalm 39, verse 6. And there are other examples also. It was their practice to use the two words 'for sin' to convey the idea of 'as a sin offering', or 'as an offering for sin'. Another interesting bit of evidence is found in the 10th chapter of the Epistle to the Hebrews, verse 6. In the Authorized Version we read, 'In burnt offerings and sacrifices for sin thou hast had no pleasure'. You will observe that the word 'sacrifices' is in italics, indicating that it was not present in the original but has been added by the translators. In other words, what they found in the Greek was, 'In burnt offerings and for sin thou hast had no pleasure' but they very rightly translated it as 'sacrifices for sin'. But they were inconsistent; for they should have done the same thing in this 3rd verse of the 8th chapter of the Epistle to the Romans, because they were confronted by the same words. The same applies to the 8th verse of the 10th chapter of the Epistle to the Hebrews, 'Above when he said, Sacrifice and offering and burnt offerings and offering for sin' – again it is supplied. Instead of just saying 'for sin' they have rightly introduced the word 'offering' which helps us to understand exactly what they mean. So Romans 8: 3 means: 'God sending his own Son in the likeness of sinful flesh and as an offering for sin . . .'.

The New Testament teaches throughout that the main purpose of our Lord in coming into this world was to deliver us from sin and condemnation by becoming an 'offering' for us – 'an offering for sin'. The whole of the Old Testament teaches the same truth. All the types in the Old Testament, all the burnt offerings and sacrifices, the killing of the animals and the presenting of the blood – all are a foreshadowing of the coming of the Son of God into this world. Why was He going to come into this world? To be 'the Lamb of God that taketh away the sin of the world'. This is the teaching everywhere in the New Testament. Take Galatians 1: 4: 'Who gave himself for our sins, that he might deliver us from this present evil world', says the Apostle. Then in 2 Corinthians 5: 21 he says: 'He hath made him to be sin for us, who knew no sin; that we might be made the righteousness of God in him'. 'God was in Christ reconciling the world unto himself'. How did He accomplish this? By making Christ 'to be sin for us, who knew no sin'. Take further what we are told in the Epistle to the Hebrews, chapter 2, verse 9: 'We see not yet all things put under him, but we see Jesus, who was made a little lower than the angels for the suffering of death, crowned with glory and honour; that he by the grace of God should taste death for every man'. The purpose of our Lord's coming into the world was that He should 'taste death'; in other words, that He should be made 'an offering for sin'. It is stated by the Apostle Peter in his First Epistle, chapter 1, verse 19: 'Forasmuch as ye know that ye were not redeemed with corruptible things, as silver and gold, from your vain conversation, received by tradition from your fathers; but with the precious blood of Christ, as of a lamb without blemish and without spot'. That is precisely what the Apostle Paul is saying here. The Son of God did not come into the world to teach us primarily; He came to save us. And to do that, He had to make expiation, and to be a 'propitiation' for our sins.

The Apostle's chief concern, as we have seen, is to show that there is 'no condemnation' to them which are in Christ Jesus. So he has to explain to us how that comes about. There is no condemnation because Christ has been made an 'offering for sin' on

our behalf. He has already said it in chapter 3, in verses 24 to 26:
'Whom God hath set forth as a propitiation through faith in his
blood'. Propitiation and expiation! That is the very thing Paul says
here. So the two words 'for sin' just remind us again, and sum up
again all he has been saying about the way of salvation that God
has provided by laying our sins upon His Son and punishing them
in Him, in order that we might be forgiven. 'For sin'. 'As an
offering for sin'. This explains why God sent Him into the world
'in the likeness of sinful flesh'.

This is vital because you cannot possible understand the phrase
that follows, namely, 'condemned sin in the flesh', unless you are
clear about the meaning of 'for sin'. The Law could not do that,
but God has done it. How? By sending His Son in the likeness
of sinful flesh, and for sin, He condemned sin in the flesh.

What does this mean? Here again many go astray. They say that
it simply means that our Lord, by living a perfect and sinless life,
condemned sin; that He showed how wrong sin was, how vile,
how evil. He showed His disapproval of it, He showed God's
disapproval of it. So they hold that it means no more than that
He expressed disapproval by living a holy life in the flesh, 'in the
likeness of sinful flesh'. Others are Perfectionists and do not
hesitate to say that this means that Christ destroyed sin in the
flesh. They teach that the Apostle is asserting that sin is entirely
eradicated out of us. Having taken that wrong view of 'the law
of sin and death' in verse 2, they are quite consistent with themselves when they say that, here, Paul is saying that sin was destroyed in the flesh by our Lord, and if we but believe in Him and
have the experience of the baptism with the Spirit, sin will be
entirely destroyed in us, taken right out of us, so that we become
sinless and perfect.

What of these suggestions and interpretations? I answer: they
are not true, not correct, for the following reasons. If Paul simply
means that our Lord, by living that perfect life, expressed disapproval of sin – His own disapproval and God's – then I say
that the Son of God did nothing that had not already been done.
The Law had already been given by God in order to do that very
thing. The Law was given to express disapproval of sin, to condemn it, in that sense, completely; to show what God thought of
it, and to reveal His holiness. There was no need for the Son of
God to come into the world to tell us what God disapproved of

sin. Paul has already told us in chapter 5, verse 20, that the Law was added in order to do that very thing – 'it was added that the offence might abound'. Indeed, he had said it earlier still in chapter 4, verse 15. These verses alone, it seems to me, puts that interpretation right out of court.

When you come to the question of 'destroying' sin, all the arguments against Perfectionism come in again. Let me give you one which I think is sufficient. If sin is 'destroyed' in us, why does the Apostle have to say later in verses 12 and 13, 'Therefore, brethren, we are debtors, not to the flesh, to live after the flesh. For if ye live after the flesh, ye shall die: but if ye through the Spirit do mortify the deeds of the body, ye shall live.' That is a meaningless exhortation if sin has already been destroyed in us. Perfectionists whom I know are ready to admit that they cannot answer that argument; they do not understand Paul's statement and cannot explain it. But I will adduce some further reasons. Sin is obviously not destroyed in us. We find that stated in chapter 6, verse 12: 'Let not sin therefore reign in your mortal body.' We are not to allow sin to reign, we have to 'mortify' the relics and the remnants and the activities of sin which still remain in our mortal bodies. Indeed, there is a further argument which is quite conclusive on this matter. Consider this word 'condemned' – 'condemned sin in the flesh'. It is exactly the same word as the Apostle used in the first verse, where he says, 'There is therefore now no condemnation to them which are in Christ Jesus'. So if 'condemnation', here, means 'to destroy', it means to destroy in verse 1 also, and you would have to read, 'There is therefore now no destruction to them that are in Christ Jesus' – which is ridiculous. Paul means condemnation – and condemnation means the same in the 1st verse as in this verse. It means 'to pass judgment upon', 'to punish'. Now the Law could not punish sin in that sense. The Law expressed its disapproval, but in expressing its disapproval it did not finally 'punish' sin in the sense of passing a final judgment upon it, so as to put it entirely out of court as far as the believer is concerned. So what we are told here is, 'God sending his own Son in the likeness of sinful flesh, and for sin, punished, passed judgment upon sin in the flesh.'

What God did was to condemn and to punish our sins in His own Son who was in this world 'in the likeness of sinful flesh', in the body. The Apostle is saying that this is God's way of dealing with this problem. He sent His Son into the world in the flesh, and there He punished, condemned sin in His flesh. So we must emphasize 'in the flesh', which means, as we have seen, 'in our nature'. Sin was condemned in Him as a man. As the Apostle Peter puts it in the First Epistle, chapter 2, verse 24: 'Who his own self bare our sins in his own body on the tree, that we, being dead to sins, should live unto righteousness: by whose stripes ye were healed'. That is what we are told here. God condemned sin in the body of His own Son. He was in the flesh when our sins were laid upon Him; and they were punished in Him. Man had sinned 'in the flesh', sin was punished 'in the flesh'. He came on earth so that sin might be punished and condemned in this way. The judgment on sin has been passed, and has been meted out, upon Him. This is, of course, the heart of the gospel, the very centre, the glory of the gospel. God by punishing our sins in His incarnate Son remains just, but can nevertheless be 'the justifier of him that believeth in Jesus'. The Apostle said it in that way in chapter 3, verses 24 to 26, and he says it in this way here.

The next step is to ask, Why did it happen in this way? Why was it necessary for God to send His Son in the likeness of sinful flesh, and to make Him an offering for sin? The answer, as we have previously noted, is found in the very next phrase at the beginning of verse 4: 'That (in order that) the righteousness of the law might be fulfilled in us, who walk not after the flesh, but after the Spirit'. We must therefore look at this once more. 'That the righteousness of the law might be fulfilled in us?' The first meaning of the statement is that the Law can no longer make any claim upon us. The righteous demands of the Law have been satisfied in the Person of the Lord Jesus Christ. The Law demands obedience. He gave it perfectly. The Law insists upon punishing sin. He has borne the punishment. The righteous demands of the Law have all been fulfilled in Him.

First and foremost this means our justification, and that we are 'clothed with the righteousness of Jesus Christ'. But again I insist that we must not stop at that point, as some of the great commentators do. There is more involved here, and I would remind you as to why we must insist upon this. Go back to chapter 7, verses 4 and 6: 'Wherefore, my brethren, ye also are become dead to the law by the body of Christ'. 'By the body of

Christ'. That is another reminder that God sent Him as a sin-offering that 'sin might be condemned in the flesh'. Because of that we have become dead to the Law by the body of Christ. But that is 'in order that' – the same argument as we have here in the 4th verse of this 8th chapter – 'we should be married to another, even to Him that is raised from the dead, in order that we should bring forth fruit unto God'. The blessing does not stop at justification. It is not merely a declaratory statement to the effect that we are righteous and clothed with the righteousness of Christ. There is more; we are to 'bring forth fruit unto God'. Paul has already said that, so why should he suddenly drop it? But look at it again in verse 6 of chapter 7: 'But now we are delivered from the law, that being dead wherein we were held; that (in order that) we should serve in newness of Spirit, and not in the oldness of the letter'. 'Serve', notice; and 'serve' in a new way! In other words, the Apostle does not stop at our justification, at the fact that we are declared to be righteous by Christ's righteousness. No, there is more than that 'imputed' righteousness; there is this 'imparted' righteousness also. We are to bear fruit in this life, we are to serve in this new way – 'not in the oldness of the letter, but in the newness of the Spirit'.

I must next show – for this is the question likely to arise at this point – why it was necessary that the Son of God should be made 'a sin offering' in order that we might serve in this new way and bear fruit unto God? The answer is, that before we can possibly live in this new way and 'bear fruit unto God' we must be delivered from the Law. We cannot 'bring forth fruit unto God' while we are 'under the law'; we must first be delivered from the Law. And that is exactly what is said in verse 2: 'For the law of the Spirit of life in Christ Jesus hath made me free from the law of sin and death'; and verses 3 and 4 are nothing but an exposition of that statement in verse 2.

So the Apostle now goes on to show why it was essential that we should be delivered from the Law, and how that was actually accomplished through the Lord Jesus Christ being 'made an offering for sin', and sin being 'condemned' in that way in His flesh. Look at the matter in terms of the following question: How does the death of Christ as our Substitute, as our sin-bearer, as an 'offering for sin', as 'the Lamb of God' – how does that death enable 'the righteousness of the law' to be fulfilled in us? By nature we are all under the reign and the dominion and the power of sin. I need not prove that again as it is all in chapters 5 and 7.

How, then, can we be delivered from sin? That is the question. Obviously, in the light of that teaching, the first thing that needs to be done is for the sting to be taken out of sin. The sting of sin, the strength and power of sin, is the Law. So if I want to be delivered from the power of sin, I must find what it is that can take that power out of sin. My problem therefore is, How can I get rid of the Law which puts power into sin? There is only one solution to this problem, and it is the one which God has adopted. It is the death of 'his own Son' for sin. 'Christ is the end of the law for righteousness to every one that believeth' (Romans 10: 4).

How does He do this? Christ has fully satisfied the demands of the Law, both in the keeping of its precepts and in the bearing of the punishment that it had pronounced and demands should be meted out upon sin and the sinner. And because all this has happened in and through Christ there is no more that the Law can do to us who are 'in Christ'. We can say, therefore, with the Apostle, that we are 'dead to the law'. Christ has exhausted all the possibilities of the Law with respect to us, He is 'the end of the law'. So the Law can say nothing to me, and, as far as the believer is concerned, it is powerless.

But, in addition, as the Law is the strength of sin, when the Law is eliminated, sin is shorn of its power. Hence the Apostle does not hesitate to say, as we have seen in chapter 6, verse 2: 'How shall we that are dead to sin, live any longer therein?' He says, 'I am dead to the law', and also 'I am dead to sin'. That is because Christ deals with the Law, and in dealing with Law, sin is also dealt with, because 'the strength of sin is the law'. The result is that we are taken out of the 'realm' and 'reign' and 'rule' and 'power' of sin. That is in chapter 5, verse 21, once more, 'That as sin hath reigned unto death, even so might grace reign through righteousness unto eternal life by Jesus Christ our Lord'. It works in this way. Sin condemns the natural man through the Law; but by the death of Christ it, itself, has been condemned. That is the first thing. But there is more. As it was the Law that aggravated and inflamed sin within me, when the Law is taken away, as it is by the death of Christ, the aggravation of sin is also taken away. That which was working in me to aggravate and inflame 'the motions of sins in my members' has gone; I am dead to it, it is no longer a power as far as I am concerned. We are delivered from this rule and reign and tyranny of sin, not only in general, but also in this very practical sense.

Then comes the third, and in some ways, the most wonderful step of all. My position as a Christian is not only that I am no longer condemned, nor that in addition the aggravation of sin, which the Law produced in me, has been taken away; something still more wonderful has happened, something positive. The Apostle has already mentioned this, first of all in chapter 5, but very explicitly in chapter 7, verse 4, where he says that 'we are married to another', to Christ – we are joined to Christ. In this 8th chapter he says it again in verse 1 by saying that we are 'in Christ Jesus'; in verse 2, by referring to 'the law of the Spirit of life in Christ Jesus'. Our position in Christ is not negative only; it is also positive. I am now positively united to Christ, He is the Head and I am part of His body; His power and His life are in me; and He has put His Spirit into me. But you cannot be joined to Christ while you are still joined to the Law and to Adam. The first thing that must be done before I can be married to Christ is that I should cease to be married to the Law. That is the argument at the beginning of chapter 7.

So the Apostle had to bring in the death of Christ again, He had to say that Christ was sent 'in the likeness of sinful flesh, and for sin' – as an offering for sin – that sin might be condemned in the flesh', because if that had not happened the Law would still be there; and while the Law is there I cannot be joined to Christ. But the Law having been removed, Christ having fulfilled it in every way, I am free to be married to the Other, I am married to Him. His power is now in me delivering me, and enabling 'the righteousness of the law to be fulfilled' in me. That is the argument; that is what Paul is saying. The life and power of Christ, the reign of grace, are now in us as Christians, and working in us actively. Thus it becomes possible for me to 'bear fruit unto God', to 'serve' in a new way, 'in the newness of the Spirit, and not in the oldness of the letter'. Thus is the righteousness of the Law fulfilled in me. We do not stop at justification, we go further. The moment the Christian is 'in Christ' sanctification has begun.

The learned commentators with whom I am disagreeing are at great pains elsewhere to say that you must never separate

justification and sanctification, yet they themselves separate them
here by saying that the theme here is justification. But you cannot
be justified without being placed 'in Christ', and the moment you
are in Him sanctification has already started within you. Indeed,
it is a simple matter to prove that all the greater statements in
the New Testament about the object of our Lord's death upon the
Cross include this further, this second element. Let me quote
some of them. Look once again at 1 Peter 2: 24: 'Who his own
self bare our sins in his own body on the tree, that we, being dead
to sins, should live unto righteousness'. In the earlier parts of
that chapter Peter has been telling those Christians how to do so.
'Dearly beloved, I beseech you as strangers and pilgrims, abstain
from fleshly lusts, which war against the soul'. He tells them
also how to regard kings, and masters, and tells them what to do
when they are threatened and when they suffer. That is all a part
of the teaching of sanctification. Take, likewise, the great statement in Titus 2: 14: 'Who gave himself for us, that he might
redeem us from all iniquity, and purify unto himself' – not when
we die, but here and now; it begins here and goes on, and will
finally be perfect – 'purify unto himself a peculiar people, zealous
of good works.' Those words are not true of any and every
sinner, but they are true of all Christians – 'peculiar people,
zealous of good works'. That is why Christ died, why He 'gave
himself for us'. 'It is the will of God', says Paul in 1 Thessalonians 4: 3, 'even your sanctification'. This starts in this world,
in the here and now, and progresses; it starts the moment we are
'in Christ'.

This teaching does not imply any question of perfection in
this life. Dr Hodge and others seem to be so alarmed at the danger
of perfection coming in. They contend that, if you say that this
means anything more than justification, you are saying that it
means that we become entirely sanctified. But that does not follow.
All it means is that the process of sanctification starts, and that it
will be carried on until finally we shall be perfect in heaven,
'without spot or wrinkle or any such thing', without any vestige
or relic of sin remaining, even in our bodies which shall be
glorified. 'Waiting for the adoption, to wit, the redemption of
our body'. The Apostle is asserting that the moment we enter
into Christ this process starts. The Christian begins to bear fruit in
this world, fruit unto holiness, fruit unto righteousness. Paul

has been arguing about that very point in chapter 6, where he has been urging us to yield our members 'servants unto righteousness, unto holiness'. So our sanctification goes on progressively. The object which God had in view in sending 'his own Son' into the world 'in the likeness of sinful flesh' and 'for sin', and condemning sin in the flesh was – What? He has already told us in chapter 6, verse 6; 'Knowing this, that our old man was crucified with him' – Why? – 'That the body of sin might be disannulled, that henceforth we should not serve sin', in other words, 'that the righteousness of the law might be fulfilled in us, who walk not after the flesh, but after the Spirit'. The Law having been put on one side – or we having died to it, and being separated from it – sin is thus deprived of its power to reign and rule over us. Though it remains to trouble us in the body, it no longer is our master, we are no longer under its rule and reign. It worries us, it troubles us, but it does not reign over us, for we are in this new realm; we are joined to Christ, we are married to Him, and His power is in us. We can now begin to 'work out our salvation with fear and trembling, because it is God that worketh in us' (Philippians 2: 12 and 13). He is doing that now 'of his good pleasure'.

In the next phrase the Apostle will substantiate and prove still more conclusively what I have been saying, and that, in turn, will lead on to the verses that follow, which are nothing but an exposition and an explanation of it. The big central principle we must grasp, thank God, is this: The Law could never save us. It had failed completely to do so, it was never intended to do so. Indeed, because of what is true of us 'in sin', we are in a state in which we have to be set free from the Law. That is the first problem, how to be set free from 'the law of sin and death'. There was only one way. It meant that the Son of God had to leave the Courts of Heaven, and be born 'in the likeness of sinful flesh', and live in this world. His soul must be made 'an offering for sin', and our sins must be laid upon Him, and punished in Him. He had to be smitten, 'to be delivered up for us all' by his Father in order that sin might be condemned 'in him'. That having been done, we can be united to Him, and the power of His life. And the Spirit that was in Him is in us, and thus the righteousness of the Law is fulfilled in us.

Twenty-seven

For what the law could not do, in that it was weak through the flesh, God sending his own Son in the likeness of sinful flesh, and for sin, condemned sin in the flesh:
That the righteousness of the law might be fulfilled in us, who walk not after the flesh, but after the Spirit.   Romans 8: 3–4

In these words the Apostle proceeds to give us a further description and elaboration of the Christian life. It is one of those pregnant statements which contain the basic essentials of the Christian faith. God has done something that 'the law could not do because it was weak through the flesh'. And what He has done is to make it possible for the righteousness of the Law to be fulfilled in us; and we are in process of seeing how He has done it. The ultimate object of it all is that 'the righteousness of the law may be fulfilled in us.

The question arises, Who are these people in whom this is taking place? The answer is, 'in us, who walk not after the flesh, but after the Spirit'. Here we have another of Paul's key phrases, and in particular from the standpoint of the doctrine of sanctification. The two best-known and prominent schools of thought with regard to sanctification differ essentially at this point in their interpretation of this particular expression; therefore we must examine it very carefully. Fortunately, we are in a position to do so, because from verse 5 onwards, to the end of verse 13, and especially to the end of verse 11, the Apostle himself tells us what he means by the expression.

Let us begin by observing what the Apostle says about those whom he describes. The first word that engages our attention is the word 'walk' – 'who walk not after the flesh, but after the Spirit'. This is one of the crucial points, as we will see, and I

[343]

suggest that it is a description of the Christian's general way of living. I emphasize the 'general' aspect. It is a word used in the New Testament to describe the general tenor of a man's life. In other words, it tells us something about what governs and regulates a man's life, both in his thought and practice. A man walks in this particular way, we are told; and that means that he is governed by certain principles which control his life – his thought, his judgment, his feelings; the objects he is interested in, his purposes, everything. Many illustrations of this are to be found in the Scriptures. For instance, in the Acts of the Apostles, chapter 21, and verse 21, we read: They are informed of thee' – that is the Apostle Paul – 'that thou teachest all the Jews which are among the Gentiles to forsake Moses, saying that they ought not to circumcise their children, neither to walk after the customs'. It was a charge brought against the Apostle that he was teaching the Jews which were among the Gentiles to forsake the teaching of the Old Testament, the Moral Law, the Levitical law, saying that they ought not to circumcise their children, nor to continue to observe the old customs. That means, obviously, that their mode and manner of life, and of worship, and of everything else, was not to be governed and controlled by the customs taught in the Mosaic Law. Or take the beginning of chapter 2 of the Epistle to the Ephesians: 'You hath he quickened, who were dead in trespasses and sins; wherein in time past ye walked according to the course of this world'. He is describing, there, the general tenor of their life. They 'lived' according to the course of this world would convey exactly the same idea. Another interesting word is used in the 3rd verse there. He says, 'Among whom also we all had our conversation in times past'. Now, as used in the King James (A.V) translation, the word 'conversation' does not mean what it means today. We mean that we are talking with someone, but 'conversation' in Ephesians 2 means the whole way of living. It means virtually the same thing as 'walk'. It is not a specific term, but a very general one. The same idea is found at the end of the 3rd chapter of Paul's Epistle to the Philippians, verse 20: 'Our conversation is in heaven'. He means our 'polity', our 'home', our 'commonwealth' is in heaven; that is where we belong, that is where we are really living. A most interesting term used about Christian people in the Acts of the Apostles is that they are 'the people of the Way'. They are people

who are walking along a given way, who are walking along 'the
narrow way', and no longer on the 'broad way'. The term 'walk'
then is a description of the totality of life, not merely of practice,
but of thought, of desire, and all else. So the Apostle is saying that
'the righteousness of the law' is to be fulfilled in those of whom
it can be said that the general tenor of their life is that they 'walk
not after the flesh'.

The second word is the word 'flesh'. We looked at its meaning
in some detail in our study of the 5th verse of chapter 7, and
noted that it is a word that is used in different senses in the New
Testament. I remind you that we discovered three principal uses
of the term 'flesh' – it is used for 'mankind' in general, it is also
used to mean 'the body', and it also stands for 'unrenewed human
nature'. In the last of these it stands for human nature as the
result of the Fall, human nature as it is before the Spirit of God
begins to work upon it. Paul says that we were all in that state
at one time, we were all 'in the flesh'; then we were quickened
by the Spirit at our regeneration. It is surely clear that the meaning it carries in this 4th verse of this 8th chapter in this Epistle
is the last one. Paul is describing 'unrenewed human nature' in
general – 'who walk not after the flesh, but after the Spirit'. In
other words the best way, perhaps, of describing this use of the
word 'flesh' is to say that it is always used as a contrast with 'life
in the Spirit'. So it stands for man's life apart from, outside the
influences and the work of, the Holy Spirit of God. Christians,
he says, are no longer walking 'after the flesh'; they are walking
now 'after the Spirit'; and they are the people in whom the righteousness of the Law is 'to be fulfilled'.

We need to exercise great care at this point. When we say that
people are 'walking in the flesh' it does not mean of necessity that
they are living a very sinful life; it does not of necessity refer to
flagrant immorality, or gross evil. Very respectable people who
are never guilty of what we call gross 'sins of the flesh' nevertheless may be 'walking in the flesh', or 'after the flesh'. The Apostle
has already used the term in that sense in the 7th chapter, verse 5,
'for', he says, 'when we were in the flesh' – that is to say, all of us,
all mankind which is unregenerate – 'the motions of sins, which
were by the law, did work in our members to bring forth fruit
unto death'. He does not mean by that, that he and all others
were drunkards and adulterers and murderers, and guilty of all

the gross sins of the flesh. What it does mean is that we were in a state and a condition in which the Holy Spirit was not leading us and guiding us. So that you can say of the most gross and obvious sinner and of the most respectable moral man, that they are both 'walking after the flesh'. Neither is a Christian; the Holy Spirit is not influencing either of them. One is in rags, as it were, while the other is very decently clothed; but they are both 'walking after the flesh'. This is a most important distinction.

A further instance of the same thing will help to establish this point. Take the Epistle to the Galatians, chapter 3, verse 3: 'Are you so foolish? having begun in the Spirit, are you now made perfect by the flesh?' It is obvious that 'flesh' as used here does not mean that you fall into gross kinds of sin, because even the foolish Galatians, at the height of their folly, never imagined that any man could improve his Christian standing and his Christian life by plunging into sin. No, what they were doing was to go back to circumcision, and to put themselves 'under the law' again. So when Paul says, 'Are you so foolish? having begun in the Spirit, are you now made perfect by the flesh?', he means, 'Having started in the Spirit, are you trying to perfect your Christian life by going back under the law and back to circumcision'? 'Flesh' there cannot mean gross, obvious sin, but a return to their old outlook and their former relationship to God. But there is a yet clearer example in the Epistle to the Philippians, chapter 3, verses 1 to 3: 'Finally, my brethren . . . beware of the concision; for we are the circumcision'. Who are we? The answer is given that we are those 'which worship God in the spirit (not in the old ceremonial law, but in the spirit) and rejoice in Christ Jesus (not in our own works) and have no confidence in the flesh'. It is clear that 'flesh' as used here again means the general tenor of one's life. Paul is not thinking of gross sins in the flesh because he goes on to say, 'Though I might also have confidence in the flesh'. Why? Because I have been a great drunkard or an adulterer? Not at all. 'If any other man thinketh that he hath whereof he might trust in the flesh, I more: Circumcised the eighth day, of the stock of Israel, of the tribe of Benjamin, an Hebrew of the Hebrews. . .' .

That should be enough to establish that when the Apostle says that the righteousness of the Law is fulfilled in us 'who walk not after the flesh', he is not saying 'is fulfilled in us, who no longer are guilty of the terrible sins that we once committed'. That is not at all what he is saying. To 'walk after the flesh' means that you view yourself and your relationship to God in a manner that is entirely opposed to God's way of salvation in Jesus Christ through the Holy Spirit; that you are like the Jew who thinks he is right with God because he is a Jew, because he has been circumcised, because he is a moral man, because he is studying the Law, because he is not doing certain things – in other words, because he is a Pharisee. The Pharisees were all men who 'walked after the flesh'. They were not walking 'after the Spirit'. That is why they disliked our Lord, and that is why they finally crucified Him. He convinced and convicted them of 'walking after the flesh'; and they would not listen to His spiritual message.

This term 'the flesh' is not primarily descriptive of evil acts or sinful actions; it is descriptive of an outlook upon salvation that is the complete antithesis of that which is taught in the New Testament gospel. It is a viewing of salvation from the carnal, fleshly, human standpoint; it is not 'the glorious gospel of the blessed God'. In other words, it is the typical outlook and attitude of the unregenerate man, whether he is a 'good moral man' or whether he is the most profligate and vile and filthy sinner. They are both in the same category; they are both 'walking after the flesh'. They do not understand the need of the work of the Spirit, and of regeneration, and the continuing operation of the Holy Spirit in them. That is what the Apostle means by 'walking after the flesh.' It must not be thought of in terms of conduct and behaviour primarily, or of particular actions. It includes the general outlook.

But walking 'after the flesh' is contrasted with walking 'after the Spirit'. We must now look closely at this second term. It is, of course, a reference to the Holy Spirit to whom the Apostle has already referred in verse 2, 'The law of the Spirit of life in Christ Jesus hath made me free from the law of sin and death'. He is just saying it again, and referring to people who are now in the realm of the Spirit. They have been enlightened by the Spirit, quickened by the Spirit, regenerated by the operation of the Spirit; and their life, their walk, is one in which they are being led and guided by the Holy Spirit of God. As I have previously reminded you, Paul had actually said this in the 6th verse of chapter 7: 'But now we are delivered from the law, being dead to that wherein we were held; that we should serve in newness of the Spirit (the Holy Spirit) and not in the oldness of the letter.' He had combined 'the law' and 'the flesh' in chapter 7, and now he combines 'the Spirit' and 'life'. So the righteousness of the Law is to be fulfilled in us, 'who walk not after the flesh,' and who do not attempt to serve God in the oldness of the letter, but in newness of the Spirit. We are the people who have been set free by the Spirit of life in Christ Jesus; we are 'in Christ' and we are led by 'the Spirit'.

Having now looked at the terms used, we move on to the crucial question of the identity of the people whom the Apostle is describing. 'The righteousness of the law' is to be fulfilled in people of whom it is true that they no longer 'walk after the flesh', but 'after the Spirit'. Who are they? There are two main ideas, as I have said, about this. The one school, which is very popular and well known, teaches that this applies to certain Christians only. They divide Christians into two main groups – those whom they call the 'carnal' Christians, and those whom they call 'spiritual' Christians. There is the Christian, they say, who has certainly 'been saved', but who is still 'walking after the flesh'. But it is possible for him to have another experience which will then bring him into the position in which he walks no longer 'after the flesh' but 'after the Spirit'. The Christian who is 'walking after the flesh', they say, is the man described in the 7th chapter of this Epistle. But, they urge, you can go out of chapter 7 into chapter 8; you can have another, a 'second experience', a 'second blessing'. Then you will no longer be a Christian who is walking 'after the flesh', you will become a Christian who is walking 'after the Spirit'. So to 'walk after the Spirit', according to this view, is something optional. You can be a Christian who does not choose to walk in this new way, or you can choose to do so. Once you have heard about this new possibility and you like it, all you have to do is to surrender yourself and receive it, and then you become a Christian who is now walking 'after the Spirit'. All depends on your decision and choice.

In my view this interpretation directly contradicts what the Apostle is really saying in these four verses of this chapter. He is talking about people of whom it is true to say that there is 'no longer any condemnation' for them. He has told us so in verse 1: 'There is therefore now no condemnation to them which are in Christ Jesus.' But they are the people whom 'the law of the Spirit of life in Christ Jesus hath made free from the law of sin and death'. They are the people for whom God sent His Son into this world 'in the likeness of sinful flesh', and 'as a sin offering', in order that their sin 'might be condemned in the flesh' in order that 'the righteousness of the law might be fulfilled in them'. These are Christian people, all Christian people (the same people the whole time). It is true to say of all Christians without exception that for them there is 'no condemnation'. There is no indication whatsoever given here that the Apostle recognizes two types of Christians; he is talking throughout about the same people. He does not say, 'Now there are some Christians who remain at justification only'. No, he is making a statement about all who are 'in Christ Jesus', and every Christian is 'in Christ Jesus'. As he will show at great length in the following verses, you cannot be a Christian if you do not have the Spirit, for 'if any man have not the Spirit of Christ he is none of his' (verse 9). All who are 'in Christ Jesus', everyone who is a Christian, is one who is walking 'not after the flesh but after the Spirit'. There is no indication of two distinct groups anywhere here.

Let me put it positively, and give further reasons for asserting that the Apostle is describing here every Christian and not merely some Christians who have chosen and decided to advance further in the Christian life. Take for instance, what our Lord Himself said to Nicodemus. You will find there the self-same contrast that we have here in these verses. In John 3, verse 4, we read: 'Nicodemus saith unto him, How can a man be born when he is old? Can he enter the second time into his mother's womb, and be born?' There you have a man thinking 'according to the flesh'. Jesus answered, 'Verily, verily, I say unto thee, Except a man be born of water and of the Spirit, he cannot enter into the Kingdom of God'. Then, 'That which is born of the flesh is flesh; and that which is born of the Spirit is spirit. Marvel not that I said unto thee, Ye must be born again' (John 3: 4 to 7). There, you have the contrast established once and for ever. It is the contrast between 'the flesh' and 'the Spirit', between walking after the flesh and walking after the Spirit. According to our Lord, Nicodemus, in trying to understand the re-birth teaching, was betraying himself as 'walking after the flesh'; his whole outlook was a 'fleshly' one. Our Lord was speaking about something spiritual, and one has to be 'born again' and 'baptized of water and the Spirit' before one can enter into this. Our Lord shows Nicodemus that his whole outlook is wrong, that he is 'in the flesh' and thinking according to the flesh. He needs 'the Spirit', he must be 'born of water and of the Spirit' before he can enter this spiritual realm – 'That which is born of the flesh is flesh, and that which is born of the Spirit is spirit'. This is the very distinction that we have here between 'who walk not after the flesh', but 'after the Spirit'. To walk 'after the Spirit' is true of every man who is regenerate.

For a final proof of my contention you must turn to the verses that follow. I have indicated already that from verse 5 to the end of verse 11 the Apostle gives us an exposition of this phrase. We hope later to look into it in detail, but we must glance at some of the statements now. Take verse 5: 'They that are after the flesh do mind the things of the flesh; but they that are after the Spirit the things of the Spirit.' That is exactly what our Lord said to Nicodemus. Nicodemus was unregenerate, but any man who is 'after the Spirit' and who 'minds the things of the Spirit' is a regenerate man. That is true of all regenerate men, of all Christians. 'To be carnally minded' – that is the same as being 'after the flesh' – 'is death' (verse 6). Note that it is not just poor Christianity, but 'death'. 'But to be spiritually minded is life and peace'. Then, in verse 7, 'Because the carnal mind is enmity against God'. That is not and cannot be true of any Christian. You cannot be a Christian and 'at enmity against God'. But he goes on, 'it is not subject to the law of God, neither indeed can be. So then they that are in the flesh' – those who 'walk after the flesh' – 'cannot please God' (verse 8). In other words, they are under His wrath. 'But you are not in the flesh, but in the Spirit, if so be that the Spirit of God dwell in you. Now if any man have not the Spirit of Christ, he is none of his'. He is not a Christian at all (verse 9). Surely that ought to be sufficient. This phrase then is not a description of certain Christians only, who have chosen to go in for a higher Christian life; it is true of everyone who is a Christian at all. Paul is describing anyone or everyone who is born again, who is regenerate, who is 'in Christ'.

I sum the matter up by putting it in the following way. By

nature we are all 'in the flesh', and we 'walk after the flesh'. That is the realm of the 'natural man'. But now, as Christians, we are in an entirely different realm, we are in the realm of the Spirit. We belong to it, we have been put into it, and it is the one in which we live and in which we walk. And that is true of every single Christian, whatever his actual behaviour and conduct may be. Take the way in which the Apostle states that in the 2nd chapter of the Epistle to the Ephesians: 'You hath he quickened, who were dead in trespasses and sins' (verse 1). He also says, 'He hath raised you together with Christ' – quickened you, and raised you. Not only that, Paul goes on to say that they, Christians, are 'seated together with Christ in the heavenly places' (verse 6). Of whom is he talking? Is he only referring to certain Christians? No; he is talking about every Christian. There are not two groups of Christians in Ephesians 2; and there are not two groups of Christians in Romans 8. This is true of every Christian; of every Christian, no matter how unworthy a life he may be living; because he is 'in Christ' he is 'seated with him in the heavenly places'. It is not true only of Christians who are supposed to have 'passed from Romans 7 to Romans 8'. There is no such thing here. All Christians are 'in Romans 8'; you cannot be a Christian without being 'in Romans 8'.

I repeat my point. There is no such thing as a Christian who is 'only justified', who has merely believed on the Lord to forgiveness and to salvation from hell, but who goes on living afterwards 'in the flesh'. No such thing is described in the New Testament. Regeneration, and being 'in Christ' and 'having the Spirit of Christ' in us make that quite impossible. You cannot be simply a forgiven Christian; if you are a Christian you are regenerate, you are 'in Christ', you are 'in the Spirit' and the Spirit is in you.' That is true of every Christian. There is no such thing as the merely justified Christian who has not yet 'taken his sanctification'. 'Christ is made unto us wisdom, and righteousness and sanctification and redemption' (1 Corinthians 1: 30). Paul is addressing all Christians in that 1st chapter of the First Epistle to the Corinthians – even the Corinthian Christians!

But perhaps the clearest statement of all on this matter is to be found in the First Epistle of John, chapter 3, verses 8 to 10: 'He that committeth sin is of the devil'. He belongs to the devil, the devil is his father, he is of the progeny of the devil. 'He that

committeth sin is of the devil; for the devil sinneth from the beginning. For this purpose the Son of God was manifested, that
he might destroy the works of the devil. Whosoever is born of
God' – here is the contrast – 'doth not commit sin; for his seed
remaineth in him: and he cannot sin, because he is born of God.
In this the children of God are manifest, and the children of the
devil.' There are the contrasts once more. 'Whosoever doeth not
righteousness is not of God, neither he that loveth not his
brother.' Now there is only one conceivable interpretation of all
these statements. 'He that committeth sin' means he that 'goes on
doing' it, he who lives in it, he who 'walks' in it, he whose
general tenor of life is in it. 'Whosoever is born of God doth not
commit sin.' John cannot be referring to individual acts of sin
there, because if he were, there would not be a single Christian,
there would never have been a Christian. Every Christian falls
into sin at some time or another; but John says, 'Whosoever
is born of God doth not commit sin'. He obviously means 'does
not live in it, does not walk in it', he does not spend his life in it;
that is not the general tenor of his life. The Christian may fall
into sin, but that does not mean that he is then 'walking after
the flesh'. He is still 'walking after the Spirit' but he has fallen into
sin, He has not changed his realm, or state; he is still 'in Christ'
though he has fallen into sin. He does not cease to be in Christ
because of an act of sin. He may fall into sin, but he does not
abide in it, he does not go back into that realm, he does not become a child of the devil again. No, he has been translated 'from
the kingdom of darkness into the kingdom of God's dear Son'
(Colossians 1: 13).

The Apostle, I say again, is describing here, in general, the
realm in which all who are Christians live. When he wants to
talk about the particular way in which we live in detail, in actions,
as Christians, he uses a word which is also translated by 'walk'
in the Authorized (K.J.) Version but which in the Greek is a
different word. In Galatians 5: 25 we have this interesting statement, 'If we live in the Spirit, let us also walk in the Spirit'. There
we have a specific injunction as to what we are to do, and what
we are not to do. Paul is not describing the general tenor there;
he is more particular, and it is interesting to note that, when he
wrote that, he did not use the same word as he uses in Romans
8: 4; he used a different and more particular word, which means

'walk orderly'. The picture is of a number of soldiers standing in a line, with someone drilling them to walk orderly. They are meant to walk all together, and in line. Is it not interesting that when he comes to that aspect he deliberately chooses and uses a different word? You find it again in Galatians 6: 16: 'And as many as walk according to this rule'. Again he is writing about detailed actions, and he uses the same word as he uses in Galatians 5: 25, not the word he uses here in Romans 8: 4. There is one further instance of this in Philippians 3: 16: 'Nevertheless, whereto we have already attained, let us walk by the same rule, let us mind the same thing.' Again it is the word that he had used in Galatians 5: 25 and 6: 16, and not the word that he uses in Romans 8: 4.

That seems to me to be the final and the conclusive argument. Here, in Romans 8:4, the Apostle has deliberately chosen the word which describes nothing beyond the general tenor of the Christian's life, the word which denotes that he is no longer in the realm of sin and law and death; he is no longer governed by sin and led by sin and the flesh. On the contrary he is now 'alive unto God', he is 'in Christ', in the realm and under the rule of grace. He is governed, he is led by 'the Spirit' – as the Apostle will tell us later on in this same chapter in verse 14, 'For as many as are led by the Spirit of God, they are the sons of God'. In sum, this is true of every Christian. He is now controlled by a new power, and that power is none other than the Holy Spirit who dwells in us and who works in us. The Holy Spirit is in every Christian, the Holy Spirit works in every Christian. That is why it is true to say of every Christian that he walks 'after the Spirit, and not after the flesh.'

But one more point arises. What is the Apostle's reason for adding this description of the Christian to the statement 'that the righteousness of the law might be fulfilled in us'? I believe there are three reasons. He adds it in order to show us how 'the righteousness of the law' can, and will be fulfilled in us; it is the work of the Holy Spirit. Secondly, he was eager to show the certainty of all this. When we analysed the whole chapter I said that his theme is assurance, certainty. 'There is therefore now no condemnation' – never can be, never will be. If you are 'in Christ' you will become perfect and entire, 'without spot or wrinkle or any such thing'. In other words, it is not enough that we should realize that we are forgiven, and free from the Law. Before we can enjoy the benefits of salvation we need a positive right-eousness, we must be holy. 'Without holiness, no man shall see the Lord.' How can I be sure that that is going to be true of me? The answer is, 'The Holy Spirit will make it sure and certain.' Christ had to come, Christ had to bear our sins, as a sin-offering, and to receive their punishment and condemnation, not only to deliver us from hell and to justify us and to make us righteous, but so that the Spirit might also come and do His work in us; and it is He who will bring us to that final glory and perfection. The certainly of it all! The Apostle has introduced this to show how it is certainly going to be perfected by the continuing work of the Holy Spirit. We have new life in us, he says; we are living in the realm of the Spirit; we are 'translated' from one kingdom into another kingdom, no longer to live 'after the flesh' but 'after the Spirit'. Paul is proving the certainty of it all.

The Apostle's third reason is that this description of a Christian is a very good one which we must all apply to ourselves. He wants to make quite certain that none should take hold of this teaching in an intellectual manner only. He wants to warn, and disabuse the mind of the kind of man who says glibly 'I believe in the Lord; all is well with me'. If you have really believed in the Lord there are certain proofs that all is well with you. If you have really believed on the Lord Jesus Christ you are in the realm of the Spirit, you are walking 'in the Spirit'; your whole mind and outlook, your desires, your whole conduct – everything is dif-ferent. The Apostle constantly repeats that.

The Apostle John makes the same point very plainly and clearly in his First Epistle, chapter 3, verse 22: 'And whatsoever we ask, we receive of him, because we keep his commandments and do those things that are pleasing in his sight. And this is his commandment, that we should believe on the name of his Son Jesus Christ, and love one another, as he gave us command-ment.' An intellectual man may say, 'I believe', but if he does not love his brother he is not a Christian; he is 'in the flesh' still. But John says further: 'And he that keepeth his commandments dwelleth in him, and he in him. And hereby we know that he abideth in us, by the Spirit which he hath given us.'

The man who is no longer 'under condemnation', the man who is 'in Christ', the man who has been 'set free from the law of sin and death' by 'the Spirit of life in Christ Jesus', is a man who has evidence in himself that he is a new man. If we lack that evidence we had better re-examine our supposed belief. A mere intellectual belief in these doctrines is of no value to us. If we really believe we shall have the evidence in ourselves; and it will be manifest also to other people. This is the answer to Sandemanianism, or, to call it by its modern name, 'believe-ism'. That was the error taught by Sandeman in the 18th century and there is much evidence of its reappearance at the present time. The favourite verse of the Sandemanian teaching was the statement in the 10th chapter of this Epistle in verse 9: 'If thou shalt confess with thy mouth the Lord Jesus, and shalt believe in thine heart that God hath raised him from the dead, thou shalt be saved.' This is how the Sandemanians put it: 'Are you prepared to say with your mouth, to make confession with your mouth, that you believe that Jesus Christ is the Son of God and that He died for your sins? If so, then you are saved. Do not worry about your feelings, do not worry about anything; if you are prepared to make this statement, you are saved.' Such a doctrine is the exact opposite of what the Apostle is saying, not only in chapter 10, but also here in chapter 8. Notice the emphasis on 'the heart'. 'If thou shalt believe in thine heart'; and if you believe in your heart your life will be affected, and you will know that you are in the realm of the Spirit, and that 'the law of the Spirit of life in Christ Jesus' has set you free. You will know that you are a new man. We must not rest content with a belief that does not provide any evidence at all, either within or without, that 'the law of the Spirit of life' is operating in us and that we are walking 'after the Spirit' and not 'after the flesh'. However much you may desire to do so, you cannot stop at forgiveness, or stop at what is called 'salvation'. You cannot be justified without the work of sanctification starting at the same moment. The moment a man is regenerate the process of sanctification has already begun; 'the Spirit of Christ' is in him, and He is a sanctifying Spirit.

God's ultimate reason for sending 'His own Son in the likeness of sinful flesh, and for sin' and for 'condemning sin in the flesh' was 'that the righteousness of the law might be fulfilled in us who walk not after the flesh, but after the Spirit'. And if you are not 'walking after the Spirit', the righteousness of the Law is not being fulfilled in you; you are still 'in your sins', you are still 'under condemnation'. Therein lies the importance of this phrase, 'who walk not after the flesh, but after the Spirit'.

Thank God, it is not added to depress us, but to safeguard us against dangerous heresy, and above all, to give us an absolute assurance that 'He which hath begun a good work in you, will perform it until the day of Jesus Christ'. The righteousness of the Law shall be fulfilled in us, because it is God who sent His own Son into this world to live and die and rise again in order that we might be reconciled to Him, in order that we might be born again and be His children, in order that His Spirit might dwell in us and work in us until we are glorified. It is God's plan, and God's work in every phase and detail.

> *The work which His goodness began*
>   *The arm of His strength will complete;*
> *His promise is 'Yea' and 'Amen,'*
>   *And never was forfeited yet.*
>
> *Things future, nor things that are now,*
>   *Not all things below nor above,*
> *Can make Him His purpose forego,*
>   *Or sever my soul from His love!*

Appendix

In addition to the case of Bunyan and many others, it is clear that the kind of experience described in chapters 19 and 20 was quite common. Indeed the whole question of the steps and stages in conversion had received much attention from the Puritans in the latter part of the 16th century and the early 17th century; and there had been much debating concerning whether conversion was sudden or gradual. Many of the writers such as Richard Rogers, Richard Greenham, Arthur Hildersam and William Ames dealt with it. Perhaps the clearest account is to be found in the writings of William Perkins who deals with it in several of his treatises. Of particular interest is what he says in his 'First Book of Cases of Conscience' (*Perkins' Works*, Vol. ii, p. 13) where he writes as follows:

'In the working and effecting of man's salvation, ordinarily there are two special actions of God: the Giving of the first grace, and after that, the Giving of the second. The former of these two works, hath ten several actions.

i. God gives man the outward means of salvation, especially the ministry of the Word; and with it, he sends some outward or inward cross, to break and subdue the stubbornness of our nature, that it may be made pliable to the will of God. This we may see in the example of the Jailor, Acts 16, and of the Jews that were converted at Peter's Sermon, Acts 2.

ii. This done, God brings the mind of man to a consideration of the Law, and therein generally to see what is good, and what is evil, what is sin, and what is not sin.

iii. Upon a serious consideration of the Law, he makes a man particularly to see and know his own peculiar and proper sins, whereby he offends God.

iv. Upon the sight of sin, he smites the heart with a legal fear, whereby when man seeth his sins, he makes him to fear punishment and hell, and to despair of salvation, in regard to anything in himself.

Now these four actions, are indeed no fruits of grace, for a Reprobate may go thus far; but they are only works of preparation, going before grace; the other actions which follow, are effects of grace.

v. The fifth action of grace therefore is, to stir up the mind to a serious consideration of the promise of salvation, propounded and published in the Gospel.

vi. After this, the sixth is, to kindle in the heart some seeds or sparks of faith, that is, a will and desire to believe, and grace to strive against doubting and despair. Now at the same instant, when God begins to kindle in the heart any sparks of faith, then also he justifies the sinner, and withal begins the work of sanctification.

vii. Then, so soon as faith is put into the heart, there is presently a combat: for it fighteth with doubting, despair and distrust. And in this combat faith shows itself, by fervent, constant, and earnest invocation for pardon: and after invocation follows a strength and prevailing of this desire.

viii. Furthermore, God in mercy quiets and settles the conscience, as touching the salvation of the soul, and the promise of life, whereupon it resteth and stayeth itself.

ix. Next after this settled assurance, and persuasion of mercy, follows a stirring up of the heart to Evangelical sorrow, according to God, that is, a grief for sin, because it is sin, and because God is offended: and then the Lord works repentance, whereby the sanctified heart turns itself unto him. And though this repentance be one of the last in order, yet it shows itself first: as when a candle is brought into a room, we first see the light before we see the candle, and yet the candle must needs be, before the light can be.

x. Lastly, God giveth a man grace to endeavour to obey his commandments by a new obedience. And by these degrees doth the Lord give the first grace.'

Perkins then goes on to deal with the *second work of God tending to salvation* which he calls the Giving of the Second Grace, and which, he says, 'is nothing else but the continuance of the first grace given'.

The first four steps described by Perkins seem to me to be an exact description of what the Apostle Paul teaches in Romans 7, and, as he says, these are 'indeed no fruits of grace' and 'a Reprobate may go thus far'. What is surprising to me is that Perkins and other Puritans, in spite of this, when they actually comment on Romans 7 regard it as being a description of the regenerate man. Their pastoral theology often seems to be superior to their actual exegesis of Scripture.